And Music at the Close:

Stravinsky's Last Years

AND MUSIC

AT THE CLOSE

STRAVINSKY'S LAST YEARS

A Personal Memoir by LILLIAN LIBMAN

W · W · NORTON & COMPANY · INC ·

NEW YORK

The manuscript reproduced on the endpapers is Stravinsky's holograph of the *Double Canon: Raoul Dufy in Memoriam.* Copyright 1960 by Hawkes and Son (London) Ltd. The dedication reads: "To Lillian Libman this manuscript / page which was premiered in our / Town Hall concert on Dec. 20/59. / With affectionate thoughts / Yours cordially / I Stravinsky / Christmas / 1959"

Library of Congress Cataloging in Publication Data

Libman, Lillian.

   And music at the close.

     1. Stravinskiĭ, Igor' Fedorovich, 1882–1971.

I. Title.

ML410.S932L44   780'.92'4 [B]   72-4499

ISBN 0-393-02113-0

Published simultaneously in Canada by George J. McLeod Limited, Toronto

DESIGNER: ROBERT FREESE

Wallace Stevens, *The Planet on the Table,* copyright 1954 by Wallace Stevens, from *The Collected Poems of Wallace Stevens,* by permission of Alfred A. Knopf, Inc., publisher.

Sophocles, *Oedipus at Colonus: An English Version by Robert Fitzgerald,* copyright, 1941, by Harcourt Brace Jovanovich, Inc.; renewed 1969 by Robert Fitzgerald. Reprinted by permission of Harcourt Brace Jovanovich and Faber and Faber Ltd., London.

PRINTED IN THE UNITED STATES OF AMERICA

1 2 3 4 5 6 7 8 9 0

CONTENTS

Illustrations follow page 208

ACKNOWLEDGMENTS

Printed thanks to the many who made it possible for me to write this book are inadequate. Those who pass through these pages have my eternal gratitude, and those whose names do not appear but whose spirit sustained me through every line, know who they are and prefer only that acknowledgment.

For help in confirming the data on certain public events, travel schedules, itineraries, programs—all the information that gave strength to my own memories—I thank Claire Greenberg and her staff at Hurok Concerts; Frank Milburn, Press Director and Music Administrator of the New York Philharmonic; José Sánchez-Mayáns of the Institute of Fine Arts, Mexico City; the staffs of the concert managements to which I refer in this book; and the three anonymous gentlemen who checked my information on the technical aspects of recording. Sheila Wolbrom, who patiently typed and re-typed thousands of words from a difficult manuscript, has a special place in my thoughts.

As for my publishers, my pride in their faith goes deep, and my thanks to them for having granted me as editor the knowledgeable and understanding David Hamilton are immeasurable.

L.L.

PROLOGUE

This book is about the last twelve years of a great composer's life and how I watched him live them, both as a public and a private figure. But there is nothing in these pages for the student or scholar of musical composition—I lay no claim to expert knowledge in this area. Nor are there any revelations concerning the nature of "genius"—no light is thrown on what took place within the four walls of the studio where the creator of *The Rite of Spring* and *The Firebird* and *The Rake's Progress* and the *Symphony of Psalms* and a treasury of other masterpieces labored to hold his right to immortality.

It is, instead, a personal book about a man and his household, and a little about some others who were around him in the twilight of his life: ordinary people, for the most part, more than extraordinary ones, for his contacts with the latter, save for one or two, were generally sporadic—first, because such meetings were dictated by the circumstances of his position; and second, but more significantly, I think, because he never *needed* this kind of audience as a witness to his ideas.

The period of time covered—specifically, from July 1959 to the day of his death, April 6, 1971, and a few months beyond—has been chosen because it was then that I worked for him and was, for the most part, close by. I do not say "knew" him, for I don't believe anyone ever did, except perhaps Vera, his wife; though she too, by her own admission to others as well as to me, was left outside the door that shut him in with his music.

When I met Stravinsky he was seventy-seven, and was just then completing *Movements for Piano and Orchestra,* which he himself was to describe in print as his most advanced work to date in the field of serialism (though in actual fact he despised such categorical words). This was to be followed in the ensuing years by—but by no means only—*A Sermon, A Narrative, and A Prayer; The Flood; Abraham and Isaac; Variations;* and *Requiem Canticles,* the last com-

11

posed when he was eighty-four years old. This mental advance in the face of encroaching physical decline has suggested the division of the book into two parts: the six years from 1959 to 1965, during which his activities as composer and "performing artist" on the podium were at one of their highest peaks; and the final six years, when he fought hard to keep up the pace in a world that grew more and more lonely for him.

Some pages in this volume deal with the relationship between Stravinsky and his associate and literary collaborator Robert Craft, who since 1948 has been the second permanent member of the composer's household. There were others before him who occupied a comparable position of intimacy, but none whose relationship was the same, and none who lasted to the end. In the period with which we are concerned here, Robert Craft's rightful place in the Stravinsky annals was already established for various reasons, and no account of the composer's last years would be valid without including them in its perspective.

As for my own *raison d'être*, since this should be explained, what began as a professional relationship between Stravinsky and myself, involving my functions as personal manager and press representative, developed into a privileged position. From arranger of many of his concerts, writer of most of his performing contracts, disseminator of information about his activities, guardian at a number of his recording sessions, traveling companion for most of his North and Latin American engagements, I came to be, happily, sometimes his secretary; occasionally his cook, his valet, his seamstress; frequently his chauffeur; very often his companion; and, before his final illness, his "nurse." Afterward, toward the last, I was entrusted with other tasks—the retrieving of his manuscripts which had been withheld from him, the dismantling of his California house, the disposal of some of his possessions, the preparation of what was to have been his permanent residence in New York, the witnessing of his last will (as I had witnessed his first), and, finally, the closing of his eyes. We never wrote a contract with each other and we never talked of one.

The nature of this book explains the absence of a formal bibliography. Aside from personal experience with the composer and my own voluminous memoranda, diaries, files, records, and correspondence with the many who sought him for as many purposes, I have relied on material contained in several hundred letters and other written communications covering the entire period from Robert

Craft to me, and some forty-odd letters, notes, messages from Stravinsky, sent between the beginning of 1960 and the end of 1965, although after that I received some mail not directly composed by him. After 1965 I was with Stravinsky for more sustained periods than formerly, and when we were not together, I had very frequent communication by telephone to Hollywood or points abroad.

But in point of fact Stravinsky, personally, wrote fewer letters in English during the time in which I worked for him (although his correspondence in the American years was, indeed, huge), always having someone nearby to whom he could dictate or explain what he wished to have conveyed via the typewriter. In the early sixties his son-in-law handled most of his "Anglo-Saxon" mail; from 1966 on, Robert Craft undertook the major part of this task, and from time to time, when I was on the spot, the chore fell to me. But the letters I *do* have from Stravinsky are precious because it was always easy to detect when he himself had pecked away at the old Smith-Corona—he had his own particular brand of English prose, enriched and colorful with his Russian-accent spelling and Russian grammatical construction. And then, there were those little extra messages in the margins, hand-written in red or purple or brown ink!

Specific passages from Stravinsky's correspondence with me are paraphrased in Part I, because permission to quote directly was refused—not by those who hold the publication rights to the Stravinsky Archives, but by the composer's widow, who retains the power of veto. According to her representative, this action resulted because on March 3, 1972 *The New York Times* printed a story based on an interview held with me about this book. Exception was taken by both Mrs. Stravinsky and Robert Craft to certain of my views about Stravinsky's activities and attitudes during his final years. My position has remained the same since that time and is to be found in this book, unchanged in any way.

For the rest, from time to time my duties also included typing (with two fingers but at extremely high speed) parts of the original and re-edited manuscripts of the Stravinsky-Craft books, as well as letters to editors, articles, interviews; I have sometimes drawn conclusions from these drafts rather than from the published versions. And finally, since almost three-quarters of my time over twelve years was spent with Stravinsky or on matters that were his concern, much of the material relating to the final years (though not all, by any means) now in the closed Estate Archives became more or less familiar to me, and, therefore, in some cases I have taken the direction in which these records point.

I have begun with Stravinsky's end—his death *was* a part of the final years of his life, and different versions of it have been (and will yet be) told, as is the case with the end of all great men. But it is placed at the beginning of this book because the events surrounding his death were as far removed from him as he was from the scene, and therefore the proper mood of objectivity for the remainder of my recollections may be established—a condition of which, I think, he would have approved.

And Music at the Close:

Stravinsky's Last Years

EPILOGUE

New York, July, 1971

I HAVE just returned for the second time from the island of San Michele, where I came when Igor Stravinsky was laid to rest, scarcely three months ago. It is a good-sized cemetery (it must serve all the city), not five minutes ride by *motoscafo* (fifteen by gondola) after one leaves the canals of Venice on its north side. The even line of the low, yellowish-white walls that surround it is interrupted occasionally by semipointed arches, and more abruptly by the dazzling epiphany of Istrian stone that is Coducci's church—that supreme reminder of the ecclesiastical Renaissance. But, chiefly, one is aware of the hundreds of massed deep-green cypresses, sober, disciplined, forming a noble frieze against the always startling blue light of the Venetian sky.

Stravinsky sleeps in the Russian corner, a fair walk from the fifteenth-century Gothic doorway adjoining the church, crowned by a sculpture of Saint Michael complete with dead dragon and scales of justice. There are cloisters through which one must pass, and then groups of graves—for nuns and friars, for little children (these are painful to see: their photographs adorn the gravestones), for the rich and for those not so rich, for men of war and men of the sea. And then, in a special section, to the right of a tiny chapel where final prayers are said for the Russian and Greek Orthodox, beneath a clump of overhanging green, is Stravinsky's grave, and beside it another, unoccupied. He is alone there: he did not know any of his neighbors, and his impresario Diaghilev has a place some distance away, to the left side of the chapel, beneath a pompous, rectangular monument with a rotund canopy of stone. A small wooden cross identifies the composer's grave now, obviously hand-sawed, perhaps by one of the workmen, or (I think) by his eldest son, Theodore, who must surely have come back alone not long after the burial. The horizontal crosspiece reads STRAVINSKY IGOR, lettered roughly in black paint. And on the vertical board,

17

marked in pencil, crayon, ink, here and there, are words—"love"; *"au revoir"*; "farewell." Flowers are strewn about, dried from the July heat, but a bed of pansies on the mound flutters in a lively manner.

His wife Vera, Robert Craft, and I have returned together to visit this place, which for each of us represents a totally different experience. What we recall, after all, is what our own memories dictate, and, like fingerprints, no rememberings can be the same. Standing over that grave, I could feel only his loneliness, and not just the loneliness of someone lying deep in a far-off place, but the loneliness of his final illness and the loneliness of his last years. And ironically, another memory intrudes—of how often he used to mention that his great-grandfather had lived to the age of 111. Implicit in this remark was the conviction that at least a century would be his lot.

What we three speak of, however, are practical things. We measure the space the plot covers, for a headstone is to be created and executed by the Italian sculptor Manzù. Stravinsky knew him well and admired his work, at least enough to have once agreed that the artist could do his bust. Plans were made, but the composer did not find time to sit—though in the years I knew him, he somehow managed to do the things he wanted to do—and the project came to naught. Mrs. Stravinsky had met with the sculptor in a strike-ridden Rome (where we had stopped for this appointment en route to Venice), visiting him with Robert and an old friend, Adrianna Panni. The studio was a forty-five-minute drive from the center of the baking city, and tempers were apparently short on arrival. Reporting the whole affair to me later in the hotel, where I was trying to arrange the next day's departure for Venice with an unwilling personnel, she could only remember that Manzù still spoke an Italian that was hard to follow, and that he had a new Cadillac, imposingly occupying two-thirds of the narrow street. A decision had been made that the stone would be a curved marble slab, with the letters of the name in colored tiles. Her suggestion, that it should also carry the very simple cross Stravinsky had drawn in his personal notebook on the day Giacometti died, had not seemed to make much of an impression on the sculptor, though Manzù did not object to it, remarking only that it must be executed in pure gold. Now, in San Michele, she appeared troubled, staring down at the grave. "How can we tell a great sculptor how to sculpt?" she asked, and it occurred to me that she might be thinking, as I was, that her husband would have taken a dim view of the proposed use of that precious metal.

We wandered about the ground, going separate ways. Robert turned to the left of the chapel, where a narrow inlet might later permit the unloading of the gravestone, and I to a thought-provoking sight, that of a naval casualty pressed to his eternal sleep by an enormous granite block bound with a huge anchor and its chain. (Stravinsky would have said that it had intentionally dragged its ship and crew down to oblivion.) Then, rounding a corner, I came upon his place again. His wife, unaware, was crouched at the foot of the grave, head and back bent, scratching at the earth with both hands, in a kind of frenzied haste. And when she had made a deep enough space, she took some violets she had brought with her, and with infinite care planted each one in the dirt.

On April 6, 1971, the first Tuesday in the month of spring, Death finally defeated Stravinsky. The end came in the pre-dawn hours— which scientists refer to as the time of least human resistance (the sun then being at its greatest distance from the earth)—climaxing a long series of hard-fought contests that had begun formally in 1967 and from then on had made the two combatants familiar adversaries. Officially, Stravinsky was pronounced dead at 5:20 A.M., by the intern assigned to stay the night, who made all the necessary tests of death in my presence. But in point of fact he must have breathed his last sometime before that, making his exit alone, with no audience to cheer him on or offer arms for support. His wife, exhausted, had fallen asleep in her adjoining room at midnight, and Robert, whose bedroom was on the other side of the sickroom, had finally retired at two o'clock. At three-thirty I had left my own bed, set up seven days before in the "office" where I worked, for I wanted to sit with the Master. He lay on his left side, his face away from me, and his breathing was faint and very irregular. His body, beneath the bedsheet, was so small (he weighed scarcely eighty pounds at his death) that it hardly made an outline, and when I placed my hand on his lower limbs there was no feeling of warmth. I wanted to call his wife, but the elderly night nurse who sat reading near the bed assured me that there had been no appreciable change for several hours, and that none was expected for several more. In the manner of night nurses (and they have a certain right), she hinted I was being a nuisance. (Her young colleague, a pretty

Scottish girl, was fast asleep in a chair, and the intern was taking some relief by dozing in the living room.) To my everlasting feeling of guilt, I permitted the night nurse to persuade me. I went back to my cubicle and sat down on the bed with a book. (The next day I noticed it was Alan Moorehead's *The White Nile,* which had fascinated Stravinsky to the point of a dozen rereadings.) I held it without switching on the light. It seemed only a few moments, though it was actually 5:15 A.M. when the young nurse shook me awake. "Come quick. There's been a change."

When I reached his bed, Stravinsky lay on his back, his eyes fixed—they had been filmy for days, so that one could not really detect their true color—his dry lips partly open. His fingers were curled like those of a child scooping sand, and his legs, to my touch, were enveloped past his knees in the dreadful characteristic cold of death. Most significantly, the mask (well known to those who have had some experience with the dying) which, to me, had begun to show its signs two days before, had settled on his features forever. "What happened?" I asked, stupidly; we had all known well for at least thirty-six hours what was going to happen. "He simply stopped breathing," the intern said. "*When?*" "Just now."

But that hardly seemed true. What lay on that hospital bed, with its pulleys and electrical switches, banked by oxygen cylinders, intravenous apparatus, suction pumps was not Stravinsky, but only a body from which the meaning had departed a timeless hour ago, and which I saw now as though it were in some kind of specimen frame. In the moment before I went to call his "Vera," I tasted bitterness—at myself for having left him alone, and at the sight of that tiny room in which only his small upright piano, and one or two religious medals and icons, and an old empty book cabinet (from the landing outside his studio in Hollywood) could be identified with him. And bitterness (unjustified, no doubt) at the impersonality of the medical supervisors who held the mirror to that mouth, and the needle to the skin, and the stethoscope to the chest, keeping me for a few seconds to watch "because somebody from the family should be here."

I wakened Mrs. Stravinsky carefully, because I was afraid; she has always kept her real feelings hidden, and even those as close to her as Robert, and as I in the last few years, cannot ever say for certain what she is thinking. She sat up and whispered, "Yes? He is gone?" I said, "Yes." "Call Bob," she said, and began to get up with a pathetic deliberation. I ran to Robert's room. He thrust out his hand as though to stop me and said, "No."

The bedrooms gave onto a long corridor. At her door Mrs. Stravinsky stood waiting, leaning against the jamb, regarding us with wide-open, staring eyes. I left her alone with Robert and they went into the room together.

Stravinsky's death at eighty-eight could not have come as a great surprise to the press or the world in general, beyond the shock of loss: one of the most influential forces in the history of music had gone from us. His health, never entirely sound, had long been a newsworthy item because he was who he was, and from the moment of the first real thrombosis during his Berlin concert in 1956, his mildest cold, as well as the several mild-to-serious occlusions that plagued him in the succeeding years, was reported in detail around the globe. The rare blood disease, polycythemia,* with which he had also been afflicted, probably for fifteen years or more, was referred to frequently by both musical and medical writers (who cited him as a victim); and when he took to his bed or entered and left hospitals, whether for a simple cold or a minor ailment, the wires hummed, and I would become slightly distraught trying to reach the Stravinskys in Paris, or Buenos Aires, or Moscow, or the outback regions of Australia, to get at the truth of the matter. In fact, from 1967 on, after the first truly frightening hospitalization for a bleeding ulcer occurred in Los Angeles, to the very end, I would regularly receive calls from two major news magazines and an international syndicate "just to check." In 1969, before he miraculously recovered from two embolectomies of the left leg and a left lumbar sympathectomy (three operations performed within twenty-four hours of each other), and had virtually been "given up," other calls were concerned with the clarification of details that would be included in his obituaries. Actually, on one occasion, not long before an astonished doctor and Lenox Hill Hospital staff saw him into his car for his return, discharged, to the Essex House (the Stravinskys' Manhattan residence at the time), I was talking to a BBC reporter in London who had telephoned to ask me, "How

* A superabundance of red corpuscles in the blood, which must be kept from forming clots.

soon after Mr. Stravinsky dies will Mr. Craft be available for an interview?"

And in all honesty I cannot say that I was shocked by the actual event of his death. For three years, interrupted only by intervals when work as a Hurok press agent took me away from him, I had watched Stravinsky failing. During the previous six months, my prayers had been that he *would* die. The humiliation of his illness must have been more terrible for him than any defeat he might have suffered privately in the composition of his music. To lose control—he, whose whole esthetic and physical being was dedicated to the principle of control—would have been synonymous, for him, with living death. Sometimes, when I would be called by one of the nurses to help lift or turn him, or (worst of all) to hold the suction pump that relieved his breathing, the look of embarrassed apology in his eyes was unbearable, and I would shut my own.

On some other evenings, when Mrs. Stravinsky and Robert dined out or fulfilled a necessary social obligation, he and I would sit together in front of the television set, where I would search for a film or documentary about animals—his attention span for detective dramas and mystery plays, which he once enjoyed, having long since passed. This entertainment, desirable because it involved movement from his bed to the living room, provided the hardest occasions on which to observe him. He would sit in his wheel chair, wrapped in blankets and in silence, his sore feet on cushions, his chin on his chest, and then, suddenly, when I was certain he was sleeping, he would reach a hand out to touch me, and, like a child who is satisfied that someone is with him in the dark, would return to his own dreams. In those moments it did not appear to matter who was with him. It seemed to be enough for him that someone familiar was.

During the last year of his life, Stravinsky withdrew more and more with each passing day, as though out of acute boredom he constantly sought another environment. Nevertheless, though his visits to this one were brief, for he tired very quickly, they were usually characteristic. The effort he would make to "join in," to conquer his dimming eyesight and deteriorated hearing, was almost superhuman. Robert, compelling him alive, would play recorded music as they always had, after dinner, and Stravinsky would sit beside him with his finger on a score, though it remained unmoving, nodding against the drugs that were given to sustain and assist him but that only (it seemed to me) plunged him more and more into his private world of silence. Now and then he would summon enough strength to mouth a phrase, as though he must do what was expected of him, but usually only his wife could understand what he said in that voice reduced by weakness to a labored whisper.

I cannot say whether Stravinsky knew he was dying, and I do not believe anyone else has the answer. It seems inconsistent with the character of the man that such a thought would have been permitted to enter his mind. Stravinsky's sense of immortality was one of his most notable traits. He was deeply religious, and whatever that religion might have been (for no one really knows), it defined his gift for *him* as "God-given" and therefore everlasting. He was also a man of the theater, and he always knew he had command of the stage. He may have felt himself removed temporarily from a particular scene, a condition that was rather like a standing-in-the-wings interval, but he was always certain he would be cued in for another entrance. Thus, the *act* of composition was what interested him, and when a work was completed, he was no longer concerned with it but moved immediately to the next. He was, in his own oft-quoted words, "a maker," and "making" is infinite, identical—as it was for him—with creation.

But though Stravinsky superstitiously avoided funerals (especially in his later years in America) and kept away from cemeteries (he once refused to step out of a gondola to visit Diaghilev's grave), his death-awareness was very strong, and clearly present in his music —but always as a circumstance occurring to others. The number of his compositions that are "in memoriams" or epitaphs is large and important,* and so are those in which the idea of death occurs without any personal dedication.† His final major work, *Requiem Canticles*, has been described by Robert in his diaries as Stravinsky's "call of death," but nowhere is there any indication, nor did I ever hear the composer express the idea, that he intended this work (destined to be performed at his bier) for himself.‡ One of my tasks for

---

* Those that come to mind are *Symphonies of Wind Instruments* (for Debussy), *Variations* (for Aldous Huxley), *Introitus* (for T. S. Eliot), *Ode* (for Natalia Koussevitsky), *In Memoriam Dylan Thomas*, etc.

† *Perséphone*, the graveyard scene in *The Rake's Progress*, etc., are suggestive. (*Cf.* Roman Vlad, *Stravinsky*, London: Oxford University Press, 1960, pp. 8 ff.)

‡ It was, in fact, commissioned in 1965 by Stanley Seeger, as a memorial to his mother.

him in the early years was to collect any newspaper accounts that might have escaped his own attentive eye of the demise of a friend or musician, and he kept a file of such unhappy material in the little office across the hall from his bedroom in Hollywood. He would also make note on his own daily calendars when someone he knew had passed on, and occasionally would draw a simple cross above the notation (as he had done for Giacometti). But he accumulated that newsprint, I am sure, purely as a reminder that certain persons were afterward to be referred to in the past tense. Once, when we were composing a condolence telegram to Pierre Monteux's daughter, he said to me rather slyly, "Ah, but what shall I wire to Ansermet's widow when *he* goes?"—referring, of course, to an old feud with his former friend, but never imagining for a moment that his own turn might come first, although he was the elder of the two. "I will not go on like this," he would say at times when he became disgusted at his inability to function without the aid of medical machinery. *Never,* "I will not *live* like this."

His death brought with it many complications, and not only those created by his position as one of the great public figures of the century. Because the subject was taboo in his household, the matter of funeral services and cemeteries, should he die suddenly, had never been considered except vaguely, and then not by him. On an evening in March 1970, following one of Stravinsky's poorer days, Robert, prompted by the visit of a friend whose mother-in-law had just died abroad and who spoke of the innumerable details involved, brought the topic into the open. We talked the next day about San Michele and also about the appropriateness of a memorial concert, which would include the *Requiem Canticles* and another Stravinsky work, possibly the *Introitus* (composed in memory of T. S. Eliot). Later, Robert gave me the draft of a letter, to be signed by Mrs. Stravinsky, addressed to Arnold Weissberger, her husband's attorney, expressing these wishes and requesting that he inquire through proper channels into the possibility of San Michele. Also in the lettter was an alternative proposal for a site—the "Keats cemetery" near the pyramid of Caius Cestius in Rome, should there be no place on that island in the Venetian lagoon. The letter clearly stated that this idea did not come from Stravinsky, but that his wife felt it would have been acceptable to him.

The subject was not referred to again in my presence. I learned from Mr. Weissberger, on my follow-through some weeks after he had received the letter, that he had looked into the matter and there would be no problem at San Michele. The simple purchase of a plot was all that would be required. As to the services, Mrs. Stravinsky had told me, on an occasion when tragedy was far from our minds, that these would probably be Russian Orthodox—her husband had been baptized in that Church and had rejoined it as a communicant in 1926, after sixteen years of absence. She mentioned at the same time that if he should die in the United States, she would enlist the aid of Natasha Nabokov, an old friend * whose brother was an archbishop in that faith and who would advise as to the arrangements. What might have occurred if Stravinsky had died abroad was never actually discussed in my hearing, but undoubtedly the religious services would have been the same. (Cremation was never considered. The composer regarded this as a heinous practice.)

Another and graver complication was the estrangement that had developed, in the year preceding Stravinsky's death, between his wife and his children by his first wife (who had died in 1939). These details have their place in another part of this chronicle, but on the morning of April 6 the situation had come to a head. Mrs. Stravinsky now felt she would be unable to meet with the children or receive them in her home. A few moments after Stravinsky died, in accordance with her wishes, I had sent wires to his daughter Milène Marion in Hollywood; to his younger son, Soulima, in Urbana, Illinois; and to Theodore, the eldest, who lived abroad in Geneva. The message was signed "Vera"; it simply gave the tragic news and included one of our two telephone numbers. But now I was the one who had to tell them, on their arrival in New York, that they would not be able to come to the Stravinsky apartment, and that no one there except myself could speak with them. In fact, this rule—although for different reasons—applied to everyone, including old friends and associates of long standing. Mrs. Stravinsky, who was in a numbed condition (she had never *really* believed her husband would die), was under doctor's orders to keep to her bed and talk to no one. And indeed she did not, beyond two telephone conversations with Mrs. Nabokov, a brief one with a dear friend, and a conference with Mr. Weissberger on

* Mrs. Nabokov was the first wife of composer Nicolas Nabokov, and had known the Stravinsky family for many years.

that first morning. It was determined then that the public service would take place at the Campbell Funeral Chapel on Good Friday at three o'clock. This was to be preceded, as is customary in the Russian Orthodox Church, by three private family services on the three prior evenings, in the small chapel of the funeral home.

Robert was even less approachable than the widow, and, never able to cope with practical situations except those connected with music, kept to his room, refusing to give out any statements to the press, which, quite naturally, regarded him in his position as the composer's longtime associate and, therefore, spokesman. It is pointless to speak of his grief—the whole reason for his existence had been taken away.

Rita Christiansen, Stravinsky's Danish nurse, who had been his devoted attendant since October 1968, when the Stravinsky's had engaged her in Paris, had remained with us to help. The only other person admitted to the apartment during the following week was Edwin Allen, a close friend of Mrs. Stravinsky since their first meeting in Santa Fe in 1962, who commuted from Connecticut, where he worked as a librarian at Wesleyan University.

The job of organization fell to me, more or less automatically—that had always been my province, and I was used to acting as buffer. Moreover, I was the only one in the household, except for Rita in her professional capacity, who had had any direct experience with the details of death. Such terms as "casket," "hearse," "burial attire," "on view" (wisely changed to "no view") might as well have never existed in any vocabulary. The ancient custom that the bereaved should be troubled as little as possible with such macabre minutiae is indeed a humane one, even though it spells escape from responsibility. The task ahead for me was enormous, and I had no time for my own grief.

But the qualms were there. One of the first came when Rita, who had gone with the body and its caretakers to the funeral home, returned with an estimate of the preliminary costs. Stravinsky would have read as far as the first item, an ebony and solid-silver-handled casket with a price tag in four high digits, and an endless correspondence would immediately have been initiated between the seller and himself, his letters demanding a complete itemization of every plank, nail, lining-stitch, metal ounce, and labor hour, with accompanying arguments against profiteering. He would not have *refused* to pay if he had wanted the article, and he *would* pay when he received the explanation. After that, all would have been entered in a diary he kept of daily expenses, its purpose being to confound the Bureau of Internal Revenue. Still, I approved the bill without much hesitation. There was no time to do otherwise, and in reality it was a small amount in terms of what had been put into circulation to make the new apartment—impulsively purchased and occupied by its owner for one brief week—moderately livable.

On that Tuesday, and thereafter until we left for Venice, the phones never stopped ringing. A world-wide press required details; statements had to be issued; friends and associates had to be mollified because they could not offer their sympathies directly to Mrs. Stravinsky or Robert; hundreds of telegrams and boxes of flowers had to be listed for later acknowledgment. The petty cash consumed in tips to messengers, elevator men, delivery boys mounted to impressive heights.

Two particularly trying decisions for Mrs. Stravinsky concerned the question of what jewelry should remain with the composer and the matter of a death mask. The first was less difficult for her than the second, which Robert, in private, asked me to arrange. Stravinsky kept his gold cross and the two religious medals that had hung on a chain about his thin neck to the very end. A sapphire ring which his Vera had once given him in Paris, and which he had treasured, she took as a keepsake. To Robert she gave his Cartier wrist watch, presented to him many years ago by an old and dear friend; it had been his favorite in a large collection of timepieces, and he had worn it throughout his illness, although his wrist was far too wasted to keep it in place. (An old gray tweed jacket that had hung on a chair by his bed, which I loved because he had traveled in it on many tours, she later gave to me.)

The death mask was a concession to history. Such souvenirs were not for Stravinsky, who was a storeroom for volumes of Old Russian superstition. A particularly unpleasant recollection makes me certain of this. In Toronto, in 1963, he sat in Massey Hall following a score while Robert rehearsed the orchestra for a recording of Schoenberg's *Pelleas und Melisande*. I was somewhere near the stage making myself disliked, as usual, by holding off a battery of photographers, who always haunted these sessions. Suddenly that deep, reverberant voice calling my name rose above the horns. I rushed. With shaking hands Stravinsky thrust a portrait-sized, mounted photograph at me, and in the light attached to the music

stand that held his score I could see that it was a rather striking
picture of the death mask of Beethoven.

He was livid. "Give it back! What have *I* to do with this! Why
does he give this to *me!* I detest such things. . . . I do not accept
such presents. . . . Give it back!" The donor, a shy, soft-spoken
man who had been photographing at previous rehearsals, stood
rigid and aghast a few feet away. I went to him and mumbled some
words of explanation. But what does one say to the bearer of a
"treasure" he feels should be possessed only by someone as great as
its subject? Sitting beside the composer while the rehearsal continued—Robert's concentration had kept the musicians in their
seats, although they were craning their necks to see what the "old
man" was up to—I noticed that it took some time for him to calm
down. Later, during a Scotch break, while he and I sipped from
our lone paper cup, he said: "A barbarism. Why to photograph an
absolute barbarism!"

By mid-morning, on Tuesday, calls had come in from the
shocked Stravinsky children. The only one of the three I knew
really well was Milène, the younger of his two daughters, and the
only surviving one (Ludmilla's death in 1938 had preceded her
mother's by only a few months). Milène lived with her French-
born husband, André Marion, a ten-minute drive away from the
Stravinskys' Hollywood home, and I saw her very frequently during the periods of my visits there, for she would come every day
when her father was "in residence." But I did not become more
than acquainted with Stravinsky's sons until the final year, although
I had met Soulima and his wife in 1964 and knew their son John.
Theodore had come from Switzerland to visit his father on two
occasions in the sixties, but I missed him both times, and we did not
finally meet until late in 1969, and then again in the spring of 1970,
when he and his wife, Denise, stayed at the Essex House for several
weeks, during his father's critical hospitalization at Lenox Hill.

Except for Milène, then, I was really a stranger, although the sons
knew of my association with their father. But nothing in their attitude betrayed the natural resentment they must have felt when I
transmitted the messages and gave the details of the arrangements
in which they had no part. They were very gentle with me. I had a
difficult time, nevertheless, with my own conscience, for I was

torn between my duty to Mrs. Stravinsky, who felt sincerely justified in the position she had taken (indeed, felt driven, at that point,
to take it), and my own conviction that her husband—regardless of
any momentary feelings of anger or hurt toward his children—
would have considered it their moral right to see the room in which
he had died. He had been a man with a deep respect for "family"
—a formal and, in a nineteenth-century sense, a conventional man
in his behavior toward everyone, even those very close to him.

Although the children's telephone calls on that morning bespoke
neither criticism, advice, nor reproach, *that* was not lacking in
other quarters. Everyone who had ever spent ten minutes with
Stravinsky felt he had a right to dictate funeral protocol. And yet
most of these people had not seen him at all since the onset of his
final illness. Perhaps a round dozen of visitors had come to the
Essex House in the very last six months, and those usually found his
bedroom door closed. One or two did spend some time with him:
Nicolas Nabokov and his French wife, Dominique, would come
occasionally to lunch or dinner, and Stravinsky would be wheeled
to the table, but he was never very comfortable during these intervals, which were urged on him mainly out of regard for the feelings
of the guests, and he would soon have to return to his bed. On the
other hand, he would respond to Natasha Nabokov, who came as
often as she could to read to him in Russian or tell him Russian
stories, judiciously limiting her visits to twenty minutes. She would
also sometimes take over the evening "baby-sitter's" role (Mrs.
Stravinsky called it "papa-sitting"), which gave the substitute nurses
time to catch up on their magazine reading. Other callers would be
told that the patient had just received a blood transfusion (very
often the case) or that he was resting, and Mrs. Stravinsky would
then perform the social amenities. She was marvelous at these times
—cheerful, gay, amusing, behaving as though nothing in the world
bothered her except the temperature of the cocktail or tea she was
serving. But if alone in the apartment, she was helpless in the face
of an onslaught of persuasion, and once when a well-known composer dropped in unexpectedly, about four or five weeks before the
end, his pleas forced her to admit him to the sickroom—a circumstance that would have thrown Stravinsky into a frenzy of embarrassment (two years before, he had been apologetic about his
appearance even to his old friend Balanchine), had he not been too

ill to care. No mirrors, except one small one in his bathroom, were hung where he could see himself, from the time he moved into the Essex House in 1969.

There were, of course, constant calls from well-wishers, fans, diplomatic emissaries, musicians, and cranks. But I had become a practiced hand at "brush-off" by the end of the first year of my association with Stravinsky.

First signs of unrest came from the outside when I made public the time and place of the services. Why a funeral home? Why such a small chapel? Why not Carnegie Hall? Why not a Russian Orthodox Church? There were logical answers, of course, the principal one being that because of the particular day, the high altars in all Catholic churches were occupied with Good Friday services. The Russian churches, which probably would have made their chapel altars available, were considered by Mrs. Nabokov to lack the facilities for handling what would surely be an above-capacity attendance. Then, too, most of them were inconveniently located, and the necessity at this time of making things as simple as possible for Mrs. Stravinsky was pre-eminent in all our thinking. But as the week wore on, the seating-plan in the funeral chapel (which could accommodate only about two hundred) provided a real headache. Publishers' representatives, composers, political figures, diplomats and their adjuncts, musicians who had performed with him (and these were legion), members of the ballet world, Broadway actors, front-men from record companies, literary figures, to say nothing of friends and acquaintances, and, lest we forget, the public itself, called to request places. Initially, the press also presented a problem. Stravinsky's attitude toward reporters, and about interviews, photographs, television was celebrated in his lifetime, particularly in the United States. (Abroad, he was somewhat more amenable.) He summed it up himself in two famous sentences, employed when he felt badgered: "I don't need *you*. You need *me*." But on this point his widow's understanding was praiseworthy. "He didn't like it when he was alive, but he is dead. He belongs to the world, and the world has a right to know." I was thus given carte blanche for the press and television, and it was a consolation that in New York their representatives, for the most part, observed the ground rules, did not climb over seats, limited their flashlight pops during the service, and kept as far away from the family as possible without neglecting their assignments.

However, the news that Stravinsky would be buried in San Michele, released on the day following his death, provoked a hurricane of telephone calls, beginning with one from Moscow that was disconnected. This was followed, not two seconds later, by a successful ring from the Soviet Embassy in Washington (which poses an interesting question about coincidence or hot lines), and then by others throughout that day and the next from Rome, Paris, London, Hamburg, Warsaw, Athens, Tokyo, Sydney, Mexico. These came through on one of the two telephone numbers, while, it seemed to me, every city, hamlet, and town in North America belabored the other. Why Venice? Because of Diaghilev? Had Stravinsky ever stated or written this as his wish? And if not, who had made the decision? Motive on the part of most callers was curiosity; on the part of several who had known him, objection; on the part of the Soviets, unexpressed (but detectable) skepticism that he had not definitely ordered his burial to take place in the land of his fathers.

In fact, the final decision was made jointly by Mrs. Stravinsky and Robert on the afternoon of April 6. Instructions were then given me to proceed with all arrangements for Venice. (The memorial concert, which Robert ultimately conducted, was not discussed at length until the following day.)

There is nothing much to go on in supplying an answer to the Italian question. In one of his drafts for the addenda to his diaries, on which I had been working, Robert (in an entry for March 5, 1970) referred to the letter to Arnold Weissberger dealing with the burial at San Michele, and also recorded that, shortly after the letter was sent, Stravinsky's nurse came to call him, as "Maestro" wanted to speak to him "about Venice." This led Robert to reflect on Stravinsky's "psychic" propensities. But on the few occasions when Robert and I had talked together about the inevitable future, it was rather in terms of what would become of Mrs. Stravinsky and of him.

The only information I have about what *might* have been Stravinsky's personal inclination comes from Nicolas Nabokov, who visited me with his wife at the Gritti Palace Hotel in Venice the Saturday following the funeral, after Mrs. Stravinsky and Robert had left for Paris. Nabokov could not understand (and neither, he said, could two other old friends—Eugene Berman and Vittorio Rieti) the choice of Venice; he remarked that once, some years before, when he was describing to Stravinsky certain architectural changes in Leningrad which he felt did not add to the beauty of that city, the composer had said: "Say no more. I will someday lie there next to my father."

Nevertheless, even though I remember clearly how profound an effect his visit to the USSR in 1962 had had on him—for months following his return he preferred to speak Russian almost exclusively and later would frequently lapse into his mother tongue (in which he always addressed his wife, toward the end) while carrying on a conversation in another language—Venice was not an illogical choice. He had loved Italy, and especially that water-bound place where so earthy and vital a stream of life contradicts the celestial stones of its surroundings. Such contrasts were the very soul of his music, and certainly the works he began or completed during the many years he lived in Venice, on and off, are witness to the inspiration he found there. This was, after all, where he had first played the piano score of *The Rite of Spring* to Diaghilev; where he composed *Agon;* where, at La Fenice, the world première of *The Rake's Progress* took place, and where he led the premières of his *Canticum Sacrum* in St. Mark's (the only non-Italian granted the privilege of conducting there), *Threni* in the Scuola di San Rocco, and *Monumentum pro Gesualdo* in the Great Council Hall of the Ducal Palace, borne there, as was customary, on a litter. And Venice was where so much music he admired began, the spontaneity of whose forms he loved.

His own great objectivity was apparent in this feeling for Venice, for nowhere did he receive such bad reviews as in Italy. The *Canticum* was excoriated, the *Rake* was vilified, and his other works were consigned to the back pages. And in the manner of Italian critics, which is to say with a hooting kind of contempt and a loud noise. It is curious that bad reviews from other countries (when he read them, far more often than he liked anyone to believe) would bring down a wrath like God's even though they might be less violent in their attack than the Italian reviews. And no judgment could be formed from the degree of his anger, since German reviewers, who might be laboriously negative but often knew a little something about the musical scene, fared far better than certain French critics who knew nothing and should not have commanded his attention; and certainly much better than American critics, who, in the early part of the last decade, bore the full brunt of his outbursts. Doubtless, too, this latter attitude had something to do with the fact that, of all countries which would gladly have opened their doors to him when he fled Communism, and later the world the Nazis tried to create, he chose the United States—which, he felt, from that point on paid little attention to him "except for taxes."

And as for Los Angeles, where he had lived the better part of thirty years and where he had owned two homes, he would not have wanted to rest there, although in the beginning he had been very fond of his West Coast life. After his eighty-fifth birthday year came and went without any public acknowledgment from that "musical" community, even in a program by its principal orchestra, and very little from other sources except the Monday Evening Concerts, under the direction of his old friend Lawrence Morton, and the *Los Angeles Times*, where music critic Martin Bernheimer remembered him in his column, he never made any comment beyond a sardonic grunt about the city in which he had established residence. Several times thereafter I was approached by representatives of the mayor's office, wishing to honor him in a public ceremony, and also by others close to the musical director of the Los Angeles Philharmonic, who asked to see him to explain what was being done *now;* but the moment I would even hint to him that acts of contrition were proposed, the subject would be changed, if not by the "Maestro," then by Robert.

And although Russian diplomacy left the question of his interment unasked, speculation might provide an answer by another question. Why Russia, if not the United States? He had lived here almost as long. Only in 1961, when news of the first USSR performance of his *Symphonies of Wind Instruments* made the top of the international music pages, had there been printed indication of a change in Soviet musical officialdom toward the Master it had denounced. Moreover, after an absence of more than fifty years, it would be hard to say whether *anyone* might not consider his native earth to be "strange," let alone a man like Stravinsky—whose work, no matter which direction it had taken in the intervening years, was part and parcel of an opposing tradition.

Venice, then, a "non-political" city, or—as Mrs. Stravinsky herself put it in her letter—"neutral." Much has already been printed about the Doge's funeral he received there, since more than two hundred members of the international and local press were present. Costly as a Doge's, too, but far less so for the municipality of Venice than for the Stravinsky estate. Although the generosity of the former extended to the very important granting of permission (by special dispensation from the Roman Catholic authorities) to hold the service in the Church of Ss. Giovanni e Paolo (or, as it is called by the Venetians in their dialect, San Zanipolo), where, the guide-books tell us, forty-six doges are entombed; and some of the expenses of the memorial concert (the RAI Chorus, the Fenice Orchestra, and two rehearsals), the rest of the bill was footed by "Maestro." And at tourist prices!

In fairness, some of the ensuing nerve-wracking spending resulted from the necessity of making arrangements by transatlantic telephone. Conversations were four-way, between funeral homes on both sides of the ocean (the Venetian one found by Campbell), an interpreter, and myself. The procedures for transporting a body abroad are colorful with red tape. Death certificates ran to twenty-five copies. (No doubt some of these will turn up on the auction block a few years hence, offered by dealers with ghoulish tendencies.) Nor is death immune to time limits: there are domestic and foreign regulations marking the earliest and latest periods of embarkation and debarkation (loading and unloading) of the remains. Furthermore, Italian law in this instance "suggested" that the landing point for those decedents flown to Venice must be Rome rather than Milan, to conform to local policy of doing things the hard way. A long overland journey by hearse was thus necessary, for the Italians, displaying an admirable streak of realism, warned that trains were not reliable as far as cargo was concerned, and the casket might therefore arrive two or three days after the services. In the course of our talks I was treated to an extended discourse on the types of plots available, but this was interpreted in such loving and poetic English, and with such an esthetic appreciation of the fine points of the San Michele landscape, that Ruskin would not have been ashamed to include it in *The Stones of Venice.* Due warning was given, too, that we must look ahead twelve years, when the "lease" would be up and the *osse* must be transferred to another boneyard. This, of course, could be avoided by the observance of certain understandable conditions, modesty, at this point, forbidding the use of such a vulgar term as *lire.* In any case, I purchased two adjoining plots by phone (I knew this was Mrs. Stravinsky's wish), but later, when the final bills were settled, discovered that the two had become three—because, in the words of the reporter who described the scene for the Rome *American*, the "typical American casket" was too large for confinement within the dimensions of the "normal" grave.

Very important in our discussions, apart from the essentials of the final service (set for noon on Thursday, April 15)—the officiating priest (Archimandrite Cherubim Malissianos of the Greek Orthodox Church); the location within the huge Gothic edifice (longer in the nave than St. Mark's by half a dozen meters) where the body would repose until the appointed time; the hours for preliminary masses and prayers, and the interval to be allotted between the church service and the private interment (at three o'clock on San Michele)—were certain Italian "musts." Flowers! There apparently is an Italian protocol about flowers that, if written up, would challenge any monograph on heraldry. Woe betide a widow who chose a modest wreath of hyacinth instead of a blanket of red and white roses, or a sibling who preferred a bouquet of carnations to a sheaf of gladioli. Friends had a little more leeway, but good taste dictated either red or white flowers; and since these must not duplicate the posies in the immediate family's province, a treasure hunt was obviously in order so that the two-color limitation would prevail. (On this point I decided we would exercise the "ignorant foreigner" privilege.) Also, it was expected that every close friend and relative be represented by an individual offering. This was "face," and I observed it; later, on the impressive array in the transept, wilting rapidly under the television lights, I saw with relief that the requirements of society were served well enough to satisfy the most exacting of Venetian Emily Posts: cards were prominently attached, large and imposingly inscribed in purple inks, in a fine Italian hand, bearing such legends as "*Moglie* Vera," "*Figlio* Theodore," "*Amico* Robert Craft," and so on.

While the international telephone cable rang up dollar after dollar, I approved such items as the binding for the books that would record the names of those attending (very beautiful, incidentally, when I finally collected them, in green and red tooled leather, with "*Onorazze a Igor Stravinsky*" in gilt letters on the front covers, and, at the bottom of the same—credit where it is due—"*Servizio Municipalizzato Trasporti Funebri—Venezia*"); the hiring of the "honored gondoliers" for the cortège to the cemetery (naturally we must have only these, and naturally they came much higher, "honor though it is to escort so great a figure"); the fee for the

organist whom we would surely require to play a background of
sacred music in the church from the moment "the Master's" body
arrived there until the service (I agreed to this since he would not
hear it); and, at last, the number of gondolas for the private procession to San Michele. This was a poser: I could not predict how
many "friends" would travel to Venice. Dozens had already told
me they planned to make the trip, but my better judgment (at that
point, in very short supply) suggested that such decisions, made in
the first flush of grief, would be reconsidered with more prudence
in the light of passing days. Trips to Venice, after all, are not quite
like following a hearse in one's own or someone else's car to a
nearby cemetery. But I ordered twelve gondolas, each to carry five
people. And this decision terminated a series of six far from brief
telephone calls to and from Venice in two days.

The concert arrangements, however, would have provided material for an opera librettist. Following the first private service on
Tuesday evening, Robert had given voice to all our feelings with a
protest that none of the Russian ritual and song seemed connected
in any way with Stravinsky, who, indeed, would have remained
quietly reading in his dressing-room. On Wednesday, therefore,
Gregg Smith, who had worked with the composer and Robert on
many concerts involving choral music, was asked to prepare his
chorus to perform two of the Master's sacred works—the *Pater
Noster* and the *Ave Maria*—at the Friday public service. At the
same time Robert agreed to conduct the *Requiem Canticles* in
Venice. This meant securing—again by telephone and at practically
no notice—an orchestra, chorus, soloists, and the music materials
(which would have to be delivered abroad immediately). I turned
for help to Carlos Moseley, president of the New York Philharmonic, and William Weissel, the Philharmonic's assistant manager,
who spoke fluent Italian, to contact Mario Labroca, longtime impresario of the Fenice Theater, now in his eighties. After several
abortive attempts, Mr. Weissel reached Signor Labroca on Thursday morning and determined that the latter "would be honored"
to make the arrangements, but unless the music could reach Venice
by Friday morning at the latest, we had better forget the entire
project, as the Easter weekend would empty all offices. The orchestra would pose no problem, said Labroca, as the Fenice complement would, of course, be available. But the singers and the
choir! Another matter entirely . . . the difficulties of the music

were well known . . . etcetera. However, he would make every effort . . . call back later.

Fortunately, Stravinsky's publishers, Boosey and Hawkes, had the music materials in their Long Island warehouse. Stuart Pope and Henson Markham telephoned the directors of Alitalia and arranged to place the package on a Thursday night flight to Milan, whence a courier would personally deliver it to Venice on Friday. Armed with this positive information, Mr. Weissel contacted Labroca again and, after a nervous-making hour, reported back to me that the impresario had indicated . . . after reflection . . . after careful reflection . . . there wasn't a singer in Italy who would be able to learn the score in time . . . let alone sing it. Therefore, *he* (Labroca) had decided that it would be far better to perform the composer's 1948 *Mass*—a work which was not only thoroughly inappropriate to the occasion, but one which Stravinsky most certainly would have vetoed. Robert said no. I said no to Mr. Weissel, who called Venice and said no. Well, said Labroca, well . . . we will see when the music arrives . . . the orchestra is in order . . . don't worry. As a euphemism this reassurance reached a new high.

At eight o'clock on Friday morning Mr. Weissel called me and in a slightly shaking voice delivered the news that he had just spoken with Labroca's secretary at the Fenice Theater . . . that the music had arrived safely and in time . . . that Labroca had departed for the week-end . . . that he was now unreachable (anywhere!) . . . that the orchestra, regrettably, was suddenly unavailable . . . that Italy, unfortunately, was entirely devoid of singers, players, in fact anyone at all who could read the music. "We are very sorry." Mr. Weissel was so devastated that at that moment my concern, especially in the face of his really heroic efforts on our behalf, was for *him;* but then he came up with the suggestion that we send our chorusmaster to Venice to recruit "on the spot" and begin rehearsals. He was confident from experience that as much, if not more, would be achieved as had been promised in the first place. Gregg Smith was pressed into service. It was arranged that he would discuss technical points with Robert immediately after the funeral and would fly to Venice at eight-thirty on Friday evening. As it turned out, he learned on his arrival that the mayoralty (on whom light had finally dawned, as a result of the descent of a horde of newspapermen assigned to report on preparations) had miraculously materialized Labroca, the RAI Chorus, the Fenice Or-

chestra, and had even printed programs. With a devil-may-care
gesture, the Scarlatti *Requiem* and a speech by His Honor were
also listed. This heartening news was delivered to me by phone
from Venice on Easter Sunday, a feat deserving of attention, for at
the time the city was in the throes of one of her numerous hotel
strikes; any visitor to Venice who has ever tried to make a call,
even under normal conditions, will appreciate the force of Mr.
Smith's personality.

After the first private family service on Tuesday evening—which
was attended by the Soulima Stravinskys and Milène (Theodore's
plane was not due from Geneva until the next morning), and such
close friends as Natasha Nabokov, Lucia Davidova, Samuel Dushkin
and his wife, George Balanchine, Lincoln Kirstein, the Elliott Car-
ters, Paul Horgan, and a few others—Mrs. Stravinsky and Robert
had decided not to be present at the other two. On those evenings
I was asked by other "friends" if they intended to come to the
funeral! Such thrusts are not at all uncommon in so-called artistic
circles, but they were hard on my temper, since anyone seeing Mrs.
Stravinsky on Tuesday evening would have realized that her attendance, even at that first service, was a cruelty her husband would
never have tolerated. Besides, the freak snowstorm that had occurred in the middle of the chanting, with its explosive thunder-
bolts and "supernatural" lightning flashes, had completely unnerved
her (as it had, indeed, the rest of us who were prey to fancy). She
was not much better as the funeral hour approached, suffering from
both a virus and an edema of the legs, and it was decided that I
would telephone from the funeral home—I had gone there at
eleven o'clock—about fifteen minutes before the service was scheduled to begin, to give the signal for her to come and thus obviate
any unhappy family confrontations.

By one o'clock on Friday, a large crowd had gathered on Madison Avenue and on Eighty-first Street, where the television crews
had set up their cameras at the rear of the chapel. Those doors,
leading to the street, had been opened for air and space. Stravinsky's
bier, covered and surrounded with flowers, not only from heads of
governments but from many anonymous music-lovers, had been
knelt to and prayed before and wept over, all morning, by some
who had known him and more who had not. Now the chapel could
not be entered except by those on the priority list I had had to
compile out of the hundreds of requests. Refusals were difficult,
but most people understood and joined the line in the lobby and

around the block. These included several small boys carrying Stravinsky records (a pre-teen-age group of budding composers?); other young people in jeans and jackets with solemn faces; many who had driven from Connecticut and Delaware and Washington and points South and West to pay tribute; two limousine drivers from the service Stravinsky had sometimes used; three stewardesses from American Airlines with whom he had flown; the man who had lately supplied him with his thirty-year-old Ballantine's; a taxi driver who reminded me that he had twice taken us to a recording session at the Manhattan Center many years ago; and so many others whom I recognized, and so many who felt gratitude for what he had given them.

Campbell's is a very well-equipped establishment, and I was grateful for the two family waiting rooms provided there for the bereaved. Also, the chapel itself was divided by a center aisle into two sections, and I did not foresee any problem in seating what had so sadly become two factions. The Stravinsky children filed in first, after the chapel was filled, and sat to the left side of the bier: Theodore and his wife, Milène and her husband, Soulima and Françoise with their son, John. On the right, Mrs. Stravinsky and Robert were supported by Edwin Allen and Rita, as well as by Natasha Nabokov, Mr. Weissberger, and, from London, Rufina Ampenoff of Boosey and Hawkes, who had cared dearly for the composer and had guarded his interests for many years. There were famous faces in that audience—Artur Rubinstein, Leopold Stokowski, Werner Klemperer, Sol Hurok, Isaac Stern, Sylvia Marlowe; and President Nixon's representative, as well as emissaries from the Soviet, French, and Italian embassies. And there were composers—Elliott Carter, Roger Sessions, Milton Babbitt, Claudio Spies, Marvin David Levy —and some members of the press not there in a reporting capacity, and Francis Steegmuller with his wife Shirley Hazzard, and Sarah Caldwell and Deborah Ishlon, and all his faithful nurses, and some strangers who had loved him. Balanchine, who had knelt and prayed at all three private services, did not come to the public one; his absence was questioned by a few newsmen who did not know of his abhorrence of crowds. An aged former member of the Ballet Russe sat in a corner and wept. After the service, Rubinstein waited in line twenty minutes to say his prayer before the bier, and not far behind him was playwright Bella Spewack, who had been with us once in Mexico.

The Stravinsky children returned to their hotel after the service,

and Mrs. Stravinsky, Robert, Rita, and Ed left for Florida that
evening, finding it difficult to remain in the apartment. They were
to fly to Venice Tuesday morning, and I was to go with the body
and the Campbell representative in charge, on Monday night. At
the empty apartment I took the phones off the hook, prepared the
press releases for Europe, and returned to my husband and my own
three-room flat for the first time in a week.

The flight on Monday was a nightmare. In the end, all of us were
aboard, for Mrs. Stravinsky had changed her mind, wishing to
travel with her husband. I pulled strings to secure seats on the
TWA flight, since a conclave of priests (headed by Cardinal
Cooke) was bound for Rome and the 747 was solidly booked. By
the time we boarded Mrs. Stravinsky was very ill and passed the
night in a daze that frightened us all. At the Rome airport the *papa-
razzi* were out in full force, and their cameras clicked like bon-bon
snappers as they stumbled over each other to catch her. Ten minutes of hysteria occurred when our luggage could not be unloaded
in time to travel with us on the connecting plane for Venice, and
the airport manager, wringing his hands, insisted he could not predict when it *would* arrive—the next plane to Venice was hours
later, and full. I told a lie: the music . . . the music vital for the
service . . . was contained therein. *"Dio mio, Signora,* which bag?"
All of them . . . distributed because of the weight. "What shall we
do? One perhaps could be found quickly, but seven! Impossible!"
Well . . . something must be done . . . rehearsal was at eight
(nine, actually) . . . rehearsals are costly . . . we did not wish
the city to be further taxed . . . the RAI chorus would be there,
especially . . . and so on. "Alas, *Signora!"* The bags were delivered to the Gritti not long after our own arrival, a testimonial
to Italian ingenuity and native respect for the municipal budget.

On former visits, and for long periods of time, the Stravinskys
had usually stopped at the Bauer Grünwald, situated on the Grand
Canal three or four *palazzi* away from the Gritti in the direction of
St. Mark's. But too many people knew of this custom, and the
smaller, more exclusive hotel promised the necessary seclusion. One
of the first calls, however, came from that veteran prince of con-
cierges, the Bauer's Tortorella, whose ability to solve any problem,
including the provision of a special Paris-bound train for guests
who have missed the last one, has made him a favorite subject for

some writers of travel literature. The Stravinskys had been his special pets for many years, and when they came to the Bauer, he would not have been daunted if they asked him to secure Tiepolo's gondola for use during their sojourn. Now his heartbroken voice begged me to assure "*Signora* Stravinsky" that his happiness depended on serving her, whether at his hotel or not. I mention all this because on Saturday morning, when all ceremonies were over, and families and friends had departed, I was stopped in the Gritti lobby by a handsome gray-haired gentleman who announced that he was a certified public accountant, sent as a gift from Tortorella, to help me decipher the final bills!

The hearse was due to arrive from Padua, its overnight stop, at 7:30 A.M. on Wednesday. In the Campiello San Andrea, around the bend from the Piazzale Roma, in front of the little church door where I went with Ed Allen to meet it, Theodore stood with his wife and his wife's niece, the daughter of a former mayor of Venice. He was bowed down with grief. The deep love he felt for his father had made a great impression on me during the weeks of his New York visit, and later at Évian, when he came daily from Geneva to see him. Of the three children he seemed to me the one most openly stricken, for he lived far away and was not wealthy enough to make many transatlantic crossings. He had come when he could, and had written often—had, in fact, begged to come in May 1969, when his father was on New York Hospital's critical list, but was asked to remain away because the doctors did not wish their patient to experience any undue emotional strain.

A small group had gathered, attracted, no doubt, by the presence of a couple of motorboats docked at the tiny quay, in which some television cameras and their operators were visible. While Ed waited in our *motoscafo*, I went to Theodore, and though his manner was distant at first, he relented, seeing my distress, and put out his hand. But when I asked if he would come to see Mrs. Stravinsky, who had indicated to me before leaving New York that she wished to have a talk with him in Venice about the feelings which had prompted her actions, he replied in French that her refusal to receive the family then had made such a meeting impossible now, and there could be no further contact "except through representatives." No pleas, explanations of her condition, nothing would make him change his mind. A Reuters reporter interrupted with some questions, and after a moment Theodore waved him off in my direction, saying that I could supply the rest of the answers. I recall little of that interview, for I was concerned with what Mrs. Stravinsky's reaction would be to Theodore's words. I knew she had had afterthoughts about the position she had taken in New York. Very well aware of Theodore's love for his father, she often spoke of it, even during the period of strained relations. And she seemed to understand his feeling of frustration at not being able to be with his father during his illness—having to watch from the opposite shore of an ocean, while this prerogative was taken over by others.

The hearse, an hour and a half late, had finally arrived, and the casket had been transferred to an old-fashioned motor launch hung with black crêpe. Three black-cassocked priests stood in the prow alongside a black-clad chauffeur. I was about to ask Theodore to take his place here when the niece whispered, "Theodore wishes to know if you would mind if he rode alone with his father." The very fact of this request, with its implication that a stranger might have the effrontery to object to it, was difficult to bear.

Our small procession up the Grand Canal, now joined by a few more private boats and *motoscafi* (in one of which I saw Nicolas Nabokov and his wife), turned into the canal at the right of the Palazzo Grimani, and proceeded through various smaller canals toward San Zanipolo. All along the way people stopped in the process of going about their business, and stood respectfully, heads bowed, some making the sign of the cross. As we approached the dock in front of the church, a woman in a window threw some flowers toward the coffin, but they missed their mark and fell into the water, where they were sucked up by the backwash from our own boat. Her look of disappointment is vivid even now; she must have been waiting patiently for hours to send her little offering. On the Campo San Zanipolo about a hundred people stood in silence, making a path for us to the huge church doors (with the notices on either side in blue letters on white paper announcing the "Homage to the Great Musician") and then following us down the long nave to the Chapel of the Rosary on the left side of the transept, where Stravinsky would lie in state until the services on Thursday.

Now, in retrospect, the brief ceremony in that extraordinary sanctuary, with its strange Gothic sculptures of saints blackened and mutilated by the great fire of 1867, and that marvel of a ceiling, where Veronese's *Annunciation* and *Adoration* and *Assumption* presided over the ebony and silver box, was for me the most impressive part of the entire Venetian affair. The solemnity of those few moments when the bearers, with instinctive gentleness, placed the coffin on its trestle, and the delicacy with which the sacristans adjusted the wreaths of flowers, and the noiseless busyness of two little boys, who with housewives' feather dusters whisked away the merest suspicion of anything that might have marred the casket during its travels—these are the things in the forefront of memory. And also the figure of Theodore, kneeling and weeping, so like his father in profile that it was startling to recall why we were there.

First meetings with representatives from the mayor's office, which took place that evening in San Zanipolo during Robert's rehearsal, were as full of old-world gallantry as a Longhi drawing room. The mayor's deputy could also easily have sat as a model for one of the painter's more accomplished seducers. He greeted me, seized both my hands, kissed them almost simultaneously, and, thereafter holding them in a firm grip, dragged me the length and breadth of the transept, enthusiastically outlining all the seating arrangements in lightning—and, need I say, totally incomprehensible —Italian. The least sign of struggle on my part was silenced with two more salutes, and after a while I resigned myself and strained my ears instead of my hands to catch a word or phrase that might make me feel less like an idiot. *Famiglia* figured frequently in the monologue, and I finally gathered that the family pews would be set up (only the nave was equipped that evening, with some makeshift rows of seats) to the left of the transept, where the bier would be placed; "*giornalisti*" (I am able to recognize *that* word in all languages) would be seated to the right, and there would be "*molti*" of those (here I was ahead of him; something like twenty-two calls from the press had come in between midnight and 4:00 A.M. that day). A general wave of the hand in the direction of the transept end of the nave, covering an area with what seemed to be the dimensions of the Colosseum, was assigned for the "*ufficiali municipali*" . . . only a few; this last statement was made clear to me by the sudden release of one of my hands to enable my instructor to display five fingers on his. "*Il pubblico*" would be admitted to the nave. And then, the lecture over, he looked at me with a slightly apprehensive eye and said, in my own native tongue, "No object?" I assured him that all was "*molto, molto bello*," received a battery of *baci* on my worn-out gloves, and off he went—to be replaced, just as I was collapsing onto a bench with exhaustion, by two gentlemen in dark suits who spoke a brand of English. Despite my insistence that all was as clear as the Venetian sky, the entire procedure was repeated, and I was told that on the morrow there would be interpreters aplenty to assist me. In the face of all this estimable Italian efficiency, I dismissed as calumny that malicious fiction about disorganization in Mediterranean countries. Even my vague feeling of unrest, when I counted thirty-three pieces of television equipment and almost as many cameras, being set up at the transept corners, on the altar, near the family area, and facing the nave, vanished. Mrs. Stravinsky, attending the rehearsal, was duly presented to the mayor's messengers and expressed her gratitude for the gift of the concert and the noble legend on the *affiches* announcing the hours of the services and the tribute to her husband: thousands of these decorated walls, kiosks, ramparts, pavements, docks, and even the sides of houses throughout the city.

And in the midst of all these graces, behind those chapel doors, the man who could not attend his rehearsal slept.

Funeral officials came early the next morning to take me to San Zanipolo, for the casket was to be transferred to the transept at ten o'clock, at which time a brief Mass for the Poor would be said. When we arrived, the Campo was already filled with those who had been unable to find places in the church, and from his immortal position on Verrochio's horse Colleoni seemed to maintain order. Doorways of shops, windows of houses, rooftops, and bridges were filled with people, conversing in hushed tones as they waited and creating a sound like the swarming of bees.

The nave was jammed when we entered, and *carabinieri* were posted grandly at the base of the steps leading to the altar and in front of the tapes that confined the crowd. All television lights were ablaze for tests, and their glare erased Lombardo's monuments and the bust of Bragadin, and blotted out Bellini and Piazzetta and Vivarini.

The casket was moved precisely at ten (as stated in the advertisements)—a union operation, I discovered, requiring nine men (on the bill), though the function of four of them remained forever a mystery. (I remembered Stravinsky's reaction on one occasion when I had to explain why two stagehands, who never did appear at all, must be included in a Carnegie Hall accounting for a concert he had subsidized himself!) The transfer was accomplished without mishap, since it involved only the lifting of the casket to a platform set on wheels, after which, with its burden, it was easily drawn from the Chapel of the Rosary to its place in the church. Ezra Pound followed it with his eyes, never moving from his (symbolic?) position near the monument to the Doge Malipiero, that marble "farewell" to Gothic art and "hail" to the Renaissance. And I recognized many old friends from the American and British press, who also stood and waited silently.

But after the Mass for the Poor, I noticed that the *famiglia* pews were occupied, and not by *famiglia*. The press section as well was filled with a hundred or so individuals armed with guidebooks and thus easily identifiable as foreign contributors to the local economy. After much persuasion, an interpreter (one of those appointed by my dragomen of the previous evening) was prevailed upon to ask them to move, but, lacking the talent of Cicero, he gave up after two minutes and vanished with a pout and a helpless shoulder shrug. Fortunately four RAI cameramen, requiring additional space for their cranes, came to the rescue, and both sections were cleared in a trice by a flashing of badges and an explosion of high-speed threats. The clean-up, however, exposed another defect. The family rows —about eight of them, to accommodate friends as well—were long, narrow-backed benches, providing a sitting-depth of six inches at the outside; despite the fact that the Greek Orthodox service is celebrated mainly while standing, this austerity seemed as hard as the wood of which they were made. Furthermore, these hair-shirts were apparently the prescribed wardrobe *only* for the family; about twenty comfortable pews with sectional seats stood ready for the arrival of the mayor's guests, and of these, the first two rows (for the highest dignitaries) were composed of armchairs equipped with fat red velvet cushions. I thought of Mrs. Stravinsky and her poor, swollen feet and decided I would exercise my Berlitz Tuscan; needless to say, no interpreter was in sight. But it seemed that even to ask such a thing was an indication that grief was not present where it should be, and the usher to whom I appealed displayed a reaction worthy of a Salem housewife accidentally presented to Hester Prynne.

It was too late to argue, for by now hundreds of people, all bearing "official" invitations, were storming the right lateral door, opened for these guests only. The "few" turned out to be anyone who had stopped by the municipal offices for an admission pass, and more of these had been issued than there were seats. The over-flow—a variety of types, including several fashion models in see-through shirts and slacks accompanied by good-looking bronzed escorts, a few *principesse* more formally dressed (they wore gloves), and a group of businessmen with briefcases (uneasy pur-veyors, perhaps, of the accoutrements of the proceedings)—moved belligerently to the family section and remained there. The first row awaited the mourners, and in the second and third friends were seated—Eugene Berman, Vittorio Rieti, Francis Steegmuller, the Robert Patersons, Alain Daniélou, Ahron Propes, Mrs. Nicolas Nabokov; and representatives of Boosey and Hawkes, the Polish composer Penderecki, and a few musicians from other countries. At that moment a kindly friar came rushing forward with a collapsible chair for the widow (*someone* had understood me!) which he pushed into the front pew, the only one made up of two benches placed together.

The cameramen had now finished focusing, and the roving photographers were taking up their positions within inches of the bier—some betraying considerable annoyance at not being per-mitted to climb on top of it. A few were squatting directly in front of the mourners' row, cameras pointed upward, lenses alert to cap-ture any interesting sign of weakness. (The widow disappointed them—her eyes were hidden by large dark sunglasses, and her face remained graven.)

Both branches of the family arrived simultaneously at the side door, where I met them and led them to their places. With Milène, Soulima and his son John, Theodore and Denise, and the niece, was Kitty, Stravinsky's granddaughter by Ludmilla, whom I knew from her one visit to the West Coast house in 1965. Mrs. Stravinsky, on Nicolas Nabokov's arm, was followed by Robert, Rita, and Ed. The awkwardness of placing both families together in the first row was alleviated by settling Nicolas, like the conciliating Prince in *Romeo and Juliet*, in the exact center of the two families, where his handsome head, with its shock of white hair glistening like spun sugar under the television lights, took command of the scene.

Recollection of the concert is dim now, probably because San Zanipolo lacks in acoustics what it possesses architecturally, and the final bars of Stravinsky's powerful vision of Death seemed wafted away through the great window that backs the apse. The Archimandrite Malissianos, whose gestures would have outdone those of John Barrymore and whose voice—chanting, singing, reading in the antique, mysterious tones of the Greek Orthodox liturgy—seemed like three voices, did indeed suggest another time and place. But his awareness of the television cameras, demonstrated by certain studied turns this way and that as their operators moved in for close-ups of his superb, black-bearded, black-browed Tiziano profile (in living color!) was as contemporary as the jewelry with which Peggy Guggenheim, visible in the third *famiglia* row, was hung. This impression may be somewhat prejudiced, however, for prior to the service I saw him in a small office (where I had been taken to sign the gondoliers' bills) administering a smart box on the ear to his tearful young acolyte for handing him his brilliant robe with adolescent clumsiness.

But it was indeed a macabre feast for the eye—that catafalque heavy with its black velvet coverlet beneath the coffin, and its encircling forest of flowers; the brocaded robes of the archimandrite and his attendant, sparkling with gold and silver embroideries; the scarlet and gold throne for the priest, the glint of swords and belt-buckles of the *carabinieri*, the flash of the gold incense burner, and the silvery smoke of the incense itself floating over the bier. Stravinsky would have found some of it intriguing, for he had a sybaritic fondness for antique fabrics and owned a few old Venetian and East Indian embroideries; and he admired the panoply of ecclesiasticism: his collection of silver-encrusted icons, some on antique velvet panels, was a source of pride.

Toward the end of the service the crowd in the nave, which had been exemplary during the Scarlatti, the mayor, and the Stravinsky, became less orderly, and an ascending hum disturbed the solemnity of the final rite, when the family filed to the head of the coffin and kissed its glossy surface in farewell.

Outside, the black-draped gondola—with its gold lions of St. Mark and oars trailing black crêpe, heading the cortège with the casket, archimandrite and cross-bearing acolyte in attendance—was also decorated with a half-dozen cameramen, each standing with one foot on the craft's ledge and the other on the dock. The chair-providing friar again manifested himself from nowhere, literally shooing them away by using the front of his cassock like an apron, as though they were chickens with nomadic tendencies, and carved a route for Mrs. Stravinsky to enter the second gondola with Rob-

ert. This arrangement had been determined in New York, for both
wished to travel together the road that the trio had so often taken—
to the island and beyond it to Torcello for a dinner at the inn with
friends, or a visit to the Teotoka virgin in Santa Maria Assunta. The
daughter and sons, to whom I had to explain this, had been tight-
lipped, but they and their families divided themselves between the
next two gondolas with only one comment from Soulima: "We
would not mind if Vera traveled alone."

Friends took their places in the remaining gondolas, and, as was
to be expected, others who had no business being there but saw
some empty spaces also joined the procession. Until we left the
small canal that empties into the lagoon past the Church of the
Mendicanti, I saw only an ocean of faces—hundreds and hundreds
of them everywhere—solemn, profoundly respectful, some wet
with tears, some with fingers on their lips as though imposing
silence. They were the faces of people of the town, not those of
curiosity seekers, and the expressions they wore were reminders of
their own heritage, for they paid tribute not only to Death and the
death of one who, they had been told, was a great man of music,
but to Art itself, visible in every stone that surrounded them.

San Michele was crowded when the cortège arrived. It is a much-
frequented island under ordinary circumstances, for it is not the
Venetian nature to deny a certainty, and the citizens are perpetually aware that to this place most of them will finally come. Families often lunch here, spreading comestibles neatly on the ground
on white cloths while their children race around the gravestones.
Today three other funerals had occurred, and their mourners remained out of respect, joining the group of sightseers and newsmen. The mooring dock swung precariously as a group of these
bystanders eagerly rushed forward to render assistance in transmitting the heavy casket to *terra firma*. The archimandrite, with a
dexterity I shall always envy, leaped out of the gondola-hearse like
Le Spectre de la Rose—no mean athletic display, since he wore
about thirty or forty pounds of brocade. On the rather long walk
to the Russian Orthodox section the pallbearers almost dropped
the casket at one point, necessitating a halt while additional help
was secured to lift it up a short flight of stone steps. It was a welcome stop for Mrs. Stravinsky, who by this time could hardly
move her legs. Inside the tiny chapel there *was* a chair for her;

Robert stood at her side and the rest of us waited, half in, half out, until official word came from the mayor's office granting "permission to bury."

The interment service is mercifully brief, and the gravediggers were ready. The coffin was lowered. The widow, summoned by the archimandrite, stepped forward like an obedient child, threw her handful of "dust," received the priest's blessing, kissed his ring, and, suddenly clutching my hand, said, "Let us leave this place." And we did, pushing through the crowd, turning our backs to the photographers standing on the wall and the curious on the paths and the acquaintances and the reporters, and some who stayed to watch until the gap was covered and he was left alone.

A young newspaperman, keeping pace with us on the way out, pulled at Robert's jacket and said aggressively, "Aren't you even going to visit Diaghilev's grave?" And Robert, with admirable control, replied, "We've been there many times. Not today."

In the bar of the Gritti Nature produced her antidote—that euphoric numbness that delays reality, for a while anyway. Champagne helped, too. There are excellent reasons for wakes, not the least of which is that they stimulate a flow of speech pent-up for too long. Mrs. Stravinsky and Robert talked with Berman, Rieti, Steegmuller, Nabokov, reminiscing, reviewing the events of the past week. From an adjoining table where I sat with two of Stravinsky's London acquaintances, I could hear snatches of Mrs. Stravinsky's conversation with her old friend, the painter Bill Congdon: "He was terrified of water. He was so nervous in gondolas . . . and you know how impossibly he behaved every time we crossed the Atlantic . . . always sick . . . never poking his nose out of his cabin." "But Venice is *full* of water," someone said as though transmitting a bit of startling information. "But he did love it here very much," she went on. "St. Petersburg, after all . . . it reminded him of St. Petersburg . . . all the canals . . . the audiences, no . . . he didn't like them, or the critics either . . . soooo nasty!"

On the following day she left with Robert and Ed for Paris. There she would see Pierre Souvchinsky, Stravinsky's old friend, who had been unable to travel to Venice. And from Paris she and Robert would proceed to Morocco to spend a few days with her

husband's niece Ira Belline, who was the only "family" relative
she now had in the world, outside the USSR. I was to remain in
Venice a day or two to settle matters before my return to New
York to work on Estate affairs.

The accounting, expressed in Italian *lire* as these invoices were,
would have been enough to cause a permanent stoppage of breath
had I not already been familiar with the rate of exchange. And it
occupied most of Saturday, since such unexpected items as special
rubber wheels for the platform that had borne the casket and
"contributions" of various sorts turned up in a column whose heading was translated as "Miscellany." But finally, in the late afternoon, when the Nabokovs had come and gone, I walked alone to
San Zanipolo. The great doors of the façade were closed but un-
locked, and I went inside. The temporary pews had been removed,
the enormous nave was empty. And to the rear of the transept
Sant' Antonino was now clearly visible, dispensing alms in Lotto's
masterpiece. There was nary a trace of television scaffolding nor
any scrap of paper from a writer's notebook. Near the altar two
Dominicans were industriously laying out the paraphernalia for
Vespers. One of them suddenly picked up an altar cloth and, carrying it to the better light of a votive candle-stand, appeared to examine it microscopically—perhaps, I thought, to make certain it had
not been damaged in the course of those recent non-Roman
prayers.

PART I

1959-1965

His self and the sun were one
And his poems, although makings of his self,
Were no less makings of the sun.

Wallace Stevens, *The Planet on the Table*

CHAPTER ONE

ON August 18, 1959, Robert Craft, writing from Hollywood, asked whether or not I would be interested in managing and promoting a series of three concerts that Stravinsky and he had just decided to co-conduct in New York at the end of the year. The letter marked the actual beginning of our professional relationship, although I had met both gentlemen (and Mrs. Stravinsky) in New Mexico early in July, and had, in a particular sense, worked for them at that time.

As head of my own modest publicity firm, which then boasted a staff of three (including myself), I had been engaged for several years in the precarious business of representing and publicizing various institutions, as well as many stars, in the classical music field. Among the former were two organizations with summer seasons, and one of these was the remarkably progressive Santa Fe Opera, founded in 1957 by John Crosby. My contract with this company had been signed the following year, and my duties included several weeks of work *in situ* prior to the formal opening. In 1959 our promotion was to include, as a feature additional to the regular opera offerings, a special concert in the Santa Fe Cathedral at which Stravinsky would conduct his *Threni*. Also, Robert Craft was one of the scheduled guest conductors, his responsibility being the rarely performed Donizetti opera *Anna Bolena*.

The prospect of an in-the-flesh confrontation with a legend aroused mixed feelings in me, prominent among which was a definite *soupçon* of terror. The name Stravinsky (like the name Kastchei *), apart from having various controversial spellings, conjured up for me a number of awe-inspiring visions, among them one in which a flock of exotic firebirds was engaged in studying a concordance of psalms. I had had a fortunate childhood in a music-

---

* In Russian folklore, Kastchei (or Kostchei or Koschei) is an evil demon. He is, as everyone knows, the villain of *The Firebird*.

loving home, and had been introduced to Stravinsky's works by my
father at a very early age. We owned whatever recordings were
available, and saw most of the performances by the Ballet Russe
de Monte Carlo during its visits to this country, both in Boston
(where I was born and raised) and in New York whenever trips
there were possible. But concerts were the special medium. As a
student at the Girls' Latin School, I was duenna for my younger
sister and two of her "best" friends every Friday afternoon, when, as
soon as classes were over at two-thirty, we would trudge through
the windy Fenway to Symphony Hall, where its manager, Mr.
George Judd, who knew my father, had someone hold our places in
the long line of second-balcony admissions. With our feet hanging
over the percussion at right stage, we would dampen the players
with tears of excitement as Koussevitzky launched into the Intro-
duction to *The Firebird,* clinging to each other for dear life in
anticipation of that initial thunderbolt of the *Infernal Dance.*

As time passed, such adolescent experiences were augmented by
articles and books about Stravinsky—which I was stimulated to
read by a very close friend who had attended the Charles Eliot
Norton Lectures that the composer delivered at Harvard in 1939
and 1940—and later by his "autobiography" (which, I think now,
is not "auto" at all). Happily also, a personal interest in contemporary music plus the profession I had chosen (at the end of a long
line of others) had kept me fairly up to date by the time I was to
meet him. One of the few commendable aspects of the music publicity business is its requirement that everything printed be read,
everything performed be heard, to avoid disillusioning clients who
consider that every dime they are spending entitles them to the
services of the Delphic Oracle.

And, of course, I had been treated to a great deal of music world
gossip. In Stravinsky's case, however, it should be made clear at once
that the locution is as inapplicable as it would be to the authors of
Leviticus and Deuteronomy. Nevertheless, tales had reached my
ears of his outbursts of temper, his arrogance, his "fantastic" capacity for Scotch, and his equally "fantastic" love of money—
among the latter, the very widespread story that he had once refused to go onstage at Dumbarton Oaks because his check had not
been handed to him *before* the performance, whereupon a personal
payment had to be made on the spot by one of the major board
members before Stravinsky would make a move in the direction

of the podium. I knew also that a new book, *Conversations with Igor Stravinsky*, was about to come off the press, and that it represented a collaboration between Robert Craft and the composer, a fact that had made me take stock of my mental catalogue of collected second-party data: Robert was his "secretary," "amanuensis," "assistant," "aide," "errand boy," etc., etc.—but one does not "collaborate" (at any rate, in a literary sense) *sans* respect for the mental capacities of his partner. All of this folklore was enveloped in my own emotion of reverence, inspired by what *I* knew I knew— that Stravinsky was the greatest musical personage of our time, and one of the greatest of all time.

There were also some preconceived notions as to his physical appearance. When I saw Stravinsky in the pit—and this had been only once, in the thirties—conducting a ballet performance of *Jeu de Cartes* at the old Metropolitan Opera House, he appeared to be of average height, spare of figure and gaunt of profile. His movements and gestures seemed extremely disciplined—that is, he was definitely not a "thrilling" or a "romantic-type" conductor. Yet when I left the opera house, I recall my strong feeling that the music had been *performed* . . . the score had been *read* precisely, measure by measure . . . and what one had heard was the truthful reporting of an idea. The idea was of massive proportions, naturally, for this was implicit in the presence of the "legend" in person.

As for *Threni*, the work that was to be the principal subject of my Santa Fe promotion, I only knew (having missed its American debut in New York's Town Hall the previous January) that Stravinsky had led the world première at the Scuola di San Rocco in Venice in September of 1958; * that its German hearing, following immediately thereafter in Hamburg, had provoked critical attacks; and that in Paris it had been so badly prepared, "disaster" was the word almost unanimously applied to the performance. The same sources of trade gossip had it that Stravinsky, in a fury, had left the French capital vowing he would never again conduct there (a dictum that, sadly, came to pass, despite many Gallic efforts in the ensuing years to reverse it).

When I first saw him at Santa Fe, Stravinsky was standing in the

---

* *Threni* had been completed in January 1958, on a commission from the Norddeutsche Rundfunk. According to Robert Craft, it was unofficially dedicated to Stravinsky's friend Allessandro Piovesan, director of the Venice Biennale, which had also commissioned the *Canticum Sacrum*.

portico of the ranch house that served as both residence and offices for the opera administration. He had just alighted from the car that had brought him there from his downtown hotel for a rehearsal, and was talking with the singers' coach, Bliss Hebert. He stood at ease, hands thrust in the pockets of his slightly baggy-kneed gray tweed trousers, a book tucked high under one arm, his shoulders hunched a little forward as he looked up from his five-foot-two to Bliss's nine-inch-taller height. He wore a blue shirt open at the neck, into which a black and white ascot scarf was tucked, and his jacket was slung nattily on his shoulders (a habit so endearing at first sight that forever after any conductor who did the same looked absurdly pretentious to me). Dark glasses concealed his eyes, and another pair of clear ones was pushed back to shine, like the horns of Moses, high on his forehead, where a few wisps of sandy-colored hair were carefully brushed in a straight line from mid-crown neckwards. I was struck, of course, by his gnome-like stature —he had seemed so much taller in the pit!—and then by his head, placed by a trick of perspective on the summit of one of the Santa Fe mountains in the panorama behind him. It was all forehead, and as I approached with John Crosby, the furrows forming there as he emphasized a point in his discussion seemed as deep as wind-shaped lines on sand. A few light-colored "eyebrow feathers" (his phrase) stirred gently in the breeze above the rim of his sunglasses. His ears were fascinating: outsize for that ascetically bony countenance; they protruded like those of one of Caravaggio's *bacchi*, their outer flanges peaked by faintly blunted points. His voice, which I was now near enough to hear, was as deep and resonant as the echo produced by a stone dropped into a "bottomless" well, and seemed to enrich itself with its Russian accent, which, far from sounding heavy (as indeed it was), succeeded in sounding elegant.

By this time he had been surrounded by a group of adoring company members whom he greeted with obvious pleasure, especially those he seemed to recognize from previous encounters. It was now my turn, and John identified me as the Santa Fe Opera's publicity director. Up went Stravinsky's left hand to move his sunglasses, just long enough for me to catch a glint of a "What's this?" in those keen gray-brown eyes, his lips came together in a closed, pro-truding *o*, he extended his right hand graciously, and then he smiled. I was to discover that the Stravinsky smiles were as care-fully catalogued as his collection of medications. This one came from the file marked "Smiles, pertaining to publicity, particularly individuals engaging therein." It consisted, without any unpursing of the *o*, in a broad upward turn of the corners of the mouth and an absolute immobility of the remaining facial muscles. Introductions over, he grasped Bliss's arm and moved off toward the nearby rehearsal hall, giving me my first glimpse of the slight limp inherited from his 1956 thrombosis, although he did not seem to need the crook-handled cane he carried. The rest of us brought up the rear.

When we arrived, and before he sat down in the chair placed on a wooden platform that served as a podium, he assigned the singers their positions for the rehearsal, using his forefinger to make short stabs in the air (designating places to within a fraction of an inch, incidentally), after which he turned with a polite look of inquiry to Bliss to see if he agreed. (He did, and I wondered at the time what would have happened if he had not.) Stravinsky then removed his sunglasses and placed them in his trouser pocket, at the same time withdrawing another spectacle case, which he set down with a precise snap on the lower left corner of his lectern; removed his jacket from his shoulder and, refusing assistance from a hovering worshipper, hung it neatly on the back of his chair; took a huge wad of Kleenex out of another pocket and pushed it under the open covers of his score, making sure that several edges protruded for easier access; asked John Crosby, who had been carrying his white cardigan, "kindly to put it just around me," meaning on his shoulders; and sat down. He opened the spectacle case, muttered "conducting glasses," put them on and discovered he was still wearing the other pair like a tiara. Out came another case, this time from the handkerchief pocket of his jacket, and in went the truant pair. Then, and only then, did he lean forward to examine the score for a moment, after which he looked up, waved a general greeting, both palms turned toward his face, and with a smile extracted from the folder marked "Pleasure" said, "Let us begin at number . . ."

But I forget the number. Those other "rituals," however, have remained with me to this day, clear as the lucent Santa Fe air, forming one of my favorite memories. (Stravinsky was always a "detail merchant" when he prepared to rehearse or conduct—a qualification, incidentally, with which he often mischievously endowed one of the officials at Columbia Records.)

A photographer from one of the local newspapers had joined me at the side of the hall, where, unnoticed, we could have a clear view of Stravinsky's profile. At a particular point about halfway through the work, we both began to kneel in order to select an angle shot to include two kittens from a litter of six that lived in the hedge just outside. They had strayed within—attracted perhaps by some of the more mournful passages—had taken up a position near the composer's platform, and were regarding the proceedings with the attention of honor students at the Juilliard School. I made a sudden move to prevent myself from slipping to the floor, and, like a buzz-bomb, the sound of ripping cloth penetrated the air—at that moment full of deathly silence while Stravinsky paused to study the score. One leg of my slacks—a practical outfit, in view of the numerous fences that had to be maneuvered during photo sessions —had split up the side clear to the waist. Panic took hold when I saw the "Maestro" gaze in my direction, fish for something in his pocket, hand it to a bystander, and point to me with anything but enthusiasm. That's it, I thought, he's sending me a cyanide pill.

It was a safety pin—diaper-size!

Later in the day, I met a besplinted and arm-slung Robert Craft, *hors de combat* by virtue of a chipped right elbow and a few strained ligaments. The accident had occurred a week or so before, when—in an enthusiastic desire to take some exercise—he had leaped over a fence at the rear of the open-air opera house, although other, more convenient methods of exit were readily available. Apart from the acute discomfort to the victim, the mishap had thrown the administration into a morass of complication, since *Anna Bolena*, which he could not, of course, conduct now, had been chosen for the season partly at his suggestion. Prior to meeting him, therefore, my own impressions were somewhat negative: an impetuous fellow . . . immature . . . not inclined to think things out carefully . . . well! When he did turn up for a press conference at which Stravinsky permitted pictures to be taken, his physical appearance, first of all, contradicted impulsiveness. Perhaps it was the care in walking necessitated by the bandages, or perhaps the horn-rimmed spectacles decorating that highly sensitive, wide-browed, narrow-jawed "boyish" face, or the voice, which was unusually soft and unobtrusive—at any rate, he looked and behaved far more like a young college instructor trying hard not to talk down to his class than like a musician in his late thirties, and especially a conductor. He began to enlarge on *Threni* for the benefit of the press and the cast, delivering an impromptu and enlightening analysis of the work while its creator sat, hands folded on the table in front of him, nodding approval from time to time. He had the ability, moreover, to appear to be addressing his remarks to an individual while encompassing the entire group within his scope—a talent which immediately demolished the notion that he did not think things out carefully. It was also clear that a large contingent of the female singers were casualties of his charm.

Mrs. Stravinsky, I was told, had been painting and was present only the next day. We met in the patio of the La Fonda Hotel, at a lunch attended also by her husband, Robert, John Crosby, the novelist Paul Horgan, and Miranda Levy. It was due to Miranda that the Stravinskys had become interested in the Santa Fe Opera. They had known her for some time—in fact, at her instigation they had visited Taos, where she introduced them to Frieda Lawrence and Mabel Dodge Luhan. Miranda had been a Santa Fe resident until her marriage to movie producer Ralph Levy brought her to Hollywood and made her the Stravinskys' neighbor as well as their friend. Both Miranda and Paul Horgan were members of the original group that had helped, by fund-raising, the development of John Crosby's project, and when *The Rake's Progress* was suggested as an appropriate highlight for the Opera's first season, Miranda had secured the composer's promise to supervise a new production, which Robert was invited to conduct.

Miranda had informed me that Robert addressed Mrs. Stravinsky as "Madame"—pronouncing it in the French manner—a title with which (someone said) she had been christened by Lawrence Morton, then director of the Ojai Festival as well as the Monday Evening Concerts at the Los Angeles County Museum. Miranda, however, called her "Vera," as did many of her other friends (I was to learn), but after that initial meeting I followed Robert's lead and never lost the habit. Besides, the title suited her perfectly—she could have been the central figure in a Russian or French romantic novel of the last century. And it was easy to see why Bakst and others had wanted to paint her. She looked that day as though she were on her way to sit for Renoir—a pastel blue dress clung to a generous, curvaceous figure; a blue gauze scarf was wound around her blondish hair and about her throat. Her eyes were (and still are) the largest I have ever seen, blue-violet in color and very ex-

pertly accentuated at that time by heavy makeup. At first her statu-
esque height and carriage seemed to overshadow everyone at the
table, especially her husband, who sat beside her concentrating on
an old-fashioned glass full of Scotch. But this was an illusion, for
nowhere can there be a more feminine woman than Madame! By
some coquettish magic she receded voluntarily into the background,
emerging only at those moments when color was called for in the
scene.

As for the composer, I had discovered the day before that everyone at Santa Fe addressed him as "Maestro." Everyone, that is, except Robert, who, in fact, did not call him by any name at all.
Robert's designation was simply the pronoun "he" (or "you" if he
spoke to him directly), carried through in all its proper declension
forms. The only departure from this practice occurred when he
talked of Stravinsky to his wife, in which case the phrase used was
"your husband." But for me, after that day, it would always be
"Maestro." That was a term I had previously employed in addressing any distinguished conductor, in accordance with music business
protocol, but I was never to use it thereafter except with Stravinsky.

I had looked forward to this lunch with great interest, not only
because it would be my first social contact with the Stravinskys, but
also because I was sure that many pearls of wisdom would be
dropped, and my mental notebook was already open, its first page
headed "What He Said." But it remained blank. The composer sat
relaxed but silent, only holding his glass high when it needed re-
plenishing, which was accomplished from his special bottle on the
table. I never saw a fifth of anything disappear so fast; the rest of us
drank martinis and gin-and-tonic in more discreet amounts. Conversation, in English, centered chiefly on several intramural in-
trigues rampant at the moment, with Paul making valiant but unsuccessful efforts to involve Stravinsky by diverting the talk to the
more conventional subjects of music and literature. Finally, thoroughly befuddled (though I would not have dared voice this
then!), he tugged gently at his wife's sleeve and whispered loudly in
French, "Can we go? I am very sleepy." And off they went, after
kisses of good-bye were bestowed on everyone, their receding figures reminding me of Juno and her peacock, the latter with tail
feathers tucked in and at rest.

Beyond this occasion and one or two other dinners, more heavily attended and more full of bottled cheer, I had no further personal contact with the Stravinskys. The *Threni* performance on July 12 was a tremendous success; the composer was escorted into the cathedral, as I recall, by Paul Horgan, robed in black (he was shortly to be appointed a Knight of St. Gregory), and by an ecclesiastic, and he looked, for all the world, like a bride being conducted to the altar in an Orthodox Jewish ceremony. I remember, too, that the faces of the ladies in the chorus—fixed on Robert as he heroically led Bach's *Trauer-Ode* with his left arm—all wore the expressions of dedicants witnessing the martyrdom of St. Sebastian.

The Stravinskys and Robert departed a few days thereafter, and I buried my recollections of these events in a comfortable catacomb.

And now this letter from Robert. It relayed, in two and a half pages of what can only be described as *petit point* in ink, the interesting information that Stravinsky wished to conduct two concerts at the end of that year, and one at the beginning of the next; that Robert would share the conducting chore in works from the contemporary and baroque repertoires; that one of the programs would include the world première of *Movements for Piano and Orchestra*, and that on another Stravinsky would also lead, for the first time in New York City, *Les Noces*, for which four "name" pianists would be required.

Stravinsky's motives, Robert explained, comprised a wish to record, a tax justification for his stay in Manhattan, a proper locale for the première (the composer had broken a contract to perform it first in Europe), and finally, a desire to "jolt" New York a bit. The letter also included proposed dates at Town and Carnegie Halls; other works to be performed (Bach, Monteverdi, Schoenberg, etc.); a list of preferred solo singers; suggestions for chorus, contractor, ticket scale, as well as budget (very small) and rehearsal time (very big). In conclusion, he told me that Stravinsky expected to *make* money, and that if I agreed to handle the proceedings he (Robert) would see me briefly in New York on September 2, when he would be enroute to Europe with the composer and his wife. The letter gave me my first experience (I was to have a few hundred others in the course of the following years) with that extraordinary handwriting—to which the regulations of the Burano Lacemakers' Guild should have been applied as a protection against

blindness—and with his equally extraordinary gift of conveying ten
pages of important information in less than two.

It also inaugurated Mr. Stravinsky's New York "jolt" with me.

In the twenty-four hours that I allowed myself for reflection
after the arrival of this communication (force of habit—what manner of fool would have said no?), two telephone calls came in.
One was from Bliss Hebert at Santa Fe, checking to see whether the
letter had been received, and the other from Deborah Ishlon, publicity director for Columbia Records. I had known Deborah for
some time because of the allied fields in which we were engaged,
and was aware that she was very close to the Stravinskys, beyond
the duties her office carried out vis-à-vis the company's most distinguished (if not most revenue-producing) piece of property. It
occurred to me not long after, as it does now, that both she and Bliss
were in major part responsible for this turning point in my life.

As it developed I talked with Robert only briefly prior to his
departure for Europe, and I did not see the Stravinskys at all until
the *Liberté* docked at Pier Eighty-eight on November 19, one
month and one day before the first concert at Town Hall. However, in the interim, thirty-four letters crammed with detail (I
knew the daily temperatures in Venice, Hamburg, London, and
Paris) had passed between Robert and myself; Stravinsky had participated in four long-distance calls, indicating his presence on the
wire by a resonant "hmmmmmmm," or a groan-like clearing of the
throat if he disagreed with something. At gangplank time our books
showed a sold-out first concert (Town Hall, December 20), a
fairly-well-selling third concert (Town Hall, January 10), and a
jitters-making middle one (Carnegie Hall, January 3).

In the course of arriving at this point, several lessons ranging
from fascinating to hard had been learned. They became the basis
for a kind of lexicon that was to serve me well in the future, and
to which, during the first three years of our association, appendix
after appendix would be attached. Here is a small part of the
glossary:

1. Stravinsky was not fond of the celebrated portrait Picasso had
made of him. According to Robert's letter of September 21, the
composer thought it not striking enough and too common, so the
idea of using it in our programs was abandoned.

2. All correspondence, however addressed, went first to Robert
and afterward into a file kept by Stravinsky. In an earlier letter

written from his parents' home in Kingston (September 3), Robert had advised me not to bother to send separate letters, as he always saw "Mr. S.'s" mail first.

3. Stravinsky expected the press to pay for their tickets: No complimentary tickets, everyone would have to pay, from Miss X (an august name!) down, was the order (October 5). I protested this, and was grudgingly granted permission to allot the resident press their usual free tickets.

4. Robert had definite views on what he would and would not conduct. He wrote that he was sick of all-Stravinsky concerts and did not wish to conduct them. This information arrived in a very early letter, written on August 24, when Robert was at Princeton with Stravinsky to address a Fromm Seminar. It was prompted by the composer's "sudden" feeling that the three concerts should be reduced to two, because he thought the third concert impractical. This would mean, Robert added, that he (Robert) would probably have to conduct the *Rite,* scheduled for the Carnegie Hall concert, as the *Movements* première would be moved to that hall.

In point of fact Stravinsky had wanted only *one* concert, and this was the most interesting revelation of all, since it now became clear that the idea of the series had been Robert's alone, and had grown to these proportions out of Stravinsky's original wish to première the *Movements* in New York. The composer had two significant reasons for this desire: first, his pleasure over the Manhattan reception accorded *Threni* the previous January, as against his displeasure over certain developments in Germany, where *Movements* had been scheduled to have its first hearing; and second, a promise from Margit Weber's husband, who had commissioned the work in which his wife would be piano soloist, that he would help should there be a financial deficit.* Stravinsky, in fact, had no actual backing for these three concerts, and the command to me was "budget according to sold-out houses."

Budget! This was a word, I soon discovered, that was not to be interpreted in its normal sense, as determining financial boundaries to stay "within," but rather in a special Craftian sense: to wit, fixing financial limits firmly and staying "within" although all costs might increase "without."

---

* I learned later that this offer was the decisive factor in the presentation of that series of three concerts.

By October 10 I was able to submit an all-cost budget for the series totaling $24,216.94—this covered everything on which we had positive figures: orchestra (including rehearsals), artists, leases, dress rehearsals, payroll taxes, extra personnel in the auditoriums, chorus risers, piano tuning, ticket printing, cartage of instruments, programs, printing, promotion, advertising, mailing costs, music material rentals, fees for music preparation, fees for vocal preparation, copyists, and my office. It also included everything on which we did *not* have positive figures, such as the chorus for all three concerts (about $2,500), extra space for additional rehearsals, insurance, and so on. Our houses were scaled to bring in a net ticket income (after entertainment taxes and with certain seats sold on a series basis at a slight reduction), of $24,860.94—that ninety-four cents was like a talisman, but that's the way it came out! *

In clarification, especially for any readers foolhardy enough to be currently engaged in the concert business, I should mention that this absurdly low figure for the three concerts, one of which would use an orchestra of ninety-five musicians, was arrived at thanks to several unusual circumstances, the principal one being the name "Stravinsky." All orchestra personnel, a body including the first-desk men of major orchestras in and around New York, played for the minimum union scale; singers such as Mildred Allen, Elaine Bonazzi, Loren Driscoll, Robert Oliver, and Regina Sarfaty accepted token fees ranging from seventy-five to one hundred dollars, depending on their degree of participation; Baldwin supplied pianos, waiving cartage costs (which were considerable, since four pianos had to be moved around quite a bit), and Stravinsky music materials were, of course, to be without rental charge. (I *was* billed by the composer's principal publisher, Boosey and Hawkes, but received strict instructions in a letter from the creator himself not to pay!)

And the composer-pianists—Samuel Barber, Aaron Copland, Lukas Foss, and Roger Sessions—refused even to consider a fee of any kind, but union regulations forbade their performances without one, and I have the delightful recollection of sending each of these distinguished gentlemen a check for seventy-five dollars on the afternoon of the first rehearsal for *Les Noces.*

(In connection with their appearance hangs a brief tale. When

---

* In 1971, prior to Stravinsky's death, Robert planned to do a concert of Stravinsky works involving a chamber-sized orchestra. The budget I drew up for this single program at Carnegie Hall came to $28,000!

Eugene Goossens conducted *Les Noces* in its London première with the Ballet Russe in 1926, the four pianists were composers Vittorio Rieti, Georges Auric, Francis Poulenc, and Vladimir Dukelsky (Vernon Duke). It seemed a good idea to reproduce the latter situation with American composers, and Stravinsky was in favor of it. He sent notes of invitation to each gentleman and I followed this up with telephone calls to explain in detail. Mr. Foss agreed enthusiastically on condition that he could play Piano Number One. Mr. Barber conceded gracefully and said, "Of course he'd want that!" Mr. Copland merely laughed and accepted, while Mr. Sessions was concerned only with the fact that he *must* have the *easiest* part, and he was absolutely sure he wasn't good enough to play it! A cablegram from Stravinsky, in response to mine giving him all this news, reduced protocol once and for all to its proper level: "All pianos equally important . . . greetings." (In the end, Pianos One and Three were played by Mr. Foss and Mr. Barber, and Two and Four by Mr. Copland and Mr. Sessions in that order.)

It should be remembered, of course, that certain prestigious benefits would accrue to all participants, particularly the younger singers, and lest anyone raise a hue and cry over the exploitation of performing artists, the fat fee that went along with the recording was not to be belittled. All of the Stravinsky works programmed— not only *Les Noces* and *Movements,* but also his arrangements of three Gesualdo motets, the *Epitaphium,* and the *Double Canon to the Memory of Raoul Dufy,* completed in Venice not long before, were scheduled for "capture" by Columbia Records. Additional icing on the cake was the inclusion in the recording sessions of Bach's *Trauer-Ode* and other non-Stravinsky, Craft-conducted works as well.

Needless to say, Columbia Records was not being over-generous in offering to record those latter works (they were committed by contract to do Stravinsky's music). Because of the concerts, they would not have to schedule any extra rehearsal time, although without bearing any financial responsibility for the concerts at all—an aspect of the whole affair that pushed me into my subsequent actions, without the slightest notion of how much support Stravinsky would give me. Possessing neither the monetary resources nor the moral right to call myself an "impresario," I had felt that someone else should "present" the series, and suggested to Stravinsky (he had concurred) that, since Columbia was involved with the recordings (and also because he did not want me to approach any foundation), we might print on all material "Columbia Records Has the Honor to Present. . . ." Surely the kudos and the ensuing publicity would inspire an immediate contribution toward defraying some of the costs—at least those of the rehearsals. Columbia accepted "the honor" promptly. Nothing further happened. But one has one's ideals, and I waited patiently. Patience on the other side of the Atlantic was not in abundance, however, and on October 5 Robert wrote me from Venice that "I.S.," thought—and so did he —that at the moment Columbia Records was receiving all the benefits. In fact, he expounded, in the public eye Columbia appeared to be not only the benefactor, the "Maecenas," but even the instigator of the idea! Both Stravinsky and he felt that Columbia must contribute to the choral costs of the concerts: fifty-fifty, said "I.S.," would be fair, and this was small money indeed for Columbia—not to be argued about since the composer, according to his contract, could oblige them to record *Les Noces* starting from scratch, without any "free" performance. Armed with this information, I appealed to an executive of Columbia, and after several days received word that the munificent sum of one thousand dollars would be sent shortly. Somehow this information did not go down too well when cabled to foreign shores. Stravinsky was more than disappointed; he was furious, reported Robert, master as usual of understatement, on October 15.

The composer's fury was soon to be matched by Robert's, for not long after this Columbia summarily decided that it would be too costly to record anything except the Stravinsky works. Apart from the fact that several of our artists had been contracted on the basis of the Bach recording and had cancelled other concerts to accept our offer, the Carnegie program on January 3—composed of Schoenberg, Webern, and Berg works as well as the *Rite*—had been undertaken on Columbia's promise that the entire concert would be recorded. This situation produced a Gargantuan headache, which I nursed in silence after discussions with John McClure, head of Columbia Masterworks, who said he would cable abroad immediately with an explanation. My clients were then enroute to Hamburg, and at least twenty-four hours would elapse before this unpleasant news could reach them.

I mused during this waiting period, contemplating the hardest lesson of all: it was not Stravinsky's music but the other works that were driving our costs beyond the budget by at least one-half again as much, and most of this overdraft was contingent on the slowest seller, the Carnegie Hall concert. This program was initially to have included, in Robert's half, Schoenberg's *Die glückliche Hand*, Webern's *Six Pieces for Large Orchestra*, Opus 6, and Berg's *Three Pieces for Orchestra*, Opus 6—a formidable array, and expensive. Materials, especially for the Schoenberg piece, were very high-priced; rehearsals for this concert, originally intended to be no more than three, now leaped to five. One saving grace: *The Rite of Spring* utilized ninety-five players, and the other works needed no additional forces beyond that. Still, a series of letters and telephone calls from Loren Glickman, our orchestra contractor, expressed uneasiness about the difficulties of the music—in particular, the Webern works (his early *Trio Satz* had now been added to the first concert!), and his anxiety trebled mine because staring me in the face was that dread word "overtime." And this overtime was not going to be concerned with the composer of *Les Noces*. Furthermore, because of the promised recording, the Bach works had necessitated a switch from a good mixed amateur-professional chorus (courtesy of AFTRA)* to a fully professional one. We had, therefore, signed Margaret Hillis's American Concert Choir, resulting in an increase of almost two thousand dollars over the original amount set for choral singers.

Having had minimum contact with my client, I could only assume that all of this had been made known to him via his amanuensis, but a tiny misgiving began to haunt me on receipt of two letters out of Hamburg. In the first (October 27), Robert justifiably complained of Columbia's two-month-long silence regarding final recording dates, and about the fact that none of the dates I had sent him (a tentative schedule) showed any time for the Schoenberg, Webern, and Berg works. He assumed, therefore, that these works had been dropped, and he wrote that this infuriated him since he had changed the program *to* these pieces because of recording; besides, they were too expensive, were costing rehearsal time/money, and were *not his ideal choice of music to go with the* Rite *anyway*. News of Columbia's "perfidy" must have reached him as soon as he had posted this letter, for within an hour I received the second epistle, in which he instructed me to find another recording company promptly, fire the chorus, break the contracts, get ready to

* American Federation of Television and Recording Artists.

change the programs, get ready to cancel everything, in fact, cancel *everything*. Indeed, he ended on such an abysmal note, I was certain that as soon as he had sealed the envelope the staff of the Hotel Vier Jahreszeiten must have rushed to eliminate all traces of a fallen body from its *porte-cochère*.

In my office, where my regular helpers had been augmented by three for the Stravinsky assignment, the atmosphere suggested Valhalla after the immolation. Nevertheless, following instructions in the order in which they had been given, I reached for the telephone to call RCA while my mournful retainers dug into the filing cabinet where the traditional bottle was kept for important visitors.

And in the midst of this, lo!, a call from John McClure . . . all was well again . . . no need to change anything at all . . . a little confusion . . . keeps things on the *qui vive* . . . regards to the Stravinskys and Bob when next I wrote . . . and *au revoir*.

I never quite learned how this problem had been solved (and before we had to call back the printing!), but the incredible speed with which the news came from Ghent to Aix pointed to its genesis in another, more secluded room at the Vier Jahreszeiten. True, there had been a compromise—the particular Schoenberg work would not be recorded (expense again!)*—it was changed to the composer's *Begleitungsmusik*—but the Webern and Berg would.

Stravinsky had indicated, at the inception of our verbal agreement, that he would like a very close check kept on the ticket sales. The most practical method was to sell tickets directly from our office, since neither Carnegie Hall nor Town Hall would look with favor on telephone calls every ten minutes for figures (and after the first five letters, it appeared to me that this was a conservative estimate). Such a procedure meant securing a resale license, and called for New York City's Department of Licenses to swear me in, take my fingerprints, bond me, and check the area I use for a box-office—a space, by the way, that had to be completely separated from the regular office area (we rented another room). The far-reaching power of Stravinsky's name, even in locales where one supposes the only really familiar music to be either *Take Me Out to the Ball Game* or the sound of a bell at the end of a round, gave us all pause. Mr. Stravinsky was going to give concerts? Wonderful! Just what New York needed. He wished to sell tickets through

---

* Not just recording expense either. The rental fee, set down by Schoenberg's widow, was prohibitive.

his own agency? Perfectly understandable, and a wise move. And the usual six weeks for the processing of such an application was miraculously reduced to five days.

But I experienced a potpourri of emotions about the privilege when we tried to open the office door the day after our first advertisement appeared in the *New York Times* (November 1). We couldn't budge it. The mail, dropped through the door-slot (by a postman who, I am sure, must have thereafter resigned his job) had piled up to the door's mid-section and jammed the hinges. The maintenance engineer (a Madison Avenue euphemism for "janitor") and his assistant, whose sly grins implied that we must be in the business of mail-order pornography, took one hour and twenty-five dollars to remove the heavy steel-reinforced door carefully, so that no single envelope would be damaged. (A zealous part-time employee had already passed on the interesting information that these thousands of missives contained thousands of dollars.) Then the business of opening, recording, stamping, entering, filling orders, and depositing money commenced. Respect for that tribe of caged human beings working our theaters, our concert halls, our stadiums and arenas, and dealing with the public *directly* (a condition we escaped, at least by half) increased proportionately as our eyesight diminished. At least a third of our patrons regarded the inclusion of the order blank as happy: it gave them an opportunity to describe in detail in the margins various physical weaknesses such as infirmity in the right or left ear, claustrophobia if not seated near an exit, excessive height necessitating aisle seats, and the like. Still, huge as the mail was, we soon discovered that all those envelopes were a snare and a delusion. There were a lot of tickets to sell!

Trepidation, therefore, was present in large quantities as I waited with Deborah Ishlon and a stray photographer or two at Pier Eighty-eight on that chilly November morning. An additional worry nagged: a few days earlier news reports from abroad had indicated that Stravinsky had suffered another thrombosis, though it was described as being of a "minor" nature (if any thrombosis *can* be that). He was then on the high seas, and it did not seem wise to phone shore-to-ship to inquire about his health, particularly since Robert's voluminous correspondence had made no mention of this. Rumors had reached us from "friends" too, suggesting we make plans to cancel the concerts.

Indeed, when he came down the gangplank escorted by two ship's officers, one holding his arm at the elbow, his limp was more noticeable than it had been at Santa Fe. Despite this he seemed to tug ahead, almost scampering in front of his aide, and his face was ruddy and healthy with the cold. A woolen scarf was wrapped high on his neck covering his ears. He wore a fur-lined, fur-collared blue overcoat and a marvelous gray borsalino (this particular piece of millinery retained a place in his heart to the end). We moved to greet him. This time he gave me a Russian double kiss and said, "I am happy you are going to be with us."

Joy! . . .

His wife, exotically costumed in a blue velvet turban and a black fur coat, followed right behind, her arms slung with various satchels, vanity cases, parcels, and coats. No persuasion on the part of the steward accompanying her would make her part with a single item, and this tendency of hers to "hoard" baggage was to be my *bête noire* for many years. (She claimed it was a hangover from the days when she fled the Russian Revolution, carrying all her belongings on her person, but I think it was part of her always intense desire to be independent of everyone.)

Robert was nowhere in sight, and a frantic search, urged on by Mrs. Stravinsky, who had given him all the passports and declaration cards, finally disclosed him standing under the letter *C*, absorbed in a book; he had slipped past us somehow, even though our eyes had been glued to the gangway, and responsibility for my present shortness of breath rests on Robert's talent for dematerializing at airports, docks, and hotels.

The first rehearsal involving Stravinsky was not scheduled until December 11, at which time he would meet with the four composer-pianists on the Town Hall stage. The Stravinskys, who were living at the now-demolished Gladstone Hotel in the East Fifties (their New York *pied-à-terre* for many years), were occupied during the preceding three weeks with social activities. They had many friends in the city, and others were expected from abroad, including Sir Isaiah Berlin, Stephen Spender, and Eugene Berman. Robert plunged headlong into pre-rehearsal activities, recording discussions with John McClure, meetings with singers, the preparation of program notes, articles, letters, most of which were farmed out to our office for typing. He still found time, however, to deal expertly with a Manhattan contingent of female casualties that had replaced the one at Santa Fe.

Stravinsky's hotel-life routine became familiar to me during this period: rise early (between 7:30 and 8:00 A.M.), breakfast with his wife (usually tea, a soft-boiled or poached egg, *rye*-bread toast), shower and shave, back to bed to read or work until lunch; then, a large Scotch, lunch in or out; rest until four and work or read until twilight, when drinks were again in order; dinner with friends, sometimes a theater or movie, and usually a look at television that lasted just long enough to bore him into retiring.

Of course there were visitors—I learned rapidly that the ones he was really glad to see were those with whom he could discuss music. Alexei Haieff, Milton Babbitt, and Claudio Spies were always welcome, and later, at rehearsals, I began to discover that they fulfilled other functions for him. Goddard Lieberson and his wife, the former ballet dancer Vera Zorina, were also at the top of the list. I met his personal physician (New York branch!) the late Dr. David Protetch, and several Russian friends, among them Lucia Davidova and Natasha Nabokov. Samuel Dushkin and his wife Louise would come often as well; Dushkin was, of course, the old friend for whom Stravinsky had composed his *Violin Concerto* in 1931 and with whom he had collaborated and toured in the thirties. Of the entire Stravinsky entourage, Sam was the kindest and gentlest; I never heard him say a disagreeable word about anyone, and he was always the first to defend anybody who was under attack— from out-of-favor colleagues or acquaintances to critics. There was a rapport between Stravinsky and him, although it was based entirely on remembrances of things past rather than anything in the present. Two other callers who evoked pleasure-filled smiles were Richard Hammond and George Martin, a well-off, quiet, intelligent duo (Mr. Hammond is a composer) whom the Stravinskys had met in Venice in the twenties, and who had lived in Hollywood a number of years, although they were now residents of Manhattan. They were always full of great ideas about where to dine and what to see at the theaters and concert halls. Mrs. Stravinsky also visited with several friends who were connected with art galleries.

For the many others who came, Stravinsky did not have too much time. He would remain in the living room for half an hour at the most, or would not emerge from his bedroom until the visit was almost over and his wife would summon him to "come and be sociable." But clearly he enjoyed people—or rather, it seemed to me, the *idea* of people around him—because they provided amusement for Mrs Stravinsky particularly, and he could be left, after convention had been satisfied, to devote himself to his work or his reading. In my entire experience I have never run across so voracious a reader, unless it be Robert. When I came to know the Stravinsky library, which in Hollywood contained about ten thousand books, I learned with incredulity that the composer could locate, in a flash, almost any volume, although his own favorites (Russian books) were stacked on shelves in his studio and in cabinets in the hall adjoining his bedroom. Moreover, the actual and intriguing fact was that the myriad of books downstairs in the library, living room, and den had been selected and ordered by Robert, not by him (the Stravinskys had a London book-dealer as well as two principal ones in New York, who usually received an order for about four out of every six new titles, as soon as the latter became known!), and Stravinsky had taken the trouble to learn their dwelling-places. He would never use the library steps, though, and would always call someone to reach some far-off treatise or dictionary whose title was practically indiscernible to even the distance-eyeglassed eye.

My own visits to the Gladstone became more regular as the date of the first concert approached, and one appointment stands out in my memory in full relief. I had come at Stravinsky's request to bring him some important mail and also to leave a revised budget for his later perusal. It was about four o'clock; a heavy snow had been falling for an hour, so that the short walk from my office, made hatless, had brought me to his door looking like that celebrated drowned rat. He admitted me himself with a smile of welcome and ushered me into the living room, moving with the deliberation I already knew. Every table surface, windowsill, and corner was stacked with floral offerings, fruit baskets, cartons of the rarer Scotches and Dom Perignon champagne, books, papers, magazines, luggage (the Stravinskys had arrived this time with eighteen pieces). Apparently he had been reading in an armchair by the window, for the only lighted lamp stood nearby, and an Agatha Christie paperback lay open and face down on the seat. He wore a sweater, rather wrinkled trousers, and leather T-strap sandals over white socks. Two pairs of eyeglasses decorated his head, and this time both were pushed high. He regarded my dripping state with a sympathetic eye, left the room and returned after a moment with two towels, one of which was used to mop me and the other the rug, a chore which I hastened to take over. A glance at his watch satisfied him as to the appropriateness of the hour for imbibing, and he asked me to pour two Scotches. He was fully aware that I stood in great awe of him, and with infinite politeness occupied himself with carefully marking the place in his book, while my frozen hands knocked glasses together, dropped the ice from the tongs, and otherwise behaved as if they had a life of their own. He accepted a short glassful with one ice cube—a preference I had noted in Santa Fe—rewarding me with an approving nod. He then explained that "Vera" had gone to an art gallery with a friend and that he had no idea where "Bob" was. I reminded him that "Bob" was with John McClure, and this led to a few emphatic remarks about Columbia's penuriousness. Then, without warning, he leaned forward in his chair and shot a question at me:

"Carnegie Hall . . . how many rehearsals are there for *not* my works?" (No one could have expressed it more exactly!)

I replied that the time was divided equally for the entire program, and that winds and strings would each have a separate rehearsal before the *tutti* rehearsal. "And what are the exact works on this program?" I told him with increasing apprehension.

"But that is impossible. There will be no time to rehearse my music."

I began to elucidate. "Maestro, we have five two-and-one-half-hour sessions. . . ."

"Five!" I never heard a word so completely endowed with disbelief, indignation, and fury, all at once, and furthermore, delivered in a resounding whisper (have you ever heard one?) that was louder than any shout imaginable.

Oh, for the manifestation of a fairy godmother who would snatch up that too-detailed batch of budget papers just within reach on the table!

"*I* did not ask you to make five rehearsals!" There was certainly no answer to *that*. "It is *I* who should have been asked. . . ." And at that point the fairy godmother did indeed appear, in the person of Mrs. Stravinsky, exhilarated by the weather and the pictures she had seen. She was, I learned, a master at taking things in at a glance. A few words were exchanged in Russian, and the fire began to die down. I put aside the towel, which I found I was clutching like a lady in *accouchement*, and said I must depart. But no, at this point another Scotch was necessary. I don't know what sorcery Mrs. Stravinsky had performed, but obviously her effect on her husband's temper was that of a miracle ointment, for he had become as soft as a dove and dropped all reference to the subject of rehearsals. Back at my office, several skipped heartbeats later, I tried to reach Robert, but was unsuccessful. The next day he phoned and said, in answer to my questions, that all was well and that I was not to refer to the Carnegie Hall rehearsals again.

The period before the work began passed without further incidents of this nature. My office was completely occupied with pushing the ticket sale as well as with some other affairs: the American Opera Society, also a client, had launched an important season, and a performance of Part II of Berlioz's *The Trojans* was imminent. (I avoided any reference to this assignment at the Gladstone Hotel —the work and its composer did not occupy a position of importance in the thinking of the distinguished resident.) Among other things, the Berlioz opus shared many of our musicians and Miss Hillis's chorus. The Society's director, Allen Sven Oxenburg, had shown a tolerance remarkable in the concert business by cooperating (which meant giving way) on rehearsal times—a generosity that stood everyone in good stead, for when I reminded Stravinsky of it in 1962, it had a great deal to do with his agreement to permit the use of the printed phrase "production supervised by the composer" for the society's concert presentation of *The Rake's Progress* without benefit of fee.

As we progressed, it became increasingly clear that our office was regarded by Columbia Records and other Stravinsky adherents as a necessary evil. True, we were doing all the work, but that was no matter. We were instructed not to annoy Stravinsky with any "superficial" details such as money. The cordon around him was strong, but the tighter it became, the more aggressive I decided to be. I could still hear the ring of that "Five!" in my ears, and I was not going to run the risk of experiencing it again. Consequently, as cartage charges and overtime mounted to heights not far short of astronomical, our memoranda addressed directly to Stravinsky burgeoned, and I began to have each one delivered by hand. He seemed almost to appreciate knowing the worst in advance, and I soon discovered that his major objection was to "surprises."

CHAPTER TWO

STRAVINSKY'S first rehearsal with the composer-pianists had an air of affability and good-fellowship that was particularly noted by the photographers from the *New York Times* and the *Herald Tribune,* who were permitted to attend and snap away without interruption (though reporters were barred). In fact, the *Times* headed its picture-spread "Stravinsky and His Merry Men," although in one close-up the face of each participant was a study in solemnity!

The concert itself was a *succès fou,* with house and standing-room sold out and several hundred disappointed devotees turned away. The audience was almost entirely composed of Stravinsky admirers—musicians, students, scholars, music publishers, musicologists, including a sizable foreign representation. A few concert managers put in an appearance (out of curiosity, I feel sure). Other patrons came for the sole purpose of seeing the great man whose eightieth birthday would take place two years hence. The standing ovation he received, when he forged to the podium after intermission with the intensity of the holder of the world's championship for walking races, lasted at least five minutes and was terminated only when he turned from audience to orchestra and raised his right arm to give the downbeat for *Les Noces.* On the other hand, applause for the premières of his two small works in Robert's half, *Epitaphium* and *Double Canon,* had been only polite, while Webern's *Trio Satz,* performed (without conductor) by Messrs. Felix Galimir, Walter Trampler, and Charles McCracken, had elicited bravos. The Bach cantata proved to be a perfect opener, and *Les Noces,* of course, revitalized a worn-out phrase and brought down the house. The twenty-minute shouting and stamping tribute was acknowledged by Stravinsky only after he had stepped down and turned to encompass pianists, singers, orchestra, and chorus in one superb sweeping gesture that literally gathered everyone into his private circle of glory. Only then did he turn back to the crowd, which he thanked with stunning bows from the waist, feet close together, hands smartly at his sides, each obeisance held for a solid minute as though he felt it were being captured in marble. To me, he looked like a very well-brought-up little boy bowing to his partner at the start of a dancing class. He returned to the stage four times, bringing his whole cast with him on the first three safaris, and then remaining alone with bowed head while thunder crashed. On his fourth exit, he snatched the towel I was holding, threw it around his perspiring neck, and made for his dressing-room, escorted by Columbia Records officials chopping a path for him through crowds of well-wishers who had run backstage as soon as he had put his hand down on the score.

At a reception afterward, arranged by my office and given by Mrs. Kenneth Simpson and the late Albert Rothschild, he was more than jovial, greeting, thanking, and toasting everyone, talking animatedly to a great many people. He discussed with Milton Babbitt an electronic synthesizing of the *Epitaphium* (a project which, incidentally, he had thought to realize at that day's performance, but had abandoned because it would be too expensive for Columbia's record); talked about jurisprudence with my brother-in-law, recalling his own youthful law studies; agreed with Claudio Spies that someday soon all four preliminary versions of *Les Noces* should be performed; and ate and drank an inordinate amount. Robert, who had departed for a recording session looking as though he could use a six-month vacation, was, alas, not present, to the great disappointment of the contingent of enchanted ladies. As for Mrs. Stravinsky, gorgeous in black chiffon and silver fox, her only comment was: "Two more to go. I *hate* concerts!"

Critics the next day were unanimous in the opinion that it had been "a rare musical occasion," and all commented on the power generated by that seventy-seven-year-old "wiry" figure, whose "physical height" was such a contradiction to his "gigantic stature." All found him looking well, though each remarked on his sloweddown march to center stage. *Les Noces,* of course, was a "masterpiece." As for the two "firsts," they were uncertain. "How can you judge anything that lasts only forty seconds?" one writer asked. (As a matter of fact, both *Epitaphium* and *Double Canon* are clocked at one minute, sixteen seconds.)

I had been told by supposedly informed persons that Stravinsky did not read reviews and had no interest in them. Therefore, I was somewhat surprised the following day to receive a telephone call from him, an hour or so before we were to leave for the *Les Noces* recording session, asking me "kindly to bring some programs and the critics [*sic*] for my own files." A reading of one very complimentary review during an interval of waiting evoked only a long-drawn-out sound, midway between a "hrmmmmmph" and a growl. But on the whole he seemed well pleased with the results, and in fact was all in favor of Robert's suggestion to add another concert on January 23, which—infected by the same impetuosity—we promptly announced.

Carnegie Hall, however, was a house of another color. We had a cushion in the "series-of-three" sale, it is true, but the rest of the tickets were not moving well, and despite the success just enjoyed, and an increased advertising and publicity campaign, we reached two-thirds of capacity and there we stayed. Of course, our top price at Carnegie *was* higher—$6.90 as opposed to $5.95 at Town Hall, both sizable tariffs for concerts a decade or more ago; there *were* 1,262 more tickets to sell at the larger house; it *was* the holiday season and people were away; the *Rite had* been performed very recently (although Stravinsky had not conducted it in New York since the forties); the weather *was* unpredictable, thereby preventing visits to the box-office—any number of alibis but the right one, immortalized in a phrase by a prominent figure from another side of the concert business: "If they're not going to come, nothing will stop them." *

Up to this point, Stravinsky had given me a total of six thousand dollars, which, with the windfall of one thousand from Columbia Records and the receipts from the first concert, had taken care of half the bills. But now we had a huge orchestra to pay before the dress rehearsal and we could not touch the public money on deposit for the next two concerts. Suddenly "everyone" felt that my client should be told the worst. Such situations have a way of clearing the premises of advisors, and I was left alone to face the dragon, whom I found playing Patience and not winning.

This time I learned about Stravinsky silences. The condition was marked by a limpid gaze that, to the uninitiated, might have appeared to express complete boredom. But it could be prolonged

* Impresario S. Hurok.

to a breaking-point. On this occasion, at the conclusion of my explanation about union regulations on payments to orchestras, and why we could not use the public's ticket money (which, naturally, he considered his), he heaved the deepest sigh on record, made a gesture indicating utter hopelessness, fell into a reverie, elbows on the table and hands supporting his forehead, and murmured, "How strange." The quiet in the living room brought Robert out of the bedroom, where he (the coward!) had been talking with Mrs. Stravinsky. He addressed Stravinsky in French:

"Did you give Lillian a check?"

"Before I give a check it is necessary first to have the cash in the bank . . . then the check."

"We have a dress rehearsal tomorrow. The orchestra won't step on the stage. It's a union rule."

"To hell with the unions!"

"All right. We'll cancel the concert." Turning to me: "Lillian, cancel everything." Exit.

Stravinsky had resumed his game of Patience, but with pursed lips. He was in a stubborn mood. I sat immobile until, a few moments later, his wife emerged from her bedroom, signaled to me (unseen by her husband) to leave, and framed the words, "Don't worry" I left in a state of acute depression.

But the following day there *was* a Stravinsky check to give to the contractor, and the dress rehearsal began under the most agreeable circumstances. The composer, in a very good humor, arrived in the limousine provided by Columbia Records (this was no great effort for them—apparently everyone at Columbia had a limousine). He sat between Milton Babbitt and Claudio Spies following Robert's rehearsal of Schoenberg's *Begleitungsmusik*, which went very smoothly, and at its conclusion stood up and raised his hands to applaud Robert and the orchestra.

Webern's *Six Pieces* came next, a difficult work in any case—but Robert had chosen the composer's 1909 version, scored for a large orchestra and far more complex than the later, economical one. This had provoked some of the players into complaining to the contractor about the amount of time they had had to spend in preparation. Perhaps these factors stimulated Robert into greater than usual interpretive demands, for he stopped the orchestra repeatedly to go over passage after passage. The minutes flew by, and by the time the required break occurred, Webern was finished but Berg had not been touched. The schedule called for Stravinsky to have the final hour; however, he generously conceded the nineteen minutes' playing time for the Berg to Robert, and I kept my eyes fixed on the sidestage clock.

The two-and-a-half hour rehearsal had begun promptly at 2:00 P.M. and it was now three-thirty. Stravinsky rose from his seat in the auditorium and proceeded, with Claudio on one side and me on the other, to right stage, a process that took approximately five minutes. There we took up a position of anticipation. But Robert did not stop; in fact, he ordered the orchestra to go back to the beginning of the third piece. 3:40 and 3:45 came and went. *The Rite of Spring*, as conducted by its creator, consumes about thirty-five minutes, and allowing for an occasional stop or repeat—this was, after all, the first time he would lead the orchestra that Robert had prepared—we were down to a chillingly fine line. "He must stop . . . *now*," said Stravinsky, emphasizing the final word with a pull at my sleeve that almost detached it. I looked wildly about for the contractor, whose business it was to deal with such situations, and then suddenly remembered that he was playing bassoon. There was an audible rumble from Stravinsky presaging things to come, and I began to sidle past the players toward Robert, pointing frantically at my watch. Without missing a beat he hissed "Overtime!" But overtime was impossible; Carnegie Hall had warned us of a choral event scheduled for that Saturday evening, and stagehands were already in the corridor waiting to remove chairs and music stands, and convert to risers for the singers. At five minutes to four, I clambered over the string section and corralled Loren Glickman. He stood up and stopped the orchestra. Robert, in a fury, snatched up his score, towel, and jacket, and stomped out, passing Stravinsky, also in a fury, stomping in. We went half an hour overtime and nobody stopped us, notwithstanding a battalion of Carnegie Hall officials who had now joined the stage crew. Awe was an emotion not unique to me.

But the impression from this incident raised questions in my mind as to the actual relationship between Stravinsky and Robert. It was certainly not a case of hero worship, nor was it the more understandable association of master and pupil. Whether restrained by respect or timidity, no one in that hall, including two highly regarded composers, would have presumed on Stravinsky's prerogatives as Robert had done. Obviously, then, the two considered each other colleagues, at least when it came to sharing the podium. I had not yet been granted any real opportunity from which to draw conclusions about their communion on an intellectual level,* nor had there been anything particularly revealing in the hotel-life-at-home-with-the-Stravinskys episodes, beyond the fact that money was important (in varying degrees, depending on whose it was). And certainly the correspondence with Robert thus far (for my correspondence with Stravinsky had not yet begun) would have made me think—except for the few inconsistencies described earlier—that Robert's function was similar to that of an executive assistant who specialized in music.

Stravinsky got his own back during rehearsals for the final concert. He was the first in line for the *tutti* session on January 7, and for the "dress" two days later. Both times he refused to budge when his hour was up, and when he finally did, he engaged in discussions with several of the musicians while Robert swore *pianissimo* and vainly tried to call the orchestra to order.

The audience at the Carnegie Hall concert glittered, one-third of the effulgence caused by "silver paper" (i.e. "expensive" free tickets), and the cheering reached a new high, in which could be detected the big question: Will any of us ever again see and hear Stravinsky conduct the work that changed music? † Reviewers also made note of this, causing their subject to remark sharply the next day, "Tell those idiots I am not yet dead."

The final concert on January 10, 1960, featuring the world première of *Movements for Piano and Orchestra*, proved to be the exception to the rule that you cannot have too much of a good thing. We were left with about one hundred unsold tickets, a large number for a house just short of fifteen hundred capacity, and these were given away to some of the many who could not afford a third concert and whose interest in the music was known. (Without consulting anyone, I had already cancelled that fourth venture proposed for January 23!) Everyone was tired, and no wonder—twenty days of concertizing and recording, not to mention the concomitants, were bound to produce a sullen and lowering atmosphere. Furthermore, it had been difficult for the piano soloist to accept the composer's conception that the piano was an *obbligato*, not a solo,

---

* *Conversations with Igor Stravinsky*, the first volume of the dialogues, had already appeared, but very little could be discerned from that beyond the fact that the questions asked of the composer were both intelligent and leading.
† In fact, he conducted it for the last time in Mexico City in April 1961.

instrument in *Movements,* and this had caused a few touchy moments, brought into full perspective on one occasion by the sound of the palm of the hand being slammed down on the score, and a vocal explosion, *crescendo:* "No. . . . NO. . . . *NO!!!"*

The reviews for *Movements,* which Stravinsky had described in the program notes (edited by Robert) as "my most advanced work to date," ranged from raves to reflection. "In this latest piece he has surpassed his predecessors as much as he did many years ago with the first performance of *Le Sacre,*" wrote Jay Harrison in the *Herald Tribune.* "This listener is willing to admit that an initial encounter does not cause him to warm to this work," quoth Howard Taubman in the *New York Times.* And two other important voices from the past, those of Miles Kastendieck and Louis Biancolli, veterans of the now long-gone *Journal-American* and *World-Telegram,* reported, respectively, that, "Stravinsky may well have created music for the Space Age"; "Yesterday's advanced music sounded pitifully barren of meaning . . . unless it serves as a warning of what lies ahead." And so on.

And the audience was startled into bashfulness by this "antitonality" (Stravinsky's description)—so startled, in fact, that the sparse applause did not warrant a repetition of the work, as had been originally planned. The ovation was also noticeably spurred on by a group of the dedicated at the rear of the hall.

With the recording of *Movements* * two days later, the New York concert project was officially at an end. Our net loss was close to fifteen thousand dollars, with the Carnegie Hall concert responsible for more than two-thirds of this sum. Stravinsky's subsidy, now about eighty-two hundred dollars, plus an additional contribution from Columbia Records of fifteen hundred dollars (thanks to the efforts of Schuyler Chapin), plus the waiving of my own fees and expenses (the desire to please can sometimes produce a state resembling lunacy), reduced this figure to about two thousand dollars. The concert had been an artistic success and a financial disaster. Columbia Records had come out ahead of us all, and my office faced ruin.

Stravinsky's resilience merited as much attention as did his capacity for work. After these killing three weeks, Robert developed a virus (it turned out later that he had had both hepatitis and mono-

* This recording was not released; another version was made in Hollywood in 1961.

nucleosis!) that raised his temperature to 102 degrees; Mrs. Stravinsky fell a victim to conjunctivitis; both my permanent staff members demanded holidays to ward off nervous collapse; and I had two wisdom teeth that had been bothering me for more than a month extracted. But Stravinsky was more vigorous than ever. He was thinking about the *Monumentum pro Gesualdo,* soon to be transferred to manuscript paper, and was entertaining other ideas for a composition based on a Biblical theme (which was to see light as his dance drama *The Flood*). He fell into the habit of telephoning my office in the mornings, sometimes with a question about the final accounting, more often with some untroublesome request—he needed a fine-line notebook, or would "one of the young men kindly to take a parcel to the post office for me . . . thank-you-very-much." It was always thrilling to hear that sonorous diapason announcing "This is Mis-ter Stra-vin-sky. . . . Would you please . . . ," each word pronounced with exactly equal care but different emphasis, so that not one single letter was slurred or lost, nothing was ever monotonous, and even a simple phrase became weighty with meaning.

An identical precision characterized his physical movements, especially at that time, since he would not admit the minor disabilities of his recent illness. When he rose from a chair, for example, it was like a yoga exercise: 1) hands on chair arms, breathe deeply; 2) bend body forward; 3) stand erect; 4) move ahead . . . with speed!—as though he were reminding the nerve centers of his brain that *he* gave the orders and nothing must move until he said so. In his immediate environment, at that time a hotel bedroom, he was without doubt all-time winner of first prize for neatness. Scraps of paper—infinitesimal—on the floor, specks of dust on a window were immediate victims of those eagle eyes, and he would stop whatever he was doing to consign the offending object to wastebasket oblivion. His dresser surface and that of the table by his bed were sectioned by invisible lines protracted by his own mental compass: hairbrushes north-north-east, traveling clock due south, water glass and carafe east-by-northeast, medications (I recall seven small plastic containers at that time, filled with multicolored pastilles, lozenges, capsules) directly on the equator. A swift glance on entering his room would tell him at once if anything had been moved by maids or other intruders, and with a click of annoyance he would reassign the article to its proper latitude. The only objects which seemed to have their own way were books: these reposed in small, easily movable piles which, after making the pertinent selection, he would gather up, and carry from room to room as needed. Dictionaries of practical size—Russian-English, French, German—were always in evidence, and consulted constantly; detective stories ran a close second. Of the latter, Miss Christie's brain-twisters ranked high on the popularity scale at the time (the only period, I believe, when he was unfaithful to the immortal Simenon), a taste we shared, and I was continually searching for titles by that empress of crime that he had not yet read. I remember, too, that he kept his own scores in a locked rectangular case of black leather when they weren't spread open on the tiny excuse for a desk provided by the hotel.

His personal meticulousness was characterized by the same precision. "Freshly scrubbed" is the phrase most apt, I think, and all the more because it applied to the basics: outward show was never important to him, although he liked to look well. His broad hands, with their unusually large knuckles and well-kept nails (which he always manicured himself), and his short, powerful fingers, were in curious contrast to the fine, almost transparent texture of his skin, and were always cool and fresh to the touch—I remember this quality particularly because it stayed with him throughout his last illness. He was very fond of pure French eau de cologne, with which he used to rub himself after his shower (he abjured the bathtub until he no longer had a choice), or I would rub him after concerts and rehearsals; the clean, fresh scent was as much a part of him as his unobtrusive mustache, silvery-sandy in color and more like an artist's suggestion of shading than a facial adornment. (He trimmed his mustache himself with a special pair of scissors, and made a final, unsuccessful attempt to do so only a few days before his death.) He preferred white shirts, although he was fond of blue and knew it was very flattering to him—but that was his wife's special color. These must always be pristine: the slightest sign of perspiration and off the shirt would come, to be replaced, from body out, with a whole new set of haberdashery. Usually we kept such "extras" in the rehearsal bag but one or twice we forgot, and the trip home, if it lasted more than ten minutes, was agonizing to him. He was also inclined, then, to bow ties—not the large butterfly kind, but neat, straight-edged ones which he wore on formal occasions; otherwise, he was comfortable at home in an open-necked shirt. The bows had the effect of instilling in any companion a desire to take care of him. This was one of the most intriguing aspects of any contact with Stravinsky: one knew and recognized the "great man" for what he was, but always one felt like swooping him up and carrying him off to some quiet spot where he could repose and think in peace.

A dislike of conspicuous sartorial effect did not prevent him from being vain of his appearance, however. He always took great trouble with his hair, now very thin, and several minutes were reserved for carefully smoothing back each strand. (He would sometimes keep an audience applauding for a good spell while I held a mirror until he was satisfied that his curtain call would not be made "indecently.") His morning shower was a ritual, and he spent time in it, but if something came up that demanded his rapid attention, he could make himself ready like Jack-Be-Nimble. (Never once did he keep me waiting downstairs when I came in a car to fetch him!)

Stravinsky was an extremely courteous man, in the great tradition of nineteenth-century gentlemen, and especially with women —except when he was involved in the business of rehearsals or conducting: at such times, everyone was equal! He would step aside at elevator doors, even when the lifts were waiting (as was everyone else) specifically for him. He never sat down at the table, either at home or away, until his wife and other females had taken their places. This habit could occasionally lead to Alphonse-Gaston situations, especially when the other guests included people almost sixty years younger than himself, who considered being with him tantamount to being presented at court. The homage was pleasing to him, provided it kept within reasonable bounds. ("Enclose a nice note," Robert advised me early in our relationship. "He loves that sort of thing.") But if it didn't, and involved a great deal of hand-kissing, obeisance, and open worship, he would be witheringly voluble about it later. Stravinsky always responded to any service performed for him, regardless of its importance (it could be the placing of an extra piece of soap in his bathroom by the chambermaid) with a "thank-you-very-much . . . you-are-very-kind." And the quaint pairing of phrases, and the courtly manner in which they were delivered, could make one feel knighted.

He was a deeply affectionate man, despite this formality that made any such demonstrations from him vitally important. And he welcomed signs of affection from those close to him. His Russian-fashion kiss of greeting (one of my great joys, especially on those mornings before he left the Essex House for the last time) could be full of love and a need to have it returned, but it was always given with dignity—nobility, really—and with a broad, regal gesture of the arms in an embrace, and a marvelous smile. It was no mean peck, either, and had a delicious smacking sound. And as for his wife—whom he loved more than anything in the world after his music—when she would return from an excursion or an errand, or even enter a room, he would greet her in this same majestic way, but as though she had just arrived after a long stay in Siberia. At these times he was kindness itself, and whoever happened to be present became the collateral beneficiary. The bequest was normally in the form of an invitation to quaff from his best bottle. Sometimes it would be a more important souvenir.

He had not referred to the concerts again after the final accounting, and I did not know what his thoughts were about either the quality or the results of our work. True, he had asked me to look into several matters for him, one of which involved a commission, but the discussions had been tentative, and I would have had no right to assume that he had given me more work to do. A few days before his scheduled departure for Los Angeles, he interrupted a talk I was having with Mrs. Stravinsky, and asked me to come to his bedroom.

"Here is a sheet of my music," he said. "I give it to you as a remembrance of our association." It was the holograph of his *Double Canon*, premièred at the December 20 concert, and on it he had inscribed a message to me. I was speechless, of course, and I cannot remember exactly how I behaved, but after he had presented it, he dismissed me with a nod and went back to his reading.

It seemed then that he was saying *adieu*.

CHAPTER THREE

Y ET what finally cemented my relationship with Stravinsky was, ironically, money again. This time I made it for him.

The pall of gloom shrouding my office after the Stravinskys' departure for Los Angeles on January 21 had been somewhat dissipated, first, by a promising business trip to Mexico City, and second, by some communications from Robert—two ordinary postcards, each containing at least 250 words, which conveyed the startling news that Stravinsky was delighted with the results of the concerts—his tax accountant had just informed him that he was going to come out ahead. Moreover, he had decided to do two concerts in New York again in late 1960. Was I willing, queried Robert, or should they look for someone else to ruin? (February 10, 1960).

Surely this was begging the question, and besides, the dates were sufficiently far in the future for me to settle comfortably on Cloud Nine. Collectors, bills, summonses aside, Stravinsky was not angry with me!

I was authorized, at the same time, to pursue some business, one aspect of which was a commission proposed to Stravinsky, several months before we first met, by the CBS Special Projects Division, which then fell under the jurisdiction of Robert Graff. This commission was to become *The Flood*, although that was not its title then. Mr. Graff and I began to hold meetings.

But on February 15 I received a visit at my office from a gentleman whose calling card announced that he was Mr. O. Alcazar, president of Conciertos Asociadas, located in Lima, Peru. This, I remembered, was a relatively new office concerned with bringing artists and attractions from other countries to Latin America, and aspiring to rival the already-established concert agencies of the

Quesada family (Conciertos Daniel) and Bernardo Iriberri, who shared a monopoly of sorts.

Mr. Alcazar, in his early forties, had a manner that was both agreeable and suave. He had been successfully involved in the recent Leonard Bernstein–New York Philharmonic tour that had included his city. The purpose of his visit was to offer Stravinsky (with Mr. Craft, of course) a tour of seven or eight capitals south of the border. Did I think the composer would be interested? And how much would he want?

Short acquaintance with Stravinsky—and, therefore, total ignorance as to how to reply to both questions—should have made me suggest (in the manner of all *great* concert managers) that such proposals must be considered over a period of months; that a priority waiting list of similar requests already existed; that, anyway Stravinsky was booked solidly six seasons ahead (at least). Where can I reach you? . . . Thank you very much for coming.

But, *grâce à Dieu*, I was *not* a great concert manager. Placing performing artists in newspapers, magazines, television, rather than on stages, was my real business, and there is one rule peculiar to this profession of publicity that would make any self-respecting impresario (with one exception *) shudder: emulate Charles A. Lindbergh.

So . . . 1) I said, yes, I thought Stravinsky would be interested, and 2) he would want four thousand dollars per engagement. Mr. Alcazar's immediate reaction was that of someone suddenly confronted by an escaped madman, after which he laughed in polite acknowledgment of my sense of humor. A moment later he took his leave, unconvincingly bestowing the information that he would "think it over."

Alcazar's shock was quite consistent with concert conditions in 1960. Four thousand dollars was an almost-unheard-of-fee for performers who were not movie, television, or recording stars (popular), and in the classical music field only a Callas, Rubinstein, or Horowitz had been known to approach, let alone exceed it; phenomena such as Van Cliburn were rare. As for conductors, they sat on the bottom rungs, save for a few who occupied permanent posts as musical directors of important symphonies, which positions, also in terms of today, commanded modest annual stipends.

* S. Hurok again!

Nevertheless, Stravinsky had long before entered the lists as a touring artist, for purely financial reasons. Between 1922, when he completed *Mavra*, and 1927, when he composed *Oedipus Rex*, his appearances in Germany, Switzerland, Italy, France, and the Netherlands, and his first United States tour, kept him so busy that he produced little more than one work per year, a very small ouput for this most prolific master. He composed chiefly during the summer months, and during the remainder of the year appeared as piano soloist in his *Sonata, Serenade, Concerto,* and *Capriccio,* although he also began to conduct a certain amount after 1923. In that year he led the première of his *Octet* at the Paris Opera House in one of Koussevitzky's symphony concerts * and was pleased with the experience. In the thirties he composed his *Concerto for Two Pianos* so that he and his son Soulima, who had been establishing his own reputation as a pianist, could tour together. That decade also found him fulfilling commitments in North America, together with Samuel Dushkin, and he did some concert traveling in the early forties as well. During the period of the *Rake*'s composition, he toured hardly at all, and then resumed this activity in the fifties, covering a great deal of insignificant territory. The enormous number of appearances over-all soon qualified Stravinsky as a barn-stormer, and he knew every backwoods concert hall, small town auditorium, and provincial theater in the United States (the circuit hasn't changed much, incidentally) as well as the more august metropolitan houses. On the basis of his conducting talents Stravinsky could never have been a great "draw." He was not a spectacular figure on the podium, and as for his own attitude, it could hardly have been more businesslike: conducting was a money-making expedient. For the managers who presented him, Stravinsky's value lay in the fact that people would buy tickets chiefly to see this celebrated figure, and, for the most part, were not too much concerned with what or how he conducted.

Perhaps what prompted my courage with Alcazar was something that had come to light during the New York concerts. I discovered that Stravinsky was then earning an average of fifteen hundred dol-

* Ernest Ansermet is supposed to have given Stravinsky his first conducting experience in 1914, when, during a rehearsal of the composer's *Symphony in E-Flat* with the Montreux Kursaal Orchestra, Ansermet handed him his baton and asked him to take over.

lars for each concert appearance, and rarely more than two thousand. There were conductors and instrumentalists of far less importance who did better. Stravinsky, in my books, did not fall within the bounds of either category, and *composer* is a foreign term on any managerial roster. Where was the logic in the fact that others were pocketing more because they performed music which, in many cases, *he* was supplying? *Ergo,* his fee should be higher than theirs . . . *much* higher.

These rather simple ideas had occurred, I am sure, to the imperial heads of New York's two major concert managements, both of which had booked Stravinsky from time to time, but of course their administrators could not be as rash as I. They had too much experience, too much responsibility, and too much money to lose.

However, I suffered a loss also—of my self-confidence—the moment Mr. Alcazar shut the door. Why had I sneezed at a commission of ten percent on, say, twenty-five hundred dollars?

The telephone rang. It was Mr. Alcazar. He had thought it over. Would I make one concession? The fee would be four thousand in cities where only one concert would take place, six thousand for an identical pair. An appropriate moment was occupied with musing. Well, yes, I thought that was fair, but at the same time he would have to be responsible for the transportation—three first-class jet tickets, since Mrs. Stravinsky always traveled with her husband and Robert. The musing was now at the other end of the line. Then, an affirmative: provided Stravinsky would take care of his hotel bills. That, I thought but did not say aloud, was as it should be, since such expenses were completely tax-deductible. But it brought another point to mind: the composer would not, of course, pay any *local* taxes. Well . . . all right. Then: Mexico City must be included in the itinerary (this, I confess, was because it was *my* favorite city, and during my recent visit I had promised the Institute of Fine Arts cooperation in securing artists). Alcazar agreed.

At this point I decided to be a *great* concert manager. "Naturally you understand this is purely speculative . . . he is heavily committed . . . *seasons* ahead . . . so many other managers are waiting . . . I will bring it up with him only because I know he is sympathetic to your landscape . . . you will hear from me as soon as I hear from him . . . you understand, I am sure."

He did. Moreover, he understood so well that he had already, with a foresight that made me think for one fleeting moment I hadn't been so smart, sublet a flat on the East Side so that he could wait comfortably.

That night I sent Stravinsky a letter dealing largely with the matter of Mr. Graff and the proposed commission. Toward the end, I included a cautious paragraph outlining Mr. Alcazar's proposition, and indicating that I "thought" I might be able to get thirty-five hundred dollars (talk is talk, and terms were not on paper) for each of a minimum of seven concerts.

Stravinsky's reply—my first actual letter from him—arrived three days later (we *did* have a remarkable postal system once!). First I looked at the signature, which was the characteristic *ISTR* used for his personal correspondence, and then saw the words just above it: "With best wishes, your cordialissimo [*sic*]" and I thought, "South America, here we come!"

The body of the letter was a lesson in specifics:

1. He was interested in a tour of South America only on condition that his fee would be *guaranteed* by the Alcazar agency in every city.

2. He would be unable to leave before June, and although he knew that June was the season in Buenos Aires, he thought it was *not* the season in Caracas, Mexico City, and Rio de Janeiro (no one had mentioned a single city!).

3. He would require reports on the orchestras in the various cities, for when he had last conducted those in the four just mentioned, they had been far from good; therefore, the programs would be determined by this report (not, "I will not conduct if the orchestras are bad!"). And, incidentally, he informed me that Rio was always the worst (*sic*) orchestra of all.*

Then came a provocative question, which gave me an inkling of the *coup* I had pulled: Would the Conciertos Asociadas help with the travel expenses? And finally, the most interesting query of all, that answered a long unasked one on my part: he wanted to know if the $3500 was to include Robert Craft's $500 or not.

In both Santa Fe and New York, any general discussion of Robert Craft's relationship with Stravinsky had sooner or later led to speculation on whether any financial arrangement existed between them. Busybodyness aside, Stravinsky's background included a sizable list

---

* On this tour it was the "second" orchestra for the second concert in Buenos Aires. Stravinsky stopped *Petrushka* at the beginning of the Fourth Tableau and made the orchestra start all over again!

of people who had worked for him for practically nothing *or* nothing. But that was not *his* fault. Except when he directly solicited offers of service, he had a right to conclude that any independent suggestions were made in expectation of nothing more than his gracious acceptance. Those who wish to be near great men must be prepared for demands on their selflessness—and they must also be willing, incidentally, to withhold their own opinions.

During my tenure, Robert *never* fulfilled the latter requirement, but he certainly met the first, at least until I was able to increase his share of the revenue. In fact, *apropos* of an engagement that had been agreed to orally before I ventured onto the scene, Robert wrote me (November 2, 1960) to say he had forgotten about discussing his own fee, and asked if I could remedy this, because "Mr. S." didn't give him anything out of his money. He was sure the management had made no provision for him, thinking that "Mr. S." split his money with Robert, which—he emphasized—was not the case.

True, Robert had no substantial living expenses even before the Stravinskys moved into their last and larger California house. He occupied rooms above the studio Mrs. Stravinsky rented at 1218 North Wetherly Drive in back of the Baroness d'Erlanger's residence (the old Stravinsky house was at number 1260), for which he paid a modest rent. He took most of his meals with the Stravinskys, and was looked after by their Russian housekeeper, Mrs. Gate (Evgenia Petrovna), not as a guest but as an accepted member of the household, sharing the various advantages (and disadvantages) that such a privilege entails. As a conductor it is unlikely that he could have earned a great deal of money on his own; few conductors made large fees anyway, engagements for Craft-without-Stravinsky were far from plentiful, and his single-minded attention to the composer's interests had limited them even further. After the 1956 thrombosis in Berlin, Stravinsky had no longer wished to conduct full-length programs, and Robert's regular chores as a conductor had started not long before our first meeting in Santa Fe.

But managers wanted Stravinsky, and the truth is that they accepted Robert because they could not have one without the other. Any foraging he did on his own presented problems—he was, in the eyes of most symphony managers, an adjunct, not a separate entity, and none of them was in a position to estimate the burden of work that fell on him. His own reputation as an expert in the field of modern music (he was later to conduct a fully staged performance

of Berg's *Wozzeck,* and to introduce Berg's *Lulu* to this country)
did, of course, lead some thinking musical societies to seek him out.
But since these were chiefly organizations concerned more with the
music and the quality of the performance than with the size of the
audience, Robert would find himself conducting for love plus his
expenses, or very close to that.

Stravinsky's question, however, was revealing as far as occasional
pocket money went, and it could be called only that, in view of
the fact that the sum of five hundred dollars diminished when the
two conducted abroad, where very often the total fee (pre–Mr.
Alcazar) was not even fifteen hundred.

How did Robert manage, then? My conclusion at this time was
that additional sums must have accrued from the various services he
rendered in the recording studio and as a writer, although neither
area provided a consistent source of income. And—he was thrifty.

Several telephone calls and another letter from Stravinsky followed on that first one, and then he suggested that I come to Los
Angeles as his guest to discuss the details carefully. The truth of the
matter was (as I subsequently learned from Robert) that he had
been so astonished at the size of the fee, he was curious about my
possible tendency to hallucinate. Armed with an air-tight contract
(which thereafter would serve as a model) drawn up by one of New
York's leading law firms, I arrived at the Los Angeles airport on
March 4 and found a message from Mrs. Stravinsky saying that I
was expected to lunch the following day at one-thirty and that a
reservation had been made for me at the Hollywood-Roosevelt
Hotel. I spent that evening reviewing the contract and a letter from
Mr. Alcazar, who agreed with the terms in principle, and stated
that he would pre-sign as soon as Stravinsky approved the contents.

The "old" Stravinsky house, purchased in 1941 after a year or so
during which the composer and his wife had resided in various hotel
apartments, was a one-story wooden structure of nondescript architecture, long rather than broad. Its inclination to ramble downhill
in the direction of Sunset Boulevard indicated that a room or two
had been added to the original dwelling, and in fact this was the case
—Mrs. Stravinsky had designed a den and studio area. A few stone
steps, curiously outlined in white paint, and a short cement walk
were bordered on the right by a jungle-like garden of, I believe,
oleander bushes, Judas flowers, plumbago, tulips, petunias, and a host

of other blossoms I could not immediately identify. Near a very small front porch were several unoccupied bird cages, some on stands, and more were visible hanging in the garden—enough to accommodate a good-sized aviary.

I was admitted by Mrs. Gate, an elderly, forbidding-looking female retainer of twenty years' standing, who nodded acknowledgment that I was expected and ushered me into a large living room reached by descending one or two steps at the right of the tiny entrance hall. Books were everywhere, in shelves, heaped on the floor, stacked on credenzas. The room also seemed full of oversize, comfortable-looking sofas (there were actually only two, I think), innumerable chairs of no particular period, and quantities of small, spindly-legged tables about to collapse under their burdens of newspapers, magazines, needlework baskets, and ash trays. I recognized a Klee, a Léger, the Picasso portrait of Stravinsky, several of his wife's water colors of flowers and shells, some sketches by Eugene Berman of sets for *Danses Concertantes* and *Pulcinella*, and Theodore Stravinsky's portrait of Madame—all of them cramming the few spaces untenanted by the library.

A handsomely befurred black-and-gray long-haired cat, which I had mistaken for a pillow, suddenly unraveled itself from the sofa and, dismissing me with a look of disdain, strolled to the threshhold, where I was startled to see Stravinsky, whose soft leather slippers had muffled his approach. "*Bonjour,* welcome." He kissed me Russian-style, and introduced me to Celly (short for Céleste), who was polishing her coat against one of his trouser legs with such intensity that I was afraid he might fall over. But he reached down and picked her up by the scruff, holding her thus until he settled himself in a *fauteuil,* informing me that "Vera and Bob are coming now from her studio." Celly, after three turns in his lap, had plunked herself down facing him, paws on his chest, from which position she then exchanged a few confidential words in cat-Russian with him. Stravinsky inquired about my health, my trip, my office staff, my husband, and since he obviously was not going to introduce the subject that had brought me to California until the other two members of his household had arrived, I made some very ordinary remarks about the charm of the living-room and the furry occupant I had found there.

"I, too, have a cat."

"What do you call him . . . her?"

"Pusspartout."

"*Ce n'est pas vrai!*"

"Yes, truly."

He was delighted, and for one moment I thought he would break into a laugh. But Stravinsky never really laughed—that would have been to do something "in excess"—he grinned out loud.

My cat's name had definitely melted whatever slivers of ice remained, and he said he would like to show me Vera's garden. Mrs. Gate stopped us at the front door saying something rather sharply in Russian. He replied in an equally sharp monosyllable and, as we went outside, said to me in an abashed tone, "She is annoyed because they are late for lunch." Upon looking at his watch, *he* then became slightly annoyed, but nevertheless led the way into the midst of a petunia bed, where he stopped to point out, in the adjoining neighbor's garden, a plum tree with fat, round leaves. "Mouses' ears," he said, "very large mouses." He also cleared up the mystery of the white lines on the steps, and the empty bird cages. "Our dear friend Aldous Huxley comes to visit us often and now he is almost totally blind, you know. Vera made the white lines to command his attention and prevent accident to him. It is possible, you know, for a blind person to see white, which has no color, when he cannot see anything else." As for the absence of feathered inhabitants, he explained that the last of some forty winged pets had been "placed elsewhere" not long before. Apparently the covey of parakeets, goldfinches, lovebirds, canaries, parrots, *et al.* had taken over the house (they were permitted to "fly free") to such an extent that book bindings, rugs, lampshades, chandeliers, draperies, and window curtains (to say nothing of the dinner table, where they assumed the prerogative of honored guests) resembled the floors of their cages. Besides, Mrs. Gate would never take a vacation, leave the house when its other residents were absent, or perform several more important chores, because the birds came first. "Their music must have been distracting," I said. "No. It made me concentrate harder."

Since there was as yet no sign of either Mrs. Stravinsky or Robert, we returned to the living room, my host throwing a cautious glance in the direction of what I assumed was the kitchen. But just then the truants arrived, breathless from climbing the hill. Mrs. Stravinsky wore a painter's smock and a gauze turban knotted like a Sikh's, while Robert, despite the ninety-degree heat, had not left off his jacket and tie.

We lunched in a pleasant small dining-room at the rear of the house. Large windows revealed that it abutted on a steep hill where lemon trees grew. There were hundreds more books on shelves, and a cabinet containing a silver samovar and several pitchers, platters, bowls, etcetera, of what I took to be Russian silver.

Robert introduced the subject of the South American tour thus: "This manager . . . is he on the level? Thirty-five hundred bucks! He must be some kind of nut."

I dropped my first firecracker—the fee was going to be four thousand dollars for "singles," six thousand dollars for a "repeat." Even Mrs. Stravinsky looked at me rather suspiciously. Then I pointed out that in the event that Mr. Alcazar did not have all his marbles, the contract stated he must place $10,500 in escrow by a date four weeks hence, which would be forfeit if the tour fell through. Also, if the money were not produced, nothing would be lost except the waiting period, which Stravinsky, in any case, had planned to spend at work in Hollywood.

Mrs. Gate appeared with a platter of meat patties resting on a bed of some kind of *pasta*. She marched to the master of the house and filled his plate (while he made himself very small in his chair), after which she set the remainder down in front of Mrs. Stravinsky and exited.

Robert: "Didn't we have this yesterday?"

Mrs. Stravinsky showed her two celebrated dimples and blandly went on serving. "She does not have much variety, but she is a good friend," she twinkled at me.

Further discussion of South America was postponed when Robert directed at Stravinsky a monologue in French concerned with the technicalities of some Gesualdo motets (the composer was then completing *Monumentum pro Gesualdo*). He interrupted himself long enough to give me a concise and fascinating history of the mad Gesualdo, his profligacy, debauchery, murderous character, and marvelous music. I was struck, as always, with the store of information he carried about with him: thus far in our acquaintance there had been no subject on which he could not supply precise details, almost as though he had photographed in his mind the contents of the entire pertinent bibliography. It was genius of a sort.

Dessert was a floating island which Stravinsky pushed away (but only after Mrs. Gate had left the room) with an expression of the most acute distaste I ever saw. "She cannot bake anything," his wife elucidated.

Back in the living room, I soon discovered that Stravinsky's

youthful ventures into the field of jurisprudence had left an indelible
mark. There was no clause in the contract that he did not examine
microscopically, nor weigh from every possible angle; and his
scrutiny of every one of those five legal-size, closely-typed bond
pages, to make certain that a stray speck could not be interpreted as
a comma, was worthy of the editor of the Harvard Law Review.
The clause referring to Alcazar's responsibility for all transportation
was obviously a very pleasant bit of news, but he controlled himself (to keep me from getting too cocky, I felt sure) and proceeded
to look for loopholes:

"He will pay all three transportations?"

"Yes, Maestro."

"How will we know he does this?"

"Page four, Maestro . . . he has to send you the tickets one
month before the first date, or he forfeits the escrow money."

"But from which point to which points? He supplies us with
tickets, but these could be only round trip. What about from city
to city . . . must *we* pay?"

"Page four. . . ."

"Ah, yes, I see. . . ." Page four was then duly examined and
approved.

Then, "Ah . . . he does not pay for the hotels?" (Which, of
course, Stravinsky would never in a million years have either expected or intended that he should; *that* would have eliminated any
tax deduction excuse for the tour.)

Robert, who had been reading pages as Stravinsky discarded them,
said to him impatiently, "*C'est une question stupide.*" Then, in
English: "What *more* do you expect? This is a great contract. Sign
it. Where's a pen? Madame, bring a pen!"

Stravinsky threw him a look as full of meaning as a dictionary
and went on reading, while Mrs. Stravinsky obediently put down
some needlepoint in which she was absorbed and began to search
about on a cluttered table.

But I was suddenly embarrassed by this revealing little contre-
temps, and, since it was then close to four (and I knew Stravinsky
liked his catnap), I suggested that we leave all decisions until the
next day, which would give the composer a chance to consider
everything at his leisure and without my being there. Robert began
to protest, but I rose and asked if I could call a cab. Stravinsky
said, "*A demain,*" and marched off to the one bedroom, located

opposite the living room, where an open door disclosed more book-shelves and a bed with an Indian blanket thrown across it. Mrs. Stravinsky, relieved that business talks were over (she hated them), kissed me *au revoir* and went back to her studio.

As Robert put me into a cab a few minutes later, he said: "It's senseless to wait until tomorrow. The important thing to remember with *him* is that one must do things immediately. You never know how long his interest will last. There's always something new that comes up, and five minutes later it's yesterday's column."

The wisdom of Robert's advice was manifest many times there-after. Anyone spending more than half an hour with Stravinsky would have to be aware of the incredible speed with which that mind worked. "Don't waste time, especially *my* time," was the premise; state the facts clearly and laconically, and come to an im-mediate decision. If this is not a possible procedure for you to fol-low, "thank-you-very-much-I-don't-need-it."

Robert's peremptoriness with Stravinsky (after all, he had now known him for more than a dozen years) was forgivable on this basis, although I thought his behavior rather rude—not because Stra-vinsky was Stravinsky, but because he was a much older man. On the other hand, I argued to myself that perhaps this approach was deliberate: what I had observed of Robert's conduct with the com-poser up to this point made the question of age inadmissible, and thus in any contact with the two together (at least while Stravinsky was in reasonably good health), one regarded the older man without thinking of the passing years. The real astonishment came in the recognition that Stravinsky, so old-world in the formality of his manners and the orderliness of his personal environment, should have accepted Robert's tone with no more than a flashing look of reproach. My presence could not have been a real deterrent; I al-ready knew enough to realize that nothing would ever prevent Stravinsky from speaking his mind if he wanted to, and no opinion—however uncomplimentary—would be withheld, regardless of the rank or distinction of its target.

From another angle Robert's impatience was entirely human. In a desire to increase *his* fees as well as Stravinsky's, I had written him into the contract as being "supplied" (in legal terminology) by the composer. I had also been very specific about the portion of the fee he was to receive, which was considerably higher than former stipends (one-third of the total, to be exact).

Robert need have had no qualms in this instance, however, for apparently Stravinsky's thinking was already affirmative. That evening he telephoned me at the hotel, explaining that his wife and Robert had gone to visit a friend, and indicated one or two changes he wished made. But at the same time he told me to wire Alcazar that he would then be prepared to sign. This instruction was typical of his own approach to everything: now that we are willing, pay immediate attention to your part of the contract, as I will to mine. The telegram was to be worded in such a way that Alcazar would not lose a minute in confirming the engagements and arranging for the deposit of the escrow money.

Thus my first visit with the Stravinskys at home came to an end the next day, during which, in the morning, Mrs. Stravinsky toured me about Beverly Hills and Bel Air, sitting at the wheel of her new Jaguar, and looking more like a full-blown rose than any I saw in the dozens of fantastic gardens we passed. Before I left with her and Robert for a visit to the nearby house of Miranda Levy (after which I was to catch my plane), Stravinsky conferred a signal honor. He showed me his studio—a rare privilege in the "old" house, though in the new one I had only to knock on the door at the appropriate times.

This sanctuary was reached by crossing to the far end of the living room into the added wing, after passing through a den completely wallpapered with books, and turning left through two sets of doors. My recollection now is that the room was long and narrow, perhaps about fifteen by twenty-five feet, and that—though almost every inch of wall and floor space was occupied by furniture, pictures, volumes—it was as neat and disciplined as a monk's cell. An upright piano, with a bracketed drawing board replacing the regular music rack, took charge of one wall; large sheets of manuscript paper as well as notebook-size leaves were clipped to this board with metal tabs. The top of the piano (contrary to the rule that such instruments should be unadorned) provided a showcase for half a dozen or more framed photographs, pencil drawings (unidentifiable), and other memorabilia. An enormous, voluptuous-looking sofa covered in a red and white fabric was bounded on one side by a table equipped with everything to make a reading or meditating hour comfortable—lamps, books, papers, carafe and glass, pencils in a jar, some notebooks; and on the other by low shelves offering more volumes within easy reach of the recliner's hand. I remember some framed Picasso drawings above the sofa, and shelves with bound portfolios—perhaps music, for I could make out Stravinsky's identifying script on the labels. One or two easy chairs and a table desk with two uncushioned maple chairs (the hard kind!) are also among my impressions, as well as an orderly array on other nearby surfaces of trays for pens, styluses, a compass, a myriad of colored pencils, rulers, some bottles of ink eradicator, and a number of different sizes of scissors. There were, I think, several icons on another shelf and some paintings that had a "Russian" flavor. From the top of a credenza near the piano Stravinsky picked up a peculiar, cartridge-shaped instrument—it resembled a metal cigarette-lighter with five small wheels at one end and a handle at the other, and explained that he drew his staves with it. "I have invented one similar but better," he told me. "This is the one I used in Russia."

The South American contracts were the first of several foreign and many domestic ones I negotiated for Stravinsky-Craft in the next seven years. Each had its own particular hazards, but most were very profitable. The hazards began, actually, with the Alcazar tour. Until all was well underway and the Stravinsky party was admiring the various views of South America from the windows of its sometime-jet aircraft, Alcazar's letters to me displayed a remarkable ability to stave off heart attacks. He persisted, won out, and thereafter turned up from time to time with even more lucrative offers.

Before the end of 1960, Stravinsky fell into the habit of referring to me those requests for his conducting services in which he was interested; most of these would be relayed through Robert. And thereafter many managers began to contact me directly. I kept increasing the fees, particularly in the United States, so that by the close of 1966 Stravinsky was receiving between seventy-five hundred and ten thousand dollars (Robert continued to take his one-third) to conduct as little as one work in some cases; and for the privilege of having him in a supervisory capacity, the *asking* price was five thousand dollars.

But of course there were exceptions to these rules, as for example the Washington Opera Society, with whom he conducted *Rossignol* in December 1960 for a small fee because it was to be recorded (Robert's half of the program was Schoenberg's *Erwartung*, also recorded); or the American Opera Society's concert performance of the *Rake* (conducted by Robert) in November 1962, on which occasion, *sans* fee, Stravinsky not only sat in the audience but permitted the program credit line indicating that the production was prepared under his supervision.

Stravinsky himself, however, rarely *sought* engagements in the sixties, except in Europe; for one thing, despite lower fees, he always felt he had more receptive ears there, and for another, he could justify on his tax forms the traveling to out-of-the-way places that his household enjoyed. Italy was the main area of operations—as it had always been—with eleven cities in that country having him as a frequent guest, and these were handled by more than one Italian impresario. Zurich, Hamburg, and Berlin appearances occurred more sparingly, and London hardly at all (but then he never did conduct much in England). As for other continents, he made his first tours of Australia and South Africa and conducted in Israel for the first time during my tenure.

But for the most part, his normal reaction to touring in the United States was, "Who needs it?" And indeed, he did not need that outlet nor any other save the one that was his alone. The pursuit of these public appearances, in North America particularly, was stimulated by Robert, as most of the correspondence indicates, but this was done not only because the latter shared Stravinsky's healthy and honest respect for money (after those Alcazar fees, my clients were spoiled!), but because from the start of his association with the composer his set policy had been (and remained) to keep Stravinsky publicly active.

CHAPTER FOUR

THE importance of Robert Craft to Stravinsky in the final twenty-three years of the composer's life could be surmised, even if all documentation were lost, from the number of people who claim responsibility for bringing the two together. There are at least a half dozen candidates, offering as many different accounts of the original encounter. The truth of the matter is that the first contact which could be considered personal came about as a result of a correspondence inaugurated by Robert, with impressive effects on the composer who followed it up. If one wished to be exact to the inch, Robert had been introduced even earlier to Stravinsky, by Claudio Spies during a rehearsal for a broadcast of *Perséphone* in New York in 1947; however, it is safe to say that since several others were also there and were presented at the same time, the very shy young man could not have remained in Stravinsky's thoughts at all after that perfunctory "how-do-you-do."

Robert had just matriculated at the Juilliard School and was then involved in conducting a series of concerts for the Chamber Arts Society, a progressive musical group concentrating chiefly on contemporary works and on masterpieces of the pre-Bach period. Stravinsky's compositions figured largely on one of the programs, and Robert wrote him about the *Symphonies of Wind Instruments*, materials for which happened to be unavailable at the time. According to Mrs. Stravinsky, her husband was struck by the contents of the letter, which seemed to him to reveal a profound knowledge of music in general and his own in particular. He went so far as to show it to his attorney and advisor, Aaron Sapiro, who was equally impressed. There was general agreement that its author was an unusual individual, worthy of attention, and Stravinsky thereupon replied, offering the Chamber Arts Society his assistance with the missing materials (he had just prepared a revised version), *and* his services as a co-conductor for that program. A meeting between

the correspondents was suggested, and this ultimately took place at
the Raleigh Hotel in Washington on March 31, 1948, at a lunch
in the Stravinsky suite. Another guest that day was W. H. Auden,
who had brought with him the completed libretto for *The Rake's
Progress.**

The joint concert at New York's Town Hall came about in April,
and in August Robert went to Hollywood for a visit with the Stravinskys. The friendship ripened, and in 1949 both shared a second
concert at the same auditorium, which included the American
première of the *Mass*. By that time it was agreed that Robert should
come to the West Coast to live and work as the composer's assistant,
at a modest salary. He began his apprenticeship by coordinating and
cataloguing some of Stravinsky's manuscripts and sketches, which
had just arrived from Switzerland. For several months Robert lived
at the "old" Stravinsky residence, bedding down on one of the
numerous sofas, but by the end of December he was installed in a
house rented from the actor Vladimir Sokolov, whose wife Lisa,
until her untimely death the previous year, had been Mrs. Stravinsky's closest friend. In 1951 Robert moved to rooms above what was
to become Mrs. Stravinsky's studio, in the guest house behind the
composer's last home in Hollywood.

Robert's sudden appearance in the Stravinsky milieu did not go
down too well, I was told, with those who comprised the "circle" at
that time. For one thing, he was an advocate of avant-garde music,
whereas they represented an opposed "Franco-Russian" element.
The name of Schoenberg was unmentionable in Stravinsky's house,
and those of Webern and Berg were not even acknowledged. The
term "twelve-tone" did not enter into Stravinsky's vocabulary in any
language, and it is unlikely that he was very familiar with any
twelve-tone music at all when Robert first met him, although he
must have come in contact with much of it at the Evenings-on-the-
Roof concerts in Los Angeles, which had attracted him shortly
after his arrival in Hollywood. In fact, probably the first serial work
he listened to with interest was Webern's *Quartet*, Opus 22, which
Robert played for him in 1952. Prior to that, his usual reply to questions on his attitude toward the "new music" was, in substance, that
he had quite enough to do with seven notes of the scale, let alone

---

* Along with the libretto, Auden brought the rather startling news that he had
a co-librettist, Chester Kallman—an announcement not anticipated by Stravinsky on any occasion, according to Robert.

twelve—an observation that has been quoted and requoted innumberable times since.

But apart from Robert's intrusion of a radical note in the established Stravinskyan environment of musical conservatism, who *was* this young "Yankee" * Protestant who could not even speak French? The Stravinskys themselves, Robert told me, spoke virtually no English when he met them, and although they had several Anglo-Saxon acquaintances and one very close Anglo-Saxon friend (Aldous Huxley), they had shown little inclination to learn the language thoroughly. Conversation was carried on chiefly in French, if not in Russian, although when they first arrived in Hollywood, German was favored, for their non-musical friends included the Thomas Manns, the Franz Werfels (she was Alma Mahler), and Max Reinhardt. Stravinsky was especially fluent in German, which he had learned as a boy from his beloved nurse, Bertha.

What was the rapport, then? For rapport there certainly was, and from that very first meeting at lunch. Then and there Mrs. Stravinsky had asked Robert (whose bus-travel reading to Washington was a volume of Kafka and another of Freud) to compile a list of English books for her husband and herself. He did so on the spot, and he has told me that when he joined the Stravinskys briefly in Denver in July, prior to his West Coast visit, they had both read every single book on the list and were eagerly awaiting another set of recommendations. Robert also applied himself to French, and, in Mrs. Stravinsky's words, "he had courage." If he couldn't think of a word, he would invent one (e.g. *vache-garçon* for "cowboy"), and this enterprise, coupled with his natural intensity in the pursuit of any activity, mental or otherwise, has made it possible since then for him to discuss vintage wines in French, argue with gondoliers in Italian, and engage in philosophical discussions in German.

But he was not as quick a "study" as Stravinsky, who learned English before Robert learned French, and thus the latter became the composer's first English-speaking intimate. That in itself was unusual, for Stravinsky never really felt at home in the language, and throughout my association with him I noted that there were very few people with whom he liked to converse in English. In any case, during the American years—that is, from 1939 on—Stravinsky had very few intimates altogether, certainly none whose relationship to him could

* Robert was actually born and raised in Kingston, New York, close enough to the scene of revolution to be designated by that noun!

be compared to that which Diaghilev or Ramuz (his collaborator on *The Soldier's Tale*) or his old friend Pierre Souvchinsky had enjoyed. There were one or two people for whom he did feel deep affection, however, as was apparent from occasional remarks. Lawrence Morton's quiet, intelligent approach in conversations about music always seemed to stimulate Stravinsky. Composer Alexei Haieff enjoyed a position of great intimacy, and Stravinsky was very fond of Pierre Boulez, whom he had met some years before through Souvchinsky. But he did not see much of these two after the beginning of the sixties. They fell prey to his possessive strain—so Robert told me—which did not permit a division of friendship (in the first case) or criticism of some of his music (in the second).

Nor was the work Robert performed for Stravinsky in the beginning, as an organizer and cataloguer, a decisive factor in the relationship. Stravinsky was always asking someone to work for him, at a salary of sorts. Such a proposal was once made to Lawrence Morton, who was invited to live in the house, and later, a similar suggestion was made to Edwin Allen when he began to catalogue the library after the family moved to its new home at 1216 North Wetherly. Stravinsky was always willing to use anyone who could be useful, and he made no bones about it.

The fact of the matter was that the composer liked Robert immediately, and so did his wife. He represented a world with which they had not yet become acquainted, and he arrived in their lives at a point when everything and everyone they knew had become rather stale. Apart from the Huxleys, the Artur Rubinsteins, and a few others, Hollywood no longer offered the stimulus it had provided at the beginning of the forties, when they were involved with a dozen or more "old-world" contributors to the "new-world" intellectual scene. Robert stirred them up; his cauldron of new events and new suggestions was kept at a continual boiling point. He filled the library with new books, brought young composers and musicians into a house that had almost resigned itself to age. He suggested to "Madame" that she stop sewing and resume her painting, and he suggested to "him" that it might not be a bad idea to lend an ear to some new sounds in the area of musical composition. But, most of all, he relieved the composer of certain professional burdens that had occupied a large portion of his time, and certain social obligations that he had felt compelled to assume because he did not want his wife to live as a recluse. And all of this meant only one thing: Stravinsky had much more time to compose.

Although Stravinsky did not generally inaugurate suggestions for concert tours, he usually concurred in whatever ideas Robert produced. As soon as I had investigated a potential engagement on the basis of such a request from Robert, Stravinsky would take an active interest in it, outlining in letters his conditions, program suggestions, and taboos.

They would not stay in private homes (invitations were always plentiful), but required only the best hotels everywhere. A suite with two bathrooms was preferred by the composer for himself and his wife, and a single with bath for "Bob." (I.S. to L.L. Feb. 24, 1960). There must always be twice as many rehearsals scheduled in territories outside the United States (in this case, Australia; I.S. to L.L. March 27, 1961).

Nor did he always agree *in toto.* Occasionally, a program worked out by Robert, as in the case of one of the South American cities, did not please him, and he would order the program *he* (italics were his) wanted. And sometimes he was pointedly rebellious: he refused to appear on a program listing Rachmaninov or Tchaikovsky concertos, he wrote me regarding the Seattle World's Fair concert where one of these works was contemplated (I.S. to L.L. February 7, 1962).

There were also times when Stravinsky's personal wishes were overridden. With regard to a proposed tour of South Africa in 1962 he sent me dates, appealing that I keep within them, as "I have lost too much time from composing." I immediately contacted the South African sponsors requesting a change of date, as well as an upgrading of fee, which, they replied, they could not grant. I then prepared a letter sending our regrets, and the hope that the tour could be made another time and on higher terms, but before it was dispatched Robert instructed me to confirm the original agreement: "Concede, concede, we *must* go!" he pleaded, and I did.

And with regard to the Seattle World's Fair, despite his objections to Rachmaninov, Stravinsky did conduct his *Firebird Suite* on the same program in which Van Cliburn played the Rachmaninov *Second Concerto,* and Robert led the *Symphony in Three Movements.*

The merry-go-round of touring on which we all had seats, beginning with the South American *Reise* on August 1, 1960, was bound to be the target for some poisonous arrows aimed by the Stravinsky claque, especially the Russian-American team. All barbs were directed at me: I was "killing" the "old gentleman" in a passionate desire to make millions of dollars. . . . I had "neither the understanding nor the feeling for Stravinsky's mission on this earth." . . . I did not "comprehend the character of an artist." A few letters expressing even more negative sentiments as to my intellect and character found their way into my anguish file, including a choice one from a member of the medical profession, ending with a denunciation worthy of Zola: "I accuse you of slowly murdering him!"

Needless to say, such attacks had to be borne in silence. Only once, when an over-eager Stravinsky friend was faced with a veto delivered by me, to a request that the composer accept some public honor, did Stravinsky acknowledge that he had an inkling of man's inhumanity to personal managers. The friend, in his presence, pointed a shaking finger in my direction, saying, "You are trying to worm your way in as his manager. Stravinsky does not *need* a manager, *do* you, Igor Fyodorovitch!" And in a tone that sounded to me like the baritone section of a choir of angels, Igor Fyodorovitch replied: "But I *do*. And this manager has expressed *my* wishes perfectly."

The plain truth, as the written record shows, is that never once in our entire association did I directly solicit any engagements unless asked to do so. And the further truth is that there were times when I did make money, but more times when I lost so heavily that I was never able to recoup. This was not Stravinsky's fault. His so-called fanaticism about money (justifiable in view of the fact that he was well into his seventies before he did not have to worry about money), was not restricted to himself. He was scrupulous about his financial obligations, once he had agreed to them, and paid me my 10 percent on each engagement, or on any commission I handled for him, usually even before I sent him a bill. He was also very prompt about reimbursing me for my expenses when I accompanied him on tours or trips, or when normal ones were incurred in the general conduct of his business. But there were some occasions when managers (usually extra–United States) could not produce total fees on time, or defaulted, and it was too late or would have been too scandalous to cancel the contract. At those times, out of a fear that the relationship between Stravinsky and myself would come to an unhappy end, I would make up the difference, or pick up bills for music rentals and hotels that managers had neglected to pay, despite the contracts. These forays into my exchequer piled up over the years. Stravinsky suspected some of this foolishness, I am sure, but he never referred to it openly. He had his own ways of showing that he understood.

He would send me a letter, for example, complaining bitterly in the first sentence about some money delay, but enclosing a check (as in the case of our second Mexican tour in March 1961), with the explanation that it was an advance on my commission to help me buy my tickets. And at the bottom of the page was one of those little personal messages that made the rest of the day cerulean blue: what was my own flight number, for he would not leave Los Angeles until he knew I would be waiting at the other end? Another time, when he decided to wait a year before delivering the completed score of *The Flood*, he sent me one-third of my total commission, saying that he was sorry about the delay for my sake, but assuring me that it was only a postponement, not a cancellation, and that therefore he was enclosing, etc. (I.S. to L.L. February 20, 1960).

However, concern about Stravinsky's health, on the part of two or three truly devoted old friends, was entirely comprehensible if one undertakes a brief study of a few of his activities in which I was involved directly or indirectly during the first two and a half years. Here are some highlights:

Following the conclusion of the South American tour (August and early September 1960), which, incidentally, included a total of eight concerts (with a five-rehearsal minimum in each city) in Mexico City, Bogotá, Lima, Santiago, Buenos Aires, the Stravinskys and Robert alighted in New York for a few days before proceeding to Venice via Rome. There Stravinsky conducted the world première of his *Monumentum pro Gesualdo* on September 27, after which he began work on the cantata *A Sermon, A Narrative, and A Prayer*, commissioned by Dr. Paul Sacher (to whom it is also dedicated).* The two-month Venice stay (which provided an excellent tax deduction) was followed in November by concerts in Genoa and Rome. In December, in the midst of a snowstorm that left New York looking like a map of the prehistoric South Pole, I met this hale and hearty trio at the S.S. *Rotterdam* pier and installed them in the St. Regis. Trains, buses, and planes having been at a standstill for days, I rented a car and drove the party, their twelve pieces of luggage, and an adoring female friend of the younger of the two conductors to Washington (the Stravinskys sat in front with me!). This was not intended as a joy ride—although a two-hour delay in the Lincoln Tunnel did provide an "unforgettable experience"—but

* This was the work that delayed *The Flood*, although commissioned after it.

was due to the contracted appearance of both with the Washington Opera. Christmas was thus spent in the nation's capital and was followed by recordings (*Le Rossignol* and *Erwartung*).

Stravinsky, back home in Los Angeles, worked hard at the cantata throughout the month of January 1961, and did, in fact, complete it on the thirty-first, while Robert occupied himself with a recording in Toronto and a final polishing on the third of the literary collaborations (*Expositions and Developments*). In this year we made two more tours of Mexico, one following Holy Week (a big success) and one at Christmas (a total debacle), for the latter of which Stravinsky composed, as a *cadeau*, a forty-nine-second orchestration of his *Tango* (achieved during the flight to Mexico City). There were also some other firsts that autumn: a concert tour of Australia and New Zealand (route: Sydney, Auckland, Wellington, Sydney, Melbourne, Sydney, New Hebrides, Fiji Islands); a visit to Tahiti (for nothing except an entirely extracurricular course in the insect life); and a sightseeing tour of Egypt, about which Robert wrote from Cairo that it was so fascinating, they would pay their own way to come back! But before all this Stravinsky began to compose *The Flood* in May, worked on it in June, departed for Santa Fe in July (where he conducted *Perséphone*, the costumes designed by his wife); sailed for Göteborg/Stockholm in September to see Ingmar Bergman's production of *The Rake's Progress*, about which he waxed almost enthusiastic. (He told me later that the staging, with Bergman's technique of having one scene melt into another without interruption, as though the characters were on a perpetually moving stage, was "striking and non-detracting from my music.") He also flew to Helsinki to conduct—and was coerced into visiting the home of Sibelius (he had not intended to do so) in acknowledgment of the Sibelius Gold Medal, for which he had been named, and thence to Berlin, where, with the Santa Fe Opera Company on tour, he conducted *Perséphone* and Robert conducted *Oedipus*.* After a concert in Belgrade and *The Soldier's Tale* in Zurich, this astonishing man traveled to London and conducted *Perséphone* again, this time for the BBC!

In 1962 Stravinsky marked his eightieth birthday year with an itinerary that would have hospitalized a dozen people I can think of who were two decades his junior. He began by conducting a

---

* Robert told me it was to have been just the opposite, but Vera Zorina, who was the speaker in *Perséphone*, requested that Stravinsky lead that work.

program of his works in Los Angeles on January 6, flying the day after to Toronto for preliminary filming of Franz Kramer's CBC documentary of his life and career; * spent the next two weeks in Washington rehearsing and conducting the *Oedipus* with the Washington Opera, was honored at a dinner by President Kennedy, decorated by the State Department in a day-long ceremony, wined and dined by friends; returned to Los Angeles, but only after stopping in New York long enough to record *Renard* and other works; completed *The Flood*, which was then taped during the final week in March; opened the Seattle World's Fair on April 21; returned to Toronto, where during that same week he participated in a CBC program in his honor, featuring the Western Hemisphere première of *A Sermon, A Narrative, and A Prayer*, and recorded it thereafter; returned to New York to attend an exhibition of works pertaining to his ballet scores at the Wildenstein Gallery; and then flew to Europe for some serious touring!

Between May and December, Stravinsky made his first tour of South Africa (negotiated because, he wrote me, he wanted to see the impalas in Kruger Park), conducting with Robert in Johannesburg, Capetown, and the Bantu country (the latter on his own—it was "forbidden" †); flew to Rome, and then to Hamburg for his eightieth birthday concert, at which the New York City Ballet performed *Orpheus, Agon, Apollo* (the latter conducted by the composer); then back to New York, where he touched off a series of summer concerts beginning with one at the Lewisohn Stadium, followed by others at Ravinia and the Hollywood Bowl; then on to Santa Fe to conduct *Perséphone* again. After this he flew to Israel for his first appearances there, conducting three concerts at the Festival of Israel in which Robert shared the podium, and directly thereafter, via stops in Venice and Paris, he returned to his native country for the first time in almost fifty years. This tour took place during the final weeks of September and would have been a good time to pause for a vacation. But instead, the Stravinskys and Robert went on to Rome and Perugia, where there were more concerts, and finally, at the end of October, via New York to Caracas, where a series of three concerts brought them into the next month. On November 20 Stravinsky sat fidgeting in his box at Carnegie Hall (Ansermet was in the house!) while Robert conducted *The Rake's*

---

* The following year Stravinsky conducted *Symphony of Psalms* for this film.
† Because of *apartheid*.

Progress for the American Opera Society. The composer concluded the year by recording his *Symphony in C* and other works in Toronto, after which he returned home. There, in December, he shut himself in his studio and began to work on *Abraham and Isaac*.

Noteworthy . . . in any touring artist's book, let alone Stravinsky's!

There was another noteworthy event in 1962, but of a highly disturbing nature to me. When I met Stravinsky's plane from Rome on the twenty-third of October, he descended the steps with a wonderful smile of greeting, but I saw for the first time that he truly relied upon his cane.

Nevertheless, such itineraries as those just described showed no signs of diminishing (although the number of concerts did) in 1963, 1964, and 1965. Instead, during those years the trio, like a family of undecided sea gulls, flew Los Angeles–New York–Los Angeles something like eighteen times, using both cities as jumping-off places for half a dozen trips the length and breadth of Canada, by car, plane, and train; for more than a dozen transatlantic crossings by air or ship; for incidental flights to Honolulu, Rio, and Jerusalem. While Venice, Paris, London, Rome, Hamburg, Stockholm appeared on their vouchers with the frequency of bus stops on a commuter's ticket, there was still enough time for concertizing in Berlin, Budapest, Zagreb, and Warsaw, to say nothing, of course, of such commonplace cities as Chicago, Vancouver, Cincinnati, Cleveland, Boston, Washington, Denver, Philadelphia, to mention a few. And, of course, there were always "fillers" such as recordings and documentary films.

And what did Mr. Stravinsky the composer think of all this gadding about by Mr. Stravinsky the performing artist? On the whole he thought it all rather boring: the crowds, the press, the enervating social obligations, the endless circuit of medium-to-bad hotels, the indigestion-provoking food, the drafty concert halls (most of them acoustically poor), the concerts themselves (sometimes with indifferent if not inferior orchestras). For, of course, he regarded his *alter ego*'s career as a terrible waste of time. There was only one thing *he* wanted to do: stay home and compose.

But he resigned himself, first because this "secondary" life provided an excellent source of income and therefore eliminated worry, and then because it made those around him happy. (Not everyone disliked constant changes of environment as much as he did; not everyone was untroubled by restlessness.) The good humor of his household spelled peace for him. To think about composing required an atmosphere of peace, and every moment of all the years I knew him, that was *all* he wanted.

CHAPTER FIVE

STRAVINSKY as a "resigned" performing artist was the least troublesome client who ever existed. Having made up his mind to accept the inevitable, he would proceed through these tours with the persistence of an explorer who realizes that a jungle must be cleared before he will make his discovery. And always with a minimum of fuss.

The starting point was his baggage. For brief trips Stravinsky used only one bag—a twenty-inch air-weight valise that looked as if it would just accommodate one suit of clothes, a change of linen, and possibly a shaving kit. But Houdini could not have possessed a box with properties as magical as these. Usually Milène helped him pack, but on occasions when I was around (in the early years in hotels, later at home in Hollywood), ritual called for my presence in his room the day before a scheduled departure. Under his watchful eye and specific directions, I could make disappear into that pint-sized piece of luggage: two suits complete with waistcoats, his *frack* (the conductor's uniform of torture), dress trousers, stiff shirts, dress waistcoat, half a dozen changes of underclothing, walking shoes, dress shoes, pajamas, lounging robe, two cases of toilet articles, shaving equipment, eau de cologne (a huge bottle), two sweaters, boxes of studs, ties, scarves, handkerchiefs (numerous), two or three small towels (why, I never knew, but I suspect that they reminded him of his comfortable bath at home), his truss (the one that never fit and caused all sorts of trouble), extra medication bottles, pencils, notebooks, and on top of all this, as a "flattener," two or three large scores. There was still room for Mrs. Stravinsky and Robert to tuck in a few extra books if need be. It was incredible! I once tried to execute the operation alone when he was busy in his studio, but failed miserably and broke all speed records for putting things back in drawers where I had found them before he returned.

It was a Russian puzzle to which only he had the key . . . a system that didn't work unless he was there to code it.

For long trips—absences of two months or more—another valise would be added for adjustment to possible seasonal changes, and also a third small satchel, furnished with everything he required for composing: pencils, manuscript paper, compasses, colored pens, paste, etcetera (the bag we packed thus for Évian in 1970 was still in the closet of the room in which he died when I returned from Venice for the second time). But normally only a crushed brown leather zipper bag was carried aboard, containing more pill bottles, a small neck pillow, his white cardigan sweater, one or two Simenon mysteries, and an extra flask of Scotch; it was used, also, to hold necessities at rehearsals and concerts.

Nevertheless, the total baggage usually came to fourteen or fifteen pieces. (Robert had one suitcase in which he carried, on every trip, however short, the library-size *Oxford Dictionary of the English Language!*) And of course there were four or five items of hand-luggage plus a sack of books. After Stravinsky began to use a wheel-chair in airports, to help cover long distances—Indianapolis in 1965 was the first time—he would insist on making room on his convey-ance for all addenda, as well as everyone's extra coats, and would then be pushed through the air terminal looking like a luggage truck, albeit a distinguished one. Robert would already be seated in the waiting limousine while Stravinsky and I were just passing the third-of-the-way mark, and Mrs. Stravinsky, leisurely, elegant, and refusing to rush, would trail behind, loaded down with those ever-lasting items from which she could never be detached.

Stravinsky was the ideal seat companion on a plane, instilling calm by his own "cool," although he never looked forward to flights. My air trips with him were the only ones when my mind was not com-pletely occupied with visions of wings dropping off, leaks in fuel tanks, pilots prone to heart attacks, or birds colliding with the fuse-lage. Once esconced in the window seat, sweater handy, book opened, pillow tucked behind his neck, he rarely moved, no matter how long the trip—reading, gazing with concentrated interest at anything below that could be seen, pointing out unusual formations of clouds, mountains, sunlight. I remember a fascinating five-minute discourse on the Finger Lakes, a sight that always intrigued him, on one of our trips from Toronto to New York. (He was thoroughly informed on the flora and fauna of that region, as he was on almost anything that had to do with wildlife.) He would become annoyed only if we had to wait an unusually long time to be airborne, which meant a consequent delay in the arrival of that first comforting drink, or if the food were particularly poor (but these reactions were shared by all other passengers, needless to say). And the only indication that he might be just a wee bit thoughtful about the whole idea of taking to the empyrean was a slight gesture toward his chest just before take-off, to make sure Saint Christopher was alerted to the "fasten seat belt" sign. Stewards and stewardesses generally adored him, made a great to-do over his comfort, and collected autographs before the landing—*he* never made any unusual demands on *their* services.

We always traveled V.I.P., which did make things simpler; these arrangements were made by me several days ahead of departure time and included permission to proceed directly to the plane, sometimes in a limousine or in the car that had brought him; expedited porter service and transportation at arrival and departure points; rapid customs clearance; quick baggage release; waiving of documents in certain areas; and so on. Official delays of the latter type would have infuriated him; he always felt that since he was on *his* way to please the public, there should be no senseless deterrents in his path. *He* never kept anyone waiting; certainly authorities should be equally considerate.

Visas always bothered him—where were they to be gotten, and what did they need, and was I sure of my facts about visas? And so did health certificates—he detested vaccinations, recalling with bitterness an occasion when, for lack of that inoculation, he was held up for two hours in Caracas (I.S. to L.L., February 24, 1960). And another time he asked me to look into the matter of special "eye's" certificates and police certificates, which Venezuela and Argentina had had the effrontery to require when he had been there before! To insure that I would apply the proper degree of seriousness to this request, he concluded with the information that he was not kidding! (*sic*) (I.S. to L.L., May 10, 1960).

His wife, across the aisle, slept through almost every plane trip, assisted by a tranquilizer taken beforehand, but Robert, despite all efforts to conceal his unease (books, notebooks, the *London Times*, on his tray table), was neurotic from the moment we left for the airport ("we should have gone a different way . . . we're late already . . . there's a traffic jam ahead") until we had checked into the hotel at our destination. Everything connected with traveling threw him; he was helpless with baggage (Mrs. Stravinsky would take care of this department if I were not there), had a hatred of crowds that surpassed Stravinsky's, suffered from claustrophobia, never had any change for tips. In this area Stravinsky was usually very good. The preparation of what he referred to as "blackmail" was part of his travel routine, and dollar bills were tucked into various pockets in the event that I might need extra ones. (He always complained that I overtipped—probably a deserved reproach, but, after all, fifteen pieces of baggage for one dollar? No!)

Sometimes not everything went smoothly, and I would have to deal with overweight on a scale suitable for a moon landing, or trace a lost piece of luggage, or argue that we *were* on a manifest list when the airlines clerk said we were not. Once, in the Acapulco airport, when Holy Week had created a seating priority problem comparable to wartime conditions, I spent half an hour screaming in Spanish that Igor Sikorsky *was* Igor Stravinsky: "Don't you *dare* bounce him off this crate or I'll call Alemán!" At such moments Stravinsky, who usually remained with me while the other two members of our party were collecting every newspaper and current magazine on the stands, would gaze steadily down at the floor, or look off into the distance as though he had absolutely no connection with the screaming harridan beside him. After it was all over, he would point to the brown satchel and say, "Now let us have a Scotch."

Check-ins were never a problem; the hotel's chief executives rolled out enough red carpet to furnish a Loew's theater lobby, and the family was escorted upstairs immediately, while I remained below to read to the desk clerks the regulations about "no calls, no visitors, no press, no pictures, no autographs . . . ring *my* room."

My first tour with the Stravinskys and Robert, which happened to be to Mexico City (the initial lap on the South American trip), established a work pattern for the future, although the engagement itself could hardly be called typical: not many cities in the world provide so magnificent a background. It was Stravinsky's first return to the land of the Mayans and Aztecs after a ten-year absence, and the city made ready as though for the arrival of the world's greatest *torero*. I had come from New York about ten days before, at the request of the sponsoring Institute of Fine Arts (*Instituto Nacional de Bellas Artes*), to assist with the press, rehearsal arrangements, and social plans. The visit of so distinguished an American citizen had other ramifications as well: the United States was then in the midst of promoting its good-neighbor policy through the instrument of cultural exchange, and government-sponsored samples of American theatrical and musical achievements had already toured Mexico (some with, more without, success). But here was a high quality, made-to-order event of note, and the embassy reacted by supplying a competent press officer and a cultural attaché who, wonder of wonders, not only knew who Stravinsky was, but also were somewhat familiar with his music.

The crowd at the Mexico City airport when the composer's plane was due required not only the embassy's efficient organization, but all the assistance available from airport officials, a contingent of the military, and the local police. When Stravinsky emerged from the plane, right arm held high in greeting, Hollywood dark glasses glinting in the afternoon light, and wearing his broadest commercial smile, the explosion that followed resembled the opening of the Veracruz Mardi Gras. Led by Mexico's minister of education and the director of the Institute of Fine Arts; delegations of musicians; representatives of the National Orchestra; a party of high-ranking government officials; the American Embassy's first officer (the ambassador was out of town); two other executive officers; and a group of diplomats from other embassies (not, however, that of the USSR) marched onto the airfield followed by a huge crowd of fans who broke through the tapes and, waving American and Mexican flags, shouted "*Viva* Stravinsky!" Above this roar of welcome, a high-school band, stationed at the head of the lane that led to the terminal building, rendered a *fortississimo* version of excerpts from *Petrushka*.

Stravinsky was delighted. Standing at the top of the landing stairs, he placed his beret on the crook of his cane and, raising it aloft, twirled it like a pinwheel, as he gave his jerky palm-toward-face conqueror's salute with the other hand. Then, his small frame completely hidden by the throng around him, he proceeded without protest to the airport lounge, where, for fifteen minutes, during which I feared he would be crushed, he permitted photographs from every angle, posing graciously and expressing over and over, in somewhat unrecognizable Spanish, his appreciation of the Mexican people and their overwhelming welcome.

And he meant all of this sincerely. Stravinsky was not unaccustomed, of course, to enthusiastic receptions outside the concert hall—they occurred in practically all countries (though rarely the one in which he resided) whenever the public had been informed that he was coming. In fact, and despite his sometime remarks to the contrary, he derived great satisfaction from public recognition, which, whether the participants were conscious of it or not, was to him an acknowledgment of his status as a great composer, and not simply as a celebrity.

This occasional need for reassurance was a strange one, and manifested itself once or twice in odd ways, within the concert hall. When Robert conducted the American Opera Society's performance of *The Rake's Progress,* Stravinsky was restless during rehearsals, raising many questions about interpretation with two composers who sat with him during these periods. He was also nervous throughout the performance (Ansermet's presence, perhaps), although the cast was excellent (Betty Allen and Donald Gramm, among others), the orchestra was good (though it *had* been somewhat intractable), and Robert's conducting was acclaimed with enthusiasm. Stravinsky departed from custom that evening by consenting to leave his box in Carnegie Hall to take an onstage bow with the librettists (W. H. Auden and Chester Kallman), usually an unthinkable act on his part when he was "in attendance." He would generally have considered it bad taste—as indeed it seemed to be on that night: it would have been far more dignified to have remained where he was, receiving the ovation in the spotlight customarily turned toward him on such occasions. For those of us who had seen his reaction at rehearsals, his rush to the stage emphasized an insecurity, as though he felt he had been wrong to appear negative when the production was in the throes of preparation, and now wished to be assured by the public adulation that his opera was, after all, as important a work as he had conceived it to be. This seeming need of public approval was driven home to me in later years, when it became more and more difficult for him to walk or even to rise from a chair without support. During a performance of his music at the Los Angeles Music Center in 1968, which he attended although he felt very ill, he was anguished that the audience saw the tremendous effort it took for him to rise from his seat and acknowledge its applause.

In the case of Mexico his pleasure was due in great measure to the fact that his music was so often performed there; during the time that Carlos Chávez held the post of musical director of the National Symphony, Stravinsky's later works had received as much attention as the early masterpieces that had established his reputation. Besides, he thought that the Mexicans were "one of the world's most dignified people, however poor . . . they do not hold out their hands," which remark, made to the late Don Celestino Gorostiza, director of the Institute of Fine Arts, one night when we all dined together, received front-page attention in *Excelsior* (without the phrase "however poor," though), and necessitated expansion of the standing-room area for the concert.

Stravinsky's willingness to cooperate—a facet of his character not often acknowledged by those who write about him—was especially noteworthy in Mexico, and particularly revealing at rehearsals. He was, fortunately, not bothered by the altitude—Mexico City is eighty-two hundred feet above sea level—although it did affect his wife, who is inclined to a slightly high blood pressure, and Robert, whose fervent approach to everything (including walking) kept him breathless in the thin air. Stravinsky never had to avail himself of the cylinder of oxygen kept handy at stage right for foreign artists, and he explained to me once, when I asked him why he had been less comfortable in Santa Fe, which was two thousand feet lower, that Mexico City, built on a lake, had a flexibility that affected the atmosphere and made it "suave." *

Rehearsals in Mexico began at the ghastly hour of 8:00 A.M., and at seven-thirty I would find Stravinsky dressed, "breakfasted," sitting near the door of his room with his scarf, top coat, hat, and rehearsal bag aligned on a bench nearby (the city was hot, of course, but he remembered the drafty damp of the hall), and impatient to be off. The Hotel Bamer, where we always stopped, is directly across from the Alameda—that handsome park where sculptures, contemporary and colonial, peer startlingly out of clusters of foliage—to the right of which stands the baroque structure of the Palace of Fine Arts, with its strange *fin de siècle* iridescent dome. We always used a hotel taxi to make the five-minute trip across, however, since at the stage entrance four steep flights of stairs had to be scaled in order to reach stage level. There was an elevator of sorts but it was never in order, at least in the dozen years I knew that theater, and every bit of one's wind was required for the climb. The night before

* However, he *was* bothered in Bogotá, which was the next stop on that tour.

Stravinsky's first rehearsal, representatives of the institute had been apologetic about this inconvenience, promising to try to work something out (what, I could not imagine, as the approach from the front of the house, where elevators *did* work, necessitated a descent to the stage via a spiral stairway, fraught with peril).

Whatever anxiety Stravinsky might have experienced thinking about that mountain of steps was not apparent during a very cheerful dinner the night before his rehearsal and a ride thereafter around the Zocalo to see the magnificently illuminated cathedral and government palaces. The next morning when we reached the stage entrance, its guardian for generations, an eighty-three-year-old descendant of Moctezuma, bent to kiss Stravinsky's hands, but the composer recognized and stopped him in order to give him the Mexican *abrazo*, which consists in encompassing the recipient's shoulders in a bear hug and, at the same time, slapping his back heartily with both hands. It is as grand a gesture of brotherly love as ever existed, and when administered by a non-Mexican it seals a friendship. Close behind this venerable gatekeeper stood two enormous *muchachos*, built like wrestlers. They bowed shyly, crossed their arms, clasped each other's hands, and signified to Stravinsky that he was to occupy the seat thus formed. The administration had indeed fulfilled its pledge to solve the embarrassing problem of the uncooperative elevator. However, Stravinsky, who was more terrified of being dropped than of losing his breath, contented himself with grasping each Hercules by an arm and accomplishing most of the ascent by stopping to breathe deeply, for a minute, at every third step. But when the final flight was reached, he suddenly tucked his legs under him and permitted himself to be conveyed to the top in one fell swoop by his supporters, who then deposited him within inches of the stage. As he straightened his jacket and smoothed his hair, he said to me almost gleefully, "Now I know what it feels like to be an eagle."

To a man, the members of the National Symphony rose to greet Stravinsky, whose approach on the arm of the librarian, another ancient friend, was announced by a ten-year-old advance runner shouting "*Viene! Viene!*" ("He comes! He comes!") Hererra de la Fuente, the musical director, moved to meet him as the musicians stamped their feet and the string players tapped their instruments with their bows. The homage prolonged itself when Stravinsky gave de la Fuente the *abrazo*, shook hands with the concertmaster and the first viola, waved to the winds, the brass, the percussion. This time *I* was permitted to undertake the whole Santa Fe–New York rehearsal procedure (thereafter a permanent function of mine)— Kleenex placement, eyeglass-case disposal, sweater on chair-back, etcetera—and Stravinsky began to conduct the *Firebird Suite*.

It was always very satisfying to watch the composer in rehearsal, whether for concerts or recordings. First of all, he enjoyed himself thoroughly (except when the orchestra was very bad), and no matter how annoyed he might become beforehand—whether his pique was due to inconvenient time schedules or interruptions of his *real* work—once he was on the podium he seemed to vibrate. *This* was "making music" (his phrase), and what could be more pertinent, except the act of creating music. For him the actual performance was never as interesting. During the time I knew him, he never really cared to listen to performances of his own works by others, and if he was compelled to on occasions when he was either contracted to be "in attendance" or had to as a courtesy, he did so with extreme reluctance and was inclined to be highly critical afterward. But his pleasure in rehearsing himself was apparent in his attitude toward the musicians: he was patient, never unwilling to be interrupted by a player for an explanation, and (contrary to popular opinion) gentle in his manner. He was also delightfully illustrative.* He would sing, whistle, imitate a metronome, use his hands frequently to beat measures on the lectern (he never used a baton, incidentally, and always used a score during my time). His famous sense of humor was to the fore, and he would intersperse his musical instructions with samples of his biting wit, as well as little anecdotes. What he had to say was always important, involving some change or improvement, or something new. Orchestra personnel, as a rule, venerated him, and not only for these characteristics. They admired the man who obviously knew his business and carried it on *sans* foolishness or dramatic overlay, but at the same time with a human warmth. They recognized from his behavior that he respected them, and consequently they accorded him the respect that was his just due.

There were exceptions, of course, on both sides. On two different occasions members of the second violin sections (pure coincidence!) of America's most distinguished Eastern Seaboard ensembles utilized

* Excerpts from Stravinsky rehearsals have been issued by Columbia Records (in set D5S-775).

the rehearsal time to catch up on their reading; the *Racing Form*, *Playboy*, and *The New Yorker* were some of the clearly visible titles. And I recall another string player who wrote, sealed, and stamped two letters during a rehearsal of *Symphony of Palms*, with an air of such nonchalance that it would not have been at all surprising had he asked Stravinsky to run down to the corner and mail them. Twice within my experience orchestras failed to rise (though these occasions were performances, not rehearsals) when he came on stage to conduct. Both incidents were deliberate expressions of the musicians' resentment concerning certain events for which they held the composer responsible. Once, in the Midwest, union difficulties had prevented a recording, and Stravinsky had expressed himself audibly backstage on the whole subject of non-creative individuals and their ability to damage music. The other incident took place south of the border, when rehearsals were called during the Christmas holidays and players were compelled to give up some of their vacation time (although they were well paid).

For his part, Stravinsky seemed to take no notice of the onstage reading and writing (I don't think he remarked it, actually). However, he was clearly both hurt and offended by the other insults; both times he had something to say to me in the dressing room, afterward. "The union scandal has tired them. They could not get up from their chairs." And of the Yuletide bad humor: "They are disrespectful. I, too, must work on Christmas."

In fact, there were few conditions capable of provoking Stravinsky to anger during rehearsal, but when they did occur, he was liable to one of those classic outbursts of rage that people associate with genius. Displays of unwarranted ignorance or stupidity—e.g., sloppy or incorrect readings of the music by indifferent players who had not taken even a moment of time to study it—would throw him into a passion. And if he found that the conductor's score (when he was not using his own) contained penciled notations or changes made by previous users of the material, he would quiver with suppressed fury until he could contain himself no longer, and a primordial roar would pierce the atmosphere. Using such a score once for *Pulcinella*, he did not interrupt himself, but sent each page flying, as it was completed, from the lectern to the floor with a gesture of his left hand, in an expression of contempt that was truly Olympian.

During the first three years of frantic touring, I grew to know that individual members of certain American orchestras (usually the older men) nursed strong feelings against Stravinsky because of opinions he had purportedly expressed about their musical directors or their own performances. Such comments, printed in one or another of the Stravinsky-Craft books, did not make for general good will. However, more than this, some players resented the presence of Robert Craft.

In these cases, Robert always started out with a major strike against him: he was *there* only because Stravinsky was. The musicians could not, indeed—what was worse—refused to understand why the composer would not accept as co-conductor their own musical director. Stravinsky's own opinion, as reported to me on many occasions by his wife, that Robert understood his music better than anyone else, was not always relevant, since many times Robert's half of the program contained pieces by other contemporary composers. For Robert fought hard, and understandably, to maintain his status as an individual and not an adjunct. He wrote me in May 1962 that he would not do all-Stravinsky programs after this eightieth birthday year, and *that* was definite; later, in December, relative to a proposed recording with Glenn Gould, he advised me that he would like to do it because everything he did by himself was worth ten times what he did with "Mr. S."

Orchestral and administrative animosity was not lost on him. Given his natural desire to assert himself as a person—and, moreover, as a person who knew a great deal about music—it had the unsalutary effect of sometimes producing an authoritarian manner vis-à-vis orchestras, which stood in great contrast to Stravinsky's acknowledgment of a mutual understanding. Robert would be supercritical, sometimes arrogant, and usually unable to remove the chip from his shoulder. His humor (and he was brilliantly humorous when he was with friends) generally emerged as scathing irony, and his criticisms were often more sardonic than constructive. He had another habit at which orchestras and rehearsal auditors took umbrage, and this increased noticeably as Stravinsky's health began to fail: in his sincere desire to conceal Stravinsky's weaknesses, Robert would sometimes stand behind the composer when the latter took over at dress rehearsal, and wave to the orchestra to follow *his* beat rather than the conductor's. Some musicians have told me that this was disturbing because, as a rule, Stravinsky's beat was much clearer. But such actions seemed to me more an expression, although it may have been a subconscious one, of Robert's fight for survival in the auditorium.

Robert, I suppose, knew all the time that he was waging a losing battle. Even if he had been a highly spectacular conductor (which I do not think he could be; his readings are generally remarkable for their understatement and lack of superficial emotionalism), how could anyone, whoever he were, compete with so legendary a figure or so compelling a personality as Stravinsky? And if anyone should attempt to, the result would have to be a *reductio ad absurdum.*

This logic, however, did not govern the thinking of orchestra personnel, nor did many of them realize for a moment, I am sure, that a Bernstein or a Mehta or a Maazel would undoubtedly have suffered the same fate in the same co-conductor's position. Robert, who held his feelings in a super-tight rein in public, suffered many private humiliations as a result. At the opening concert of the Seattle World's Fair, for example, because of the nature of the event and Stravinsky's high fee, the Seattle Symphony Board won out, and its musical director, Milton Katims, shared the program (leading Van Cliburn in Rachmaninov's *Concerto No. 2*)—but only one-third of it, for Robert conducted Stravinsky's *Symphony in Three Movements.* Through an oversight, however, Robert's name was left off the program entirely (as it was in Lima and one or two other places) and the audience, embarrassed, did not know who he was and did not acknowledge his entrance. Although the omission was a printer's error, in this instance Robert's insecurity did not allow acceptance of such an excuse; he felt it was a deliberate slip. I was deeply sympathetic when he said to me later, "Well, the musicians were very nice and congratulated me anyway."

But he had a large following among younger orchestra players, who openly expressed their profound respect for his knowledge of and writings on Schoenberg, Webern, and Berg. His own fan mail was heavy when his recordings of works by these composers were issued, and it is worthy of note that many of these, as well as his recordings of pieces by Varèse, Boulez, and Stockhausen, won more foreign prizes than any discs listed in the Columbia catalogue.

CHAPTER SIX

FOR those on the other side of the footlights, Stravinsky could only have been the most soul-satisfying performing artist in the business. And in my opinion, he was one of the greatest hams in the history of the theater—a medium, incidentally, with which he always claimed a strong affiliation, because of the dramatic talent his father had possessed as an opera singer. Furthermore, he was fond of saying that he *liked* to perform. Some evidence of the enjoyment he derived from treading the boards, not to mention an awareness of the effect his presence had on audiences, emerged during every engagement within my recollection.

Concertgoers who were at New York's Philharmonic Hall on December 6, 1964, for example, when Stravinsky and Robert shared a program featuring the American première of *Abraham and Isaac*, may be unable to recall exact details of either the performances or the pieces, but they almost surely will remember the following incident. Stravinsky conducted his *Elegy to J.F.K.* and some of his Russian songs, after which the *Pulcinella Suite* required a rearrangement of music stands to accommodate a larger and differently placed orchestra. Several minutes were then scheduled for stagehands to rush forward and make the necessary adjustments. Stravinsky, at that period, was making his trips back and forth to the podium extremely slowly and, of course, with the aid of his cane. When he had finished conducting *Pribautki* he turned and, remaining in his place, took his bows, while by pre-arrangement the players and singers quietly left the stage. He then stepped down from the podium laboriously, and made as though to exit via right stage; but midway he paused, appeared to be thinking for a moment, then returned to the concertmaster's chair, sat down, and lost himself in a study of the *Pulcinella* score, already opened by the librarian on the stand before him. For a moment the audience sat immobile, fascinated by the sight of that small, hunched-over figure, occupied in a secret world. Even the crew crept about on tiptoe, collapsing music racks noiselessly (an almost impossible achievement), and moving chairs as if they were bits of fluff. A coo of delight, resembling the sound that might be emitted by a pair of grandparents on observing unmistakable signs of genius in a new-born heir, rippled through the house. Stravinsky straightened up, peered haughtily into the auditorium's huge, dimly-lighted gloom, pressed down on the handle of his cane for support, rose carefully, climbed the steps of the podium, and held his pose, hands on the lectern, while the orchestra filed in and the audience roared its pleasure. "No one even went out to the Coca-Cola machine," remarked that prize disciple of Thespis as I was helping him divest himself of his *frack* in the dressing-room—and with an air of innocent astonishment that would have left a child of eight undeceived.

His knowledge of theatrical protocol, in no matter which country, was also infallible. During that same Mexican tour of beret-twirling fame, Stravinsky received the *Diana* from the orchestra at the conclusion of the program. This musical tribute (which many foreigners have heard but may not recognize as the finale to the traditional *Hat Dance*) is the highest compliment the Mexican ensemble of trumpeters at bull fights can bestow on a great toreador or a brave bull. It is sounded rarely, and only when one or the other has demonstrated such courage in the *corrida* that he is judged worthy of the title "the Bravest." In the concert hall its occurrence is equally rare, since it is usually reserved for distinguished elderly artists, and signifies not only recognition of a superior performance, but also the presence of a great personality. However, there is one difference: the entire orchestra must be well-disposed toward the object of the tribute, and according to information I have from Mexican orchestra members, a popularity poll is usually taken in advance. In other words, no unanimity, no *Diana*.

On this particular evening, for a bejeweled and brocaded parquet and tiers and a poncho-clad gallery, Stravinsky had conducted a thrilling performance of the *Firebird Suite*—so exciting, in fact, that the explosion of sound announcing the entrance of Kastchei had sent a sizable group of patrons, occupying the partial-view seats at the rear of the Fine Arts Palace, in search of speedy exits: they mistook the crashes and rumbles for the start of a *temblor!* As Stravinsky closed his score, the audience rose to its feet and began to clap rhythmically. Above the *olés* came the roll of drums which Mexi-

cans know is the prelude to the *Diana*. Stravinsky, who was
then bowing from a position to the left of center stage, turned his
back to the public—but only just enough so that he remained visible
to most of it in profile—placed his right hand on his hip and his
left hand on his heart in such gestures as would undoubtedly be
prescribed in a toreador's handbook of good behavior, and bowed
low from the waist to the orchestra. The *Diana* was repeated three
times, and he did not move a muscle, although I could see (from my
position at the downstage wing) that the back of his always red
neck was now almost purple. Fortunately, the wind players had to
pause for breath—ten minutes of hard blowing at an altitude of
eighty-two hundred feet would render even a Pheidippides senseless
—and Stravinsky made a superb exit, backing slowly as though he
were leaving the papal presence, while the palace virtually *did* shake
from an earthquake of stamping feet. Two backstage denizens
received him in their arms when his heel caught in a metal strip at
the wings, while fifteen or twenty others stood clapping in time with
the audience and hailing him with the ultimate accolade: "*Torero,
Torero, Torero!*" He bowed gravely to them all, as he had to the
orchestra, and marched off to his dressing room, outdoing Juan
Belmonte.

Stravinsky's sense of dramatic timing, as one would expect from
this master of musical time, never failed him. It was uncanny to
observe how he would control an audience and its applause, so that
after concerts he always left the public yearning for more of the
same. When it eventually became difficult for him to return to
center stage for even a second curtain call, he inaugurated a new
system. At the end of a program he would remain onstage, accepting
plaudits for himself and the orchestra and giving the audience free
rein for a maximum of five minutes. Then exit, to make use of the
articles I held ready for him in the wings: towel, hairbrush, mirror.
After this, eight paces onstage for a low bow, this time limited to
two and a half minutes. Exit again, but now I would drape his
scarf around his neck, help him on with his overcoat, button it to the
throat, turn up the collar, give him his borsalino: and on he would
go to stand downstage right waving his hat in an absolutely explicit
signal of "Thank-you-very-much-but-please-I-want-to-go-home."
(At the Hollywood Bowl in 1965, on an evening when the ther-
mometer registered approximately eighty, since he was *sans* over-

coat, we borrowed a scarf and a costermonger's cap from a thrilled clarinet player.) Audiences, without exception, went wild.

In general, during concerts Stravinsky preferred to remain alone in his dressing room for the first half of the program, where he would immerse himself in the latest Simenon opus or, sometimes, in the score he was to conduct (if it didn't happen to be *Firebird!*). To guarantee his privacy—there were always autograph hunters or "composers" carrying creations of Beethovenian or Wagnerian quality lurking about in the shadows—I would lock him in before I went to look after Robert, or post a guard if an unbribeable one could be found. But there were occasions when the composer would sit in a chair in the wings, leaning on his cane with one hand while he cupped his ear with the other to listen. (This position was the hidden picture-snappers' delight; identical thousands of such shots must now be in the collective possession of backstage personnel and their relatives all over the world.) The pieces that could draw Stravinsky outside his protected area were premières of his own compositions or works of his not often performed. Sometimes a soloist would attract his attention, as Itzhak Perlman did when Robert conducted him in the *Violin Concerto* with the Chicago Symphony at Orchestra Hall in 1966. And when Van Cliburn played the Rachmaninov *Second* (which Stravinsky had not wanted on the program) at the Seattle World's Fair, I discovered him just outside the door of his dressing room listening intently, although I am sure this was simply to verify his negative opinion of that composer's work. But he would rarely emerge to hear works by other composers, doing so only if Robert requested this of him, and he never refused his younger colleague.

There were other Stravinsky concert traditions. Immediately before Robert left for the stage, the composer would salute him with the Russian double kiss. It was a very private and moving little ceremony, and I would turn my back to avoid intruding. But I had my own moment with him, too, when I would help him change in the dressing room after the evening was over; he was human, and he liked to hear that he had done well.

Robert customarily left the concert hall as soon as his work was over, which, most of the time, was at intermission. But as Stravinsky began to restrict himself to only the final piece of the evening, Robert would have to prolong his stay into the second half. This always bothered him, and even if he finished within twenty-five minutes of the program's conclusion, he would more often than not rush off alone unless transportation provided a problem. His compulsion toward self-effacement when he was with the composer in public was ever-present, as was his completely opposite attitude of assurance, authority, and even impatience or abruptness with him at home.

To all outward appearances, Stravinsky's onstage entrance was very matter-of-fact. He would hand me whatever he had in his pockets, his wallet, and sometimes a small cross that he carried in addition to the one he always wore around his neck on a chain. On certain occasions (as when rehearsal periods had been unsatisfying) he would help himself to half a tumblerful of neat Scotch from the flask we had brought with us, proceed to the wings, take a deep breath, adjust his lapels, and dart forward, trying hard not to let his bad leg retard him. He never showed any effects from the pre-concert fortification, which was completely undetectable, even to his wife. During the final two years of intensive touring he tapered off a bit, and added more than half a glass of water to a third of a glass of Scotch. Stravinsky enjoyed Scotch as a thirst-quencher and during my years with him never took it for any other reason, certainly not to lift himself out of a depressed mood, although its occasional placement on the banned list by one or another of his physicians could irritate him into fury. His super-hospitality in offering people drinks was purely and simply because he knew most visitors were slightly afraid of him, and "Scotch makes everyone relax."

When I was able to accompany Stravinsky on tour, his wife would avoid the concert hall as much as possible. This was not out of indifference to her husband's music (though she *did* have her favorites) or to music in general, although I think she much preferred to look at or work at painting. In fact, her ideas on programming were often solicited by Robert because she had an instinct for selecting Stravinsky compositions that would complement each other and interest audiences. But her dislike of performances was the result of a constant fear that something might happen to her husband on the stage. On occasions when her presence was mandatory, either because diplomacy dictated her attendance with a group of dignitaries or because, in my absence, there was no one who understood the backstage requirements, she always suffered from nervous tension, though usually only Robert and I could discern this. She was as accomplished an actress when surrounded by people as her husband was an actor: all dimples and smiles and full of innocuous social conversation, while her blood pressure was climbing. It was impossible for her to stand or sit in the wings, and if persuaded to do so by attendants who found her wandering in the corridors, she would direct her smiling gaze toward some complex of pulleys in the flies, or "nonchalantly" smoke a cigarette, avoiding glances stageward with the care exercised by Lot's daughters fleeing Sodom. Most of the time she sat in the dressing room as though doomed to the guillotine, until the sound of thunderous applause told her all was well.

As Stravinsky's health began to decline, her nervousness naturally increased, and during several of the American engagements she would either remain in Hollywood or would leave the concert hall with Robert, giving as a reason that room service had to be commandeered well in advance to insure a proper supper when her husband came home.

My presence, therefore, was helpful to her, immodest as that may sound—and in other ways as well. For she loved to explore cities, spend hours in art galleries, shop, have lunch or tea with friends, "away from all that music business." My being along allowed her the free time she needed for these activities, and since Stravinsky seemed content that the substitute caretaker be me, her mind was relieved of anxiety (particularly in the later years) and she could enjoy her enthusiasms. Mrs. Stravinsky had, and still does have (she is now over eighty) the most youthful approach to life imaginable, and on the tours a trip to Woolworth's in Minneapolis could be as exciting as shopping for a mink coat on Michigan Avenue in Chicago; or sharing a pizza with a friend as much fun as having dinner with the president of the United States. An atmosphere of good humor has always been vital to her well-being. She could never tolerate depressing conversation or, in fact, a discussion of serious problems of any nature, or cope with topics that were not amusing. Displays of bad temper on the part of any of us would guarantee her immediate disappearance from the premises, sometimes on an excursion of unknown destination (these were worrisome!) in her car. People who were boring or unattractive disturbed her: once, when one of the two cars had to be driven from Los Angeles to New York while we made the trip by air, she voted for a driver who

looked like a cross between Troy Donahue and Rock Hudson, and
smelled as though he had just returned from a five-day "trip," in
preference to an applicant who worked for General Motors and
came with a handful of excellent references, a slightly crooked nose,
horn-rimmed spectacles, and no smile. Result: the brand-new Cadillac was ruined, and Troy-Hudson hung about the Pierre Hotel
lobby sending billets-doux upstairs for money (she had already
given him three hundred dollars) until the management, which took
a bigoted view about untidiness in its lobby, had to order him away.
She would be impervious to forewarnings in circumstances such as
these, and after the deluge, with a sweetness that was so melting one
could not scold her, she would say: "I cannot help it! I am soooo
stupid!"

On tour the two conductors remained in their hotel rooms
(usually a three-bedroom suite and a room adjoining or nearby for
me) when they were not working. Robert's extra-concert occupa-
tion was writing. There has never been a time since I first met him
when he was not engaged in applying pen to paper: on the jointly-
authored books, on addenda to new editions, on articles and book
reviews for magazines and newspapers, to say nothing of letters,
letters, and more letters (his correspondence surely equaled the ag-
gregate of Sainte-Beuve and Mme. de Staël)—to critics, editors, musicians, students (he always answered any query), friends. Chiefly
he would work in bed, in a most uncomfortable-looking half-sitting,
half-slumping position, his neck pressed against the headboard, the
entire room shrouded in darkness, except for a one-bulb lamp directed onto his work. The rest of the bed sagged under the weight
of glossaries, thesauruses, reference books, newspapers, manuscripts,
reams of manila paper, and paper clips. Piles of paper covered with
that unbelievably minuscule calligraphy attested to his habit—in
his perpetual search for perfection—of writing as many as eleven
or twelve (sometimes more) revisions of a single page, *on that single
page.* He used colored pens (as Stravinsky did in his sketches) to
trace the routes of his word and phrase changes, transpositions,
rewrites of paragraphs; and whoever was condemned to type had
to master the technique of following this rainbow spool of Ariadne
through the labyrinth.

But sometimes he would accompany Mrs. Stravinsky on a promenade or a visit to a museum, while Stravinsky and I remained
behind. Now and then the composer would poke his head out of the

bedroom and call me from the living room, where I was working, to ask the time (which he would then check exactly with his own watch in order to tell me I was two seconds wrong), or chat a bit about the concerts or other plans—simply to reassure himself that he was not alone. Occasionally we would play simultaneous games of solitaire. (By 1964 he had lost his taste for double-solitaire, or Russian bank, at which he had been adept, always beating me with his lightning perception; but as time wore on I think he began to regard them as too violent—all that slapping about to build on the aces before one's opponent arrived there was "excessive!") Sometimes we would take a walk for one or two blocks "to exercise my legs." He liked to window-shop, displays of timepieces or any kind of electrical gadget commanding priority, and he was always intrigued by electric knives or space-savers for desks, automatic pencil sharpeners, battery-powered erasers (he owned two). Once in Boston, waiting for the limousine in the dead of winter, we stopped for fully five minutes (while our ears froze) in front of an antique shop near the Ritz-Carlton, where a window full of eighteenth-century weather-measuring instruments, one almost exactly like a metronome, prompted him to remark how useful it would be if the music-clock would operate on the barometric principle: that is, by recording automatically any change in the composer's timing during the process of creation, as the weather instrument does for changes in temperature. Music and record stores were always bypassed, of course, as well as apparel shops (although his wife once told me that formerly he could not be pried away from the latter).

Such walks were brief, for when I met Stravinsky he was beginning to favor his left leg more and more, and he always had a terrible fear of slipping or falling. He would cling fast to my arm and take short, carefully considered steps. (I was later to recall these walks with deep nostalgia, when our excursions were restricted to three or four turns around the small second-floor terrace in Hollywood or, at most, a circuit of the paved area in front of the backyard garage, before dinner.)

Touring with him was not always cakes and ale, however. Fans presented a continual problem. For obvious reasons, Stravinsky never received the public in his dressing-room, often not even very close friends: his weariness after an hour of hard conducting; his fragility, which, not without good reason, intensified his instinctive hypochondria (he was prone to inexplicable rises in temperature, and caught chills very easily); his age. Usually my two-minute explanation, which I would render as gently as possible to the throngs filling the backstage and surrounding his waiting car, would be effective. People were, in general, very understanding and would call out their messages or "bravos" or throw their posies from a respectful distance, until the "old gentleman" was safely tucked in the front seat of his car (usually there, since it was easier for him to slide in, rather than step in). But then there were the diehard demanders whose attitude clearly indicated that Stravinsky had achieved the heights only because *they* had so ordained. "No autographs, please, he is very tired," would be answered by, "So are we. We've been standing here for hours" (while the concert was in progress?), or (unbelievable!) "Who does he think he is!"

Such aggressiveness could be dealt with in only one way, by summoning the door guards or, occasionally, the police assigned to help us. I was always particularly wary of the individuals who practiced "laying on of hands." Some of their back-pats, sleeve-pulls, and shoulder-rubs might have been learned at a *karate* school, and poor Maestro, clutching the back of my coat, would try to conceal himself like a frightened cat until we reached the haven of the limousine.

On a particularly trying occasion in 1964, when a blizzard had practically entombed Philadelphia and its environs, thereby producing a state of general grumpiness not only among the orchestra members, whose cars were stuck and whose fingers were frozen, but also in Stravinsky (we had been compelled to take a long and dangerous drive from New York in order to fulfill the contract), he was more emphatic than usual about observance of the backstage rules. The extra caution was prompted by a letter, lately received, informing us that a party of suburban socialites would be calling on him in his dressing room during intermission—altogether an inconvenient time: few artists, let alone Stravinsky, are inclined to be sociable when preparing to go onstage. He had, therefore, given me strict orders to advise these "inconsiderate individuals" that "if they have come to see me and not to hear my music, they can go home" —a message that, needless to say, I planned to rephrase somewhat when the time came. I was in the midst of pinning his suspenders to the back of his trousers—two occasions when they had deserted their buttons without warning having established this precaution as part of the wardrobe procedure—when the door (it was the esteemed music director's dressing room we occupied) slammed open and a sable-wrapped, sable-booted, sable-hatted lady, backed by at least a half dozen others attired in equally rare zoological remains, flung herself in with an "Ohhhhhhh, Mr. Stravinsky!" Terror that Mr. Stravinsky, whose hand was now on his cane, might lift it to deal lethal blows, moved me to push with the energy of a destroyer of the Bastille, and although I was one and they were numerous, such moments can produce superhuman strength. I jammed the door shut, not without damaging a few toes. Stravinsky was both shaken and furious. "They have mistaken me for Mr. Ormandy," said he grimly. But later, before we left the Academy of Music, this unpredictable man stood near the backstage cloakroom, signing programs for the same group of storm troopers, and looking as if butter wouldn't melt in his mouth, while I stood by in disgrace, the recipient of such looks of smug and malicious satisfaction from the furry celebrity-hunters as would have leveled a saint to earth.

In this way Stravinsky could be as capricious as the next performing artist. In Los Angeles, while I was turning away four or five picture-snappers at the Hollywood Bowl, behind my back he was "freezing" so that a sixth and seventh could preserve his photogenic profile on their film. At New York's Lincoln Center, a lady and her little boy, listening to my negative discourse beginning, "If he signs one program, he will have to sign hundreds . . ." could see over my shoulder that the unwilling signer of hundreds was affixing his "I. Stravinsky" to a record jacket advertising *Petrushka*, held by another little boy accompanied by another lady.

An embarrassing situation, fixed like cement forever in my mind, occurred at Symphony Hall in Boston after the *Abraham and Isaac* performance. I was explaining with unusual care to an eager father of five tow-headed children (they all *looked* like him), who had come all the way from Newburyport, Massachusetts, in a driving storm, that Stravinsky could not greet them because he was starting a cold (true) and this was perilous for a perspiring conductor after the heat of the hall. I had reached a point of convincing eloquence only to discover that all during this touching speech Stravinsky was not only greeting them one by one, but was drawing a beautiful sketch of "The Hub" on the smallest child's program.

There were other bugaboos of a different nature. Fans and orchestra members often brought recordings of Stravinsky works for an autograph. If the jacket advertised a conductor who happened to be out of favor, or if the composer did not like the recording, he would refuse to sign and would return the proffered disc curtly (for example, the phrase "Ernest Ansermet, conductor" made his pulse quicken). Several times when a photograph of an old pre-war portrait, which had once been widely distributed in Germany and which he detested, was presented for his signature, he drew a large X across the face, and another time he would have torn one in two if I hadn't—throwing caution to the winds—snatched it away from him with the hint (I never *warned*) that he might be sued for destroying property. Other annoyances consisted of scores, pocket- and full-size, that he had frequently denounced because they were full of printer's errors. Even as he waved his hand to sign, he would deliver a polemic against the incompetence rampant in the music-publishing business, while the owner of the score stood confused as to whether he should permit the composer to write his name or beg him not to so that integrity could be preserved. (Leeds' *Firebird Suite* used to provoke the lengthiest diatribe, but J. & W. Chester, too, came in for some pretty fancy criticism for *Les Noces*.) He also suffered the usual plague of autograph collectors who arrived minus pen or pencil and would ask to borrow his, or with blank sheets of paper (which could then be used for other purposes, such as drawings purportedly signed by him), or with records and scores of works by other composers—a sin *sans pareil!* (Nevertheless, on one occasion—the only one within my direct experience, though there may have been others—he *did* sign the work of another, but it was a book: *The Measurement of Meaning* by University of Illinois researchers Charles Osgood, George Suci, and Percy Tannenbaum. The volume was owned by the music editor of the *Chicago Tribune*, who brought it to the *Orpheus* recording session in Chicago's Orchestra Hall in 1964. Stravinsky wrote on the flyleaf: "To Tom Willis in remembrance of Igor Stravinsky who liked this book.") *

But for every problem that gave me a headache or sent me to bed in tears (the latter condition was usually related to the slow arrival of managerial money), there were twice as many events that made these tours a joy, apart from the music. (It was always a marvel to me, when I heard the music performed, well or badly, that I was with the man who had composed it.)

* He also wrote a message, I have been told, in Shirley Hazzard's *The Evening of the Holiday*.

Stravinsky could be a very good sport, in the Anglo-Saxon sense of the term, and would fall in with any leisure plans suggested by the rest of us. Of course his approval would be sought, but I never remember him saying anything except "Why not?" during the time when he was well. On our second Mexican tour, in 1961, we planned to spend Holy Week, which preceded the Mexico City concerts, by driving south to Acapulco with stops at Cuernavaca and Taxco, in the manner of all tourists. It happened that Bella Spewack—one-half of the celebrated *Boy Meets Girl* playwrighting team—was in Mexico City. She had come to investigate Latin-American television possibilities for a *Kiss Me, Kate* production, and elected to go along with us. The Stravinskys and Robert had not met her before this, and though they undoubtedly would have preferred to keep ours a foursome, their politeness on hearing the news left nothing to be desired. Bella and I sat in front with Vicente, a driver who had chauffeured me about on previous visits and who could have been type-cast as Luis Firpo. Mrs. Stravinsky, resplendent in a pith helmet tied beneath her chin with a tulle bow, and Robert, who refused to leave off his necktie, sat in the rear seat of a far-from-limousine-size Buick sedan, with Stravinsky between them. About halfway to Cuernavaca, where a famous roadside shack called *Tres Marias* marks the ten-thousand-foot altitude point prior to the descent to that perpetually sun-engulfed city, we disembarked to stretch our legs and search for conveniences. After a glance at the unisex privy, Robert returned pale-faced and advised Stravinsky to "find a nice clean bush." Mrs. Stravinsky, Bella, and I were less delicate (I learned, during my years as an archeologist, that women can muster much more *sang-froid* about these things than men, probably because a fear of snakes supersedes a fear of contagion). When we all reconvened at the car, Stravinsky was comfortably and conspicuously seated next to Vicente, who was explaining the virtues of *pulque* * as a specific for any disease from "hippincoff" to "pleg." The composer was holding a bunch of bougainvillea blooms, and presented each lady with several specimens, at the same time announcing that he had insured the growth of a new crop; but he did not relinquish his seat, and tucked Bella in beside him.

At the Casa de Piedra, a handsome old hacienda on the outskirts of Cuernavaca, Bella waded in a lily pool while we sipped drinks; and, Stravinsky, in a completely uncharacteristic burst of infor-

* A milky liqueur distilled from Mexican cactus, designed to paralyze the limbs of any foreigner.

mality, squatted and splashed his hands in the water, looking like a youngster creating a storm at sea. We lunched that day at *Las Mañanitas*, an inn equipped with a famous restaurant and table-set lawns at its rear, where many varieties of rare birds wandered or fluttered about with the aloofness of paying guests—herons with lacy crowns, flamingos the color of Pink Ladies, peacocks white and sapphire, macaws, screaming parrots, and pigeons with feather boas, almost outnumbering the clientele. We were joined there by Edward James, an old friend of the Stravinskys who lived in the neighborhood at the time, and since lunch had to be cooked to order, he swooped Mrs. Stravinsky, Robert, and Bella off to watch a religious procession enroute to the cathedral for the finale of the Good Friday services. Stravinsky preferred to remain in the garden, where he was comfortably lost in the depths of a leather-cushioned wicker chair with the largest fan-back in existence and could watch, undisturbed, the "feathered" fiesta going on about him. A half-hour passed thus before the *maître d'* told me all was ready, and I went to fetch him to our table. He was leaning intently forward in his chair, hands pressed on its arms. Two gray-haired cranes stood, in the one-legged posture of the picture-books, directly facing and about a foot away from him. "Sizing each other up" took on a new meaning for me. I emulated a fox creeping up on a busy chicken run, when suddenly the cranes materialized their second legs, arched their tubular necks in a movement so imperious that it would have aroused envy in the breast of Rameses I, and departed. Stravinsky rose, slid his sunglasses from his forehead to the bridge of his nose, took my arm, and said as we walked to the dining room to meet the others, "I have just overheard a marvelous conversation."

We passed that night in the silver-mining mountain village of Taxco, which because of the double holiday (to Mexicans, the Day of the Dead as well as Good Friday) was jammed with worshipers from nearby villages as well as several hundred Americans of the gayer type cruising the streets and bars. The main event—a sacred tradition for the former, a secular entertainment for the latter—was the conclusion of the ceremony of the *penitentes*. In this mystery (very rarely observed by outsiders), three young men selected for their extraordinary devotion to the Church throughout the year relive the Passion of Christ. Hooded for anonymity (only the priests of the parish know their names), they begin their penance the day before by re-enacting the Agony in the Garden, and on Friday undergo the actual Flagellation and Crowning with Thorns, after which they take the Stations of the Cross. The climax is the "Crucifixion." The *penitentes* are led by small boys from the village to the area of "Golgotha," symbolically located in the confines of the Convent of San Bernardino. The whole town follows, each person carrying a lighted candle in a long procession which originates on the ridge of a nearby mountain.

Bella, through the exercise of some influence undisclosed to this day, had secured access to the very secret ceremonies of the Flagellation and Crowning—rituals forbidden to foreigners, and to most natives, in fact, except a few distinguished for their piety. She now came rushing to the village plaza to find me, for it was after dark and the candle-bearers were close to their destination. I joined the Stravinskys and Robert, in the midst of a crowd of solemn-faced worshipers at the rear of the convent—the women covered by black *rebozos* draped over head and shoulders, the men with *sombreros* held against the black *sarapes* crossed on their breasts. Stravinsky, whose height prevented his total view of the ceremony, listened intently as one of the chosen three, bent under the weight of his cross, made of a huge bundle of heavy faggots, and with bleeding back gruesomely visible, knelt and chanted prayers before a man dressed in an ordinary suit. After a few moments the composer signified that he wished to leave, and once out of doors he stood silently, taking deep breaths of the unpolluted air. I was smoking, and he inhaled with relish the wisps floating from my cigarette. (Once a heavy smoker, he had given up this habit after his stroke in 1956 but still took pleasure in the odor of tobacco.) While we waited for Mrs. Stravinsky and Robert (Bella had vanished), he suddenly asked me to describe the area which had been out of his range of vision, where two huge crucifixes with life-size plaster effigies representing the thieves had stood to the left and right of a vacant cross. I could not tell whether he was impressed or repelled by this strange Passion Play, at once so physical and mystical, but I rather thought his frequently self-confessed dislike for exaggerated realism would have prevailed, even over his probable interest in the strange, primitive sound of those chanted prayers.

He was irritable when we returned to the hotel (the La Borda, located about five minutes outside the village limits). I think it was three o'clock in the morning when I opened my door to a knock and found him, pajama-clad, in the corridor. "Please, my dear, is it possible . . . can we do *anything* about this wretched guitar player who is strumming in my ear all night? My dear, I do not think I can stand it!" Loud off-key strains of *Guadalajara*, played and bellowed by someone who had obviously been glorifying God all day with *tequila*, were pelting the Stravinsky room (although Madame slept!), ascending from the swimming-pool located just below. A hasty descent and thirty *pesos* convinced the troubadour to take up a stance somewhere near Cuernavaca, and peace of a sort reigned until five-thirty, when a chorus of *burro* countertenors and coloratura pigs engaged in reveille with some yapping dogs.

There are other pictures in the Mexican memory book: one of the composer spreading morsels of bread with honey in the splendid dining room of the Hotel Presidente in Acapulco, for two youngsters named Jonathan and Jonathan, who were on a holiday chaperoned by Agnes de Mille Prude.* In exchange for this largesse, the boys regaled him with a vivid tale of a climb up the Pyramid of the Sun at Teotihuacan, which had ended in disaster: one Jonathan now had a sprained ankle.

Maestro: And have you put a strong bandage on it?

Jonathan: Yes, sir, very strong.

Maestro: Not too strong, I hope. I once had a sprained ankle and I made the bandage too strong. I was almost minus an ankle.

Jonathan: Really, sir?

Maestro: Sure. Have some more honey. It is very good for sprained ankles.

And another, at the same hotel, of Stravinsky permitting Bella to try a *sombrero* on him, while we watched Robert break all Olympic swimming records in the giant-sized pool; waving his glass in a toast and shouting "Olé!" as his colleague completed each lap. At his side, his wife, whose pith helmet was now tied with a colorful string of tassels from a burro's bridle, fanned him happily with a huge palm leaf. She had only one complaint: her bedroom in the penthouse suite, an accommodation so luxurious that it would have put a maharajah's palace to shame, was a five-minute walk from the suite's front door, and she was always forgetting her change purse. "The *muchacho* had to wait fifteen minutes for me to tip him for the tea, poor boy," she said ruefully.

* The Jonathans **are** the respective sons of Agnes and Walter Prude, and of the late Bennett Cerf and Mrs. Cerf.

There were other events of a more "historic" nature. During our third and final trip to Mexico in December of 1961, Stravinsky and I spent a twilight hour in his tenth-floor Hotel Bamer bedroom catching up on some correspondence; Mrs. Stravinsky and Robert had gone for a stroll in the Alameda, transformed into a forest fantasy of colored lights, tinsel trees, spangled crèches, *piñatas*, sparkling angels dangling from branches, phosphorescent balloons. From time to time he would walk to the broad picture-window and gaze down at the brilliantly clad, festive crowd filling the sidewalk and the avenue, which had been closed to traffic. I knew he was wondering where his wife might be and I suggested that we descend to see if we could find the adventurers.

"Why not?" said he, and was off in a flash to find his coat. Then, "No. One more moment, I have an important letter. Or perhaps a telegram is better . . . we will send it the long way." (I took this to mean a night letter.) What followed is reconstructed here to the best of my recollection.

"Dear Mrs. Kennedy . . . regret I must decline kind dinner invitation due to heavy schedule . . . I have many things to do . . . I cannot take the time from my music" (he was warming to his subject) ". . . I am very busy with concerts . . ." (a rising note of irritation).*

I had long ago stopped writing.

"Maestro, to whom is this telegram addressed?"

"Mrs. Kennedy . . . I already have told you . . . Mrs. Kennedy!"

"Which Mrs. Kennedy?"

"I only know *one*" (scathingly!) . . . Mrs. *President* Kennedy!" (he had searched for her first name in vain, and this upset him more). "She wishes to invite us to dinner because I will be eighty. It is very kind of her, of course, but I cannot go to all these dinners. I have my work . . . I must compose . . . with all this touring, there is no time to compose . . ." (This usually was the opening blast in a series of encyclicals against the terrible necessity of earning money.)

"Maestro, I am afraid we cannot answer quite this way . . ."

"Why not? I have received her letter of invitation some time ago. With all this . . . this . . . business" (a wave of the hand in the

* I still have this specimen of Stravinskyan diplomacy in my notebook!

direction of the Palace of Fine Arts) ". . . I had no time to answer. Now a telegram is necessary." (The thought of the expenditure brought on by concerts was sending his temperature up.)

"Maestro, have you discussed your reply with Madame and Robert?"

"There is no discussion. I cannot go."

But of course he did go. The invitation had resulted in part from some correspondence and a meeting I had held with State Department officials during the previous July (after the USSR had extended its invitation to Stravinsky) to find out what the United States government was going to do to honor its distinguished citizen in his eightieth birthday year.

The difficulty that evening was surmounted by the early closing of telegraph offices due to the holiday, for Stravinsky would not listen to my protests that a telegram was not the most *soigné* way to refuse a White House invitation, no matter how late his reply was. That night I consulted hastily (and alone!) with Mrs. Stravinsky and Robert.

Later, a note went off to President and Mrs. Kennedy accepting with pleasure the proposed January 18 date, two days before Stravinsky was to conduct the first of three performances of *Oedipus Rex* with the Washington Opera (Robert's half: Ravel's *L'Heure Espagnole*). Robert's brilliant account of that presidential *soirée* is most highly recommended reading,* but there were some asides, not part of the official calendar of events, that may bear recording.

The Stravinskys, Robert, and I said *au revoir* after our Christmas in Mexico, but I rejoined them in Toronto at the end of the first week in January, where Stravinsky conducted the *Symphony of Psalms* for the documentary film begun the previous year. Before this, a call from the White House had reached me in New York, relaying, through the medium of Mrs. Kennedy's social secretary, a partial list of guests who would be attending the "small dinner" in Stravinsky's honor. The names mentioned were those of Nicolas Nabokov, Mr. and Mrs. Leonard Bernstein, and Mr. and Mrs. Goddard Lieberson, all ostensibly representing "friends of the composer." I was also told that eight or ten friends of President and Mrs. Kennedy (names *not* mentioned at that point) would attend, and then, with great courtesy, I was asked if there was anyone else whom Stravinsky might wish to include at this "family [*sic*] dinner."

* *Dialogues and a Diary* (New York: Doubleday, 1963), pp. 198 ff.

I immediately corrected the glaring (but certainly inadvertent) omission of Robert Craft's name, and thought of one or two other longtime associates, but did not refer to them because it had also been explained, in the course of our conversation, that this "family dinner" could not exceed twenty people. Since the Stravinsky contingent now included eight (counting the guest of honor, his wife, and his associate) and since "eight or ten" Kennedy friends plus the hosts would make up the preferred total, I concluded (correctly) that the question was asked out of politeness. As it turned out, the White House friends proved to be Mrs. Kennedy's sister Lee Radziwill, her college chum Helen Chavchavadze, Marshall Field, the Arthur Schlesingers (Jr.), Max Freedman, and the Pierre Salingers. The Stravinskys were not well acquainted with any of them (although they had probably met one or another at some unrecalled function), and my subsequent reading of the final list to Stravinsky on our arrival in Washington on January 14 evoked a plaintive, "But I don't *know* anybody. Why should I *have* to go?" He already realized, however, that this could only be a rhetorical question.

We had put up this time at that queen of small hotels, the Jefferson, and between rehearsals the Stravinskys held reunions with old friends (St.-John Perse and Mrs. Robert Woods Bliss among them) and visited the National Gallery. There was also an impressive State Department ceremony during which Secretary Dean Rusk presented the composer with a medal bearing the following legend: "To Igor Stravinsky, in honor of his eightieth birthday year, whose music has enriched his country and the world."

But the presidential day finally arrived, and on the morning of the night, the Stravinskys sat in their salon while I went over the protocol (in which I had been instructed by officials): principally, that the evening would end when Mrs. Kennedy, at approximately ten-twenty, would rise and make some charming remarks about her charming guests of honor, after which it would be proper for the Stravinskys to thank their hosts and take their leave. Mrs. Stravinsky was a little wary about all this, knowing the recent Stravinsky tendency to nod a bit after dinner, but since the president was sending his car at seven-thirty sharp and dinner was at eight, I pointed out that the whole period of time was less than that of a concert. Besides, if ten-twenty arrived and the First Lady did *not* make any move to dismiss her guests, it would then be quite correct for Mrs. Stravinsky to present her excuses on the basis of her husband's age and need for early hours because of the strenuous day of rehearsing ahead.

A Stravinsky rehearsal of *Oedipus Rex* had been scheduled at the Lisner Auditorium at four-thirty despite my protests, for the composer should have had at least an hour to rest and dress for the evening's activities: with post-rehearsal gatherings-up, cologne rub-downs, transportation, and so on, it was all a little risky. (I did not anticipate any difficulty this time with lost dress shirt studs—one of the crises that accompanied each concert as inevitably as the scores —for I had taken particular care to carry an extra set in my hand-bag.) Also, despite the incognito registration at the hotel, prelimi-nary reports warned me that press might be on hand to cover the departure, prior to rushing over to Pennsylvania Avenue to record the arrival. This was a situation I wished to avoid, since everyone except Stravinsky was suffering from a touch of stage-fright, and the enterovioform had to be kept handy.

Nicolas Nabokov accompanied us to the rehearsal, for which I was profoundly grateful, as his humor always could produce that deep single cough of laughter from Stravinsky; but he didn't take his eyes from his watch for one moment, and reminded me every five minutes that the Maestro must leave off at five-thirty promptly. At five-thirty the Maestro was just beginning to warm up, and Jocasta (Shirley Verrett) was following suit. I approached gingerly and leaned across the footlights, whispering, "Maestro . . . time."

"I am *not* through, and I will not *be* through, until this *work* is through," was the non-whispered reply.

Oh, well, I thought, he'll be able to dress in thirty minutes.

At quarter to six, Nicolas gave me an encouraging push. This time I said, "*You* stop him." The result was silence, except from the stage where Oedipus (George Shirley) was learning the bitter truth. However, at six o'clock, when Stravinsky was informing the orches-tra and soloists that "we will now go back to five measures before" what turned out to be the bottom of the second page of the score, I decided to risk everything for the United States of America. "Maestro" I shrilled, "you will be late for dinner with the presi-dent!" And I stepped back to lessen the impact of the explosion.

Stravinsky addressed the company: "My dears, you will have to excuse me. I have a dinner engagement this evening at the White House and I cannot keep the president waiting. He is not a musician, I think, but he is a very busy man nevertheless."

As usual, he was ready before anyone else, and since he had already donned his coat, hat, and muffler, we descended to the cooler regions of the lobby (where I had been notified the coast was clear) to wait the remaining ten minutes before the arrival of the president's car. Leonard Bernstein and his wife (she was undoubtedly the most glamorous-looking *enceinte* lady on record) were checking in at the reception end of the small lobby, about thirty feet away from us, already dressed for dinner, and clearly having arrived from New York in the nick of time. The young Maestro spotted the old Maestro and made a beeline, arms outstretched:

"Who *is* it!" hissed Stravinsky in my ear.

"Lennie, Maestro, *Lennie!*" The last syllable coincided with a monstrous hug that almost lifted the presidential guest of honor off his feet.

"And what are *you* doing in Washington, my dear?" said the victim cordially when he had regained his breath. (There were, indeed, times when I longed to be selling hosiery at Bloomingdale's.)

Mrs. Stravinsky, magnificent in white bouffant *peau de soie* and a blue satin stole, emerged with Robert from the elevator. There were kisses all around while I held off an eager camera-bug whom I had spotted creeping up, intent on capturing all this charisma.

The president's car pulled up on the minute, and a moment of embarrassment occurred when Mr. Bernstein innocently suggested that everyone ride together (the car was intended *only* for the honored guests), but Mrs. Stravinsky, with unmatched aplomb, trilled, "Oh we can't. We ladies with our big dresses . . . we will be ruined before we arrive." And the Bernsteins went in search of a taxi. As Stravinsky was being assisted into the limousine by the president's chauffeur, he turned to me and said, "I am sorry you are not going with us." (There were also moments when I could have scaled Mount Kilimanjaro.)

Every minute of the evening's plans save the exact menu and the exact guest list had been reported in the early editions with stock-market precision, and the grapevine had transmitted the information that several reporters would make their way to the Jefferson as soon as President and Mrs. Kennedy led their guests in to dinner. I retired to the restaurant with two old friends from the *Washington Post* for a leisurely snack, only to discover that the Jefferson—apparently employing a superior intelligence department—had prepared a menu duplicating each course supposedly being offered in the State Dining

Room (sole, leg of lamb, strawberry mousse, and cheese). The Stravinskys would certainly not return before ten-thirty, I estimated (if protocol were observed, as everyone was sure it would be), and we settled down. In the course of the next hour and a half we were joined by a columnist, a few other reporters, and two television representatives carrying portable units. By ten o'clock it seemed more convenient to move to the bar, which was directly off the lobby (I will be forever thankful to "someone up there" for instilling in me a certain uneasy feeling). I suddenly noticed the desk clerk, who was frantically trying to attract my attention by waving a large paperweight replica of the Washington Monument back and forth like a semaphore. Foresight made me close the door of the bar tightly before I rushed out—to discover that the president's car was just turning into the hotel's crescent-shaped driveway.

But it was only ten-ten!

The first passenger to alight was Robert, who, without looking to right or left, covered the lobby in three strides and vanished into the self-service elevator, fortuitously at ground level. Mrs. Stravinsky, a wee bit flushed but otherwise as tranquilly beautiful as she had been at the start of the evening, came next. I pointed warningly to the bar door and muttered "Press! Quick! Tell me what happened. You're early."

"It was lovely," she proclaimed to me, the desk clerks and the columnist (who had a phobia for closed doors.) "Everything was lovely. The president and his wife were lovely. The dinner was lovely. The only thing *un*lovely was my husband. He got drunk and the president had to take him to the men's room." And she too glided into another elevator. The columnist, on winged feet, flew phoneward.

The "unlovely" culprit, supported by the chauffeur and the hotel doorman, was then gently delivered to me. I yearned to throw my arms around him and laugh heartily, but instead I delivered him to his bed, where he promptly fell asleep before I could finish clucking sympathy and buttoning his pajama jacket.

The press in the bar were informed that apparently the Stravinskys had slipped upstairs unnoticed, having returned a little prematurely due to Stravinsky's concern about his trying schedule; that this circumstance had been graciously accepted by the First Lady; that everything had been "lovely"; and they, too, finally went home.

When I entered Stravinsky's room at breakfast time, he was propped up in bed, his expression as mournful as that of a champion basset—abashed, contrite, and suffering from a murderous hangover. "I must send flowers to Madame President," he quavered. "I am in disgrace, No, I am *a* disgrace."

His wife, fresh as a marguerite in a fluffy white housecoat, came in carrying some cold towels which she patted down on her husband's forehead despite a groan of anguish that would have done credit to a contra bassoon. "The martinis were doubles," she told me, "and they kept coming and coming and coming. . . ."

Robert, eating his breakfast, was none the worse for wear; he related that Mrs. Kennedy was one of the most attractive women he had met, and Helen Chavchavadze even more so. He also regretted that he had lost a chance to learn the Twist, in which everyone except Mr. President, Mr. Field, Mr. Schlesinger, and perhaps (though he didn't say so) Mr. Nabokov and Mr. Lieberson, was about to indulge when good nights had to be said.

The telephone rang in the adjoining living room, and wafted from 1600 Pennsylvania Avenue were the dulcet, slightly breathy tones of the First Lady inquiring after "Dear, dear Mr. Stravinsky." Her sincere concern about the night he might have passed put me completely at ease, and I told her all about the sad patient in the next room.

Coda: *She* sent him red roses, and *he* sent her yellow ones.

CHAPTER SEVEN

ALTHOUGH Stravinsky's general attitude toward concert touring was one of resigned acceptance, one trip provided him with what was probably the profoundest experience of his last decade. In 1962, at the age of eighty, he returned to his native country for the first time in more than forty-eight years. No composer except Stravinsky has tasted the bitterness of acclaim from every nation in the world save his own. The simple act of agreeing to go home again, after almost half a century of rejection, must itself have engendered powerful emotions.

The circumstances which brought about this journey were undoubtedly various; one certainly must have been the presence of Khrushchev at the helm of the Russian government. But an influencing factor was probably Leonard Bernstein's successful tour with the New York Philharmonic in 1959, under the cultural exchange agreement between the United States and the USSR. Mr. Bernstein's program included *The Rite of Spring* and the *Piano Concerto*, the latter composed by Stravinsky in 1924, ten years after he had left his birthplace, and therefore a work totally unfamiliar to the Russian public. And although Soviet critics attacked the brief introductory speech in which Mr. Bernstein pointed out to Soviet audiences that the *Rite* also was relatively unknown, since it had not had a hearing in their country in more than three decades, and "corrected" him with examples of times when it *had* been played (in outlying regions and with little-known orchestras), it would have been difficult to prove or disprove Soviet approval of, or antagonism toward, Stravinsky's music at the time. The glowing newspaper accounts of the reception accorded his works and Bernstein's performances of them were received with no unusual signs of excitement from the composer, who, in fact, was inclined to be skeptical, in particular about the effect on the populace of his *Piano Concerto*.* There is no doubt, however, that he was deeply touched by Bernstein's efforts in behalf of his music, for he spoke of them with appreciation to me and others.

On June 8, 1961, a delegation of distinguished Russians, headed by Tikhon Khrennikov (then general secretary of the USSR's Union of Composers, and formerly in the vanguard of Stravinsky denunciators) and composer Kara Karayev, called on Stravinsky at his "old" house in Hollywood. This was the first move that could be considered formal in any way; but in fact, after the composer's seventy-fifth birthday, several feelers had been put out from time to time, to which he had remained indifferent. Prior to this first get-together, Khrennikov and company had paid their respects to him backstage in Los Angeles following a concert he had conducted; pointed hints had been dropped at this time, and the invitation to 1260 North Wetherly resulted.

Robert wrote me on June 11, 1961, that the entire press had been on hand for the visit of the Russians, as he had expected they would be, since the whole affair had been organized by a huge musical festival.† The Russians had said what they wanted to say, he reported, though all Stravinsky said was "maybe." This slightly cryptic remark was a reiteration of what Robert had told me on the telephone the evening before: that an oral invitation had been extended to Stravinsky to conduct a program of his works in the USSR on his eightieth birthday, which, according to the Russian calendar, would be observed on June 17, 1962.‡ The phrase "said what they wanted to say" simply meant that, to the disappointment of the festival organizers, no lively discussion on music took place. After the fact, Stravinsky's "maybe" became more of a "probably" in a statement to the press, supreme in its double-talk: "I do not make projects. I only fill out contracts. I am very glad that these

---

* Bernstein said that the *Piano Concerto* had moved Russian audiences to tears—but Stravinsky doubted the presence of "lachrymal liquid" (Robert's phrase) in this instance; see *Dialogues and a Diary*, p. 200.
† The First International Music Festival, held at the University of California at Los Angeles.
‡ Old Style, that is. Every century one day is added to the Gregorian calendar. Thus Stravinsky, who was born on June 17 according to the Julian calendar, celebrated his birthday on June 18 from 1901 on.

gentlemen came to see me. I will be very glad to see them again." *

This visit was followed by several birthday telegrams from the USSR, including messages from a prominent composer who had once referred to Stravinsky's music as "decadent and bourgeois," all expressing the hope that he would celebrate his next birthday on Russian soil. A family-reunion atmosphere permeated the air. But the oral invitation was not immediately followed by an official written one, and the composer kept his counsel while everyone else speculated. Mrs. Stravinsky's noncommital reply to all questions was that she and her husband felt the trip might prove to be "too emotional."

As the weeks wore on, however, there were indications of impatience at the unsettled state of things. The composer had heard nothing from Russia in the month since the telegrams had arrived, Robert informed me from Santa Fe in mid-July (where the trio was on hand for *Perséphone* (and *Oedipus Rex*, conducted by Robert, with Paul Horgan as narrator), but Robert thought it was too early to interpret the silence.

The uninterpreted silence prolonged itself throughout the following months as well, during which the Stravinskys returned to Hollywood and I occupied myself with concluding some very involved negotiations for the Australian tour (on again, off again, on again), an endless series of meetings and correspondence on the *Flood* project (which was beginning to live up to its name), and the inauguration of equally voluminous files for the South African tour and a tour of Israel, as well as other major events growing out of the forthcoming birthday year.

The Stravinskys and Robert came East at the beginning of September, preparatory to sailing on the *Kungsholm* for Sweden (to see Ingmar Bergman's production of *The Rake's Progress*), after which they would travel to Helsinki, Berlin, and thence to Australia and New Zealand. I installed them this time in the Hotel Pierre, which was thereafter to be their New York residence, until Mr. Nixon's campaigners changed its name to "The White House." The move from the St. Regis, incidentally, was due to the fact—and let this be a lesson to all innkeepers—that within ten days after their five-day stay in that hostelry during the previous December, for which I delivered to the cashier a check in four figures, Stravinsky received a pressing communication stating that he had "neglected" to pay a

* *New York Times*, June 9, 1961.

breakfast charge of $6.07. He sent me this bill with an attached check and a letter which, in an explicit paragraph, instructed me to transmit the payment to the St. Regis while saying, politely, "*Merde!*" At the bottom of the page, in brown ink, he asked me to make sure that the St. Regis meant $6.07 and not $6.08! (I delivered both check and message.)

Despite the fact that Soviet officialdom had not come through with a formal invitation, Stravinsky's attitude during the New York stay leaned more toward "Yes" than "No." Therefore it seemed a good idea to anticipate whatever business arrangements might arise, and I suggested that we secure the cooperation of the one man whose expertise in Russian negotiations had been almost entirely responsible for the successful operation of the cultural exchange agreement between the United States and the USSR, resulting in visits to the respective shores of the best in ballet and music. That was, of course, impresario S. Hurok. There was never any question of my handling the Russian contracts: at that time I was not at all informed on Soviet concert procedures, and it would have been unwise to use Stravinsky as a guinea pig. Nor was the United States government involved. During my visit to Washington the previous July, State Department officers had referred to attempts made early in 1961 to arrange the composer's visit to the USSR during that year, under the cultural agreement. But so many delays had been encountered, according to the officer in charge of the Russian Desk at the United States Information Agency, that by the time clearance from abroad reached the State Department, Stravinsky was completely booked for the season (true, indeed, but I did not recall any mention from the West of a communication containing such proposals).

Stravinsky and Hurok had not been in touch, at least in a professional sense, for several years.* According to Mrs. Stravinsky, a slight coolness existed between them "over some concert business," and I concluded that this might have been due partly to some financial disagreement and partly to the fact that Stravinsky's name had suddenly appeared on the roster of Columbia Artists Manage-

---

* Hurok had made efforts on behalf of the composer from the time of the latter's arrival in the United States in 1939. In 1940 Hurok had suggested to music publisher Ralph Hawkes that he "take Stravinsky on" and offer him a yearly guarantee. According to the impresario, Hawkes followed this advice and signed the composer, guaranteeing him $10,000 per annum at that time.

ment in the fifties, when Hurok was listing him supposedly exclusively. (But so it had appeared on several other rosters; *everyone* was always putting Stravinsky's name on his roster!) My own acquaintance with the impresario was then limited to my having acted as public relations counsel for several of his artists and to my position as liaison between his office and the Mexican Institute of Fine Arts for a proposed American tour by the Ballet Folklórico of Mexico. I telephoned Mr. Hurok and told him Stravinsky would like to talk to him about Russia, and then I told Stravinsky that Mr. Hurok would like to see *him* for the same reason.

The meeting took place at the Stravinskys' Hotel Pierre suite, in half-Russian fashion:

"Igor Fyodorovitch!"

"Hurok, my dear!"

Hurok was "honored," of course, to handle the Russian negotiations "on the basis of old friendship." He was informed that nothing official had resulted from the June visit, and he, in turn, told Stravinsky that business would take him to the USSR in January, and in the meantime he would "investigate discreetly." My trio duly departed on the *Kungsholm*, and the idea then was that the trip *would* be made, with concerts arranged to include the period of Stravinsky's birthday.

News of an increasing number of performances of post-1914 Stravinsky works in the USSR, among which was a thrilling report of an alleged ovation for the *Symphonies of Wind Instruments*, made the music pages from time to time, but the composer's only reaction to such stories was, as usual, "How did it sound? No one there has ever heard it."

The official Russian invitation finally arrived in October, but in the interim Stravinsky had become both uncertain and edgy. Robert wrote from London on October 26 that Stravinsky did not plan to answer immediately. The indecision, I was sure, emanated from one of the most consistent areas of trouble during all the years I was with Stravinsky: a compulsion on the part of all members of the *ménage* (though in the composer's case less marked) to discuss any plans they might have, however intimate, with anyone who happened to drop by. In "Mr. and Mrs." this tendency might have been defined as a Russian idiosyncrasy: let us secure advice from everyone and then we will know exactly what *not* to do. But in Robert, who in a three-day period was capable of writing fifty nervous letters to friends about the necessity of making a decision, the desire to "talk" always seemed to me to spell out his profound conviction that he might participate in a wrong decision, and therefore he would usually secure as many allies as he could by mail!

The subject of Russia was the invitation *par excellence* to such social seminars. From Berlin, Robert wrote on September 29 that Nicolas Nabokov had a 3-hour session with Stravinsky when the trio arrived there, and managed to terrify them about Russia. But many other opinions, including "Chip" Bohlen's, urged the composer to go to Russia—though not on his birthday.

The birthday objection, which came from other sources as well, including a West Coast entrepreneur who was eager to have the composer conduct at a Los Angeles Stravinsky Festival also planned for June, was justified by the objectors on two counts: 1) the double impact of arriving in his homeland both at the age of eighty and after nearly half a century of life elsewhere might produce an over-powering emotional trauma in him ("could be fatal," was one pre-diction), and 2) this dual circumstance would give the Russians extra ammunition for propaganda.

Of *course* it would all be emotional (but I did not think "fatal"), and of *course* there would be propaganda (*here* as well as *there*), but I could not see why everyone should be thrown into a state of consternation thereby. They were, however, and in the confusion of mind-changing that resulted I was forced to solve a jigsaw puzzle wherein pieces of Israel, Chicago's Ravinia Park, the Hollywood Bowl, Lewisohn Stadium, Caracas, and a few other areas had to be matched, so that what finally lay before me was a transportation map of the globe that would have kept Magellan peacefully at home. On November 24, however, in a communication which (wonder of wonders!) was also highly complimentary about the "paradise" of New Zealand and the "superb" organization both there and in Australia (a dozen letters threatening to cancel because of inefficiency and low fees lay in my file drawer), I was told to notify Hurok that he could proceed with formal negotiations during his January trip to the USSR, although not for June, but perhaps for the fall . . . and they planned to talk more carefully about this with me when we saw each other again.

Mexico at Christmastime was my next reunion with the family, but Stravinsky refused to engage in any discussion on the subject of the Russian tour. It was easy to detect that *he* was still of two minds;

Robert, however, was not; the trip, he was sure, would definitely take place. Part of his confidence had grown out of the trip to Helsinki in September, when he had detected strong feelings of nostalgia in both of his traveling companions. There was their home-land, practically next door, and the statue of Tsar Alexander II in the city's large square acted as a constant reminder of what lay to to the East. "They must go," he said to me in that intense tone I had come to know well, which virtually compelled others to accept part of the responsibility for his decision.

Save for one or two brief interruptions, I remained with the Stra-vinskys during the rest of the winter months and through the spring of 1962, and saw them off on the *Flandre* ("Flounder," according to the composer) on May 8. I was quite prepared for the letters full of pros and cons that flew in from Paris thereafter, since this was the home base of several expatriated White Russian friends, as well as some French ones sympathetic to their cause. However, as I had discerned in Mexico, minds were already made up. In fact, the seven days aboard ship had actually produced three "definite" all-Stravinsky programs (destined to undergo a number of changes, as all such "definite" programs always do), for Moscow, Leningrad, and Kiev (the latter city was ultimately dropped from the tour); one work each from the composer's "old Russian," "middle," and "new" periods was to be included in all three.

As expected, the Parisian "opposition," recognizing after a few days that a non-budge point had been reached (a positive influence on this position having been a communication from Hurok con-taining satisfactory though not exaggerated terms, plus such addi-tional benefits as air tickets, hotels, and ruble spending-money), ceased all their objecting and took up an equally bothersome line in the opposite direction. All of Eastern Europe, according to my correspondence file, began to resemble Shangri-La.

Meanwhile, I was having my own more prosaic problems with the Russian arrangements. A major network, in the person of the engaging and gifted David Oppenheim, was contemplating a docu-mentary film about the composer, and although the project was not to be realized until 1965—at which time it was made and produced for CBS by Mr. Oppenheim—the USSR tour was quite naturally regarded as a priceless opportunity for the film record. Furthermore, and much to the astonishment of everyone, including Mrs. Stravin-sky and Robert, Mr. Oppenheim produced a letter signed by Stravinsky giving him exclusive rights to any film that would be made in the Soviet Union during his tour. This was not the first time we had run into this embarrassing type of Stravinskyan generosity (nor would it be the last), or into the charm of network personnel, for that matter: during the period of the New York concerts, when all watchdogs were momentarily off the premises, Stravinsky had cheerfully agreed to conduct a CBS telecast of *The Firebird* for a fee one-half the size offered him the year before, for much less of a chore, by that network's chief rival.* Later he would complain bitterly about these lapses, placing the blame on everything except the conviviality engendered by the Chivas Regal (early sixties favorite) over which such transactions might have been made. Stravinsky in a mellow mood, especially in the last decade, hardly ever said no.

Mr. Oppenheim's sudden materialization complete with letter disturbed Mr. Hurok. It was not, as the impresario explained to me in a tone that was never (not for a moment!) raised above normal pitch, that he had *any* objection to the "contract" (or to Mr. Oppenheim). It came down to something very simple: either *he* was handling *all* negotiations on *all* activities within the USSR, or he was *not*. Furthermore, he made the interesting suggestion that the Russians might have some personal views on the subject, and that these views might be disappointing, if not to Stravinsky (who was always receiving offers for films), then to Mr. Oppenheim. Tranquility was restored after the passage of half a dozen letters between New York, Europe, and Australia. S. Hurok (who presents) was handling the negotiations, and the Russians made their own (unobtainable) film.

Another difficulty arose in the form of Stravinsky's principal publishers, who were reluctant to ship performing material to the USSR without Mr. Hurok's personal as well as financial guarantee that they would be safely and promptly returned. The works in question were, of course, the post-1914 compositions, which were not copyright in Russia. Boosey & Hawkes was highly unenthusiastic about the whole trip on these grounds alone, and had already sent a very legal-sounding letter to Mr. Hurok, in which they endowed him with the honor of being responsible for everything. On his part the impresario felt (not without logic) that since he was involved as an *amicus curiae* and nothing else, he should not be asked to risk money

* One of Stravinsky's reasons for accepting the CBS offer was that the money he received somewhat reduced his losses on the New York concerts.

as well.* The ripple that thus disturbed the sea's surface did not exactly engender a typhoon, but there was a brief squall, tempered finally by having all materials carried by the two conductors, Mrs. Stravinsky, and Jerome Hines (who was to appear concurrently with the Bolshoi Opera in *Boris Godunov*).†

A few tricky stiles had yet to be maneuvered before the passengers boarded their Aeroflot turbo-prop from Paris to Moscow on September 21, and in the course of finding the right road I entered into a correspondence with the late Ralph Parker, Hurok's representative in the USSR—a scholar and the soul of discretion. Not once in his numerous letters and cablegrams did he abandon a saintly good humor that prevailed throughout weeks of program changes (eight); a "touchy" situation involving the proposed substitution by Robert of a non-Stravinsky work for a Stravinsky work on one of the programs (Schoenberg's *Variations*—the Russians said "*Nyet*" ‡); numerous jugglings of performance dates; the disappointment the composer suffered when Kiev was dropped from the tour; and, finally, an impossible and almost disastrous mix-up over the non-delivery of the air tickets by the Soviet representatives, which prompted a call from Mrs. Stravinsky to the Soviet Embassy in Paris to inquire where they were. She reached a petty official, who expressed complete ignorance of the name "Stravinsky," knew nothing of concerts or tickets, and indicated that if Stravinsky and Company wished to visit the USSR, passage could be secured by the simple process of handing money over at the appropriate ticket office. Mrs. Stravinsky hung up, and promptly. Twenty-four hours (and several high-ranking apologies) were required to render this potential firecracker harmless, but Mr. Parker pulled everyone through and, *enfin*, Aeroflot received its distinguished passengers. But almost not. Just prior to the closing of the plane doors (wrote

* Hurok was generous in another way. He deeply felt the prestige accruing to him from his handling of Stravinsky on this tour, and this prompted him to supply the dollars that made up the difference between the rubles the Russians offered and the composer's fee.

† As it turned out, there were *no* rental charges for the USSR, since Stravinsky claimed that the box of performance material was never opened, as the Russians had their own quite satisfactory materials. He instructed me to inform the publishers of this.

‡ Parker's explanation for the negative was that the Russians had requested "all-Stravinsky"; Robert's explanation was that Schoenberg was on their "Index."

Mr. Parker), an escort, appointed to accompany the Stravinsky party to Le Bourget, delivered so negative a speech about the enterprise in which they were about to engage and expressed so much sympathy for their plight that Stravinsky actually rose from his seat and had to be restrained from making an unscheduled exit.

Mr. Parker's correspondence contained some other interesting points of information. He wrote me that he hoped there would be a "variety" of Stravinsky works, and not just *The Rite of Spring*, *Firebird*, and *Petrushka*, as "the Moscow public would be disappointed to hear only those already well-known works, and especially since the orchestra and choir knew the *Symphony of Psalms* very well." Also, Kyril Kondrashin, conductor of the Moscow Philharmonic, requested particularly a program that would include the *Symphony in Three Movements*.* It would seem from this that some of the composer's later works were, indeed, not unfamiliar to Moscow musicians, or that at least they had been boning up on a few important ones in the course of the previous months, and the Tass dispatches about the success of Stravinsky's later music appear to have been correct.

The great reception accorded Stravinsky in the USSR received wide international coverage, and accounts of ovations, concerts, sightseeing tours, social activities, digestive upsets, and the Stravinskys' visit with Khrushchev were fully reported in all languages. But not one of those stories—nor even Robert's own record of the events in *Dialogues and a Diary*, vivid as it is—has been able to reveal how that elderly man really felt when he crossed the bridge that spanned a gap of forty-eight years into a country that had rejected and vilified him, its native son, for almost the same period of time.

The Russian tour was followed by the contrast of Italy and concerts in Rome and Perugia, as well as trips to Spoleto and Assisi, and the travelers did not return to the United States until October 23. More than the usual number of reporters were on hand at Kennedy Airport; the chief interest, naturally, was in Stravinsky's reaction to the Russian visit, but there were also a fair number of newsmen who sought impressions of his first trip to Israel. The concerts there with Robert had preceded the Russian tour, a circumstance the press obviously felt (judging from questions put to me, since Stra-

* Stravinsky works finally performed included, among others, *Symphony in Three Movements*, *Orpheus*, *Ode*, *Capriccio*, *Baiser de la Fée*, and *Fireworks*. *Symphony of Psalms* was not performed.

vinsky would not talk, and his wife and Robert had already taken
refuge in the limousine) must have been a source of annoyance to
the USSR—especially since the composer had announced in Moscow
that his next composition would be a cantata in Hebrew for the
State of Israel. (Stravinsky was never one to sidestep a question on
the basis of diplomacy, unless it were *his* diplomacy!)

I could not concentrate on the question, however, because I
experienced a sense of shock when I saw Stravinsky, and not only
because he now depended on his cane—press reports from the
USSR, incidentally, had mentioned the fact that he used a walking-
stick to approach the podium—but because he definitely appeared to
have aged. The lines in his face were deeper; his stance was less
erect; and he seemed thinner, although he denied it, claiming his
constant 122 pounds. Before this, Stravinsky's physiognomy and
carriage had never seemed to change much to the outward eye, as
his photographs of the forties and fifties show; they can hardly be
identified in terms of years, but usually only by their backgrounds.
Now he looked his age to me, and as we ploughed through the airport crowd, I had to shorten my steps considerably to adjust to his.
He was overflowing with affection, too, inquiring with deepest concern about my mother, who was then very ill.

During the drive to the Pierre, Robert related details of the trip
and its emotional impact on the Stravinskys, telling me that they
had become "more Russian than the Russians." Mrs. Stravinsky
repeated over and over like a hymn, "It was marvelous . . . marvelous." Her eyes were misty as she listened to Robert describe the
walks and drives to the neighborhood of her youth. But her husband was silent, and when, in a slightly lowered tone, Robert told
me that the composer had not visited his father's grave because both
he and his wife and been fearful of the effect on him, Stravinsky
pressed the metal button that opened his window automatically, as
though he wanted the sound of passing traffic to shut out the words.
Mrs. Stravinsky remarked that "the world has a totally wrong idea
about life over there. People are *sooo* polite . . . *sooo* helpful . . .
sooo hospitable. It was cozy . . ." (a favorite word with her always) ". . . one never has to pretend." At which point Robert
interjected, "They don't realize that not everyone gets the V.I.P.
treatment they got." And at that an argument on this topic ensued,
obviously a continuation of one that had begun with their arrival
on Russian soil. Mrs. Stravinsky terminated it suddenly with: "Why

does everything have to be so political all the time? Why is there always a motive? Why can't you just *like* people?" (Poor Robert! He was always being called to task for not "liking" people!) She went on to tell me that in some of the hotels, especially in Leningrad, things had seemed exactly as they were when she visited the city in her student days. "The hotel clerks even look the same, but they are much less snobbish than they used to be. And the salespeople . . . not impatient like in New York. But there's nothing much to buy." Her only criticism was that the women wore "awful clothes," but "after all, this is not so important, and they are improving. Madame Furtseva [the minister of culture] is very chic and attractive."

From this point on, and for the next few days before the family left for the Caracas engagement—which I had arranged reluctantly because recent reports of bandits, not only attacking but also decapitating travelers, had made the financially profitable proposition not the least bit attractive—Stravinsky spoke only Russian, even forgetting himself with me until I had to remind him of my total ignorance of Slavic languages. And for quite a time thereafter, when he spoke French or English, it was with a noticeable hesitation, as though he were no longer sure of his vocabulary. This passed, of course, but more Russian expressions than heretofore continued to color his conversation in other languages, and he was now using diminutives, a "bourgeoisism" he had scorned in the past. (So was Robert. He called me "Lilliachik" until the Caracas trip changed it to "Lilliana.")

There were other changes as well. My offices were now closed, and Stravinsky and Robert were my sole private clients; bread and butter came from assignments I took from time to time to represent touring attractions for Hurok, or on one or two occasions (if the project were interesting and I could get the job) a Broadway play. These extracurricular activities were arranged, as far as possible, to coincide with Stravinsky's trips abroad, and the system worked very well except for overweight luggage problems, for I always carried all his files with me when I traveled. Much of the time my base was New York, where I worked out of the Hurok office, in exchange for which that organization handled some of our contracts.

From the time of their return from the Soviet Union, my position with the Stravinskys began to be more intimate. Mrs. Stravinsky, who had previously regarded me kindly but also as a necessary clause in a contract (the fine print), now began to treat me more like a distant relative who, astonishingly, had turned out to be a friend, and I was usually included in any family discussions. Robert had shown me his friendship almost from the very beginning, however, by turning over to me not only some of his personal responsibilities vis-à-vis the Stravinskys, and his own independent concert activities, but also many of his social problems: someone was always in love with him, and he was always in love with someone, and I had two shoulders. Besides, since I was becoming expert at deciphering his handwriting, I began to be a time-to-time recipient of drafts of articles, my comprehension of their contents being judged more important than my inability to type with more than two fingers. Because I understood what I was reading (most of the time!), I could usually feel my way through the maze. I often wished, in the succeeding years, that Robert would fall in love with some graduate of the CIA's Decoding Division who could also type at least seventy-five words a minute. (Robert did not have a regular secretary until 1966, and in Hollywood, at least in the early sixties, it was catch-as-catch-can, while Stravinsky relied on his son-in-law for the mechanical execution of most of his own correspondence.)

Between Stravinsky and myself something of a rapport had developed, all the more important since our relationship had survived two incidents in the previous year during which I had encountered "Stravinsky Enraged." One involved a contract (foreign) wherein the impresario was unable to produce the final third of his fee, thus placing the burden in terms of the agreement on me. But neither could I raise it, since I was in the process of closing my office and settling bills to avoid being branded as bankrupt. In other words, I was as broke as could be. Stravinsky wrote me a series of badgering letters—letters that almost sent me to a retreat, less for the badgering than because he signed these missives "Sincerely" or "Yours truly," rather than in his usual affectionate terms. It was no solace to me that others close to him suffered the same kind of nagging about money. Robert had written me once (January 17, 1961), regarding an advance made to him by Stravinsky on a fee due, that the composer had made him sign an IOU for $2500 . . . and that he was sure his creditor would remind him of the debt every week or so. I finally did scrape together almost the entire sum, deposited it in his private account, and received one of his little calling cards covered with red ink and concluding "With love."

The other incident was a tempest over the closing date of the Australian tour, which, according to the contract, was scheduled for November 29, 1961. The plane for Tahiti, where the Stravinskys had decided to take a week's holiday on their way back to the United States, had been booked by Milène's husband André for that same date, a discovery made only when the party had arrived in Berlin in September on the first lap of the stay abroad that was to include Australia, and long after the contract had been approved and signed. There were no other planes to the flowery island for several days; hearts had been set on going there (the resident black widows were not listed among points of interest in the travel brochures), and some despairing R.C. letters from the Hotel Kampinski indicated that if I couldn't change the final concert date to the twenty-eighth, "down under" would be devoid of Stravinsky. The latter's paternal loyalty (this time, at any rate) was beyond question. He refused to admit that the fault was not mine, and delivered an ultimatum: Change it or we won't go. The injustice of this made *me* angry, and in a mood of fatalism I replied: "I am not a mind-reader and I knew you were going to Tahiti, but I certainly didn't know your reservation was for the twenty-ninth. How could it be when the contract clearly stated, and has stated all along, that the *concert* was on the twenty-ninth!" Strong language to use to the great man!

We weathered this storm also, principally because I succeeded in changing the date of the last concert to the twenty-eighth (hosannas to my friends the Australians).

If these incidents seem overstressed, given Stravinsky's well-known reversals of attitude toward old friends, they are not. Throughout his earlier life he had been famous for terminating associations of far longer standing than the one I enjoyed, and for what would appear to be trivial reasons. For example, a longtime crony was never really forgiven for having made, as his first remark following the première of the *Canticum Sacrum* in St. Mark's, "Where are we going to have dinner?" And an impulsively-worded letter of reproach from a physician who had looked after Stravinsky for years, and who had expected to accompany the family on one of their trips abroad but was told he could not, closed the door to him forever—not for the reproach but because the letter had enclosed a huge bill! It did not matter that the physician had rearranged a complicated schedule of appointments, which now suf-

fered from this unexpected (though not unusual) change of heart.
The professional feuds arose, of course, from reasons considered
serious by the composer, and they were irreversible. His estrangement from Ernest Ansermet is a case in point. The two had met in
Clarens in 1911, and had become very good friends by the twenties.
Ansermet was the first to conduct *The Song of the Nightingale* and
the 1919 revision of *The Firebird,* and before that Stravinsky had been
very instrumental in furthering the conductor's career by recom-
mending Ansermet as successor to Gabriel Pierné and Pierre Monteux when the latter two left the Ballet Russe in 1914. But in 1937
Ansermet made an unauthorized cut in *Jeu de Cartes.* Stravinsky
was furious. His fury mounted with news of more unauthorized
cuts in other works during succeeding years, and finally reached a
breaking point as Ansermet became more and more outspoken
against Stravinsky's post-1940 works. Their last confrontation was
in 1957; after that, it became dangerous to mention Ansermet's
name to the composer. During the Stravinsky Festival at Lincoln
Center in 1966, at which Ansermet had been a guest conductor, the
latter sent Stravinsky a postcard in French on July 13, and subsequently another on July 25. The composer replied in a handwritten
card on August 6, but though Ansermet continued to write during
1967, I do not think Stravinsky replied again.

Stravinsky could never forgive disloyalty to his music, nor would
he permit a division of loyalty to himself. If one were his adherent,
not even a small portion of one's attention could be turned elsewhere. He was possessive in this sense more than in any other. But
when I knew him he was far above minor disagreements, although
he was willing to be a participant in grudges held by other members
of his household out of a sense of duty, even though he was totally
uninterested in the origins. It was more or less understood by
members of the circle surrounding Stravinsky that approval by all
three was vital if more than temporary tenure with the composer
was the goal.

At the other extreme, Stravinsky was often deeply contrite if he
recognized that he had inflicted hurt unjustly, and was quick to
acknowledge his error. A letter he sent me during the third year of
our association was worth, and always will be worth, the whole
twelve-year price of admission. It was received in response to one
from my secretary, written while I was on a business trip, correcting Stravinsky's criticism of an item in one of my accountings

(which, needless to say, were labored over for days and days to avoid any such trouble!). "Dearest friend," it began, and went on to tell me the depth of his sorrow for having caused me any grief . . . never in his life would he say such things to dear Lillian because . . . and he gave his reasons. He ended with a plea that we both forget about the whole incident and would I please permit him to pay what was due.

No wonder I would have changed the map to get him to Tahiti!!

And thereafter I remained with the trio until the end. I now had a part not only in the working program but in the leisure one as well. Movies were always a popular pastime in off-duty moments. We had already made a series of visits to the foreign prize-winners —*La Dolce Vita, L'Avventura*—in 1961, and after Stravinsky returned from Caracas in November, in between rehearsals for *The Rake's Progress* with the American Opera Society and his departure for recording sessions for the *Symphony in C* in Toronto, we went to the cinema often. In this period we saw *Ben-Hur*, during which Stravinsky told me he would take a nap if I would wake him in time for the chariot race, and we also caught, on the next trip to New York, a good many James Bond films. We never had to wait in line. I would make a preliminary visit to the theater manager's office, have a little chat about Stravinsky and his music, and four seats were always waiting for us at night when we arrived. Once a manager reversed an escalator and held up a whole theater of descending patrons so that the composer could ascend comfortably before the block-long double line in front of the movie-house was admitted. Usually I sat with him as protection against autograph-hunters equipped with cats' eyes, and, incidentally, as a supplier of additional dialogue, especially later, in the case of British-made mysteries (we "seen" every "pichur" Alistair Sim and Margaret Rutherford ever made!), for there always were a few moments of difficulty adjusting to British English.

Ethel Merman was one of Stravinsky's favorite "legit" stars, and when we went to see *Gypsy*, I had to secure seats that practically made us members of the percussion section so that he could satisfy himself that her voice—"What an instrument! It would fill Madison Square Garden without a microphone!"—was capable of conquering the liveliest combination of sound.

Mealtimes during the New York stays were always occasions for get-togethers. In those early days the East Indian room below the Pierre lobby was a favorite, and there John McClure or David Adams, or Claudio Spies or Dr. Protetch or Alexei Haieff would join us; and sometimes Nicolas Nabokov came when he was in town. We went to Arnold Weissberger's famous cocktail parties, crammed with stars of stage and screen, where Stravinsky enjoyed talking with his host's "Mama" as much as looking at Rita Gam. (But he always admired beautiful women, and was generous with his compliments to the very end.) Once, when Arnold had arranged a theater party and found himself with a spare ticket, he asked the composer if there were anyone he cared to invite. "Yes," said Stravinsky, "Rita Hayworth." (She was in town, and she came!)

I recall another time when the four of us had a delightful lunch at Lucia Davidova's, which was also attended by W. H. Auden and Chester Kallman. The entire conversation was devoted to cats and poems about cats. Afterward, on our walk to the car, in answer to my question about why he was so silent—was he feeling well?—Stravinsky said "Sure. I was only afraid that if I spoke it would be to say 'Meow.'"

CHAPTER EIGHT

STRAVINSKY, composer, was as fully occupied as Stravinsky, performing artist, during the first years of the sixties, incredible as that may appear to be on examination of the travel itineraries. Between 1960 and the close of 1965 he produced the cantata *A Sermon, a Narrative, and a Prayer;* the anthem *A Dove Descending Breaks the Air;* the musical play *The Flood;* the "sacred ballad" *Abraham and Isaac; Elegy for J.F.K.; Variations: Aldous Huxley In Memoriam;* and *Introitus,* in memory of T. S. Eliot. In addition, he finished an instrumentation of an earlier piano work (*The Five Fingers,* composed in 1921), turning the eight piano pieces into *Eight Instrumental Miniatures;* created *Fanfare for a New Theatre,* a two-trumpet gift for his friends George Balanchine and Lincoln Kirstein, when the New York State Theater was opened; and took the theme from the Finale of *The Firebird,* working it into a brief *Canon* for full orchestra. Within this period he also completed the *Monumentum pro Gesualdo* (instrumenting three madrigals by that composer), and rearranged a Sibelius *Canzonetta* for eight instruments, as an homage to the country which presented him with the Wihuri-Sibelius Prize in 1963. And he was to have the power, after all this, to compose *Requiem Canticles.*

The emphasis, easily discernible even to the layman, was on works based in religious ideas, and more consistently so than in previous decades. The most ambitious opus, from the standpoint of production (I do not say from that of composition, for only Stravinsky could supply this answer), was *The Flood.* This work, his "first for the television medium" (these are the words of publicity; Stravinsky's medium was never anything except the voices and instruments he used concretely to expose his ideas), was unique in another sense than the fact of its creation. Its world première on June 14, 1962, by way of a CBS telecast, was the only event during his eightieth birthday year that did not bring him ovations. *The Flood* was a commission I handled for Stravinsky from start to finish, and it had some aspects, as well as an aftermath of publicity, that made it exceptional.

Sometime before Robert Graff (president of Sextant Productions) had approached him in 1959 with the CBS television project, Stravinsky had turned his mind in the direction of a "large" work on a Biblical theme. Robert told me that he had, in fact, discussed this with T. S. Eliot during one of their visits together in England, at which time the poet talked of the universal elements in the stories of Noah and the Flood. Eliot had further suggested that the Miracle Plays might provide rewarding sources. Stravinsky was interested, but then his thoughts apparently took another path, for during the period of the New York concerts when he asked me to undertake meetings with Mr. Graff, he mentioned that the story of Sara and Tobias from the Book of Tobit intrigued him. Moreover, Robert must have been preparing some notes for a libretto on this idea, for he, too, referred in passing to the theme in one of his early letters to me. Apparently, toward the latter part of 1959, the composer abandoned the Tobias story and turned his attention back to the Flood legend. Eliot's suggestion had obviously made an impression on him, for he selected as the text for the Prayer in *A Sermon, A Narrative, and A Prayer,* an excerpt from Thomas Dekker's *Foure Birds of Noah's Ark.* Also, according to Robert, in Stravinsky's talks during the fifties with the poet Dylan Thomas, whose tragic death had prevented a potential collaboration between the two, the idea of a libretto based on the resurrection of the world after its ultimate destruction was discussed—a theme certainly suggestive of the Flood idea as a symbol.

In any case, in January 1960, a television project was drawn up by Graff, proposing that Stravinsky create music for a ballet based on the story of Noah and the Flood, to be choreographed by Balanchine. At the time W. H. Auden was named by Graff as a possible librettist. The project indicated that the telecast would be of an hour's duration, with a production date in March 1961. Stravinsky's first positive words to me on the subject, after my initial investigations, came in the middle of February, when he told me in a long-distance telephone conversation that I might report to Graff that he was considering the matter seriously, because "I like working with him."

But four days later he wrote from Hollywood stating that the work would have to be postponed for a year, as he had just accepted a much more advantageous commission, the result of a promise made long before, that he now found he could not put off although he had hoped to. And three weeks after this it seemed as if the postponement would be permanent, for in an over-enthusiastic move Sextant released a story to the *New York Times* (March 12) giving the following summer of 1961 as a definite videotaping date and (an unpardonable sin!) defined the uncomposed work as a "one-hour ballet"! Stravinsky, on one of his calling cards that printed his name in Japanese characters on the reverse side (which he always used when he was in an enormous hurry), told me in bright red ink what to do about this "prematurely enough announcement," adding that it would certainly not be a *television ballet* (thus eliminating the idea expressed in the original project outline). Calm was restored following the transmission of this message. A new release was prepared, with the ultimate production date so vague that no one was compromised, and CBS picked up its option to purchase the commission in April 1960.

On April 16 Stravinsky made it clear in a letter to me that he had arrived at a decision regarding the work. Noah as a subject still appealed to him more than anything else, he wrote, but the difficulty was that he now saw the necessity of restudying the various texts and compiling something that would differ from his previous thinking. (In earlier conversations, the episode of Noah's drunkenness, which became an important interlude in the completed work, was not part of his concept.) He went on to say that it was impossible for him to predict the form, for even if he were to begin to compose the very next day, *he could not tell what would happen in a work until it happened.* What he had in mind, he said, was closer—musical style apart—to *Perséphone* than to any of his other works; that is, he was thinking of including narration, chorus, soloists, and *incidental* choreographic movement. He warned me to remember at all times that the work was *not a ballet.*

Revealing, in the sense that the process of creation was underway. He gave me permission in the same letter to use its contents as a guide in my discussions, and indicated that he definitely did not plan to have the work ready for performance before an unspecified month of 1962. He then instructed me to proceed with the contract negotiations for the delivery of a piece of music that would not be more than *twenty-five minutes* in length: Balanchine would do the choreography, and, worthy of note, Stravinsky would try to work with Robert Craft on libretto during their travels, an indication that he did not intend to approach Auden or any other outside collaborator.

Mr. Graff's first draft of a contract, following lengthy discussions, was sent by him directly to Stravinsky less than a week after this concise letter, but despite my emphasis on the "unspecified" production date, it was implicit in the text that the composer would be compelled to deliver a finished score in the late spring of 1961, so that videotaping could be undertaken in the summer. Stravinsky's reaction was interesting. For the first time he talked about his age, his powers, his health, as he had never done—certainly not in the brief time I had known him, and, according to his wife and Robert, not within their recollection. It was deeply moving to hear this great man protest almost pathetically over the long-distance telephone that he had not had a commission with a positive time limit on it for more than fifteen years, and that the pressure was something he was "not young enough" to stomach. About his ability to finish in terms of the proposed date, there was no doubt in any of our minds. Robert, in fact, wrote me that *he* could assure Graff that Stravinsky *would* finish by June or July 1961. And he urged me to try and effect a compromise. But on April 23, 1960, Stravinsky was equally definite in a letter to me: if he said that he could not possibly compose the music by June 1961, no amount of insisting on Graff's part would change the matter. If Graff were willing to make the agreement read January 1962, then he (Stravinsky) would be willing to sign the agreement—but if this were unacceptable, all discussions would come to an end.

Graff was willing, and, more important, he persuaded CBS to accept Stravinsky's terms. The delivery date was set, loosely, for January 1962. During April and early May, I held further meetings with Sextant so that there would be no misunderstanding about the terms in the final draft of the contract. The overall fee Stravinsky was to have received at this point was twenty-five thousand dollars.* However, since only twenty-five minutes of music were promised, something had to be done to bring the telecast up to its required full hour of prime time, and in the course of the meetings, Robert indicated that Stravinsky would agree to appear briefly in whatever would be planned as a filler (one of the ideas was to in-

---

*A Stravinsky commission could range at this time from fifteen thousand to fifty thousand dollars.

clude excerpts from the new score, performed without ballet and conducted by the composer). For this service, another five thousand dollars were added to the fee, although I had not had any direct advice from Stravinsky as to whether or not he would concur in such a plan.

He signed and returned the contract to me on May 27 with the comment that since it seemed to be worded so vaguely as to the time of delivery, he did not feel as pressed as before. The central theme of the work was now crystal clear: the composer conceived the focal point to be the Flood itself, representing symbolically the atomic destruction of the world, and then its rebirth. The man Noah was a Christ figure, as in the thinking of the theologists of the Middle Ages. (Once, when Robert had talked about Venice, he had referred to the famous late-fourteenth-century relief at the east end of the Ducal Palace, which depicts Noah's sons covering their naked father in his drunkenness, and Stravinsky had called it "The Deposition.")

The libretto was to be based on a compilation of passages from the Book of Genesis and the York and Chester Miracle Plays, the latter supplying episodes relating to the Fall of Lucifer and the Fall of Man, as well as a passage on the Flood itself. As is generally known, the Miracle cycles were originally created for audiences that could neither read nor write, and the simple words of the texts could easily be modernized to fall within the comprehension of the widest possible television public. The universality of the composer's idea did not allow for archaic *décor*, either, and it appeared that the work would be as contemporary as the date on which American audiences were scheduled to see and hear it. Stravinsky defined the composition, incidentally, as "a musical play," to be entitled *The Flood*, although later he agreed to the subtitle "dance drama" and the expansion, for television purposes, of the main title to *Noah and the Flood*, so that the content of those glaring thirty-five minutes of as yet unoccupied, commercially-sponsored time would be covered.

And having thus expressed his plans, the composer considered that from this point what went on behind his closed studio doors was nobody else's business. His sole requirements from the "outside" were Robert's compilation of the texts and, from the producer, certain specifications of a technical nature that would provide him with the information he needed for his own time schemes. This request for specifications *only* was a surprise to the producer, who had in-

terpreted rather literally Stravinsky's message about liking to work
"*with* him." The composer's reply to a proposed conference on the
West Coast with the producer and Balanchine (who was not a party
to the suggestion) was hardly in the spirit of togetherness. He wrote
me emphatically on June 11 that he had *never* exchanged a word
with Balanchine about anything they had done together until the
music was composed, adding in a postscript that someone must have
been reading too much about meetings at the "Summit"!

Silence on this particular subject now reigned for some time. But
an intervening incidental note may be worth a mention. Stravinsky
decided in June to cancel the proposed January 1961 concert in
Town Hall about which Robert had notified me some months
before, because, he wrote me, he could not afford to lose so much
time from composition; and, further, another reason was that he had
just read the reviews of the European première of *Movements* and
the contrast with those in New York had made it very plain to
him that his music and his person were more welcome in Europe.
Hurt feelings? Maybe. But Stravinsky was not unaccustomed to un-
favorable reviews on his later music on either side of the Atlantic.
("Always bad reviews; always sold-out houses," was the uncontra-
dictable comment of one of his European impresarios.) The pure
and simple truth, in my opinion, is that he did not want to subsidize
any more concerts if recordings could be arranged conveniently in
another way. (They could—he recorded *The Nightingale*, which
was to have been included in the Town Hall program, with the
Washington Opera after the performance in December 1960.) He
only wished to complete his cantata and begin on *The Flood*. Robert, as subsequent letters to me indicate, tried his best to revive the
plan, but this was one of the few "concert" occasions when his co-
conductor remained unmoved.

Mr. Graff made an attempt in November to find out how matters
were progressing behind those sacred portals, although this rash
move was undoubtedly due to the pressures on *him* from the sponsoring network, which certainly could not have cared less about the
problem or wishes of the creator. He wrote, requesting "a full
report," something Stravinsky would never have given even to
Diaghilev! ("Full report, indeed!" reverberated from the West with
the thunder of Jeremiah!)

Robert's outline of the libretto was ready by December 16, and
although its author was sure that the final version would bear no

resemblance to it, he was wrong. Stravinsky's finished composition followed the pattern his colleague had set down with very few changes, and for these efforts Robert received the sum of twenty-five hundred dollars, plus a small share in the royalties.

Stravinsky began to compose *The Flood* at the beginning of May 1961. A near-catastrophe was barely avoided when Sextant, relying on that unfortunate slip of Robert's tongue to the effect that Stravinsky *could* finish before the end of the year, suggested in a letter that perhaps "the score or some part of it" might be made available for choreography in August. To which Stravinsky replied that I should inform the producers he now hoped to finish by January 1973!

But by the third week in May he had completed the major ballet scene of the "Building of the Ark," and Sextant was busy in another direction, working out agreements with the composer's publishers, Boosey & Hawkes, with regard to rental fees, exclusivity rights, and *their* publication date. No further waves disturbed the beach until August, when a renewal of the proposal for a Stravinsky-Balanchine-Graff meeting reached the composer by telegram. According to Robert (August 10) the house on Wetherly Drive was almost *sans* roof, and the echo of falling debris finally convinced CBS (and the long-suffering Mr. Graff) that there was to be no more prodding if they wished to have a *Flood*.

Stravinsky finished Satan's final song at the beginning of March 1962, completed the score on March 14, and at long last the meetings with Balanchine took place in Hollywood on the succeeding two days, and on April 11 and 12. Sextant was not represented at any of these get-togethers, but Robert made working notes of the discussions between composer and choreographer, which he sent to me for typing, and which, after four revisions, were subsequently published in *Dialogues and a Diary* (pp. 89–98). The score was put on tape at the end of the month, with Robert assuming the lion's share of the conducting chore—Stravinsky, in fact, conducted only a few measures to be used in the filler segment of the hour.

For Stravinsky the composer, that part of the affair which interested him was now at an end. But he did have some curiosity as to the treatment his score would be given in the two-dimensional medium, for he wrote me (April 5) prior to the final two meetings on the choreography, that he must have some knowledge of how his new work would be introduced, indicating at the same time that he was pleased with the cast, but had heard that the prologue to the whole program was "*sa*phomoronic." When the Stravinskys arrived in New York at the end of the month, he was far more concerned with the success of his wife's exhibition of works at the Galérie Internationale and would ask me, after my daily visits there, if there were "enough customers."

In any case, on Thursday, June 14, when the première of *Noah and the Flood* was telecast over CBS, Stravinsky was preparing to leave Rome for Hamburg, where the New York City Ballet—some of whose stars had performed leading roles in the production—would honor him in a birthday program with performances of *Orpheus*, *Agon*, and *Apollo*.

The publicity heralding the television première may have had a great deal to do with the negative post-mortems. Living up to the subject, it came down on the public like a tidal wave, in a deluge of stunning full-page advertisements in the *New York Times* and the *Herald Tribune*, which prophesied that ART had at last come to television. And apart from Stravinsky and Balanchine, who would have proved this point in any medium, certainly the array of talent assembled—actors Laurence Harvey, Elsa Lanchester, Sebastian Cabot; ballet luminaries Edward Villella, Jacques D'Amboise, Jillana; Rouben Ter-Arutunian as production designer; Kirk Browning as director—implied that the advertised word might for once spell truth.

Along with David Adams of Boosey & Hawkes and a small number of invited guests who were interested in either the composer, the production, or the sponsorship, I watched the first performance at the New York apartment of the producer. Time has passed and wounds have become untroublesome scars, so I will run the risk of reopening a once-sensitive area and say that it was so bad it shocked me—all the more because the effort of the producer to bring the predictions of the advertisements and publicity to pass was so evident. No money had been spared, particularly with regard to special effects: Lucifer (Villella) fell marvelously from Heaven to become a jet-spangled Satan, and Adam and Eve clung to a Tree of Knowledge sparkling with "diamonds," while hundreds of yards of costly, shimmering fabric, covering the bodies of dancers simulating waves, showed the world "overflowed with Flood." The voices (including singers John Reardon and Robert Oliver, jointly, as the Voice of God) were impressive; the Gregg Smith Choir was equally so. But the choreography suffered the restrictions of the medium, and the dances were so incidental as to be almost nonexistent (but Stravinsky had indeed referred to "incidental" choreographic movement, and he had meant just that!). Balanchine's usually effective technique of using a single gesture to express a great scope of movement —such as the touching of fingers by Adam and Eve to signify their awakening to some of life's more delightful aspects—was, alas, too subtle for the small screen. As for Stravinsky's score, it was so surrounded by Breck Golden Showcase commercials, and a hodgepodge of documentary film clips, eulogies, flood legends, and rehearsal excerpts, plus an introductory minor epic rivalling the speech of Polonius in pomposity, no amount of concentration could afford it a fair hearing. (This all came home to me later, in 1963, when I went with the composer to the Stravinsky Festival at Oberlin College and heard again, but unadorned, the Building of the Ark and the Flood episodes, performed superbly by a student orchestra.)

On that fateful evening, however, my opinion of the production was unhappy, and it was shared by Mr. Adams, who agreed with me that it was well Stravinsky had not been present. The brave producer held his head high and received "congratulations," which, in my own case at any rate, were given as a sincere tribute to his admirable perseverance and courage. He had executed a project which (I am sure) he was aware from the start would have provoked attack from the Stravinsky circle even if it had been a smashing success, simply because the cloak of ownership its members spread over the composer was often embroidered with beads of jealousy.

The printed blows fell the next day, permeated, first of all, with resentment that what had been advertised as an hour-long première had turned out to be a new Stravinsky work of less than twenty-five minutes' duration, and though much of the rodomontade placed the blame squarely on the shoulders of those who had conceived the production, there was little if any indication that the score was great enough to emerge victorious from the morass.

"In this reviewer's opinion the hour as a whole was enough to retard the progress of the arts in this country by a great deal," said the *New York Times* critic. "Literature, music, art objects, and by implication their creators, were made to seem insufferably pretentious, disorganized and dull." And, further, faintly damning, "The score Stravinsky composed for *Noah and the Flood* will surely not rank as one of his greatest achievements, but it is a serviceable and thoroughly listenable piece of work."

But Stravinsky could ignore this, as indeed he did, since his sense of restraint admitted the presence of "serviceable" and "listenable" in his own vocabulary, however useless he might consider the body of the critique. The report of another, writing for the *Herald Tribune*, was not to be ignored, however. "The whole thing is nothing but a 20-minute intermezzo, an oversized vignette in an hour-long show. . . . There is, of course, some music. . . ." This sentence undoubtedly terminated the Stravinsky reading hour, though a few paragraphs further along the critic, in what he must have considered a complimentary vein, wrote: "Mr. Stravinsky is not a dour decaphonist by nature, nor indeed by grace; compared to other living practitioners of the 'system' he is a Bohemian, and though reformed and under discipline, his glorious past is still there."

These reviews and others of the same ilk, though far from the same importance (circulation-wise), reached Stravinsky in Hamburg on the eve of the birthday tribute by the New York City Ballet, many of whose members had seen the telecast, and this circumstance was an irritant. Stravinsky had granted the first stage production rights to Rolf Liebermann, and the date of the Hamburg production, to be staged by Gunther Rennert, had been more or less officially set for spring 1963. No matter how objectively the Staatsoper administration might regard the press reaction, the atmosphere of celebration must have been somewhat dampened for the composer, whose "home country" had so belittled his new work. Besides, the *Herald Tribune* review came from the pen of a critic who had been one of two focal points of attack in the third volume of the collaboration * ("totally tone deaf" . . . "ignorant" . . . "primitive" . . . "stupid"), and who had replied, not quite in kind, but with not-to-be-ignored riposte ("The collaboration has reached a stage where Mr. Stravinsky should use the business designation 'A Division of Craft Products, Inc.'").

Stravinsky's fury on the evening he learned about this review was defined by Robert, who spoke with me from Hamburg, in one word: "*Wheeewww!*" He told me that a cablegram had gone off to the *Herald Tribune* music editor an hour before, and that he was certain the newspaper would be afraid to print it. The newspaper

* *Expositions and Developments* (New York: Doubleday, 1962), pp. 170 ff.

was not afraid, however, and set it instead in a prominent box. The text, which burned like Nero's Rome, concluded with the highly uncharitable regret that since the composer was celebrating his eightieth birthday, this would probably prevent his living long enough to attend the critic's funeral.

The private effect of this malediction on its target is unknown to me, but it certainly accomplished one thing not intended: it confirmed his immortality.

I have been asked many times by other reporters whether or not Stravinsky transmitted this message himself, and I have always given the same reply: the message, yes; the transmission, no. The cablegram was a "collaboration"—Stravinsky's views, edited for cablegram-reading by Robert, who, of course, would then transmit it, as he did most wires when no one else was there to do so. The composer's rage in the privacy of his suite must certainly have found expression in terms perhaps far more down-to-earth than the ones that whizzed across the Atlantic to the editorial desk, but I believe that, given a few hours, the whole matter would have been relegated to the wastebasket along with other items considered unworthy of more than a momentary glance (to make sure they *were* unworthy). Once having pounded his fists on the table or torn the offending page in two with limb-from-limb force, the composer would have allowed the fire to extinguish itself. (What had such printed quarrels to do with him, after all, who was really concerned only with music?) And thereafter, the mention of the adversary's name (if he recalled it at all) might conjure up only one of those loud grins with a slightly malicious twist at the corners.

Stravinsky's fame as the antagonist of critics was always a part of his legend. "The critics cannot judge me. Not only am I more important in music, but I *know* more than they do." Such views were constantly printed, reprinted, utilized as points for debate by the defense, and they kept a number of music columnists, critics, and cartoonists in business around the globe.

The press, on the whole, thoroughly enjoyed being engaged in these battles. Occasionally a writer would seek me out to see if there were in the offing some controversial thinking on any current subject—a new piece of music by an "established" composer, a new production at the "Met," or did I know Mr. Stravinsky's true opinion of Beethoven as a musician? (yes, this question was really put to me by a Boston newspaperman! *)—in the hope (vain, I hasten to add) that grist for their mills would instigate replies immortalizing the questioner in the archives.

Some victims took the barbs in the spirit of true sportsmanship. I remember a visit I made in the early sixties to the music critic of the *Los Angeles Times,* just after he had undergone an ordeal by fire comparable to that ordained for the *Herald Tribune* writer.† Under the circumstances, I approached his office shyly, although I had come on other than Stravinsky business, and found him seated at his desk wearing a magnificent sweatshirt with IGOR STRAVINSKY appliquéed in handsome letters on its back: he started a cross-country vogue. And another attackee, in Chicago (but later), had hung on the wall directly over his working space a full-face blown-up photograph of the composer, cane raised as though to demolish the cameraman. The picture was completely surrounded by snapshots of the most lightly-clad pinups of all time.

In the final five years of his life. Stravinsky would no longer be drawn into controversies with critics. He had come to look upon these arguments as a kind of game that amused those around him, and which he had been willing to play for that reason only. But he was now too old for such pastimes. No doubt his opinions about the music press remained the same until the end, and he would never have given up his own right to independent criticism. After all, in music he was "in charge," and he could not permit the "spreading of ignorance without correction or interference from professionals," as he once put it in a *Newsweek* "interview," in explanation of his attitude.

"*Shalom* is the only Hebrew word I know," Stravinsky remarked to the Israeli press when he made his second visit to that country in 1964, "and the meaning of that word expresses the idea of my new work." "Peace" had been the order of the day during the composition of Stravinsky's sacred ballad, *Abraham and Isaac,* which followed in the wake of *The Flood.* He had fallen in love with the Hebrew language, he told me and others on his return from that

---

* Not, I hasten to add, Michael Steinberg of the *Globe!*
† *Themes and Episodes* (New York: Alfred A. Knopf, 1966), pp. 82 ff. The letter reprinted there, written on January 28, 1962, was a reply to a critique of the first Los Angeles performance of the *Rake.* Lawrence Morton collaborated with Robert and Stravinsky in this one, Robert told me.

country in 1962. But I recall that, even before the question of a commission arose, he had mentioned that he was contemplating a work in that ancient tongue. When I received instructions to investigate the possibility of a tour to Israel during his eightieth-birthday year, I discovered that his friend Sir Isaiah Berlin had already spoken with members of the government of Israel about commissioning a Stravinsky piece in Hebrew and Robert had once written me that Nicolas Nabokov was encouraging the project. The time element precluded its delivery on the occasion of the first prospective visit, and as a consequence Ahron Propes, director of the Festival of Israel, called on me in New York on November 17, 1961, with a proposal that a second tour, in which the commissioned work would be featured, be planned for 1963. But money was a problem. The Israelis could not meet the regular concert fee, and the commission, as well, would have to be handled by a system of delayed payments. Stravinsky said "No" at first, took some time to consider, and, in fact, gave his affirmative reply only during his initial visit to Israel. (He did, incidentally, perform at a lower-than-usual fee on that first tour.) As it turned out, *Abraham and Isaac* did not have its world première until August 23, 1964, in Jerusalem, and later, in December of that year, it was introduced to America in New York, Washington, and Boston, before impressed audiences and approving critics.

Hebrew was the sixth tongue that Stravinsky set to music. Russian and Slavonic had been used for many of the pre-1920 works, but after *Mavra* was finished in 1922, the composer very rarely employed a Russian text.* Works of succeeding years were set to French, Latin, and English, major examples of his use of these languages being *Perséphone*, *Oedipus Rex*, and *The Rake's Progress*. Some writers have also credited him with a seventh tongue, Italian, pointing out the vocal passages in *Pulcinella*, but those actually had been set by the eighteenth-century composer Pergolesi, on whom Stravinsky drew in that work.

Stravinsky's fascination with the Hebrew text he had chosen from Genesis stimulated him to apply himself to an analysis of the language with the zeal of a Hasidic scholar. He sought help in understanding the pronunciation and sound of the original tongue not only from Sir Isaiah but also from the composer Hugo Weisgall, whose father was a distinguished cantor. Musical scholars have told

---

* He did use Slavonic for his church choruses (*Pater Noster, Credo, Ave Maria*), composed in the thirties.

me that the work is remarkable because Stravinsky utilized the
actual Hebrew syllables, with their particular accents and intona-
tions, as the principal element of the music, and with such precision
that he might have been working in his mother tongue.*

He began the composition in Hollywood in January 1963, shut
himself in his studio throughout February, and completed it at the
beginning of March. Two weeks later, when I joined him in Oberlin for the four-day Stravinsky Festival—so satisfying to him, inci-
dently, that a few months later he presented the manuscript of
Threni to that institution as a surprise gift—he told me he was
pleased with the new work, "although it is much shorter than they
expect." Not so much, however; it was twelve minutes long, but the
Israelis were more than satisfied. Stravinsky's next works (uncom-
missioned) lasted one and a half, five, and three and a half minutes
respectively (*Elegy for J.F.K., Variations, Introitus*).

Requiem Canticles (affectionately referred to by Robert as
"Requicles"), his last major work and his last commission, did not
involve me except that its composition was in progress during one
of my prolonged visits to his new Hollywood home in the summer
of 1966. The commission was sought in 1965 by Stanley Seeger, a
Princeton alumnus, who asked friends of his (Mr. and Mrs. Jascha
Kajaloff) to approach the composer. Mr. Seeger's mother had left
a generous legacy to the university with the proviso that her son
should exercise certain prerogatives with regard to some of the areas
of allocation. The Music Department became one of the principal
beneficiaries thereby, and Mr. Seeger wished some of the money to
be used for a Stravinsky work that would be a memorial to his
mother. A letter from Mrs. Kajaloff to the composer, caught by
Mrs. Stravinsky in the mail (there were so many requests for commissions, most of which were uninteresting!), brought results. The
contract, a highly complicated one, was handled by Stravinsky's
West Coast attorney, William Montapert.

One other commission, though not in the usual sense, was carried
out in 1966, and provided us all with an inside look at cultural life
in the stratosphere. United Airlines decided to fill its "friendly
skies" to capacity with passengers by tempting them into the upper

---

* He was not so patient in other languages, especially English, where often the
syllables must be adjusted to the musical accents; similar adjustments in French
occur frequently (cf. *Perséphone*). Stravinsky would not make any concessions, for he always considered that the language served the music.

ether by means of a film—intended for distribution by its makers on "a non-commercial, public service, *sans*-fiscal-gain" basis—to be called *Discover America*. With unarguable logic, Reid H. Ray Film Industries, producers for United, explained to me their decision that a film documenting the spectacular achievements of both Nature and Man on the terrain of the world's greatest country should have background music only by the world's greatest composer. But they were not asking for a new work ("Our music budget is considerably less than half a million, of course," one of the executives told me, quite seriously); they only wanted excerpts from "his established masterpieces," and for this they were prepared to offer a sum, handsome in its five, if not seven, figures, if Stravinsky would give permission and make suggestions for a score of appropriate selections. At first reluctant, the composer was persuaded to join in the sport, and I remember one delightful evening in the Stravinsky living room, following our first look at the film (during a "coast-to-coast, north-to-south flight" in luxuriously upholstered armchairs in a studio near Hollywood and Vine), when he assigned excerpts "for the public": the *Danse Sacrale* for the Grand Canyon, *Petrushka* for Disneyland, *The Nightingale* for Texas, and so on. A suggestion of mine that *Movements* be applied to New York met with an instant veto: "No one would fly there." The final, somewhat different score (*The Firebird* for the Great West, *Apollo* for the nation's capital, and *Symphony in C* for Manhattan, etc.) was assembled and edited by Robert, who also made the recording for discs United Airlines planned to distribute as gifts to patrons (ten thousand, and not one single one over that!), and I had the satisfaction of sending him (with Stravinsky's approval) the full fee.

So much for the commissions of the final years. But of course there were continuous requests. A prominent Mexican industrialist asked me to approach Stravinsky with his offer of fifty thousand dollars net (he would take care of taxes!) if the composer would agree to write a five-minute cello work for the donor's gifted son. The answer was no; Stravinsky was never interested in composing for that instrument (he found its bass register "too juicy").* On another occasion, at Stravinsky's request, I listened to a proposal from a major film studio which offered one million dollars, plus other benefits (such as villas in Rome, etc.) for a "few minutes" of new

* Nevertheless, in collaboration with Piatigorsky, he had, in the thirties, arranged excerpts from *Pulcinella* as the *Suite Italienne*.

music to be used as a theme in a projected Biblical epic. The epic came to pass, and it was indeed "Biblical", but without any melodic gospel from Stravinsky; * its other proportions, however, demonstrated that a million dollars would have meant as much to the producers as a grain of sand on the shores of their "Red Sea." The movies are persistent, and some such project would be placed before me once a year on an average, although never again on such a majestic, fantasy-provoking scale.

* Dino di Laurentis's *The Bible*. The tax bite would have left Stravinsky with very minor compensation for a major expenditure of time.

CHAPTER NINE

MY OWN impression that Stravinsky had shown signs of age and weariness following his return from Russia was borne out by a new physician consulted in New York after his arrival from Caracas, who, however, took away his Scotch and put him on a milk diet that almost killed him! Stravinsky, therefore, claimed that he had never felt better, and the vitality and concentration that produced *Abraham and Isaac* within two months stood as a testament to his own knowledge of himself. Nevertheless, I began to be wary: the letters from abroad had contained more than the usual number of references to colds, bronchial disturbances, and abnormal bloodcounts: Stravinsky always had periodic blood tests, wherever he was, because of his polycythemia. The report of his digestive attack in Moscow (from "sour borshch") * had upset me so much that a reassuring cable from him had been necessary, and the cane at Kennedy Airport had put the finishing touch on my uneasiness. From 1963 on, I began to rely more and more on my own judgment with regard to a limit on the number of concert engagements.

Nudges to action from the West Coast did not diminish proportionately, however. India suddenly burgeoned in Robert's correspondence with me, and although this is a land abundant in beauty, mystery, exoticism, and history, to say nothing of certain highly contagious diseases, it suffers a relative dearth of orchestras and wherewithal for fees. Nevertheless I investigated, concentrating especially on New Delhi, which had produced a conductor beginning to make himself felt in American music circles. I tried vainly and for some time to plough through a thick hedge of clerks at the New York–based East Indian government offices, and finally, aided by friends of the new prodigy of the baton (who turned out to be

---

* There now seems to be no question that what Stravinsky suffered in Moscow was a minor embolism.

Zubin Mehta), I came to meet a courteous gentleman named Mr. Kaul, who was willing to "contact the concert interests there personally." But though his smiles and bows displayed the noble heritage of his country, he held out very little hope of an affirmative reply: "We are rich in culture but not in sums to spend on its dissemination," was his own estimate of the situation. The whole affair came to a sudden end in the middle of the year, on my part at any rate, when a news flash from Paris, stating that Stravinsky (who was then supposed to be safely in the air enroute to Bergen, Norway, to conduct *Perséphone* with Vera Zorina!) was confined to his bed at the Ritz because of an undescribed "illness," sent me flying to the telephone. An exceptionally cheerful "Halooo" from him banished my anxiety, and I was further relieved to discover that Robert was substituting for him—the contract had been a source of endless trouble, for Stravinsky had never wanted to go, as the correspondence shows—and no legal consequences would ensue. We engaged in a chat, which consisted first of the information that mine was the second call he had taken while his wife was out shopping; the first had come from the King of Norway, inquiring about his health. Next, there were various questions about monies due and not yet received from Columbia Records and the Canadian Broadcasting Company for his recent work in Toronto (both checks, needless to say, arrived safely the next day); about whether the Ravinia program scheduled for July was suitable (a query to which only an affirmative reply was expected); and did I know the final rehearsal hours for the *Oedipus* in Hamburg on June 12 (no, I did not)—and so on. Since he did not seem in a hurry to terminate the conversation, and since there was a noticeable absence of any reference to the projected tour through the country of temple bells, I thought he was waiting to see if *I* had been as busy as he, and I reported on the status quo. "India! Who said I wanted to go to India! I am not going to India *now*, and I have no plans to go to India in the *future!*"

And although throughout that year and the next the question of pursuing the philosophy of universal love in the land of its most poetic expression, through the facility of a concert tour, was revived from time to time, my own follow-through was a shameful pretense, to which I now confess. Attention was thereafter switched to Teheran for a spell. Never say die!

But Robert, the perpetrator, was also fighting qualms. He wrote in June from Hamburg, just before the *Oedipus,* that the trip had tired Stravinsky, because every day he became more newsworthy and the constant demands of friends in every city were killing. He also reported at the same time that Stravinsky's forgetfulness about small details was proving to be a major problem, although the importance of this claim seemed to me exaggerated; like many other people past thirty-five, I have frequently been unable to dial my own telephone number or remember the name of a first cousin. In my entire experience with Stravinsky, except for those last years, he never failed to recall the exact amount of postage or taxi fare expended in a particular city.

But 1963 was, in any case, a leanish year concert-wise, although travel arrangements continued to swell the coffers of the transportation industry. *The Flood* had been staged in Hamburg, and a note from Robert, sent on April 23, contains the interesting observation that the orchestra would never be able to play as well as the "Oberlin kids" even after ten rehearsals. Trips to Budapest and Zagreb in May, where the composer did conduct, were followed by a holiday in Dublin and its neighboring counties, where he did not. After this, Milan provided a concert so lucrative that it could not be ignored.

I rejoined the two conductors at Ravinia in July (Mrs. Stravinsky didn't want to go to Chicago and was praying I would go instead, Robert wrote me on June 12), where Stravinsky, on his second visit in two years, despite a heavy rainfall drew upwards of five thousand people both under the theater's protective roof and on the surrounding lawns. After that there were concerts in Brazil—yes, organized by our good and old friend Mr. Alcazar—following on Robert's highly successful performance of Berg's *Lulu* in its American première at Santa Fe. The year was rounded out by a return to Italy until the first of December, when Mrs. Stravinsky's New York exhibit of her paintings at the Galérie Internationale brought the trio back to New York. During this year Stravinsky received the proceeds of the Wihuri-Sibelius Prize, amounting to twenty-three thousand dollars, without having to travel anywhere—which made me wonder why he wanted to bother with conducting engagements at all.

Because of these projected lengthy absences from the United States, I had signed a contract to handle the national tour of Robert Bolt's play *A Man for All Seasons* and due to a fortunate coinci-

dence of dates, it was possible for me to be in Hollywood during
the Stravinskys' brief visits home in August, and also in New York
when they returned in December. The composer finished the year in
better health than at its beginning, and my diary records that he
told me he was "pleased that all the little platelets are behaving well
and not multiplying." He had, however, been deeply affected by the
death of Pope John in April, according to Mrs. Stravinsky, and
during the prelate's illness his mood had been one of great depression, causing him to refuse all invitations, both social and professional, while he kept to his room. But after the pope's death, he
regained his spirits and began to accept everything, from the most
unimportant concerts to tea invitations, with an alacrity in marked
contrast to his previous gloom. (It was during this period, incidentally that Mr. Alcazar had his stroke of luck, for after a long-distance
call from Paris with dismal news about everyone's health and everyone's future, I had been about to cancel the Rio concerts.) Such
sudden reversals of feelings, after news of a death, were typical of
Stravinsky; his natural instinct for survival was powerful. He closed
these pages of the past with finality, and if they had ever to be re-
opened, the perusal was completely objective. But this had been a
year of other deaths as well: that of Huxley, who had been his
friend, and President Kennedy, who had been his acquaintance;
each met his end, expected and unexpected, within two days of the
other, and both were destined to be subjects for Stravinsky's music.

Although we did not know it then, the Italian trip marked the last
time Stravinsky would conduct in that country. The concert took
place in Rome in Santa Maria Sopra Minerva, and he led his 1948
Mass. The period of final appearances had in fact definitely begun.

Those 1963 digs in my ribs about the slowing-down of American
concert engagements did have some effect on me after Mrs. Stravinsky's advices regarding the revival of her husband's "conducting
mood." Consequently, with the cooperation of Hurok booking
agents, I applied myself so that the United States would be as well
represented as Europe on the routings, if not in quantity, at least in
the quality of engagements booked for the next two years, and I
selected from the lists Robert would send as suggestions. It was not
difficult to find willing managerial ears, although often this was as
far as negotiations went. Stravinsky's fee was now approaching the
point where it would double my 1960 quotations, and many musical

organizations could not meet it. Nor was he inclined any longer to make concessions, even when the orchestra was one about which he entertained a good opinion and with which—prior to my arrival— he had appeared at a lower fee. But on the other side of the scale were those in the concert business who were very conscious of what must soon come to pass, who wanted to present Stravinsky "once," or in some cases "once more." Some of these engagements were unhappy for me, not only for what they implied, but because in a few instances the sponsors, once in possession of a contract, would bombard me with demands for the composer's presence at innumerable social functions, panel discussions, hour-long lectures, on the all-too-clear grounds that if this was to be "the last time," they and their subscribers were going to get as much out of the "old man" as possible: that familiar he-owes-it-to-the-public-that-made-him attitude was always cropping up. Those managers will remember me only for my disagreeable personality.

However, apart from Hurok there were other independent impresarios, long in the concert business, who really wanted *him* and the honor he brought to them and their cities: among them the late Aaron Richmond in Boston, Harry Zelzer in Chicago, Hugh Pickett in Vancouver, Patrick Hayes in Washington, William Zalken in St. Louis, Francis Mayville in Miami. And two, far from old in experience but mature in appreciation, Velma Andrews and Robert Garner in Denver. All of these managers undertook the contracts with the almost certain knowledge that they would probably lose money or, at best, break even. (At that time, only in New York was there an audience that did not flinch at a top price of more than ten dollars; with increasing costs of orchestras—and Stravinsky/ Craft usually had extra-large ones—and smallish concert halls, even that ticket scale did not always yield enough to cover expenses.)

Stravinsky was hardly concerned with the financial fate of the concert manager, of course, but he never liked the white lie of a "papered" house, which condition he instinctively recognized when it occurred. He would purse his lips and elevate his brows as though to ask who was protecting whose feelings. *He* needed no protection from such public miserliness. If people lacked the intelligence to spend money on a good product, *tant pis* for *them*.

But in the case of the young team of Andrews-Garner, he did feel something. They had suffered a huge loss due to an act of God: the outdoor theater at Red Rocks, the scenic reason for booking the concert in the first place, had been flooded by a violent cloudburst, and the change to the Denver Arena, made at only a few hours notice, did away with a large part of the audience. In that region music is preferred under the stars, and depends largely on a last-minute "window sale." Stravinsky agreed with unusual amiability to a deferred payment of his fee (it was deferred for only forty-eight hours, to be exact), and he remarked to me sympathetically that he was certain Andrews-Garner had probably mortgaged everything they owned to produce it in that time. (He was right.)

But there never was any satisfying everyone! No sooner had contracts been drawn with the Philadelphia Orchestra for engagements in the home city, and a tour including New York and Ann Arbor; or an itinerary prepared for concerts with the Cleveland, Chicago, Minneapolis, Rochester, Louisville, Cincinnati orchestras, symphonies, and philharmonics, than those familiar post-cards would come flying out of Los Angeles or points abroad, with suggestions about tackling Dallas, Houston, San Antonio, New Orleans, Pittsburgh. One communiqué, sent on the heels of a truly titanic achievement by Hurok involving weeks of cabling for a tour of Poland at an acceptable fee (*that* was the hard part!), conveyed thanks but then told me to get busy and nail Miami, Honolulu, Anchorage, Oklahoma City, Baltimore, Kansas City, Atlanta, and—recurring like malaria—Teheran. Such "orders" were only meant to keep me on my toes, of course, and sometimes they had a sad between-the-lines ring: "We are so isolated here in Hollywood, please don't forget us." But they also were an indication that the writer knew more than just a little about the concert business, for the cities mentioned, excluding the Scheherazade territory, were "excellent potentials" on every managerial list. However, we were far from bowled over by a flood of acceptances from all these cities, even though most of them were investigated. The reasons were various, but they all boiled down to two: Stravinsky/Craft were too expensive, or the orchestra wanted its own conductor to assume Craft's position.

Refusals on the second basis were always hard for me to explain, and I would circumnavigate them by inventing some story about intramural difficulties or my own inefficiency, or whatever other reason I could think of, although I knew Robert never believed a word of it. But they were unpleasant to take, and some of them were

infuriating. One letter, from the manager of a leading Eastern orchestra, expressed in somewhat pompous terms the reaction of his
organization to a proposed recording by Robert of the *Symphonies
of Wind Instruments* and *Abraham and Isaac*, after a Stravinsky/
Craft concert. "Only Titans of the podium have ever been extended
the privilege of recording with the Orchestra, including Toscanini,
Bruno Walter and Stravinsky," it rumbled magnificently.

However, with the passage of time I became more and more
relieved when the responses were negative, and by mid-1965, when I
met Stravinsky at the Indianapolis airport, for the first time bringing
a wheel-chair along with the porter, my mind was made up that the
concerts would be reduced to a minimum as long as I was handling
them.

Indianapolis, the scene of this first real concession to his physical
condition, was the air stop for an engagement as agreeable as the
four days we had spent at Oberlin. We traveled by car from Indianapolis to Muncie, the seat of Ball State Teacher's College, which had
scheduled a three-day arts festival around Stravinsky's music at the
end of June, and had worked hard to raise the money. Stravinsky's
ill humor on arrival at the airport—the wheel-chair, of course, augmented by the innocent presence of an Indianapolis newspaperman,
who had come not to question but to pay his respects—vanished
when we were all installed in a comfortable off-campus inn: "off-
campus" meant that we did not have to smuggle the Scotch, the only
disadvantage of our Oberlin sojourn in a dormitory. Besides, he was
not conducting; Robert had that chore, and all that would be required of Stravinsky was his attendance at two concerts plus his
presence, on another day, at a small discussion group where he
would make a few remarks and answer questions put by students
and faculty from the Music Department. Mrs. Stravinsky was happy
because the inn was quiet, the town "cozy," the food far from bad,
and her husband well. As for Robert, Midwest groves of academe
were his natural habitat; on the occasions that tours brought us to
such campuses, I would recall my first impressions of him at Santa
Fe, though now he had attained a professorial status in my mind.
Students flocked to him with eager queries, and not just about Stravinsky, but about his own work in the field of contemporary music;
their acknowledgment of his authority did away entirely, if only
spasmodically, with his compulsion to turn himself into "the incredible vanishing man."

The mayor, accompanied by the president of the college, called on Stravinsky at the inn and presented him with a five-pound key to the city and a citation which, although majestically worded, regrettably lacked the fascinating Hoosier drawl of the presentor: "My-agh-ty glayd to welcome you to ahr city, Maestroo Stravinsky. . . ." The student choir and orchestra were very satisfying in *Oedipus*, even without the finesse of the Oberlin groups. The informal discussion remained informal, but had to be transferred from the opera workshop area originally set up to a large auditorium, because of the demand from outside the Music Department that the privilege of hearing the great man be shared. He sat onstage in an armchair and Robert stood at a lectern conducting the discussion, which consisted of questions submitted in advance, now to be answered by the composer. As I had come to know, when Stravinsky agreed to "say a few words," he more than fulfilled his contract, and the half-hour grew into an hour and fifteen minutes. I recall that a student who had obviously read some Stravinsky/Craft asked his opinion of Richard Strauss as a composer. Answer: "He was a good conductor. . . . I do not like his major works and I do not like his minor works."

From Muncie, we drove to Indianapolis to enplane for Chicago for the fourth Ravinia concert in as many years. That is, I drove with Stravinsky beside me. Mrs. Stravinsky, incidentally, was the only member of our party who never was guilty of back-seat-driving; Stravinsky's warnings took the form of pronounced intakes of breath audible enough to put an end to Rip Van Winkle's nap, particularly when we went over bumps or seemed to overtake cars too rapidly. But Robert, who always drove as though he were training for the *Grand Prix*, would keep up a steady stream of predictions: "Red light a quarter of a mile down. . . . You can pass those two cars . . . you have enough room to get by that truck. . . . Watch it!"—until I would heartily wish that he and I were alone in the car so that I could drive us both over the nearest cliff. He was unusually informative on that particular night, and I (who have driven all manner of cars, jeeps, trucks, ambulances, etcetera, since I was sixteen) had murder in my heart, when fortunately we stopped at a Holiday Inn to sleep. While I unpacked for him, Stravinsky explored the dresser and found a Gideon Bible lying on its surface. It was open to Psalm 38. He regarded me with wonder. "See here . . . imagine . . . here in this wilderness, these people know me. Look . . ."—and he pointed to the lines "But I as a deaf man heard not; and I was as a dumb man who openeth not his mouth . . ." which provide one of the texts for the *Symphony of Psalms.* Not for one moment did it occur to him that this might be a coincidence, and I confess that I too was somewhat startled, for I had telephoned the management in advance for rooms and explained who was coming in order to justify the list of requirements that customarily accompanied such reservations. Robert's approach was more mundane, however, and at dinner he dwelt at length on Gideon Bibles, their universal presence in all hotels, and the absurdity of considering that Holiday Inns were staffed with moonlighting musicologists from the Institute for Advanced Study. Nevertheless, Stravinsky was indifferent to this hard realism and went to sleep with that open Bible on his night-table, his eyeglasses resting on verses 12 and 13.

There were other concert events, interesting for one reason or another, as the composer approached his eighty-fifth birthday, and some of them are worth mentioning. We did finally do another Stravinsky-subsidized performance in New York, at Philharmonic Hall on December 6, 1964, when Robert conducted *Abraham and Isaac* (American première) with Andrew Foldi as the baritone, and Stravinsky engaged in his famous onstage study period. This time it was "S. Hurok has the honor to present," and with that office absorbing some of the promotional costs, no one was ruined, and we came out even. The concert was artistically successful as well, and was subsequently presented at Boston's Symphony Hall by Aaron Richmond, and in Constitution Hall in Washington by Patrick Hayes. An added feature in New York was the surprise (unadvertised) four-minute appearance by violinist Isaac Stern in Stravinsky's exquisite little *Pastorale*, composed in 1907 and dedicated to Rimsky-Korsakov's daughter Nadia. It was a sentimental moment for Stravinsky, who sat with his wife and me, concealed from view in the one-way-vision broadcasting room overhanging the stage. As for Mr. Stern, who had flown in for these four minutes from a concert engagement in the Middle West, whither, with his world-famous vigor, he flew back when his miniature tribute was over, he was— in one word—superb.

Stravinsky read one Simenon mystery on our train to Washington for that concert, and another on the return trip, while Robert worked on passages for *Themes and Episodes*. Mrs. Stravinsky had remained in New York, and the three of us stopped this time at the Hay-Adams House, where the bathrooms—always a point of interest—were equipped with large shaving mirrors on flexible gates; one could achieve facial perfection by a twist of the wrist, even while lying at a 180-degree-angle in the bathtub. Stravinsky and I spent fifteen minutes trying to figure out a way of detaching the contraption without leaving fingerprints, but, alas, the Hay-Adams administration knew the treasure they possessed and had taken ample precautions. We entertained the local manager, Patrick Hayes, his wife and some of the singers and musicians at a late supper in the suite, presided over by the distinguished host, illustrious in white pajamas. The atmosphere was gay, although Constitution Hall, that memorial to the Daughters of the American Revolution, displayed over three hundred empty seats. "They should have advertised a Republican Concert," said Stravinsky.

Vancouver in 1965 was also a high point, for its incomparable scenery and hospitality as well as the ovations. Even the gas stations carried banners reading "Welcome to Igor Stravinsky." The Bay-Shore Inn, noted for its magnificent panorama of the Vancouver mountains, was our hotel, and Stravinsky sat in the morning gazing out of the picture window for long periods of time. But a trip to the zoo, piloted by Lawrence Morton, who had come from Hollywood to be with us, had to be made in a wheel-chair. Stravinsky was thinner by a few pounds at this time, too, and the belt that supported his hernia had become a source of constant trouble. It had never been properly fitted, despite visits from the manufacturer's representative on an average of twice a month, and was prone to slips at odd moments. At the start of the dress rehearsal, notable for a special atmosphere of cheeriness on everyone's part and Stravinsky's little speech about his pleasure at being with the musicians, he had just raised his arm to begin when a look of acute embarrassment came over his face. "Lillian. . . ." As I helped him down from the podium and led him off, trying very hard to conceal his discomfort he turned to the musicians and said, "Forgive me, gentlemen, I must leave the room. Don't go away." When he returned, after Hugh Pickett had proved himself an expert in such crises, the orchestra gave him a hero's cheer.

The managerial rush to secure Stravinsky "for the record" in those final concert years was only one manifestation of the preparation of obituaries. Two important documentary films were also made: David Oppenheim's for CBS, and another by Rolf Liebermann, then director of the Hamburg Staatsoper.* Both were begun and completed in 1965; both were entertaining; both were based on scenarios that combined a "homey" atmosphere with snatches of current professional activities or reminiscences about some long past: Stravinsky at lunch discussing music with interrogators (hardly!); Stravinsky in a limousine enroute to Orchestra Hall in Chicago (yes); Stravinsky seated on a sofa with a beautiful girl holding a microphone to catch his statements on composition (???); Stravinsky addressing a group of ballet "rats" in the Paris Opera House, where *The Rite of Spring* received its famous barrage in 1913 (but surely not in English!); Stravinsky and his wife in Warsaw, viewing the stone commemorating Nazi victims (but only a view and only for the cameras); Stravinsky conducting (why not?), drinking Scotch with a friend (naturally!), wearing a ten-gallon hat in Texas (well . . . !).

Still, these documents have captured on film valuable elements of the public personality of the man and certainly some of the better shots made of this stellar example of photogeneity in his last years. And in the Liebermann film there *are* fleeting glimpses of the "other" Stravinsky. Question: "Do you like to compose?" Answer: "Do you like to be awakened?" And again, "Everyone who creates [music] does harm to something. . . ."

But, oh, for a snapshot of Maestro trying to scuttle after a lizard darting across his driveway; or working hard at gardening (he made one valiant attempt with tools and instructions provided by his wife, and that was the end of his Burbankian experiment); or looking for some of my fudge in the kitchen ("Where are those little black candies you made?"), or carefully selecting the proper pill from a dozen or more bottles, or hiding behind the door of his Hollywood Bowl dressing room to escape the visit of a familiar bore. And where can we find a picture of him checking off the items for his "composition" satchel, or hunting vainly for a dollar to give to a porter, or— later—wearing an expression as dogged as that of a mountain climber while he walked in circles around his little porch to bring some life back into his legs!

Stravinsky was fully aware that he had progressed from being "excellent copy" to the status of "historic copy." He had never underestimated his importance in the permanent scheme of things. This explains the extremely cautious wording that characterizes

* Now of the Paris Opera.

most of his letters, even those to close friends. When there was general correspondence that absolutely demanded a direct reply from him, and he would complain that he had no time for such matters, his wife would point out that all he need do was write a little note. "But I *cannot* write just a little note. I have to take time to think *carefully*. This idiot will *quote* me, if not now, then later." He was thus abstemious with written words, for he had been burned more than once, and badly.* And he was always cautious with anything that required his autograph. The speed and thoroughness with which he examined items offered to him for this purpose, to make certain they were harmless, and without arousing any suspicion in the profferer, equaled that of a well-trained treasury agent watching for counterfeit at the cashier's desk in a cut-rate department store. And he guarded even his discards: what went into his wastebasket was shredded into such minuscule fragments as might be found in heaps of dust. In short, he would give away, in words or on paper, only what he wished to give away, and that is why it will always be easy to determine the authentic ownership of his manuscripts or sketch pages: they must be inscribed in his hand, or the conclusion may be made that *he* did not actually give them.

But he submitted (for a good-sized fee) to his destiny in the archives and annals, and he suppressed his annoyance, in public at least, at being followed everywhere for weeks by an entourage of film-makers and technicians, always keeping his commercial-smile file handy. In private he was not so pliant. At the time of the world première of *Variations* with the Chicago Symphony, one of the document-makers arrived with director and crew to capture as many informal sequences as possible during the five-day stay in that city. On the morning after our arrival at the Ambassador East, Stravinsky gave me a small piece of white paper (still among my treasures) on which he had written down his exact calculations of time allowable for the intrusion of the cameras. Apparently he had had second thoughts about an original fifteen-minute allocation, for this figure was crossed out and above it "thirty minutes bet. 11 and

---

* "Music is powerless to express anything at all." This statement, made at Harvard during his delivery of the Charles Eliot Norton Lectures, kept cropping up to annoy him throughout his life. He tried often, but without success, to explain that the statement was made in an offhand manner and was incomplete. What he had meant was that music expressed *itself* (cf. *Expositions and Developments*, New York: Doubleday, pp. 114–15).

half AM" was noted down—obviously a princely amount of time in *his* book. I gently reminded him that films required many more takes than recordings because of the lights alone, but concealed the fact (as I marked time until Mrs. Stravinsky or Robert arrived to support me) that the corridor outside his suite was already jammed with cables, cameras, carrying cases, lamps, and hordes of crew. He replied that the producers had certainly secured sufficient footage of him in Austin, Texas (where, at the beginning of the year, Robert had conducted a concert at the university), and, furthermore, complete with cowboys and other Lone Star paraphernalia—enough to make ten films, in fact; he added conclusively, "No explanation is needed. That is *all* the time I have."

I escaped those lying in wait, going by various back routes to the hotel beauty parlor, but there the producer and director finally ferreted me out, adorned with curlers (unfair!), and reminded me of the fee that was being paid to their star. The reminder was unnecessary; I had sought that cosmetic haven to think of a diplomatic way in which to bring this very point home to the man who considered the stipend an overpayment for anyone else's, but a picayune one for *his*, time.

A method of securing my cooperation that always produced a rise in my temperature was then employed. The director suddenly decided that this film could not be a success without my appearance in at least two or three sequences. Such offers were not unusual in the course of my association with Stravinsky, and nothing made me angrier—less because it was matter-of-factly assumed that I was along to secure whatever personal publicity I could get than because of the implication that I was stupid enough to be taken in. Stravinsky was conscious of my strong feelings in this regard, and he could detect the approach of "unseen" cameramen in airports, lobbies, and at stage doors when he felt my grip on his arm loosen as I tried to sidle out of range.

Several times he mischievously held fast. At a reception during one of his Toronto engagements, as government officials moved forward to greet us—Mrs. Stravinsky was on Robert's arm, just ahead of Stravinsky and me—and cameras started to click, we had a real tug-of-war, which he won by announcing: "Gentlemen, this is Miss Libman, my dear friend. She has official titles as well, but they don't matter." Knowing looks pursued us to the receiving line, and he whispered to me with relish, "Now everyone in Canada will think

there is something between us!" There always was someone who
did, of course, in addition to the occasional "sightless" stranger who
would address me as "Mrs. Stravinsky." At a dinner party high up
in the Hollywood spurs—an affair, incidentally, carried out entirely
in shades of yellow: yellow sauce on yellow shrimps, yellow squash,
yellow ice cream, and yellow candles jaundicing everyone's com-
plexion—a chlorotic gentleman, whose ownership of large portions
of Beverly Hills real estate was deemed sufficient justification for a
loud-mouthed lack of manners, leaned across the table, addressing
me, at Stravinsky's left, thus: "If that's his *wife* down there"—pointing like Uncle Sam in the posters—"what are *you* to *him?*" Maestro:
"She's my governess."

PART II

1965–1971

As for this place, it is clearly a holy one,
Shady with vines and olive trees and laurel:
Snug in their wings within, the nightingales
Make a sweet music. Rest on this rough stone.
It was a long road for an old man to travel.

Sophocles, *Oedipus at Colonus*
(translated by Robert Fitzgerald)

CHAPTER TEN

BEFORE the Stravinskys moved into their new Wetherly Drive house in the fall of 1964, whenever I came to Los Angeles I would rent a small hotel-apartment on Sunset Boulevard, about five minutes away from them and almost directly across the street from the S. Hurok Building, which housed our West Coast offices. But from 1965 on, if I was with the Stravinskys for prolonged periods, I lived below their living room in a huge guest room, furnished with a fireplace, a grand piano, and stacks of records and books, as well as bedroom appurtenances. This room was also sometimes used by Robert for rehearsing singers or choruses. A short staircase brought one up to the living areas, and a door led into the back garden.

The house, which had belonged to the late Baroness d'Erlanger, was not pretentious in the Hollywood sense. That is, its white stucco two storys and basement occupied about half an acre of land rather than twenty-five or more; it did not have a swimming pool at the time the Stravinskys acquired it; and it was equipped with only a modest back patio, on whose far side stood another small, white, two-story structure containing Mrs. Stravinsky's studio and Robert's second-floor living quarters. Like the old Stravinsky house, the new one was of indeterminate architecture (no Mies van der Rohe or Frank Lloyd Wright here), and, in truth, with its black, grainy roof and occasional eaves it would have been a far more familiar sight in a Westchester or New England suburb than in that territory of cliff-hanging regional designs. A great deal of remodeling was necessary, the aging baroness having preferred to adjust her life to the comfort of a dozen or more cats; floors, walls, doors were ripped out; new plumbing and new kitchen equipment installed; and several small rooms made into fewer large ones. Within the first year a swimming pool was sunk into the rather narrow area at the rear of the house, between the patio and the downhill next-door neighbor's hedges;

and from his bedroom window, or the little upstairs porch adjoining his small office, Stravinsky could watch his wife and Robert take their late-afternoon watery exercise. He never used the pool himself; in fact, he had never learned to swim well, his fear of water dating back to his childhood.

Six months were required for reconstructing and remodeling (the house had been purchased in February), during which the touring schedule was reasonably full. In April 1964 we went to Ann Arbor for performances of *Perséphone* with the Philadelphia Orchestra (Robert conducted *Symphony in C*), and there we were joined briefly by the Soulima Stravinskys, whom I met then for the first time. Soulima, in his mid-fifties, resembled his father remarkably (although, later, I found Theodore even more like his parent despite his taller, heavier physique). I thought him a very quiet, almost introverted man, and somewhat detached even in conversation with Stravinsky. His wife, Françoise, an extremely attractive Frenchwoman and a testimonial to the "opposites attract" theory, was vivacious and amusing. One could never have guessed that she had not long before suffered a serious illness. Her son John (whom I was to meet later that year in Chicago, during the Ravinia engagement) was obviously the center of her existence; he was the chief subject of discussion during the visit. Concern was expressed by John's mother because he had taken it into his head to become an actor, and she was not at all sure she and Soulima were right in allowing him to pursue this career. Both Stravinskys evinced only mild interest in that maternal digression—grandfather merely pursing his lips, and step-grandmother commenting with unusual cynicism, "Then you will have to support him for a long time." I was struck by a certain lack of cordiality in their tones toward any mention of the grandson (and, in fact, even more by the very reserved attitude toward this particular family). But then Mrs. Stravinsky had frequently been heard to remark that neither she nor her husband were very generous grandparents—they neglected both birthdays and Christmas unless John's actual presence brought the "necessity" to mind.

There were a few hysterical moments at Ann Arbor when Robert could not find his score (the *Symphony in C*) after the performance; he sat biting his nails in the dressing room while a dozen of us hunted vainly through every other score in the librarian's possession. It was finally discovered in Stravinsky's rehearsal bag from which, at the height of our panic, the composer withdrew it with an air of Jovian calm—and to this day no one knows how it arrived there. But Robert must have lost at least two pounds.

A long and dull limousine drive from Ann Arbor (with Robert and a music-department friend leading the way in another car) brought us to Toronto for several days of recording with Columbia at Massey Hall, and after this the Stravinskys came back to New York for a short time before returning to Hollywood on May 19. We then talked long-distance almost daily, and it was apparent that Mrs. Stravinsky was appalled at the enormous job of packing that faced her. Thoughts of the books alone almost put her into a decline, as they would have anyone (ten thousand plus!) but she would not listen to my pleas that her wrapping of hundreds of small packages, containing eight or ten volumes each, carefully bundled in newspaper covers and secured by special cord from "Koontz's, an absolutely ma-a-a-arvelous hardware store on Santa Monica," was taking the food out of the mouths of moving companies.

In June I met the trio in Denver for the weather-washed concerts and after that brought them East again, where they took off for London to record *The Rake's Progress* in four intensive days. A return to Ravinia and then another transatlantic flight to Jerusalem were accomplished before they saw Hollywood again at the end of August. I was already on the West Coast, and I found Stravinsky on his arrival exhausted and nervously anticipating the move. He hated change, although most of the time it had a benign effect on him, manifested in increasing spurts of energy. But he had loved the old house dearly: his studio was arranged exactly to his liking, and he would have been content to stay there forever. Moreover, and very disturbing, his quarters would now be on the second floor, a trial because he detested staircases. Two more catastrophes were the imminent retirement of Mrs. Gate and the passing of the ancient Céleste, who had been "put to sleep." "Murder was committed here today," Robert told me on the phone after the merciful execution had taken place. "That's what *he* feels."

Stravinsky had paid only one or two brief visits to his new property, nearby though it was; his sense of order bespoke a preference for "after" views rather than the "before" ones that architects, builders, painters, and decorators always keep in brochures as testaments to the incredible miracles they have wrought. But the wisdom of investing in that neighborhood had been explained by the lawyers and real estate agents, and the moderate purchase price was attractive. In any case, who could have predicted at that time that the discreet portion of Sunset Strip (which lay just below North Wetherly Drive) would ever countenance the intrusion of hippies, flower children, and that colorful personnel which composes the narcotics industry? Also, Stravinsky recognized the convenience of additional space, especially for his wife, who now had her own bedroom, extra closets, and an efficient kitchen. Her almost childlike delight was sufficient reason for him to overcome his own irritation.

My presence provided an excuse for everyone to make a tour of the as yet unfinished premises. We found Jack Quinn, the construction engineer, eating a sandwich while comfortably seated on a pile of plaster sherds in the dining room, and he guided us over the mountains of archeological remains. Jack, who had been recommended by Miranda, was a very good-looking young man possessing a brilliant smile, no intellectual complications, a completely ingenuous nature, and a quantity of nervous-type patience. He had successfully built or remodeled several houses in the Laurel Canyon area, and from the moment he took on the Stravinsky project until the last time he saw us at the Essex House, only a few months before the composer's death, he single-mindedly dedicated himself to the Stravinskys' comfort. He had, in fact, practically destroyed himself along with the old floors and walls, by accomplishing in six months what a less sanguine but more business-minded firm would have taken a year and a half to achieve. During his conducted tour all I could think of was a champion beagle puppy who had graduated from the Flagg Dog School and was anxious to show that his diploma had been won fairly. "Maestro . . . look here! for your scores, see . . . isn't this nice? . . . over here, all these shelves . . . do you like it? . . . and see, your piano goes here . . . the light will come over your shoulder . . . it's nice, isn't it? . . . and this, for your medicines, waterproof. . . ." And Maestro, jacket characteristically slung across his shoulders, behaved exactly as a Master Trainer should (short of patting his servitor's head), pointing admiringly with his cane at vinyl-covered counters, new French windows, built-in cabinets, and never once asking the price of anything. Jack was transported beyond the bounds of the Seven Heavens.

The family moved in finally on September 8, *sans* assistance from Mayflower, the Seven Santini Brothers, Allied Van Lines, or other union members. For furniture, bric-a-brac, china, silver, pictures, lamps, wardrobe, and the entire library were transported from Number 1260 to Number 1218 by Jack, a station wagon, and two or three assistant pixies. Such items as could not be accommodated in the "do-it-urself" hauler (Stravinsky's upright studio piano, for example), were propelled by hand down the hill on dollies. It was an incredible act of devotion not included in the bill.

Jack was truly one of the unsung heroes of Stravinsky's final years in Hollywood, and I will never forget his aid and comfort. He lived on the crest of an adjoining hill in one of his own creations, containing an unforgettable bathroom that could have been used as a movie set for the jungle retreat of the heroine of *Green Mansions*. His unlisted number was inscribed on a memo pad placed in every room of the Stravinsky house. Should a rainstorm cause the trees hanging over the composer's studio to shed too many leaves, a call to Jack and the vagabonds would be eliminated before they could float down to the driveway. A blistered awning rope, a recalcitrant window pull, a clogged drain, a jammed ice-tray recovered competence in seconds after he appeared on the scene. Later he also chauffeured nurses, found them apartments, took them to dinner. Jack was agile, motiveless, and, like so many others who ask little, taken for granted.

When the Stravinskys returned from Europe in June 1965, the composer was not well. The journey behind the Iron Curtain to Warsaw had been without even the minor luxuries of travel (as well as fully encumbered by the documentary film-makers), and I was informed that the atmosphere had not been cheerful, albeit interesting because of the superior quality of the musicians and some stimulating meetings with Polish composers. Disillusionment with European concerts was beginning to cast its shadow, as a letter from Robert on June 6 out of Paris indicated: the trip had been a financial disaster, the $1,000 in *zlotys* had covered expenses in Warsaw (only!) because prices were the same as those at the Pierre, and the automobile hired to convey the party to Switzerland and back had cost more than $3,000 (!) . . . *Ergo*, about $12,000 in expenses for only $800 in income. Another major disappointment was the very low figure—forty thousand dollars—which the sale of the old Stravinsky house had brought (advisors had "promised" twice that sum). Mrs. Stravinsky had been disgusted and restless, counting the days until she could flee to Paris, and thence to her new home, in which, incidentally, the trio had spent little more than three weeks out of their four months of residence. In New York, she privately begged me to control any enthusiasms for additional concert engagements during the forthcoming year, with which plea I already had great sympathy. Not less worrisome was the schedule for the remainder of the year, which still involved all that travel to Muncie, Ravinia, Vancouver; then a long recording period in Hollywood and a Hollywood Bowl concert; then another trip to London for a concert and recording in Festival Hall. Still more recordings were to be carried out in New York thereafter.

Stravinsky was very depressed. He wanted to cancel London, where we had written a contract with a new impresario, Robert Paterson, who expected him to conduct *The Rite of Spring*. It was perfectly clear that he would be unable to undertake this work, always strenuous even for conductors much younger than he. In fact, Robert had written me from Warsaw that the plans to have Oppenheim film Stravinsky conducting the *Rite* had had to be restricted to a "take" of two measures. Now the composer was complaining not only of an increased stiffness in his leg, but for the first time about trouble with his eyes, although that difficulty did not then appear to arise from any more serious cause than the need for a new refraction. But the leg was indeed much worse, and his walk had changed radically, with the drag of the left foot very marked. "I did not conduct well in Warsaw," he told me one day, almost apologetically. "I did not feel well. . . . I do not *see* well." I was accustomed to frequent reports of bad digestion, hernia trouble, diarrhea; they were part and parcel of the Stravinsky picture, and any of us who were around for very long was sure to come down with some, if not all, of these symptoms. But those new complaints were not typical in their pointed admission of weakness, and thus they were alarming. Robert had indeed written from Paris that Stravinsky's conducting in Warsaw had been very vague, but by the time they had reached the French capital, just before the return to New York, he told me that Stravinsky was in "good shape." Nevertheless, others shared my unrest, for a letter from Rufina Ampenoff, Stravinsky's protector at the London office of Boosey & Hawkes, who had seen the travelers in Paris, commented with definite concern on the composer's weariness and general appearance of strain.

The Vancouver concerts were over on June 14. We all returned to Hollywood, and a day later I flew back to New York. This time it was particularly difficult to leave Stravinsky. The evening before my departure, when I came to his room to bid him good night, he looked at me reproachfully and said, "Why must you go? There will be no one here to help me with my 'little things,' " an expression that covered everything from important letters to trips to the movies. But my own garden was in disorder, and I had to return home, where I, too, had spent barely five weeks in six months. Edwin Allen was then living in Hollywood, and had been a great help. He had already begun to arrange the library and was assisting Stravinsky in sorting out the contents of dozens of cartons of papers and files, but he did not wish to settle permanently in California, and was making plans to come east. Ed, then in his late twenties, was quiet, shy, and gifted with a genius for avoiding all arguments, a self-discipline I often wished I possessed. He worshiped Mrs. Stravinsky, as indeed did every young man who fell within the range of her wonderful smile and enormous eyes, and his respectful adoration was also good for her spirits. Catering to the whims of two temperamental gentlemen who, more often than not, forgot she was a person in her own right, could have a very demoralizing effect. Ed cheered her, encouraged her in her own work, listened to her problems, assisted in innumerable ways.

But I had been in New York no more than a week when a joint telephone call from Mrs. Stravinsky and Robert summoned me back. The principal difficulty appeared to be anxiety brought on by the forthcoming eleven-session Columbia recording schedule, which would begin on August 19. Then there was a Hollywood Bowl concert on September 2, and though this would not be too difficult, the usual period of concert neuroticism had to be muddled through. Robert was hard at work on the final stages of the fifth volume of the "collaborations," and was barely visible. There was no servant, no driver, no secretary, no organizer, no *confidante*. Forty-eight hours later I was on a plane to Los Angeles for the first of several long visits with the Stravinskys. At this point, the four of us had been associated for six years, but it was only after I had lived near them for a few weeks that I began really to understand Robert's position in that household.

When my taxi pulled into the Stravinsky driveway at three o'clock on a hundred-degree afternoon, Mrs. Stravinsky, looking very Polynesian in an orange-and-black-printed *muu-muu*, was attempting to drag, from the front seat of the black Lincoln Continental (a new white one stood just in front of it), two supermarket grocery bags that would have vanquished an expert weight-lifter. As I rushed to help her before gravity added milk, ginger ale, rice, blueberries, and cheese to another heap of parcels already in front of the open door, she dazzled me with her dimples, two kisses, and (I hoped) a *non sequitur:* "I am so glad to see you! We have no cook." While we unloaded what seemed to be the entire stock of the local supermarket, I was brought up to date. Her husband was in a terrible mood, being acutely worried about his condition and even more about the imminence of the recording sessions, which he did not think he would have the strength to endure. A heavy burden fell on Robert, who would be responsible for most of the preparation, and Robert's mood was even worse. His book had a rapidly approaching deadline; he was writing day and night; the part-time decipherer of his handwriting lived several miles away near Westwood and the typescript had to be ferried back and forth by car, for which task Robert had no time; he was touchy, jumpy, and "soooo impossible even to talk to. . . . Life is *Hell.* I will run away."

Poor dear Madame! Her run-away projects cropped up on an average of once a week in those days and were never fulfilled, because on her way to some far-off land in her car, her attention would be attracted by a florist's shop displaying a new plant for her garden, or she would pass her art-supply dealer's and remember something she needed, or (woe!) she would spot the candy-striped facade of a Will Wright Ice Cream parlor, advertising loganberry as the month's special flavor. But the lament that surpassed all, so sorrowful in its tone that it would have moved the heart of a sphinx, was: "I never, never have time to paint!"

I sent her off to her studio, and opened every window in the house, all of which were closed, with blinds drawn, to express the prevailing temper of those within, and then I settled down to life with the Stravinskys. The comfortable residence that Jack had built, or rather remodeled, was equipped with a multitude of French, dormer, and picture-size windows—one of the first things one noticed—and the light thus admitted was underscored by white walls throughout, save for a yellow-countered kitchen and black ceiling-to-floor bookshelves in the first-floor library, immediately to the right of the front door as one entered. A spacious reception hall at the end of a small front entrance corridor led to the dining and living areas, as well as to a small den, also furnished with book-shelves and sometimes used as an office. Doors at either end of the dining room opened onto the kitchen and a conservatory. To the right of the reception hall a stairway, broken by a landing with more books, ascended to the second floor. The door to Stravinsky's studio was directly to the left at the top of the stairs, with the entrance to his wife's bedroom just opposite, across a narrow hallway. The composer had perfect solitude here, for he could pass from his bedroom at the rear through his spacious bathroom and into the studio. The door to his tiny office, across from his sleeping quarters, was partially concealed by a jutting wood-and-glass-fronted bookcase, and could be reached in two quick steps, so that even if he chose to enter it when other people were on the second floor, he could easily escape their attention. The upstairs terrace was accessible through either his office or Mrs. Stravinsky's bedroom. The same staircase led down from the first floor to the guest rehearsal room, which also had the virtue of privacy because of its own egress to the back garden and the swimming pool.

The only area that did not really remind me of the old house was the living room. Miranda had helped Mrs. Stravinsky to arrange it rather handsomely, but its white brocaded sofas and chairs, gold rug, Louis Quinze *fauteuils,* and black or white marble-topped tables always seemed to me a little overdecorated for this particular family, where elegance and formality had their perfect expression in the head of the household. Nevertheless, Mrs. Stravinsky's paintings, some Stravinsky-collected *faïence,* and a three-paneled screen covered with a blown-up photograph Mrs. Stravinsky had taken of the Villa Manin, with her husband on a bridge in the foreground, made the room familiar, although except when visitors came only one corner was put to much use. This, near a row of French doors facing the front garden, was equipped with an antique walnut game table on which patience was played and tea served, and around which Scotch was consumed before dinner. Sometimes Stravinsky would examine books of photographs here with his wife, or listen while she read snatches of Russian poetry to him in a melodic sing-song that was itself poetic. To me that little niche represented what the Stravinskys meant by "cozy"—or perhaps it was just the sight of their two heads close together, sharing the complete privacy of a forty-five-year-old relationship, that made me feel this way.

There were other corners, too, that filled this "intimate" requirement. At one end of the conservatory (so titled because of three gargantuan philodendrons, cultivated from slips by Mrs. Stravinsky and now ungratefully threatening to pierce the ceiling), an enormous, overstuffed, pillow-laden sofa attracted everyone with its promise of sensuous comfort. Stravinsky liked to curl up here occasionally for his after-lunch nap (voluntarily, those days, and not, as later, necessarily, when the staircase had become a painful obstacle), and there he would snooze, lost in cushions and peace. A rare Coptic textile (the Stravinskys owned several of these works of art) with strange hieratic–looking figures in black and ochre decorated the back of the sofa, antimacassar-fashion, and the picture of him lying there beneath it always brought to my mind the painted scenes of sleeping saints decorating the walls of the great Byzantine church at Mistra. (The conservatory was later made notable by a stentorian-voiced canary who had no respect for these daylight dozes, and had to be silenced with premature darkness produced by one of Stravinsky's old sweaters.)

The library, of course, was one of the most frequented cozy corners. Here, during the day, mail was examined, packages opened, or study carried on. A long, rectangular Venetian-style trestle table with a marbleized paper top and some captain's chairs were the principal furniture, and after dinner we would sit here while Robert played recorded music, which he and Stravinsky followed with scores. In 1965 we were listening almost nightly to Mozart, especially *Don Giovanni*. Preparation for these sessions included the padding of Stravinsky's chair with pillows—no one can sit on an unadorned captain's chair for two hours—and making certain that several quarts of milk were handy. Record-playing induced in Robert an unholy thirst for this beverage, which Mrs. Stravinsky and I tried vainly to analyze. One conclusion, offered by her, was that his system, having undergone a total catharsis through the music, demanded the calcium in milk as a binder!

Mrs. Stravinsky usually worked on her needlepoint during the "performances," and several handsome scatter-rugs of her own design, in the reception hall, living room, and den, were products of these evenings in the library. The music was always played at full volume (providing entertainment, welcome or unwelcome, up and down North Wetherly Drive), and after a half-hour or so my hostess would leave, remarking that she could hear it just as well upstairs. There, undisturbed, she would return the telephone calls that had come in during her hours in the studio, when I would rarely permit anyone to disturb her. Or she would switch on her television, tuck herself up on her blue-brocaded sofa-bed, and have a good time with "that new funny woman Carol Burnett" or her non-variety favorite, "Mr. District Attorney." Her reasons for abandoning the cultural scene were specific: "I like to listen when *I* like to listen. But when Bob starts talking about *this* modulation and *that* figuration, then I want to watch television!"

Stravinsky's studio naturally fulfilled his own prerequisites for coziness, and he had arranged it as much like the one in the old house as possible. It was roomier, however, and some of the pieces of furniture had been moved to other areas—among them the beloved red and white goose-down-filled sofa, now taking up a large part of his rather small bedroom. The area for drafting, complete with drawing-boards, clip-boards, and tables filled with that celebrated and infinite assemblage of implements for the transference of his thoughts to manuscript paper, was located near the stair-side wall and backed by a long credenza. His piano was at right angles to the wall opposite, receiving its light from a window behind him as he sat at the keyboard. A corner was devoted to a two-door, waist-high cabinet on which he kept the portrait photograph of his friend the late Pope John, for whom he had hoped to perform his 1948 *Mass*. Various medals and honors, and the State Department citation, also occupied this surface.

On top of another glass-enclosed book cabinet, containing his portfolios of sketches, stood his bust in bronze, executed by his longtime friend and personal physician Dr. Max Edell, and next to it an eighteenth-century urn of white Höchst porcelain in a reticulated design, enameled in blue and gold. (It was later transferred to the living room fireplace mantel.) This was the gift of Willy Brandt, who had presented it during one of Stravinsky's trips to West Germany. It had been carefully carried to New York by Mrs. Stravinsky in an airline handbag and had landed, to her astonished despair, in one thousand pieces. My husband, whose work as an appraiser of fine art brought him into contact with all manner of craftsmen, found a Japanese artisan who reconstructed the object with such skill that its fractured state defied microscopic detection. Stravinsky called it his "Chinese puzzle" and told my husband that he now regarded it as a "superior example of Oriental art." Another valuable object on display was a pre-Christian-era long-necked

amphora of greenish glass, found in the Dead Sea area, and given
to the composer by Teddy Kollek, the mayor of Jerusalem. Framed
photographs of Weber, Schubert, Mendelssohn; pictures of Stravinsky with Ravel and with Debussy; a photograph of Webern;
two pictures of Wagner (one a reproduction of the Renoir painting); and a dozen other mementos of composers were arranged
about the room on shelves and on the walls. Two of Picasso's
sketches of Stravinsky, together with one by his son Theodore,
were included in a long rectangular frame; another large one held
the famous Cocteau caricature, drawn in white lines on black
paper, of Cocteau, Diaghilev, Sert, and Stravinsky. A small straw
crucifix of the Mexican *arte popular* hung above another credenza,
and several icons occupied more surfaces. On the wall to the left
of the entrance door an Italian carved-wood hand, holding an electric bulb in the form of a torch, jutted from the wall.

Stravinsky's long-established daily routine had apparently changed
in one major respect by 1965: during my stay he spent less time
at work in the evenings, which formerly had often been devoted
to correspondence or sometimes passed in the studio. Now he preferred to relax with his "family," read, or listen to music. Otherwise he observed the regimen he had set down for himself years
before. Breakfast was taken in his room, and during the "cookless"
days I would bring it to him around eight-thirty. It still consisted
of tea and toast and, occasionally, oatmeal; but sometimes he would
gulp down two raw eggs, tossing his head back with a gesture of
abandon that both startled and horrified me, especially at that hour
of the morning, when one is unprepared for idiosyncrasies of diet.
Mrs. Stravinsky, already dressed and ready to leave for her studio,
usually came to say *bonjour* during this repast. She has always
been an early riser, often starting not only her own day but that
of the local greengrocer before eight o'clock.

After breakfast, if the postman made an early visit, I would
screen the mail, removing any letters to the composer that looked
as though they might be disturbing. I had strict instructions about
such mail (especially during the composing periods), which was
turned over to Robert or Mrs. Stravinsky, who would then decide
about the judiciousness of giving it over to the addressee. Letters
from friends or acquaintances enclosing bad reviews or questioning
some article that had appeared, or letters whose return addresses
immediately identified the writers as troublemakers, were on the

contraband list. But I always gave him letters from Russian correspondents or from Souvchinsky or from his children. Also, I never failed to turn over his royalty statements or anything that had to do with his business, no matter how unpredictable the contents. He knew exactly when such statements were due, and if they were a day late, a correspondence was bound to ensue, sometimes even by cable or telegram. The mail had a range from demands for hard cash to original manuscripts, and was always crammed with requests for autographs, signed photographs, questionnaires from students and professors. I removed those in the first two categories that did not contain self-addressed, stamped envelopes (wastebasket!), and the remainder would be given to him. Once or twice a week he would sign such a batch of such requests. Many of the questionnaires went to Robert, but Stravinsky would himself acknowledge, or dictate replies to, letters including original scores, drawings, poems, and other small gifts (one lady regularly sent him ten dollars every birthday!).

By ten o'clock he would be in his studio, and almost immediately Bach would make his presence known, sending faint greetings through the tightly shut door from Stravinsky's muted, slightly out-of-tune upright. The composer began every day of his life by playing two or three fugues from the *Well-Tempered Clavier;* were they his daily prayers? After that there would be silence, and one could deduce from this that the mornings were the periods of ideas. As twelve-thirty approached, the piano might sound again— a single note or chord struck several times (if he liked the sound, this could keep on for several minutes)—rarely more music than that. At that point I would stop my own work on Robert's manuscripts, or on correspondence, orders, telephone calls, which I conducted in the first-floor library or den—I rarely used the little upstairs office while he was in the studio, for fear the sounds of the typewriter or of telephone conversations might reach him. His ear was so highly sensitive that the sliding of a file drawer, I discovered, might prompt him to open the studio door with annoyance. After those few notes, silence would prevail, usually until one o'clock.

The summons to lunch was given by Mrs. Stravinsky, back from her own workshop or from an excursion to Beverly Hills or the Farmer's Market. She would stand at the bottom of the staircase and clap her hands together smartly three times. Her husband would emerge immediately, almost as though he had been waiting for this signal, get a firm purchase on the balustrade, and descend with great care. Coming down was always more difficult for him than going up; he was fearful but courageous, and it was not until two years later that he began to require the extra assurance of a supporting arm.

The lady of the house would then open the screen door leading from the conservatory, breathe deeply, and shout "Bob" across the patio. We would then sit down to lunch. Two such shouts later (from me, this time) would be followed by the distant slamming of a door and a sound like sticks being loudly dragged along a picket fence, and Robert would arrive, clutching books, clippings from newspapers, and always ten or twelve thickly-covered, hand-written pages of yellow paper (he never used white, it was too glaring for his eyes), which he would drop on the typewriter in the office before he took his place at the table, not wishing to upset my digestion by handing them to me.

I came to know that if the piano had given out forenoon sounds, Stravinsky was apt to be in a very good humor and complimentary about everything, even on one experimental occasion when I produced a Waring Blendor *gazpacho* so full of olive oil it would have repelled a Spanish peasant. Enthroned on a white-and-green-cushioned wrought-iron chair (the dining room was charmingly furnished in garden style), padded with the inevitable extra pillows, he would inaugurate the lunch hour with a kiss of greeting for each of us, and follow this up with a toast from his half-water-half-Scotch-one-ice-cube-filled glass.

Lunch was normally the first time of the day any of us would set eyes on Robert (his life began at ten-thirty or eleven with breakfast in his rooms, and lasted until two or three in the morning), and he would deliver a *précis* of news events as reported in the *New York Times*, the London *Times*, and the *Los Angeles Times*, to which everyone except Stravinsky listened intently; or he would give us ten-minute reviews of a batch of books that had arrived the day before, and which he always seemed to have read thoroughly, though when, I have absolutely no idea.

When Stravinsky's humor was exceedingly good, Robert might also secure an answer or two to questions on which the "conversations" in the books were based, or which provided a theme for the "interviews." If the composer showed no inclination to enter into any discussion, as often was the case, Robert would adopt the

Hollywood Bowl, 1965

Daily constitutional, Hollywood

Green Thumbs outside Madame's
studio

© Arnold Newman

The cast at home in Hollywood

Poetry or Scotch?—with Yevtushenko, Madame, and the author, Hollywood

Historic encounter: *Perséphone* rehearsal, 1947. Left to right: Claudio Spies, Walter Hendl, Lukas Foss, the composer, James Fassett, Robert Craft

Repose — Santa Fe, 1963

Acapulco bound, 1961

We talk backstage—Musical Director's office, Academy of Music, Philadelphia, 1964

We scan United Airlines' friendly skies while Robert talks with directors

With Carlos Chávez
— Mexico City air-
port, April 1961

With Leonard Bernstein and Carlos Moseley—Bauer Grünwald,
Venice, 1960

With S. Hurok, at home in
Hollywood

Reverie with score— Los Angeles

Bach at the Essex House, November 1969
Miriam Pollack

'ork goes on—New York hospital,
69

Venice, April 15, 1971: front row, left to right: Rita Christiansen, Robert Craft, Mrs. Stravinsky, Nicolas Nabokov, Theodore, Milène, Soulima, John, Kitty, Denise

A corner of his last room, Fifth Avenue, May 1971

San Zanipolo, Façade July 1971

San Michele, June 1971

technique of expanding on the idea himself, knowing that if there were any objection to his conclusions, we would all hear about it promptly. Otherwise mealtime was generally concerned with household problems, plans for the evening, the morning's correspondence, or, when Miranda dropped in, as she very often did for coffee, all the news of the film colony, The Bistro, the Bel Air set.

But there were occasions when the morning had not satisfied the composer. He would then sit silent and brooding over his plate, eating mechanically, unresponsive except if something irritated him, such as the clatter of dishes in the kitchen, the sudden ring of the telephone, or the presence of paper napkins on the table (he had a violent dislike of such efficiencies, which were "only for picnics"). Then he would push dishes aside with violence, or emit deep, heart-rending groans. Once he pounded with his fists on the marble table-top in an agony of frustration, causing a bowl of blueberries to take to the air, but his fabled days of book-throwing and dish-breaking were long since past. Now the rare outbursts only made one wish with all one's heart that they would return.

His wife never acknowledged these moods by so much as a raised eyebrow, but went right on chatting gaily, eating her lunch as leisurely and dreamily as though she were seated alone under a chestnut tree in the middle of a large glen. After a bit, her husband would slide his hand tentatively in her direction (although his head remained bowed), and she *might* give it a tiny pat. She was a living lesson in how to handle *any* man, let alone *this* one.

Stravinsky's afternoon nap was over at about three-forty-five, after which he and I would have a glass of ginger ale together in the studio; or sometimes he would prefer a cup of tea a bit later. Before his health began to decline, he still chose to take this refreshment upstairs, in order not to lose too much time from his afternoon's work. Then his door would be closed again, and now the piano would sound in sustained periods, on and off, until four-thirty or five. What had been conceived in the morning was being put to the test.

No one ever really knew what work he was engaged on during the studio hours. He would never talk about anything before it was finished, out of feelings that were purely superstitious. But Robert has told me that there were times when he would ask his wife to listen to what he had accomplished, and would seek her opinion or watch for its effect on her. On one or two occasions, he also asked Robert to lend an ear, but never before Mrs. Stravinsky.

Milène's visits usually coincided with the end of the studio day. She would come every afternoon and go directly to her father's studio or bedroom for the better part of an hour, stopping on her way out for a chat with Mrs. Stravinsky or with me, if I happened to be staying with them. She also executed commissions for her father: brought sheets of music manuscript to the photostater (a very sacred errand), shopped for special supplies, packed for him when he went on a trip, cut his hair. He always treated her as though she were still a very young girl (she was in her early fifties when I first stayed at the Stravinsky house), and indeed, with her "Irene Castle" clip, pert, youngish face, and high-pitched though not unpleasant voice, phrasing English sentences in a somewhat plaintive manner, she always seemed so to me. Adoration and timidity characterized her whole attitude toward her father, and a harsh or impatient word from him (not at all unusual when someone did not immediately grasp the point of what he was saying) would send her flying from his room to Mrs. Stravinsky's in floods of tears. She spoke French with him (having been brought up in France, it was to her equivalent to a mother tongue), and addressed him as *père*, referring to him thus even in English conversation with others.

Milène was a superb gourmet cook, too (her French husband was something of a connoisseur), and dinners at their house, which I attended twice, were projects to anticipate. Once she spent three days preparing a *paté* of hare as a special treat for her father, though when I knew him he did not take any unusual interest in exotic dishes (and, incidentally, knew little about vintage wines, although he appreciated a good one). He had already arrived at the stage where he chose broiled or poached seafoods or lamb and other viands of this sort for his main course. Milène was talented in other directions as well: her hobby was collecting unusual stones on the seashore, which she tumbled in a spinning drum set up in her workroom at home and polished into exquisite shapes and colors. Stravinsky had several gifts of these, and his pleasure in their beauty and pride in their creator was obvious, since he kept a box of those jasper, hematite, agate, and opaline marvels on a table in his studio, close to the stand on which his manuscript paper was placed, and was fond of pointing it out to the privileged few admitted at his invitation.

Milène's arrival was usually the signal for Mrs. Stravinsky and me to invade the swimming pool for a few moments. And just before the sun left the area, around six or half-past, and the California evening cool began to creep in, Robert would dash down that rickety staircase again, jump in, swim eight laps without pausing, jump out, dash upstairs.

Some days after my arrival, a "non-American" cook of late middle age was engaged, and the kitchen, where Mrs. Stravinsky and I had been stumbling over each other, was entrusted to her, although she had no knowledge of *soufflés, sauce béarnaise, risotto,* or (as it turned out) hamburgers. She did, however, have a *noli mi tangere* manner that brooked no criticism, and this, coupled with her complete lack of English, French, or German (the Stravinskys made their needs known to her in a mixture of Polish, Russian, and Hungarian), forced us to develop a taste for mysterious stews, parboiled potatoes, raw rice, and desserts that should have been called by any other name. Once or twice, Mrs. Stravinsky tried to explain certain simple recipes (such as plain boiled chicken), but this kindly gesture met with such insulted indignation that we ate twice as much on those evenings of what passed for noodle pudding. We also attempted to steal into the kitchen during her rest period (she lived in a bedroom-sitting room suite just below Robert's apartment, converted by Jack from what was formerly the garage portion of the guest building) in the hope that we could prepare something edible like Russian cutlets or *kasha.* Mrs. Stravinsky had even planned what we would say if discovered: that a Russian friend, not knowing of our good fortune in having found a cook, thought she would save us an evening's work. But, alas, the scheme fell through, for like all controllers of kitchens, this one had concealed utensils and implements where geiger counters could not have found them, and the precious time was consumed in hunting instead of cooking. It was a hard period, especially since the food Stravinsky abhorred above all others was this cook's specialty: goulash. Once he made the error of correcting her when she christened it with another title. "I am a lady; do not speak to me that way," she bristled, according to Mrs. Stravinsky's translation, and for a moment it was touch-and-go.

But the Stravinskys put up with it because she was a refugee
(although Robert and I were never certain, in the beginning, from
which side). And she had her virtues: the kitchen was spotless,
and her honesty and thrift extended to saving infinitesimal bits of
string and reusing wrapping paper. This latter quality may have
been the grace that protected her menus from more specific Stravinskyan denunciation, for the composer was a string-and-paper-
saver without equal. Margins of mailing pieces or advertisements
that arrived by post, backs of envelopes received, calling cards
were used for notations, reminders, telephone numbers. He even
wrote letters on smoothed-out paper bags and gave them to me
to type; one such memento, addressed to Signor Tortorella in
Venice, in response to that gentleman's query about two pieces of
Italian music, in one of which he suspected plagiarism from the
other (the composer responded succinctly that the only thing
they had in common was the 4/4 time), was composed on the
inside of a Saks Fifth Avenue bag that had contained new pajamas.
For that reason, more than for the letter itself, the scrap of paper
is very dear to me.

Stravinsky was unable to tolerate weight of any kind when he
slept (a sheet and a light blanket, with *no* tuck-ins, was the rule),
and could wear only the lightest fabric next to his body. These
special pajamas of fine white batiste were periodically purchased
by his wife from the Saks palace on Wilshire Boulevard. The last
batch was, through some error, two sizes too large, and since the
line had been discontinued, I set about altering them until we could
locate some other similar supply. Stravinsky, pajama-clad, would
sit on the edge of his bed for a fitting. He would stretch out one
arm with that ridiculously long sleeve hanging over his hand, so
that I could pin and baste it, and would read Alan Moorehead's
The White Nile, which he held on his knee with the other hand.
Now and then he would stop reading to relate some interesting
fact: Did I know that in Ethiopia the killing of a hippopotamus is
an event as important as a birth or a death? Or did I know that at
the time Napoleon landed in Egypt, the population of that country was a third of what it had been during the days of the
Pharaohs? And each item of information was delivered in a tone
so pregnant with significance that I would memorize the details
as though they comprised a catechism. These sewing-circles did
not occur very often, but they were completely relaxed moments

for both of us, and I truly believe he enjoyed them. As for me, when they were over, I would float out of his room feeling as though I could repair four dozen pajama sleeves in four minutes.

Life with the Stravinskys during the three weeks preceding the 1965 Columbia recording sessions and on my subsequent visits was astonishingly normal. We all had work to do, and all of us worked very hard. Holders of preconceived notions about the environment of genius would have been sorely disappointed, for the pattern was neither glamorous nor exciting. No great intellectual symposia took place in the Stravinsky salon. The friends who came were generally friends of either Mrs. Stravinsky or Robert, and were welcomed by the head of the house for that reason, *when* he chose to see them.

Thus, visits were informal, and frequent visitors consisted mainly of Jack, Lawrence Morton, Miranda, and, of course, the Marions, Dr. and Mrs. Edell, and Stravinsky's attorneys, the Montaperts. Also Bill Brown, an artist and close friend of Mrs. Stravinsky, who lived in Santa Barbara, was a weekly caller. Sometimes, too, Christopher Isherwood and Don Bachardy would come from Santa Monica for dinner. The most regular caller was Miranda, whose house was located on a short street at right angles to, and directly below, the rear of the Stravinsky property. She used a back route to reach the Stravinskys' patio, and would appear unexpectedly at the screen door leading from the conservatory, poking her head in like a mischievous *gamine*—but one who had learned how to be chic. Her coiffure was a sleek, boyish cut, and her clothes, usually designed by the current Hollywood "rage," went from one extreme to the other. One day it would be turtle-neck sweaters that swaddled her entire chin, worn over trousers tailored to a fare-thee-well, and the next day, the most feminine and exotic of *djellabas*. Miranda was nearsighted and always wore thick-lensed, heavy-rimmed glasses, tinted to Stygian darkness. Her wit was sharp and included a cache of stories about the hidden life of Hollywood that sometimes made me think she must have been one of Louella Parsons's secret agents. She was also a mine of useful information in every possible emergency—with apparent access to the best laundresses, the best cooks, the best caterers; to boutiques where nylons, shoes, costume jewelry, neckties, cosmetics, and bonbons were to be had at wholesale prices; and when it came to unlisted addresses or telephone numbers that might have been mislaid, she could materialize them out of her memory, and at the same time give details as to the current whereabouts—Europe, Palm Springs, Mexico, the Aleutians—of the individual in question, and tell you whether that person were on location, or getting a divorce, or having a baby nine months hence. Miranda adored the family, and the house was dotted with little gifts from her that were amusing and useful. One that produced a throaty almost-chuckle from Stravinsky was a white china hot-plate tile, decorated with a large Maltese cat and the legend "In this house even the cat is nervous," and another was a kitchen looking-glass framed exotically in gold and hung with a red velvet sash. Her conversation, carried on in a deep, throaty voice of the type to which the adjective "sexy" is often applied, was never very serious. Most of her other friends were movie stars—Zsa Zsa Gabor, Greer Garson, Doris Day—and Mrs. Stravinsky was no different from most women in her eagerness to know what they did to make them look so young (*I* took notes!). Stravinsky always had an affectionate kiss for Miranda, and she was the one person who could tell a slightly off-color story in his presence without a glance of reproof from him. Generally his nineteenth-century "ladies present" attitude would emerge when such anecdotes were related by others, a rather curious prudishness in a man whose art acknowledged the existence of every possible human emotion and act. But of course for him this type of humor had no "form."

Another very old friend and frequent visitor—though only by telephone—was the widow (since deceased) of the late ballet dancer and choreographer Adolf Bolm. This enchanting elderly lady remains only a voice to me; she had reached the age at which paying calls became too burdensome. But every forenoon the phone would ring and a delicate music-box would tinkle tender inquiries about the health of "dear Igor Fyodorovitch" and "dearest Vera," and then about *my* health and that of Milène and André and anyone else she could think of. I always delivered news of her calls very promptly to Mrs. Stravinsky, who would then begin to upbraid herself for not finding time to visit Mrs. Bolm every day. But since that lady usually telephoned again in the afternoon (forgetting she had called in the morning), Mrs. Stravinsky would make up for her dereliction in an hour-long exchange of "news."

There were occasional out-of-town visitors, too, who might be in Hollywood on business: Goddard Lieberson often, sometimes Balanchine (when his company came West), several times John McClure. And there were, though infrequently, visits from people whom the world has placed in a special category surmounted by the title "celebrity." But the latter cannot be considered an integral part of the pattern of Stravinsky's life in Hollywood in the sixties. Such encounters would occur perhaps half a dozen times a year, and lasted no more than an hour or so.

Routines were otherwise interrupted only by more such ordinary pastimes. Stravinsky made visits to Dr. Edell's office once or twice a week for check-ups or bleedings. The latter, a treatment prescribed for polycythemia, to keep the platelets at a proper level so that clots (threatening thromboses) should not occur, were not looked upon with favor by Stravinsky's East Coast physician, the late Dr. Lewithin. Cross-country calls would take place almost daily, so that the relative merits of each doctor's theory could be weighed and measured as part of the evening's program. (The same would occur, of course, when Stravinsky was at the other side of the continent, in which case Dr. Edell would be the recipient of the calls.) We also visited the optometrist and the dentist, and a sizable portion of time was spent in consultations with the hernia-belt technician.

About a quarter of an hour before cocktail time, Stravinsky and I might take a short walk around the patio, arm in arm, stopping to admire his wife's plumbago and riotous flower beds. An examination of the avocado tree was always included in these promenades. He had a passion for this fruit; I believe he could have subsisted on it for weeks, provided it came from *his* tree. On tour Mrs. Stravinsky often carried in her handbag two or three ripening samples, and these usually arrived at such a point of maturity by the time we reached our destination that I could detect her whereabouts even if she were momentarily lost to view. These walks, the longest of which took us to the rural-type post-box hung on a pole at the end of the driveway (in the event a letter might have escaped my long arm in the morning), were the hour of my wildlife lessons. Stravinsky, on my first visit, was rereading Maeterlinck's *Life of the Bee* (as well as a new book on ant life), and a glimpse of a searcher after honey would lead us into parts of the garden disastrous to footgear, stimulating the caretakers to engage the next day in extra dialogue as they smoothed down disrupted beds. He also instructed me on opossums (he could give only the Russian name, which I forget, but his English description was vivid: "a nose like a sharp pencil point and a head with Zulu hair"), deer, lions (the "wildcat" variety, I am sure), which "in the old days," when Wetherly Drive was (according to him) a "vast wilderness," were accustomed to seek haven on his estate. He related slowly and impressively the terrifying invasion of his bedroom by "a horror of a flying bat," which he had routed by thrashing about with his cane. "When I saw it, I immediately put on my beret to prevent it from becoming entangled in my hair" (those six strands?). And he would look at me with wide-open eyes to see if I were properly frightened. Reptiles and lizards had no terrors for him. Once he suddenly pulled me to a clump of fern where he had spotted (I hadn't), coiled in menace, a black snake of a size that almost threw me into a state of shock; but he assured me it was quite harmless, and besides (pointing to a slight bulge in that hideous patent-leather skin) "even if it were dangerous, we are safe, for it has just eaten probably a small rat."

The discovery of the snake provoked reminiscences of his youth. He told me that when he and his younger brother Guri were small boys and living at the Stravinsky summer residence in Ustilug, a favorite sport was tarantula-hunting. The boys would lie flat on their stomachs and drop strings with safety pins dipped in honey into the holes in the ground where these hairy predators lived, capture them in bottles, and display them to friends, who were charged admission. "Profits were excellent," he said. This saga was repeated to me with slight variations (once it was salt on the safety pins) on two or three other walks, which led me to investigate the habitat of tarantulas in a treatise on entomology I found in the library. Ustilug (and environs) did not seem to be listed among the preferred sites, although spiders of the daddy-longlegs variety could be found in profusion in that territory (as in most others around the world, according to this authoritative account).

Occasionally we took an hour's drive after dinner. Before he fell ill, Stravinsky thoroughly enjoyed car rides and would sit up front with me while his wife caught a nap in solitary splendor in the back seat. We had our choice of three non-freeway routes (the Los Angeles area is *not* filled with scenic highways), and if we were not caught in traffic, we would eventually reach either Malibu, the other side of Laurel Canyon, or the Municipal Park. Stravinsky could predict every turn in the road before we came to it, and would warn me well in advance about the hazards of curves or steep hills. Otherwise, drives in Beverly Hills consisted of climbing one mountain, only to reach a dead end or no-entry sign, and descending right back to the starting point, where the best plan, according to him, was to go home.

On Sunday nights we would spruce up and go off to Chasen's to dinner. The Stravinsky table was in a small area at the left side of that gathering place for—not gourmets, but people who liked (and could pay for) a great deal of expensive food. "Mr. Chasen" had a special door, otherwise kept locked, so that the composer need take only a few steps from his car to reach his seat in our circular booth, where we were more or less concealed from celebrity hunters and those they hunted. Robert always took charge of orders, and these meals would begin with quantities of caviar, sour cream, chopped egg, and Scotch for everyone except me. Stravinsky always gave my drink order to the captain himself: "She will have a double vodka martini," and protests on my part (single Chasen martinis were served in pint-sized champagne-wine glasses) would be argued down with "A double is a time-saver." These dinners were usually pleasant affairs. Robert was relaxed, Mrs. Stravinsky looked glamorous, and Stravinsky, as normal, was content that everyone seemed happy. We always ate too much butterfly steak or saddle of lamb or lobster, and drank too much wine at unheard-of prices. Five or six servitors hung about throughout the evening, supervising the downing of every mouthful, and if the composer paused for more than two seconds, captains came running from all directions fearfully. The composer thoroughly enjoyed attentions such as these, and adopted the imperial attitude that should go along with them (and that was, incidentally, expected), raising his arm to summon the wine steward with the grand gesture of a caliph beckoning his vizier, rarely uttering a word, but making his commands known by a wave of his hand toward the wine cooler or our glasses. This royal behavior also (and unfortunately) was applied on one or two occasions when all did *not* go according to plan—soda water *in* his Scotch, not *beside* it; a shrimp cocktail placed on *his* plate instead of Robert's; the absence from the menu of *prosciutto*, which his wife had yearned for —and then the gesture was clearly to be interpreted as "Off with your head." (If that order was not immediately understood, a

word or two might follow—"*crétin*" . . . "idiot"!). These were
moments of acute embarrassment, but more for Robert and me than
for Mrs. Stravinsky, who might reprove her husband in Russian—
but only for *his* lack of self-control, and not because she thought
his expression of displeasure was out of proportion to the cause.
The Stravinskys, one should remember, were both products of
the ruling class in a feudal society, and the social behavior patterns
of their childhood were permanently ingrained because of their
exile (forced in her case, self-imposed in his) at the hands of the
"serf." Stravinsky's autocracy with servants—in fact, with anyone
serving him whose mental equipment fell short of the mark—was as
much a part of his nature as his tendencies to hypochondria and
superstition, and as immutable. Mrs. Stravinsky's outward reaction
would take a much milder form—a gesture of irritation, an impatient word, or a snapping of the fingers to call attention, but
that was as far as it went. She was, in general, timid with domestics,
sometimes accepting poor service in public places rather than
make even the slightest fuss, but her thinking was identical with her
husband's: there were "good ones" and "bad ones," but they were
all there to serve, and serve they must.

But while I would stare fixedly at my plate during one of these
demonstrations, Robert never let them pass. Championship of the
underdog amounted almost to fanaticism in him, as though, it
seemed to me, he experienced complete identification with the
victim. His remarks to Stravinsky (or to Mrs. Stravinsky, for that
matter) would be sharp, and they were often delivered regardless
of who might be present to hear them. At the end of those first
weeks in Hollywood, I discovered to what this could lead.

CHAPTER ELEVEN

WHEN Stravinsky recorded in Hollywood, the sessions were usually held in a wooden building on Highland Avenue, midway between Hollywood Boulevard and the Hollywood Bowl entrance. It was an edifice of barnlike proportions, and resembled such constructions in one other respect: it became an inferno if the outside temperature rose above seventy degrees. There was no air-conditioning, at least during the time of that lengthiest of all Stravinsky recording schedules, when Southern California was sweltering under a heat wave with a daily Fahrenheit register between ninety and one hundred, and the long-ignored encroachment of dirty air had reached a point of enough importance to be included in the daily weather report. It was then at "eye irritation" level.

Stravinsky's fear of chills made him inclined to complain more about cold than heat, although he did not like any extremes of climate. But in his later years he was afflicted with a chronic allergy that caused an uncomfortable watering of the eyes and nose, and should have entitled him to become a major stockholder in the Kleenex Corporation. This annoyance was accompanied, occasionally, by a sneezing spell (although the ailment did not appear to be hay fever) that lasted for exactly seven spasms—if he stopped sneezing before this magical number was reached or went beyond it, we always diagnosed the approach of a cold. Air pollution was a considerable pest to him. Robert, whose myopic eyes were perpetually strained because of the close work on his manuscripts and his non-stop reading, suffered aloud. Mrs. Stravinsky has always detested hot weather with the fervor of an Eskimo (a feeling inherited, doubtless, from the Scandinavian side of her ancestry), and darkened her room and closed her door after announcing that she expected, nay hoped, to die in her sleep. (As a precaution against this, I stocked the little "cooling cabinet" in her dressing room, in which she kept her lotions and creams, with ice, milk, yogurt, and ginger ale.) For my part, I was an Easterner, and in the mid-sixties air pollution was considered a California curse, accepted as one of the hazards of travel. I wore my sunglasses at all times, and endured.

By 1965 I was well-versed in the format of Stravinsky-Craft recording sessions, having accompanied Stravinsky to all save three or four of those held on the East Coast and in Toronto (where many records were made because of the high quality of the Canadian Broadcasting Corporation musicians and the excellent acoustics in Massey Hall).

Some time before my arrival on the Stravinsky scene, Columbia Records had undertaken a project entitled *Stravinsky Conducts Stravinsky*, intended as the final recorded document of all of the composer's works, and sessions to accumulate this library took place two or three times a year during the first half of the sixties. In point of fact, Stravinsky had not engaged in very much recording from the time he began to compose the *Rake* in the forties, and the first really important Columbia recording schedules began with that work in March 1953, a few weeks after its Metropolitan Opera première.*

Because of the enormous costs of record-making (involving not only performers but a skilled and knowledgeable director, half a dozen assistants, and many others technically qualified to produce the disc itself), sessions were generally scheduled in connection with concert performances, thus eliminating extra rehearsal costs and the additional time and expense contingent on contracting musicians. Orchestra and chorus members work by the hour, at salaries established by their respective unions, while the conductor and soloists (if any) generally receive fees agreed upon by contract.

For these reasons, the number of performing artists (particularly

---

* Stravinsky's first recordings, in the nineteen-twenties and early thirties, were for English and French Columbia. In 1940, after his arrival in the United States, he recorded *Petrushka* and the *Rite* for American Columbia in New York, and in 1946 other works for the same company. A contract with RCA Victor produced some recordings in 1947–50, and there were also scattered recordings for other labels prior to the relationship with CBS-Columbia in the nineteen-fifties and sixties.

conductors) with recording contracts empowering them to request sessions without benefit of concerts is very small. Stravinsky, however, was one of them, and the August sessions were set up on this extremely expensive basis.

Robert's share of those recordings provided benefits for both sides—and this is interesting. For, along with the *Stravinsky Conducts Stravinsky* project, there was a "Schoenberg project," with Robert as conductor. Columbia was not unwilling to record the works of this major figure in twentieth-century music, but they were sometimes reluctant to allocate the necessarily large sums of money specifically for Robert—they could, after all, have used other orchestras and conductors to whom they were also committed. An arrangement was therefore made whereby a portion of Stravinsky's royalties was deducted for this purpose. It was pointed out to the composer by his West Coast attorney that such expenditures would provide excellent tax benefits for him—and he doubtless accepted the arrangement on this basis alone, since there is no likelihood at all that he, personally, would have any interest in seeing recorded, on his money, the works of a composer to whom he was far from dedicated.* On this basis (in part), Robert made some sixteen Schoenberg discs in the sixties. Exactly to what extent Stravinsky's funds were used to produce these records is unknown to me; some of the required money was undoubtedly considered an advance against royalties accruing to Robert, for I know that at several points Columbia was "dunning" him for money, the sales of the records not having brought in the necessary revenue.

On a good day a three-hour recording session, during which twenty minutes of each hour constituted a union break, might with luck produce fifteen minutes of usable tape. It can therefore be concluded that while heat and nerves were troubling the residents of North Wetherly Drive, anxieties about getting three major Stravinsky works (as well as several lesser ones) on tape within the allotted period of time were plaguing John McClure.

Although recording today is so major an industry that almost every layman has some notion of how a tape is made, it might be worth repeating that the music is conveyed from the area occupied

* Stravinsky *was* generous, however, with regard to another composer— Edgard Varèse—for he gave part of his recording time for *Renard* in January 1962 so that a work of Varèse's could be made by Robert, with the composer in attendance.

by the performers to a sealed control booth housing the director, the engineers, and a great deal of machinery to transfer the sound to magnetic tape. Microphones, hung in various spots above the orchestra, "travel" not only the music but also conversations between the recording director and the conductor. Any communications of a private nature between the two, such as "God, that soprano has got to go," or "What shall we do about that second horn?—he plays like a trombone," are confined to private telephones on their respective desks, used only when the microphones have been switched off.

The music is rehearsed perhaps several times, and when everything seems ready, a take is made, usually of a section or movement; or, if the work is a short one, the entire score. More often than not, several takes of particular sections or movements are necessary (from which the choicest is later selected), and at the union break, what the tape holds is played back in the control booth, producing moods of either elation or despair.

Stravinsky always liked to record, and if sessions went well his satisfaction was deep, for the unarguable reason that *his* recordings, under such conditions, represented the truest expression of the ideas he had set down on his manuscript paper. In this sense the three-score-plus Stravinsky listings in the Columbia catalogue form a true document. But it would be equally correct to say that after Stravinsky's eightieth birthday, Robert's assistance was vital for many of the recordings, and these discs may certainly be referred to as the end result of a collaboration. And this poses an intriguing question: how far does this collaboration extend in the final record which the public buys under the title *Stravinsky Conducts Stravinsky?*

The composer, in recording sessions, often referred to Robert as "my ears." Robert has a "mechanically perfect" ear: that is, he is able to detect immediately even the slightest deviation from the printed score—a wrong pitch or rhythm rarely escapes his attention during rehearsal or playback. It is a talent that may be compared to the photographic memory he also possesses, which used to make me imagine his mind as a library of microfilm capable of supplying, at a moment's notice, exact copies of any printed matter that had passed through his hands. This "ear" was invaluable to Stravinsky, since the conductor cannot really hear the true sound because he conducts in a confined space, and when the *Rake* was recorded in

1953, the composer must surely have become aware that this particular talent could supply one of the most important services his "assistant" would render.

So did the recording company—for a practical reason: Robert saved them money (and this is doubtless why they so readily accepted the financial arrangement for the Schoenberg/Craft project, astonishing though it is that they did!). Robert knew this well, for on March 15, 1962, with regard to the *Flood* recording, he wrote me that he could get it done in half the time Graff would pay if Stravinsky did it alone—if, in fact, he *could* do it alone. And this was true, of course, but whether or not it was *fair* to Stravinsky (or to Robert) is another thing entirely. In some of the sessions that took place before 1965, it was very apparent to me, as well as to other interested parties from the music world, that Stravinsky was accorded too few takes on tape, whereas more and more takes were made during the so-called rehearsal period. Regardless of Stravinsky's diminishing vigor, up to the point of his last public appearance on the podium on May 17, 1967, in Toronto's Massey Hall, he was capable of standing and conducting continuously for an over-all period of forty-five minutes, although it is true that the music usually involved (*Fireworks, Firebird, The Fairy's Kiss*, etc.) did not impose the strain on him that his later compositions did. But with the stop-and-start technique permissible during the making of a record, it would seem that the recording company, which was purportedly preserving musical history, was a little over-eager about these money-saving rehearsal takes. In other words, Stravinsky simply needed more time, and he did not get it.

By the time Stravinsky stood up for the final run-through and the official take, the orchestra was thoroughly indoctrinated with Robert's tempo (which was generally more rapid than the composer's) and his interpretation (which might also differ), and would therefore have great difficulty adjusting. Stravinsky's beat, usually very clear, suffered under the pressures of this situation. Add these circumstances to just time enough for a maximum of two takes and it is easy to understand the pointed questions raised in musical circles in the last five or six years about the authenticity of certain Stravinsky recordings made in the final decade. How much is Stravinsky and how much is Craft?

But surely, I have been asked, Stravinsky was able to differentiate between his takes and those from Robert Craft's rehearsals? Did he listen to all the playbacks? And how much did he have to do with the editing of the takes, and the splicing that produces the final disc?

As far as I know, Stravinsky did *not* listen to playbacks, at least not during any of the sessions I attended. As for editing, this was a task in which he had never involved himself; he relied on others whom he trusted, and from the time of Robert's association with him, he seems to have regarded Robert's judgment in these matters as final. In earlier years Lawrence Morton had often been asked for his opinion, and in the sixties both his and Claudio Spies's aid would very frequently be enlisted by Robert. (Claudio, in fact, had another important editorial role, for when a score was completed, photostated pages of it would sometimes be sent off to him to check for errors inadvertently made by the composer—a significant responsibility, comparable, let us say, to that assigned by a writer who may ask someone to scan his manuscript not just for misspellings, but for actual misuses of words or idioms.) *

But there is no question in my own mind that if Stravinsky *had* listened, he would have been able to determine immediately which takes were his and which were Robert's, and if the release of a record containing both was permitted, it should naturally be concluded that he regarded the interpretation as satisfying to *him*, as an expression of *his* wishes, and perhaps a *better* expression than he himself could have made under the restrictions of his age. He would never, when he knew of it (and once or twice he did not), permit the release under his name of a record containing none of his takes. And his attitude was made very plain to Columbia in a 1967 letter, which Robert showed me, forbidding the release— unless specifically attributed to Robert—of the *Japanese Lyrics, Balmont Songs, Capriccio, Danses Concertantes,*† *Abraham and Isaac, Requiem Canticles,* and *Chant du Rossignol,* and the 1966 recordings of the *Mass, Symphonies of Wind Instruments,* and *Variations* (the last of these the composer did record himself during the August 1965 session, but none of the takes were good enough to use). He did catch the *Mass,* advance pressings of which

---

* Claudio did a great deal of such work on the manuscripts of *Abraham and Isaac, Elegy for J.F.K.,* and *Fanfare for a New Theatre,* and also on both manuscripts and final scores of *Introitus, Variations,* and *Requiem Canticles.*

† It is interesting to note that within days of Stravinsky's death the *Danses Concertantes,* attributed to Stravinsky, was issued by Columbia (M-30516).

were sent to reviewers with an ascription to Stravinsky, provoking calls to Columbia and several letters to Stravinsky from individuals who were present at the session and knew that he was not even there during the major part of the taping. He immediately forbade its release, of course, and his own 1960 record was substituted on the disc. But these advantages taken of Stravinsky provided some (though not all) of the reasons for the cancellation in 1968 of his contract with Columbia.

Some days before the August sessions began, Stravinsky's granddaughter Kitty arrived from Geneva for her first American visit, and I moved to the Hotel Continental on the Strip so that she could have the guest room. The Stravinskys loaned me their brand-new white Lincoln (it was typical of Mrs. Stravinsky that she preferred the comfortable "old black cozy car") so that there would be no transportation problem, and for a few days the nervous hostess occupied herself with all manner of shopping to fill the guest room with objects dear to a young girl's heart (and to hers!—she bought enough fluffy powder puffs, eau de cologne, bath salts, and colored soaps to supply a seraglio). Stravinsky anticipated the visit with an attitude of paternal solemnity; it was delightful to watch him trying to evince interest in the purchases that were made when his wife spread them out on her bed, although in his mind Kitty was so very young (she was then approaching thirty) that he could not understand the need for all those cosmetics. The Stravinskys had seen Kitty not long before in Paris, on their way home from Warsaw, and had extended the invitation at that time. Kitty had lost her parents in her infancy—her mother had died when she was barely two, and her Jewish father was killed shortly thereafter by the Nazis. Kitty was "adopted" by Theodore and Denise and took the Stravinsky name rather than her paternal name of Mandelstam * (the intermarriage had not been regarded favorably by certain other members of the Stravinsky family). She was now at the age when she wished to break away and lead her own life, despite the fact that a very sheltered existence had not equipped her with much stamina for facing life's problems. She duly arrived, and turned out to be delicate, rather phthisically pretty, extremely shy, and girlish. Her awe of her grandfather went so deep that when he

* I have been told that her father was related to the Russian poet, but Mrs. Stravinsky says this is not a certainty.

addressed her she would be startled to attention like a scared rabbit, and Stravinsky took great pains (on constant reminders from his wife) to be as gentle as possible in his manner. He explained all about the recording sessions, apologizing that these were going to take some of his time during her visit, and suggested that she might like to attend one—a rather unusual invitation from him, as he never, in all the years I knew him, gave any indication that he considered the *observation* of himself at work a matter of importance to others (except, of course, for the public concerts, when, like anyone else, he dearly loved a full house). Kitty did come to the second session, but for the most part spent her time with her aunt Milène, who doted on her. Mrs. Stravinsky, lamenting continually that she had no idea how to entertain a "youngster," outdid herself with presents—a practically brand-new fur coat, new dresses, new hairdos—but she was very glad of Milène's major participation in the visit, and almost relieved when it was all over.

The first two days of the sessions had been assigned to *The Fairy's Kiss*—Stravinsky's forty-five minute ballet in four scenes, inspired by some of Tchaikovsky's non-orchestral pieces that he had admired very much.* He had a pleasant feeling about the session when we started out that morning. The work posed no particularly strenuous conducting problems, and Robert's remark, as he jumped into the car—"Well, today it's Tchaikovsky's turn"—provoked only one of those audible grins rather than the icy silence that usually followed any flippant comment on his music. But in fact it was never possible to know what Stravinsky really thought about his compositions. Replies to questions about his works were generally confined to details about their genesis, or the form they took, or the technical aspects of their construction. He rarely said anything from which definite conclusions could be drawn about his inner feelings. I believe he loved all his works as a parent does its offspring, with perhaps particular affection for one or the other, depending on its individual character—sometimes for their weaknesses, or even for their failures. Once in a great while there might be the merest hint. Claudio Spies has told me that some time after

---

* *The Fairy's Kiss*, composed in 1928 on a commission from the celebrated dancer Ida Rubinstein, was the work which terminated the relationship between Stravinsky and Diaghilev. The impresario made it known that he considered the composer had sacrificed his art for money—Mme. Rubinstein's company, in his opinion, being very inferior.

the recording of *The Rite of Spring* in 1960 Stravinsky, in a meditative mood in the car as they returned from another session, suddenly remarked to him "I would like so much to rescore the entire *Le Sacre*," and (according to Claudio) mentioned that he might use a saxophone in such a rescoring. The idea of changing the *Rite* must have occurred fairly consistently. He did revise it somewhat in the early twenties, and in 1943, when he rescored the "Sacrificial Dance" section, he made what he himself described as "many improvements in the instrumentation." But normally it was not in his nature to look back. The final manuscript page that went to the photostater was, in every sense, final—and the mark of an erasure could never be detected.

Still, did he have a favorite as a father has a favorite son? Here, too, one can only speculate, and so I will and say that I think it was *Les Noces*. Except for *The Rake's Progress*, which occupied his attention almost exclusively for more than three years (1947–51), he labored longer over *Les Noces* than any other work, although between the time he began it in 1914 and the completion of the short score three years later, he produced at least half a dozen other major pieces, including *Renard* and *The Soldier's Tale*. But the length of time is more understandable in the case of the *Rake*, which is, after all, of two and one half hours' duration and was the first of his works to utilize an English libretto, whereas the choreographic scenes inspired by wedding ceremonies in a peasant village last thirty-five minutes and are deeply Russian. He returned and returned to the latter, and did not complete the final orchestration until 1923. It drew him, it would seem, as almost no other work of his had done. And its sketches and early scores are his most beautiful manuscripts; they resemble a tapestry. During the time I knew him, the mention of *Les Noces* never failed to produce the same smile with which he greeted those for whom he felt great affection, and after one of the rare occasions on which we listened to it in the last years, when I tried unsuccessfully to express the feeling of joy it gave me, he said, "Yes, I suppose I am very satisfied with it." It has always struck me as so strange—although the reader will realize that I base this assumption entirely on my personal feeling about the composer's attitude toward this work— that the man whose intellectuality was as natural a gift as that which led him to create great music, whose works, some of which, now close to the three-quarter-century mark of their existence, are as much that and even more in advance of their time, should regard so highly the music more based in tradition than any he ever composed.

Enroute to the recording studio we collected Lawrence Morton (who usually attended all sessions scheduled in Hollywood), and Stravinsky's good humor extended, I recall, to answering some questions about Ansermet's (authorized!) performance of extracts from *The Fairy's Kiss* in the early nineteen-thirties.* For my part, I was especially pleased that Lawrence was with us, for he was always thoughtful about helping me with the half-dozen or so burdens that weighed me down. (Robert was usually inside the studio before I put the car in neutral.) Otherwise, I employed a particular technique, which consisted in hanging everything (rehearsal bag, handbag, extra sweater or coat) on my left arm and shoulder, with scores (heavy) tucked high under the same arm, leaving my right hand free for Stravinsky to cling to. The disadvantage was that this arrangement generally produced temporary paralysis of the left arm, rendering it useless for such tasks as holding a cup while I poured Scotch with the other hand.

That morning, however, help was abundant, for most of the musicians and John McClure were waiting in the parking area at the side of the studio to greet the composer—an honest tribute: despite the morning hour (it was ten o'clock), the humidity was visible in the form of a miasma that made the sun look filthy.

Along with the progressive shedding of garments, the heat generated an air of informality, and all proceeded normally. Everyone was patient, and since two days had been set aside for this one work, time pressures were relatively nonexistent. More care than usual was rendered after Robert finished rehearsing the orchestra, and takes of the first two scenes were made by the composer to everyone's satisfaction, including his own. I remember that John McClure took particular pains that day with the composer's takes. After the Prologue was completed, he remarked that he thought the beat was too slow. Stravinsky agreed. There was one more take at a slightly faster tempo, which was pronounced perfect, and the first day was chalked up as a success.

* Lawrence had a particular interest in this ballet, and had published a study of it in 1963 in Paul Henry Lang's *Stravinsky: A New Appraisal of His Work*.

Session number two, on the next day, had a larger audience, composed in part of students of composition from the University of California and Los Angeles, and this time we brought Kitty, who was made to feel useful by being put in charge of *grandpère's* sweater and towel. At the end of an hour the stifling atmosphere in the studio began to show its effect in the unguarded repartee passing between the control booth and Robert. "Let's hurry it up" . . . "That's O.K." . . . "That does it"—all indications that one take after another was being made. This did not escape Stravinsky, who remarked to me that "they may know very well what they are doing, but *I* am not so sure." Just enough time was left for him to conduct the two final scenes with two takes, and, bedraggled and drenched with perspiration, we went home.

The recording of *Pulcinella* was set for the twenty-third, a day that began badly, for Stravinsky awoke with a headache. As a matter of fact, he was rather frequently troubled by headaches after sleeping; they were not the migraine type, but could be very crashing in their effect. Robert attributed them to the shots of Vitamin B_{12} that he had been taking since they had become fashionable, and that may have enriched his already too rich blood, but a more likely explanation, according to doctors with whom I have talked, is that this chronic condition could have been the delayed result of the spinal anesthetic administered in 1953 when Stravinsky underwent a prostate operation. Certainly the anesthetic is known to have had an effect on his sense of balance thereafter, especially when he walked.

Usually the headaches would vanish by the time he had his breakfast or finished with his shower, but this particular one hung on, aggravated, perhaps, by the oppressive heat and a pair of new eyeglasses. Robert, who had been working on his manuscript almost all night, kept us waiting in the car longer than usual, and by the time he sat down (behind the wheel that day), Stravinsky was not feeling sociable. A passage in French was exchanged which ended with a quivering "I do not like to be kept waiting," to which Robert's "Then why didn't you go without me?" (in the full knowledge on all our parts that this was impossible) gave a slight fan to the flame. The rest of the journey was made in dead silence.

The studio was filled this time, not only with students, but with a cordon of soloists as well. Robert's beat during rehearsal was particularly fast. In the control booth, where I went at Stravinsky's instigation to find out how long it would be before he would take over, John McClure was remarking to the engineer, "Too fast . . . too fast . . . he's always too fast"—worrisome, of course, because Robert's speed always meant that Stravinsky's slower tempos would cause problems. However, John told me he hoped only one take would be necessary since the orchestra and soloists (Irene Jordan, George Shirley, and Donald Gramm) were in top form that day. I went back to Stravinsky and suggested that he move to a lobby-like area equipped with a leather sofa, where it seemed cooler. He refused snappishly, and from the manner in which he moved his finger along the score he was holding, pressing down on each measure as though to retard what was going on in the studio, I could see that his ire was increasing.

When he finally stepped to the platform for a run-through, time was short, and as always, under such conditions of pressure, his beat suffered. The orchestra, which had been following Robert for a lengthy spell, was in a state of consternation. Robert stood at Stravinsky's side signaling *his* beat to the orchestra, in the hope of pushing Stravinsky to *his* tempo. But the composer would have none of it. *He* knew how he wanted the work to sound, and regardless of time or anything else, it was going to be played his way. Then a wind player made an error, which Stravinsky corrected sharply. Robert said something in an undertone; Stravinsky threw him an ominous glance and began to conduct the passage again. The player made the same error. Stravinsky lost his temper and dealt with the offender briefly but pointedly, with a generalization about stupidity. I had moved closer to him by that time, although not quite close enough to hear exactly what Robert said, but the expression on his face clearly indicated that he was taking Stravinsky to task, and with intensity. (In substance, as later reported to me, he said: "Don't talk to him that way. Don't talk to *anyone* that way.") Before the now vitally interested group of musicians, and with microphones on, Stravinsky whirled on Robert and retorted, in an enraged and imperial tone, "How dare you address me in this manner!" White-faced, Robert snatched his jacket, towel, and scores, and left the studio.

Stravinsky resumed his work. But he was visibly shaken. He could not find his place, and his hands trembled as he turned the same two pages back and forth several times. No one dared approach; the orchestra sat motionless until John McClure, who had come down from the control booth at the first sign of trouble, as though his only purpose in life was to adjust the microphone hanging over the first violins, won a medal for tact. "Maestro, we were off-balance in that last bit. Do you mind if we take it again from the beginning?" "Why not?" said Stravinsky, but his attempt at joviality was pathetic.

The session was completed with one take, and after that, as I led Stravinsky to the car, he remarked: "I do not wish to record tomorrow. You must tell McClure." I reminded him that he did not have any more sessions until *Variations*, which was to follow a few days of sessions for Robert alone. Mrs. Stravinsky was waiting for us in the driveway when we arrived. She obviously knew what had occurred, but only greeted her husband with a kiss, told him his lunch was waiting, and asked very casually how the session had progressed. Stravinsky asked her in Russian where "Bob" was, and she responded with a nod in the direction of the guest house. After eating in silence, he retired to his bedroom and closed the door. Mrs. Stravinsky turned to me despairingly. "This time it is very bad," she said.

I thought she was probably referring to another occasion when her husband and Robert had clashed, only that time the quarrel had taken place in private and was not concerned with music but with a literary matter. A letter written by Mrs. Stravinsky to a "distant relative" in Moscow, in which Stravinsky's home life had been intimately described, had appeared in *Musical America* in January 1963 (and was later reprinted in *Themes and Episodes*). What had angered the composer was that Robert had used this private letter. I was not with the Stravinskys when the actual argument occurred, but I gathered, from various reports, that it had come very close to ending Robert's association with the composer. (Later, when the book was published, Mrs. Stravinsky warned all her friends not to refer to it in Stravinsky's presence.) But from that point on, whenever I was typing a manuscript, Stravinsky would ask me exactly what it was, and several times when I happened to leave the room for a few minutes, I found him on my return reading what I had finished or what was in my typewriter. He never commented on my explanations, nor did he indicate approval or disapproval, but sometimes he raised his brows, and sometimes he left in silence.

But obviously he and Robert must have had many disagreements.

Robert had really become a *fils adoptif* by this time, and between "father" and "son" it would be extremely unlikely for peace to prevail at all times. Still, a public argument of the nature of the present one had never before taken place, to my knowledge. Stravinsky's open reprimand to Robert in the studio deprived his colleague of the privileged position that others believed him to hold. Robert had been humiliated, and before almost a hundred people.

"Very bad," Mrs Stravinsky had said. And it was. For almost four days there was no communication between the two, and Robert kept to his room even for meals, or came into the main house only when he knew Stravinsky was on the second floor. Necessary messages about recordings, correspondence, and the like were transmitted by me. There was general concern. John McClure telephoned; Lawrence Morton telephoned. Mrs. Stravinsky tried to reason with Robert, and so did I, but it was very apparent after the first day and a half that Robert had no intention of giving in. "He will go away, unless my husband apologizes," she told me, and with such a desolate note in her voice that had I not already begun to see how important Robert was in the household, Mrs. Stravinsky's total dependence on him, if not her husband's, would have been revealed by this simple remark.

Stravinsky kept to his daily routine during the crisis, but as the days passed I was certain he was making ready to yield. "Has he sent me any message?" he would ask when I came upstairs in the morning. Or, "Does he not have the courtesy to excuse himself?" (He did not say "apologize.") And once, when I summoned up enough courage to tell him no, that Robert felt himself the injured party and that Mrs. Stravinsky and I thought he would stand firm, he said to me: "He has a difficult character. He has always had a difficult character." And then, almost wonderingly, "But I am much *older* than he."

It was plain that he was profoundly disturbed; the evenings were empty for him without the music sessions in the library, and he would emerge from his studio two or three times during the working hours to ask some unimportant question, obviously to see if he might run into Robert. Finally, on the fourth morning, he hinted to me that he would not take it amiss if someone let Robert know that he hoped he would come down to lunch. Robert did; the meeting had all the old camaraderie, and all was well again. But the argument had had its effects. The recording of *Variations* took place on the following day, and although Robert stood at Stravinsky's side throughout the latter's rehearsing and conducting of the entire work, and a complete tape was made, it could not be used, and Robert had to record the work again in 1966.

The significance of the entire episode (for me) lay in the fact that it was Stravinsky who had yielded. It was a simple admission that he could not—or at least certainly did not wish to—manage without Robert. No one acquainted with Stravinsky in the years before Robert's arrival would not agree that this concession represented a complete change in the composer's nature: in former days he would never have tolerated an association on any terms save his own, and such an episode as had occurred at the recording studio would have brought an instant end to a relationship.

But now, it seemed, he was inclined to think twice. And I detected behind these second thoughts a much deeper feeling, an actual fear on the part of both Stravinskys that Robert might someday leave them. It was clearly a case of two elderly people unwilling to face the fact that the "son" they had found late in life might suddenly assert his independence.

Besides, it was also apparent that Stravinsky was acknowledging an obligation that had nothing to do with paternal feelings. This was unusual in itself, for while Stravinsky was never *unaware* of obligations, they were very often considered of no importance in relation to the principles that governed his thinking as a composer. The fact, for example, that at one point in his career, when he was almost penniless, Serge Koussevitzky paid him fees for conducting the Boston Symphony that were more than treble those of the highest paid conductor at the time, did not stop him from excoriating his benefactor for what he considered "outrageous" performances of his music, and he never forgave him.* And this was not the only incident of this nature. Obligations were obligations, but the greatest obligation was to himself.

Still, here he was, feeling the onus imposed on him by a man forty years his junior. In the archives, covering the final decade of his life, there are indications that make this clear. Part of Stra-

* After Koussevitzky died, Stravinsky was never directly asked to conduct the Boston Symphony. It was a sore point with him that none of its conductors thereafter evinced much interest in him or his recent music. I *was* approached once or twice in the mid-sixties, but the negotiations came to naught.

vinsky's program of self-discipline had always included the penning
of reminders, many of them concerned with injuries he felt had
been done him, or incorrect statements that had been made about
him. Sometimes the latter took the form of underscorings or mar-
ginal notations on letters, periodicals, or news-clippings, reflecting
not only his own opinions on the contents (usually *very* negative) but also his deliberate intention to place the writer in a permanent purgatory. But there were others that revealed his *human-
ness*—the self-reprimands, the personal castigations: "I should not
be so angry with Bob," one began. (I remember this because it
was written during that August unhappiness, and it made me feel
very sad.)

Yet, too, I had the conflicting feeling that Stravinsky may have
given in more on his wife's account than his own. Perhaps because
(though he never mentioned it, of course) the law of averages dictated that he would leave this world before she did, and he did not
wish her to be alone; or perhaps more for the old reason—that his
own peace of mind depended on *her* contentment. But most of all,
I think, he gave in because he was growing old, and another need
was now keeping pace with the added years: his open yearning
for the love of those around him.

Robert surely knew all these things. Why, then, did he exhibit an
attitude of what would seem to the outsider unforgivable hardness?
Why not make a concession to the temper of an old man, and,
furthermore, one whose occasional autocratic outbursts were never
regarded as such by the bystander, because Stravinsky was a great
man and therefore entitled to certain extraordinary privileges?

But Robert could not, because to have done so would have been
to admit that Stravinsky and he had no common meeting-ground
and that he therefore occupied a subservient position in the household. And that was not true so long as Robert did not permit it to
become true. It was a question of his own integrity. It would be
well for chroniclers to remember that, from the start of his association with Stravinsky, Robert was under covert censure: from the
composer's relatives, who felt that he was assuming their position;
from "friends" and associates who claimed that access to Stravinsky
was possible only if Robert permitted it; from critics of the composer's music who attested that the work of his final years suffered
because Robert had turned him toward a new and incompatible
musical direction; and, finally, from a variegated group of indi-

viduals who "suggested" that Stravinsky was being used as a ventriloquist's dummy is used, to express Robert's views on music and other matters via the printed word.

First of all, simply to stand up under this onslaught required admirable resistance, and to defend one's self against it dictated a special brand of battle-dress. Robert felt he had to manufacture an armor-plated cape of stubbornness that would protect the principles for which he had voluntarily given up his right to any personal life. Therefore, he could *not* give in, for he believed himself to be in the right. To have bent one inch would have—in his own eyes—turned him from a person into an object, another "thing" in the long, long list of possessions, both material and abstract, that Stravinsky had collected in the course of his lifetime.

I understood Robert's attitude during this period of unpleasantness, although I was not sympathetic with it, for I now began to see Stravinsky as an aging man, and I do not think that a little flexibility would have meant the destruction of a principle. But then I was not Robert, and there was much that I did not know, although throughout his correspondence there were always little hints of situations that must have been great trials for him. It was impossible for him, for example, to take any kind of holiday away from the Stravinskys without having to go through an ordeal of reproach on their part that he should even entertain the notion of seeking amusement, however temporary, elsewhere. And the question of marriage was purely academic. Even if Robert had wanted to marry while Stravinsky was alive (and there was at least one occasion when I am sure he did), no compromise on a division of time for his private life could ever have been reached, unless it were 95 percent versus 5. On the other hand, the choice had been his and he had made it.

Robert, therefore, was both aware of and prepared for battle. When he decided to become an actual Stravinsky "in-dweller" (against the advice of several of his friends, by the way, who warned him that with Stravinsky possession would be ten, not nine, points of the law), he began to sharpen his already highly developed anti-attack antennae. And in the ensuing years, as his roots became more firmly established, Stravinsky himself supplied the alloy that made Robert's coat of mail impenetrable to assaults on him as an alleged alienator of affections, a self-appointed social censor, an exerter of undue influence, and an unauthorized ghost-

writer. Stravinsky, too, had a choice, and he made it. For, despite
any or all accusations, Robert remains a member of the household
to this day.

But what of these attacks? Was there any basis for them? Letters,
articles, conversations recalled and noted in diaries make them all
part of the record. They provoke, if not specific answers, certainly
legitimate speculations, and in my sometime capacity as an "executive bystander" (if I may coin a phrase), I entertained many of
the latter, and drew my own conclusions.

Did Robert alienate the children from their father? No, not
consciously. Did he occupy a place in Stravinsky's affections as important as that of the composer's children? Yes, and in some ways
it may have been—probably was—even more important. With
Stravinsky, who was concerned with music first and everything
else after that (provided he had any time left), it was always a case
of "out of sight, out of mind." Robert was *there* and his own children were *not* there. True, Milène, who had come with her husband
André from France in 1947, was close by, and remained so until
1969, when the Stravinskys left Hollywood permanently. A few
months after that, the lawsuit brought in Stravinsky's name against
André, charging him and Stravinsky's attorney William Montapert
with the illegal withholding of the composer's manuscripts, terminated their contact forever. (The next time Milène came to her
father, it was to attend his funeral.) Her own loyalty was naturally
to her husband. She could supply to her father (during his lifetime) on the side of feeling only a part of what was required, and
on the side of intellectual communion nothing at all. (The un-
reasonableness of the demands made in any relationship with Stravinsky is very clear in Milène's case; when the manuscript quarrel
arose, there was general shock that Milène took her husband's side
against her father, exactly as any other devoted wife would have
done.)

As for Stravinsky's two sons, Theodore had never considered living in the United States; his career as a painter was rooted in Switzerland. But had he done so, Stravinsky would undoubtedly have
helped him as he had Milène and Soulima, who came from France
in 1948 with his wife and his infant son, John, and who lived in
Hollywood for a year. At the end of that time (when Robert was
only just beginning to know the Stravinskys), Soulima made his
decision to pursue a career elsewhere, feeling that he could make no

progress living within the shadow of his father's fame. He tried New York first, and ultimately settled in Urbana, Illinois, where his present position in the Music Department of the University of Illinois was secured after the retirement of an instructor who had been acquainted with Mrs. Stravinsky and to whom she had suggested Soulima as a suitable successor. Urbana, of course, is no great distance from Los Angeles as the jet flies, or as after-six reduced telephone rates permit. In other words, if the sons had wanted to be near their father, there was no real obstacle. And even if Stravinsky had not found in either of his sons the intellectual companionship that he needed (and that Robert apparently supplied), this, after all, had been true during most of his life, and it should not have made any difference at this later date. Stravinsky indeed recognized that blood was thicker than water, and he loved his children deeply and according to the rules. It is also true, of course, that Robert, in the children's eyes, was alien—Stravinsky's other intellectual companions had been closer to the fold, and some of them had known his first wife, their mother. It is also a sad truth that, for the most part, the feelings of the Stravinsky children toward their stepmother were defined in terms of fairy tales, lacking only the adjective "cruel." Her championship of Robert was therefore the pitting of her "son" against *them.*

As for the censorship imposed on the entrée of old friends, that charge holds water in a particular sense. There were very few people whom Stravinsky ever wanted to see, especially in the final decade of his life, when he must have felt that time was running short. (My own duties also included a certain amount of censorship, though not in the same context.) Robert's decrees, therefore, were perfectly understandable in certain cases. The disciples of Stravinsky's so-called neo-classic period (roughly defined, from 1920 to 1950) entertained exactly the same feelings toward Robert as those surrounding the composer in his "Russian" period had entertained toward *them.* In plain words, jealousy was rife, and one of the effective manifestations of jealousy is intrigue. At the risk of being attacked for generalizing, I think it is safe to say that intrigue in the world of music exists on a grander and more heinous scale than it does in other branches of the arts—it can sometimes reach cosmic proportions! Robert, the passionate advocate of the "new" (and therefore the "dangerous") became the new victim. And the "Russian" predilection for gossip, shared by the Stravinskys as well as those who carried tales, helped. Like all victims, Robert defended himself with whatever weapon was handiest. And in his position as guardian of all doors, including the one that led to the studio, who could blame him for forbidding entrance to his own attackers?

The belief in some quarters that he had a "bad" influence on Stravinsky's creative output is patently absurd. Only one person could ever influence Stravinsky on anything that had to do with music, and his identity goes without saying. Whatever path Stravinsky took was directed from within himself, and was plotted by his own instincts. "*I cannot tell what is going to happen in a work until it happens,*" does away once and for all with immediate exterior influences. That Robert was an important instrument in Stravinsky's exposure to a new kind of music is undeniable. But unless the composer's own inclinations had pointed the way, there would have been no traveling in that direction. How could there be? It was "new music," and he was making *new* music. The works of others in the field could not possibly have interested him in terms of his own and of what he was in the process of creating. And whatever reactions he may have had could only have been based on pure objectivity. "Sympathy" was the strongest favorable word I ever heard him use in discussing any contemporary composer, although I was aware, of course, that after Robert introduced him to Webern's music in 1952 he felt drawn to this composer. I also recall that during the performance of Schoenberg's *Erwartung*, which Robert conducted with the Washington Opera in 1960, while we sat listening in the dressing room, Stravinsky remarked, "I have never found the music of this composer sympathetic, but it has interesting things."

For the most part, he did not listen to modern works at all, and there were very few with which he was thoroughly familiar. One that I am sure of was Elliott Carter's *Double Concerto,* and I remember that particularly because Stravinsky "visualized" it in his comments. And he knew several Boulez works well. But whatever it was that influenced Stravinsky's music, it was not in the person of Robert Craft.

The accusation leveled most frequently and most harshly against Robert was that he used Stravinsky as the "expounder" of his own views via the printed word, and it was almost one of the first conditions I encountered in my association with the family, for members of the press were already posing that question in connection with the first three collaborations.

In 1959, when I met them, Stravinsky and Robert had been literary colleagues for two years. The first volume of "conversations" was already in print; the second, *Memories and Commentaries* had gone to press; and the third, *Expositions and Developments*, was being written. Robert wrote me from Venice in October 1960 that he was "busy as Hell" with the third volume (and added that despite this he was going to Torcello with Barbara Hutton that day!). Volume III, in fact, was completed in March 1961; I note in my diary that I picked up the retyped manuscript at Virginia Rice's (she was literary agent for the authors) and proofread it, as Robert had instructed, on the plane to Mexico.

Stravinsky's interest in these first three volumes was very positive—and in the first one certainly very active. He prepared his own notes and made comments, corrections, additions on the typescripts of the next two. For those unfamiliar with the books, it should perhaps be explained that the format was chiefly dialogue between the authors, with Stravinsky's answers to Robert's questions representing the latter's compilation over a period of time of the composer's recollections, musings, opinions, afterthoughts. Stravinsky, obviously not having the time to sit down and write a book, was satisfied to be the supplier of the substance and left its expression to Robert's judgment.

When the idea of this duet in prose had been brought up in 1957 (Deborah Ishlon, incidentally, made the initial suggestion), Stravinsky saw the project as a practical method of correcting inaccuracies in previous (non-Stravinsky) publications of his own views, as well as errors in biographical details and "misrememberings" of his own.* The expression of his revised or new opinions went without saying, of course. And the books also provided an appropriate answer to certain press requests for interviews. The solution was that the interviewer's questions be put in writing to Robert, who then secured the answers. This procedure was a great timesaver as well, since Stravinsky did not have to confine himself

* It is interesting to note that Alfred A. Knopf, eventual publisher of the final two volumes (*Themes and Episodes* and *Retrospectives and Conclusions*), turned the first volume down. Goddard Lieberson brought that one to Doubleday; they published it as well as the next three.

to a set appointment. The questions could be answered at random moments, and Robert usually waited for the opportune ones. Sometimes these "interviews" would not be based on questions per se, but on a particular subject, with the interested publication giving virtual carte blanche, of course.

In the United States there were exceptions to this rule against direct interviews. In my time Stravinsky received Jay Harrison of the old *Herald Tribune* and Irving Lowens of the *Washington Star*, who came to New York to see him prior to the *Abraham and Isaac* première in Washington. Emily Coleman of *Newsweek* had a few words with him in Toronto once, and Donal Henahan of the *New York Times* had a "silent" interview, and there may have been one or two others. In the latter case Stravinsky had heard of the writer from Robert when Mr. Henahan worked for the *Chicago Daily News;* Robert thought his reporting unusually intelligent. When the *New York Times* sought an interview with the composer in the spring of 1969, I arranged for Mr. Henahan to visit the Hotel Pierre on the chance that Stravinsky would become interested and join in a conversation the reporter planned to hold with Mrs. Stravinsky and Robert. Stravinsky "joined in" to the extent of not leaving the room for one moment, and took no notice of the photographer from the *Times* as he clicked and clicked, but he said not one word! *

For the most part, Robert acted as proxy. He also had the very important role of editor. Stravinsky's English was certainly pregnant enough to be quoted directly, and in the first two volumes much of its flavor is preserved, but his exact phrasing of an answer or his more lengthy expositions on a topic always sounded better and more literary in languages over whose idiom he had a more complete command than over English. Robert, therefore, created a style that he felt conveyed the quality of Stravinsky's exact expressions. But, being a writer himself, it was bound after a while to become much more his own style. This explains in part why critics have concluded in some instances that since these may not be Stravinsky's exact words—not *sounding* like his English—they cannot represent his exact views.

I fell into the style trap myself once, when I acted as collaborator. For several years the Hurok office, which toured the D'Oyly Carte Opera Company in North America from time to time, had been

* The *New York Times*, May 11, 1969.

asking me to secure an article from Stravinsky recounting his experiences with the works of Gilbert and Sullivan. (The composer had once referred to the fact that he had been introduced to this repertory in London by Diaghilev.) In 1968 I was finally able to pry some answers out of the West Coast during one of my visits, but Robert was too busy to write the piece and asked me to do so, employing the usual technique. The *New York Times* printed the piece (after I had had it approved, of course) on October 27, 1968. But Stravinsky's recollection of events that had taken place half a century before telescoped several years of visits to the Savoy operas into one—and that great Gilbert and Sullivan expert Mr. Reginald Allen pointed this out in a letter to the *Times,* a copy of which was sent to me by the Hurok office. The letter did not appear in the newspaper—a demonstration of courtesy toward the composer that did not often occur in other printed controversies with him.

Most of the material in the first three volumes of "conversations" deals with Stravinsky's life and thoughts in the years prior to his arrival in the United States, and although some of his recollections may contradict those in his *Autobiography*, anyone acquainted with Stravinsky would recognize that the tone of the later collaborations is far, far more Stravinsky. The *Autobiography* is unique in that almost everyone in it emerges enveloped in the aroma of a rose garden, and while Stravinsky may indeed have felt charitable (as the text indicates) in certain instances, it is hardly likely that the articulation of his sentiments would have taken on such a honeysweet tone in *any* language. In fact, Mrs. Stravinsky has told me that the *Autobiography* was written because Stravinsky was in need of money, and he was advised at the time that the book would be a revenue-producing item. According to her he had two collaborators, and the book did not fulfill his financial dreams, although by this time it has, no doubt, accumulated a tidy sum for someone.

Stravinsky always referred to the "conversations" as "our books," and he was interested not only in the reviews but in the advance promotion. One memorandum I have from the 1959 period instructs me to advise the publishers (Doubleday) that he thought it would be an excellent idea if they contributed to one of the New York concert programs "a large advertisement" announcing the forthcoming appearance of *Memories and Commentaries.*

The first three books—although none of them was ever on the non-fiction best-seller lists—enjoyed a moderate success and prompted the fourth one, *Dialogues and a Diary*. At one point, however, neither author (according to my correspondence) had thought beyond Volume III. But this new book differed radically from the others in one respect: it introduced Robert to the public as a diarist. Always a chronicle-keeper, though not a daily one, Robert made notes on his own activities, the people he met, and his observations on a variety of subjects from the time of his student days. After he became associated with Stravinsky in 1948, he began to keep very detailed accounts of important occurrences and meetings with old and new friends of the composer, chiefly recorded during the course of their travels abroad together. He has told me that it was always much easier to provoke Stravinsky into reminiscences when he was away from home, because the daily regime of studio hours was more or less abandoned and everything became flexible. In the course of drives about the various countrysides and meanderings through and around the sites of ancient civilizations, Stravinsky would talk at length to him. And then there were Robert's own impressions, derived from the table-talk at get-togethers with men of art and letters and music, when, on occasion, the composer might be voluble. He was productive, in any case, no matter how laconically.

The material for *Dialogues and a Diary* was being assembled in the early years of our relationship, and I was remotely involved in it (apart from typing many revisions of the notes on Stravinsky's and Balanchine's meetings about the *Flood* production that were included therein). The most interesting experience was in connection with the always provocative question of how much direct contact Stravinsky had had with the holy trinity of new music, Schoenberg, Webern, and Berg. The first of these men provided the major point of attention, especially since he and Stravinsky, in all the years they spent as virtual neighbors in Hollywood, never saw each other. Stravinsky's own recollections of his initial meeting with Schoenberg are related in the first volume of "conversations." * He met Schoenberg in Berlin through Diaghilev, who invited the German composer to a performance of *Petrushka*, in return for which Schoenberg extended an invitation to a performance of his *Pierrot lunaire* on December 8, 1912 (it was actually the fourth performance in a series). During the preparation of *Dialogues and a Diary*—on May 27, 1961, to be exact—Robert wrote

* *Conversations with Stravinsky* (New York: Doubleday, 1959), pp. 76 ff.

me asking that I contact Edward Steuermann, who had been the pianist in the December 12 performance of *Pierrot lunaire* (which Stravinsky admits was his first contact with Schoenberg's music), to see if I could learn anything that might throw some light on the subject. What transpired is interesting, I think, not only as an example of Robert's early care in checking on details (even those supplied by the composer), but also because it is again an illustration of the fact that history is very often a matter of recollection rather than record. And because it demonstrates the exactitude with which the fourth volume was undertaken, I quote the results of my contact with Mr. Steuermann. I located him through his wife, who told me on the telephone on May 29 that her husband was "ill," though not seriously, but that she would relay my questions by "writing to him." On June 3 I received a telephone call in New York from Steuermann himself, and reported its substance to Robert in a letter written on June 6:

> In a ten-minute conversation with him [Steuermann] on the phone, this is what I got: he recalls now that on December 8, 1912, *Pierrot lunaire* was performed and conducted entirely by Schoenberg. He says that he dimly recalls the Maestro [Stravinsky] sitting with him [Schoenberg] in the *Green Room—but not in the audience.* He also recalls several dinners with Webern, Berg, and others at Schoenberg's house, but does not clearly remember anything beyond the fact that Stravinsky *was present*—probably more than once.

My letter went on to explain that Steuermann had no recollection of Schoenberg's attendance at a performance of Stravinsky's *Oedipus Rex*, and it also answered negatively some questions about Schoenberg's presence in Berlin in 1924 and in Venice in 1925, when Stravinsky played his own *Piano Concerto* and Schoenberg conducted his *Serenade*, within a day of each other. Neither heard the other's work.

When *Dialogues and a Diary* appeared, Steuermann's impressions, as given in my letter, seemed to be within Stravinsky's recollection, except that he could not remember any particular dinner at which Webern and Berg were also guests.

With the fourth volume, Stravinsky's interest in the literary collaboration began to diminish. But this is not surprising. Every ounce of his energy, the precious energy of an aging and, at that point, a somewhat tired and ailing man, was being carefully guarded for the area of work that meant more to him than anything else. And his lack of interest in the literary aspect of his life is apparent in the fifth volume, *Themes and Episodes.* During my 1965 Hollywood stay I typed several drafts of sections from Robert's diaries, as well as some previously published material (letters to editors, magazine interviews, and so on) that was to appear in that book. In fact, it was no longer to consist of dialogues in the sense of the previous volumes. Some new pages also were prominent, containing "Stravinskyan" views on longevity, the new computer vocabulary, and "do-it-yourself" music; but I cannot comment on these since I never seemed to be around when such views were expressed by the composer, or such questions posed by Robert. However, for all practical purposes most of this volume was made up of matter that had already been printed, and in that sense it was certainly a "collaboration."

The sixth and last volume—*Retrospectives and Conclusions*—was not published until 1969, and it can actually be described in the same terms as the previous book. A great many events occurring before its publication had direct bearing on its contents, and it falls into proper perspective within my record of the final three years of Stravinsky's life.

CHAPTER TWELVE

THE recording sessions came to an end on Thursday afternoon, August 26, leaving a few loose ends to be threaded together at some future date. And as though it had been involved in some conspiracy against Stravinsky, Robert, and Columbia Records, the weather suddenly decided to behave itself and live up to its California legend. Everything, including tempers, immediately became clear and balmy, and Robert actually descended from his lair to swim an hour earlier than usual that afternoon, going so far as to sun-bathe for fifteen or twenty minutes after his eight laps. (The reader will fail to see the importance of this, I am sure, but in all the years I have known Robert, I believe I have not seen him in a completely relaxed state more than a dozen times.)

The Hollywood Bowl concert was exactly one week away (September 2), and I did not anticipate that we would start worrying about that until a day or two before the first rehearsal (there were only to be a niggardly two—a very sore point with the composer every time he conducted in his home town). But otherwise the program fulfilled what he called the Bowl's requirements—it was "good and loud": *Fireworks, Scherzo à la Russe,* and the 1945 suite from *The Firebird,* none of which imposed too much of a strain. Robert's piece, concluding the first half of the evening—Schoenberg's orchestration of Brahms's *Quartet in G minor*—was actually the most demanding work, since it would be played for the first time in the Bowl, and a portion of one rehearsal was not really enough to regulate its subtleties of balance. Still, even that did not seem to be too upsetting.

But Hollywood Bowl concerts were usually more pleasurable affairs for the audience than for the performers. Backstage, which overlooked the parking area for the hundreds of privileged characters who had special permits eliminating the long uphill walk from the entrance, and who very often arrived late, with a honking of horns and a glare of headlights penetrating the dressing rooms, was not the most placid area one could find. For Stravinsky the whole business was a little too *al fresco*, also because the refreshment stand, with its pervading odor of hot dogs and mustard (an Americanization he had escaped), was just a little too close to his dressing room. Still, none of these disadvantages was really troublesome, and one even accepted them as part of the whole wonderful outdoor scene.

So . . . since there was really nothing important to worry about, we began to search for something. Robert found it: rain would undoubtedly fall on the night of the concert. This was a presentiment one did not voice in California, especially during the Hollywood Bowl season. That open-air edifice is perhaps the world's greatest testimonial to chauvinism. Let anyone imply that the heavens might give forth rain between June and September, and cudgels would be at the ready. For there is not one single spot except the stage where shelter from the elements is available.

Because of this negative optimism, Hollywood Bowl concerts generally do not contain rain clauses. Should such an act of God occur, the administration is held blameless—there are no rain checks—and all commitments, including the performance fee, become null and void. True, efforts would be made to reschedule a concert for another time or season, but in the current instance no other time was possible, and the fee was a very nice seventy-five hundred dollars. Also, we had been unable to cancel the London engagement at Festival Hall on September 14 (although Stravinsky had wished to do so), principally because the composer was committed to the Liebermann documentary film, and London was to be preceded by five days of activity in Hamburg for the same purpose. He therefore would be compelled to leave Hollywood the day following the Bowl concert.

But Robert said it would rain, and to keep everyone's mind off this dread prospect (there wasn't a single cloud in the sky on Thursday, Friday, Saturday, Sunday, etc.) we made trips to the Pancake House, where Stravinsky indulged himself in the blueberry variety to such an extent that he developed a three-day stomachache; and on another evening went with Jack Quinn and Miranda to the Luau, where Mrs. Stravinsky had so much grog (I think she liked it because the name sounded Russian) that she remained in bed for most of the next twenty-four hours.

I also remember that we dined at La Rue's with the Montaperts. I had met them on one or two occasions, but this was the first opportunity I had had to spend any time with them at all, and I recall that after a very interesting dinner, during which Mr. Montapert's unusual ability in the difficult area of tax law was clearly revealed, we stopped for a brief visit at their house. It had a rather extraordinary and very handsome kitchen—extraordinary because it was also the residence of several barnyard pets, including a huge rabbit that behaved exactly like a devoted spaniel (he came when Stravinsky summoned him), and handsome because its wood paneling and provincial accessories were the work of Madame Montapert, whose other special talents were in the direction of international law. I noticed particularly that Stravinsky listened very carefully to everything the Montaperts had to say about his business and his taxes, and it was obvious that he had complete and apparently highly justified confidence in both of them.

Wednesday, the day of the first rehearsal, rolled around, and along with it so dense a fog that is was impossible to see the far end of the driveway. Robert was to rehearse that day by himself, with Stravinsky taking the dress rehearsal on the following morning (the day of the concert). With a daring that almost gave Mrs. Stravinsky a heart attack—and me a fractured torso, since I had elected to stand near the mailbox in order to mark a path for him—he backed out the *white* Lincoln (which exactly matched the fog)—and vanished from view, "forever," said Mrs. Stravinsky. Her husband, who had come clad in pajamas and beret to see his colleague off, reassured us over some porridge, which he chose to take that morning in the dining room, that "he will appear again like *Der fliegende Holländer*." Half an hour later, when the mist had cleared a bit (it was now possible to see the houses on the opposite side of the street), George Fowler, head of Hurok's West Coast office and my good friend, came to take me to the Bowl, where we found Robert and the musicians damply at work. The box seats, as well as the benches at the higher reaches of the Bowl's circumference, were streaming with condensed fog. The musicians—the string players especially—were naturally concerned about damage to their instruments, and half of them were not playing. But Robert, as always when he worked in Stravinsky's absence, was the soul of patience, and decided to order a break until the sun came out. He was immediately surrrounded by a large group of the younger men, who engaged him in a discussion (I recall) about the just-completed recording sessions, with a particular emphasis on "the Maestro's" *Variations* tape, which (it was apparent) some of them had already heard, via the grapevine, was a total loss. The sun *did* come out and I was unable to hear how he extricated himself from this embarrassment, but as we drove home he did say to me that several of the men who had been at the sessions had remarked on a noticeable failure of the composer's vitality. Neither of us agreed, at the time, with this opinion, and neither did Dr. Edell, whose latest report only a day or so before described his patient's blood as normal and his vital organs in better condition than those of most men twenty years his junior. The leg was troublesome, but it seemed to me that even that difficulty had been improved by the walks, and I note in my diary entry for August 30, when we dined with the Montaperts, that he had climbed up and down the staircase twice in the course of half an hour to find some papers he wished to give to his attorney, and which he said no one else could locate.

That night—or rather at two that morning—I was awakened by a thunderclap that almost threw me out of bed; this was followed by a cloudburst. Robert had been right, as usual. He is, I have always been sure, possessed of a sixth sense: prophecy. Still, this time he fell a little short of the mark, for the day dawned gray but promising, and although Stravinsky started the rehearsal expecting a cancellation call at any moment, the sun did come out, and with such force that by ten-thirty the seats were dry and another heat wave had begun.

Ten thousand people came to the Bowl that evening, and ten thousand stood up and cheered Stravinsky's slow and (he told me afterward) extremely uncomfortable trip to the podium. The walk is a long one on the Hollywood Bowl stage, and I had a moment's fright as we waited for the cue, for he turned to me and said: "I do not feel my leg. I cannot walk." But he did, and conducted with even more vigor than he had shown at his eightieth birthday concert in 1962 on the same stage.

The reviews were concerned almost totally with the ovation and the tremendous power "generated by that tiny aging figure"—in this case very correctly described, for even a six-foot-three conductor and a hundred-piece orchestra appear miniature in that vast space. As I drove home alone with Stravinsky, who sat with his neck swathed in towels and with the windows tightly shut against the treacherous air, he said to me questioningly, "All the seats were full?" And when I answered yes, he remarked that those in the highest rows were probably applauding the music accompanying the movie at Grauman's Chinese Theater, on Hollywood Boulevard.

He preferred the smaller dimensions of Ravinia, of course, as most musicians would, and I thought about the concert he had just conducted there on July 8, his fourth since 1962, and the one that was fated to be his last in that theater. The audience had not been large—about four thousand people attended, in contrast to the ten thousand jamming the lawns surrounding the open-sided roofed area during the year of his eightieth birthday,* and establishing an all-time record for a program of serious music. But this time the evening had been full of enchantment, as one reporter put it, not only for the audience but for Stravinsky. He had many old friends in the orchestra and greatly admired the first trumpet Adolph Herseth and the oboist Ray Still. The program was not "popular" in the sense of those given at the Hollywood Bowl, for he conducted the complete *Fairy's Kiss* rather than the *Firebird* or *Petrushka*. And Robert led Webern's *Six Pieces* as well as Stravinsky's *Symphony in Three Movements*—not at all works to arouse excited responses in a crowd of people out for some fresh air and not-too-profound entertainment. But the ovation, supplemented by the *Tusch* of homage from the Chicago Symphony, was, in proportion, greater than that from the Bowl audience, which was to number six thousand more. That night, too, I had trouble with Robert and his curtain calls. These were always a difficulty with him—he would rush out once, bow almost as though he were embarrassed at being applauded, acknowledge the orchestra, rush off, and have to be pushed hard for a second bow. His own performance on that Ravinia evening had been spectacular (all four Chicago critics agreed on this the next day), and the applause was heartfelt and prolonged. But after his first return to the stage, he could not be budged, despite the public's persistence. In fact, Donal Henahan (then with the *Chicago News*) mentioned to me, as our paths crossed on his way out, that Robert's refusal to take his share of the limelight would eventually make him as famous as his championship of "modern" music had.

As for Stravinsky, at supper later in the Ambassador Hotel's

* In 1963, the figure was also in the neighborhood of four thousand, but this was due to rain. In 1964 there was a near-capacity house.

Pump Room (unusual, for we normally had after-concert meals via room service), he consumed a huge trout and one of my lamb chops, plus two double Scotches, astonishing the two "blacka-moors" in full oriental dress who settled him on the banquette as though he were a piece of rare porcelain. In fact, he did not even object when the dance band started to play.

We left for New York on the day following the Hollywood Bowl concert, and on September 6 I put the trio on a Lufthansa flight for Berlin. Stravinsky had a bad cold, and from that point on I began to hold my breath every time he was out of sight, although I needn't have. Phone calls to and from Hamburg (where the Lie-bermann filming was in progress) and later from London, prior to the Festival Hall concert, were reassuring—the only complaint was that the press conference in London (also documented by Lieber-mann) had infuriated Stravinsky because in his opinion the ques-tions had reached a new high in inanity. ("How does it feel to compose in old age?" "*I* do not feel in old age—*you* may feel I am in old age—but *I* do not," or words to that effect!)

But London was trying nevertheless. This was the concert he had wanted to cancel after his return from Warsaw, and a great disappointment had been in store for Robert Paterson (whose initial contact with us at the Hurok office had been early in January) when I wrote to him at the last minute that Stravinsky would be unable to conduct *The Rite of Spring*. It was also very difficult for me, since I was beginning to run out of phrases that would not give managers the impression that the composer was an invalid. The problem was that, not being musicians in most cases, none of them could realize exactly how strenuous the *Rite* was for any con-ductor, let alone a man in his eighties. I would get around it by explaining that because of his leg, works that might be lengthier but had more "rest periods" (meaning *lento* or *adagio* passages) were easier on him.

But strangely, although he certainly did not *want* to do concerts, the fact that he might not be *able* to was beginning to trouble Stravinsky. During the London stay he agreed that Paterson should book concerts for him in Brussels, Monaco, and Stockholm, and anywhere else where large sums of money might be available. And the sums were indeed worthy of the adjective, as I discovered when he turned the whole headache over to me and had me notify

Paterson that anything in the neighborhood of seventy-five hundred to ten thousand dollars would be satisfactory. In Europe!! But of course his demands were based on the fact that most of what came in had to be turned over in local taxes. (Those days when I had insisted in contracts that the local management should pick up the local taxes were gone forever!) These sudden enthusiasms, as the reader will remember, were familiar to me but not to Paterson, who immediately began to involve himself in arrangements that were to prove troublesome for everyone, but especially for him.

In the present instance, the consolation prize for Paterson was a healthy one, for he received the first London performance of *Variations*, which Robert conducted. Stravinsky also permitted Paterson to arrange a BBC television recording of the second half of the program (the *Firebird Suite*) without extra fee—although in London he had always been accustomed to receiving large amounts for any such undertaking. However, this generous gesture was profoundly regretted by the composer, because the television crew caused so much disturbance setting up lights during the *Variations* performance, and was so rude and noisy, that the music could hardly be heard. Stravinsky's fury emerged backstage, and one of his victims was a gentleman he did not recognize, who was soon to occupy a more important position than the one he then held: Mr. Edward Heath.

The costs of this BBC recording, since it involved the London Philharmonia, were sizable, and were absorbed by Paterson Ltd., a point that came into great prominence the following year when I was under fire from that manager for having to upset all the lovely promises he alleged (correctly) had been made to him. The sad but compensating factor for Paterson is that he now possesses a rare document, for the Festival Hall concert on September 14 was not only the final occasion on which Stravinsky conducted in London (where, in point of fact, he had conducted very little in the over-all picture), but also took place on the last day the composer would ever spend in England.

We were due in Cincinnati on October 10 for two concerts with the Cincinnati Symphony, with which Stravinsky was to appear for the first time in twenty-five years. The requests for his return can only be described as passionate: the variety and number of letters from Cincinnati begging him to come back exceeds anything in my files from any other city. Between February 1962 and August 1963, for example, appeals arrived from eight suburban musical organizations, five women's clubs, five high schools, two societies for the promotion of the arts, and three synagogues, as well as eighteen private citizens who wondered where and when he would be in the vicinity. Few references, however, were made to fees.

Back in 1962, when I was out of town, a call came from a gentleman named J. Ralph Corbett, who was to make the Cincinnati engagement a reality in 1965. In the intervening years this philanthropist of culture had not only established a distinguished lecture series in the Music Department of the University of Cincinnati, but had been very instrumental in helping to build the orchestra up to its present position of importance in the national picture. He now supplied the missing financial element.

We were all sympathetic to Cincinnati, especially Mrs. Stravinsky, who had had a *vernissage* there the year before and had promised several committee members that she would exert her influence with her husband to fit a visit into his schedule. Also, Stravinsky knew Max Rudolf, the musical director, from the old days at the "Met," and remembered him as a "*gentle*-man" (he emphasized his syllables exactly that way to suggest his double meaning). But he also had heard (from Isaac Stern) that the dressing rooms were "a mile away" from the stage of the Music Hall and that he would have to use a troika to get there in time for his entrance. This bothered him, and it is one thing I always remember in connection with Cincinnati: Stravinsky referred to it over and over and over, from the moment I signed the contract!

There was another more troublesome condition, however. This involved Stravinsky's delivery of a lecture in the Corbett series, and during a moment when I was off the premises, someone at the Hurok office had told Lloyd Haldemann, the orchestra manager, that no contract problems would arise because of this requirement! I had a good deal of trouble getting us out of *this* one, particularly since I again had to extricate Stravinsky from conducting the *Rite* (also promised). Mr. Haldemann heard patiently, via letter, that *The Fairy's Kiss*, besides being the masterpiece we all knew it was, would give Cincinnatians an eight-minute longer opportunity to see the composer on the podium, and that as a bonus he would open the program with *Fireworks*. (I will forever think with pleasure of Messrs. Corbett and Haldemann for the placidity with which they accepted both pieces of "negative" news.) Stravinsky did agree to greet the Corbett lecture audience and answer questions, and his colleague Robert, in addition to conducting the *Rite* and *Symphonies of Wind Instruments*, would deliver the lecture. I signed the contract in March.

The Corbett Lectures were a formal series—much more so than those requested at Muncie and other places, and the subject had to be chosen beforehand with care. It happened that, at the time the contract was executed, Stravinsky had just seen a handsome edition of the autograph of Debussy's *Prelude à l'après-midi d'un faune*, with illustrations and explanations of its development, published in Paris for the Robert Orin Lehmann Foundation. He promptly wrote his publishers, Boosey & Hawkes, that he intended to grant Mr. Lehmann (who had approached him) the privilege of producing an equally artistic volume on *The Rite of Spring*. In July I was instructed by the composer to carry on some discussions with Mr. Lehmann regarding his ideas about the presentation. This was one of Stravinsky's little strategies, employed when he felt that the people around him were not moving fast enough to do things he expected. Boosey & Hawkes had been talking for some time about publishing the *Rite* sketches (since they held the right of first refusal, as with all other Stravinsky materials in their possession, unless Stravinsky said no), and now were far from overwhelmed at the idea of an outside group's involvement in something so important. Moreover, Mr. Lehmann had some very positive notions about how the volume should be presented and distributed—he would not, for example, produce a subscription edition, but only a uniform edition to be distributed free to eight hundred libraries throughout the world. Boosey & Hawkes busied themselves without pause, and the result was that Mr. Lehmann lost out, but the preparation of the volume was undertaken minus further postponements or delays.

Robert began work on the musical analysis and the notes, and it was decided that here was a subject for the Corbett Lecture. He gave it the title *The Rite of Spring: Genesis of a Masterpiece*, and I duly announced this to the Cincinnati management. Everyone became very enthusiastic, a great deal of excitement over the importance of the subject matter was generated throughout the university, and the symphony and university publicity departments applied themselves. I have, among my records, a sheaf of news-clippings announcing *The Genesis of a Masterpiece* that, in my lengthy experience in the publicity business, still stands as a superior example of press placement by someone whom I would bribe away immediately if I were still operating my own office. The count of stories is something close to forty!

But the Corbett audience was not destined to learn about this particular Genesis. Robert, who was occupied with half a dozen other writing projects, and who always thought he could add another to the list, was not ready with this one in time, and the evening in the Music Hall (yes, the demand was so great that the locale was transferred from the university to . . .) became another question-and-answer period. This time both conductors sat in chairs, and the president of the university stood at the lectern and acted as monitor for queries from the floor. As usual, Stravinsky, who had stipulated that he would say hello and then sit back to enjoy his colleague's exposition, answered questions for almost three-quarters of the hour. (Pretty much the same questions, too! Strauss figured again.)

There was an epilogue to this incident. *The Genesis of a Master-piece* was delivered later in the year at Ohio State University during the concerts in Columbus, where the topic for the evening had been announced in the press as an analysis of *L'Histoire du Soldat*, which was changed to *Les Noces*, which was changed to . . . !

During the three weeks in New York prior to the Cincinnati concerts, Stravinsky was not well. He had several extremely bad days; complaints were specifically about severe pains in the back and an "impossible" stiffness in the leg. Doctor Lewithin came to see him almost daily. Both Stravinskys looked forward to his visits, which were more social than medical events in their lives. "Amusing" was always the determining adjective in their selection of any doctor (no matter how high his medical qualifications might be), and Doctor Lewithin filled this requirement. He spoke Russian, for one very important thing, and seemed to have all the time in the world to listen to their problems, not only about physical disturbances, but about life in general. Mrs. Stravinsky had a chance to lament her lot as the caretaker of two touring musicians who left her not a moment to herself; and her husband, whose knowledge of materia medica and syndromes equalled, if not surpassed, that of any physician (with two exceptions) who attended him throughout the years I knew him, had a captive audience.

However, there was one day at the end of September when he was so ill and depressed that I wanted to cancel Cincinnati. At the very mention of this possibility, he displayed so much energy that in the following three days we went to the theater twice (we finally saw *Hello, Dolly!*) and to dinner and lunch at the Côte Basque, which was then a great favorite.

We had a fine time in Cincinnati, even though the backstage mileage caused Stravinsky to walk so slowly that we had to leave the dressing room a good eight minutes before he was due to make his onstage entrance. But we remembered that city for another reason, too—it had one of the best French restaurants in the country, an establishment called Pigalle, where the chef was a dedicated fan who outdid himself with *crêpes* and beef stroganoff every night —almost to Stravinsky's undoing.

CHAPTER THIRTEEN

MRS. Stravinsky and I had had many opportunities to talk together during my stay in Hollywood; she had begun a very concerted campaign to bring her husband's conducting activities to a gradual end. But she was, as always, torn in two directions. Her concern for Stravinsky came first, of course; yet she was also deeply worried about Robert's future. Her references to the obligation due this friend, who had become so much more to the Stravinskys than even that term implies, always made me feel that she regarded his fate as similar to Jonah's. And the analogy is not far-fetched, for like Jonah Robert struggled desperately and constantly to be "unswallowed." He was engaged in so many projects—book reviews, the fifth volume, letters, the *Rite* sketchbook project—that we began to fear he would have a breakdown. Mrs. Stravinsky worried constantly. "He is so good a writer," she would say. "Why doesn't he do just *that?*" And she would indeed have been quite content if Robert had abandoned all other projects and devoted himself to writing on his own account. But then, in the second breath: "He is so good a musician. Why can't he do concerts on his own?" The implication always was, why can't *you* get them for him? And I did keep trying, but it was fairly clear by this time that I was not going to be successful, and that *that* source of income for Robert was diminishing rapidly.

But what Mrs. Stravinsky could never understand was that the writing and the music were two separate affairs. In the first instance I was in complete agreement—Robert's talents as a writer were obvious. He "conveyed" Stravinsky, but in his *own* prose, and whether or not the articles, interviews, and musical analyses were signed with Stravinsky's name, and expressed Stravinsky's ideas, there was no ignoring the ability of the actual author. That shone through and was recognized immediately by discerning writers with an eye for style. More and more, Robert was receiving critical appreciation of his own style even while blasts were blown in his direction for employing it as though it were Stravinsky's. But in the second instance, there was no possibility of argument. As a conductor Robert "conveyed" Stravinsky's music in Stravinsky's own musical language. There was no translation, no transliteration, no editing, no self-expression. Stravinsky had once said of Pierre Monteux and his conducting of the *Rite* that "he never looked for his own glory in it." This is an opinion I think the composer applied in his mind to Robert as well, and explains his complete acceptance of him as co-conductor in the concert hall and the recording studio. It also serves as the most truthful explanation of Robert's failure to command public attention as an independent conductor: he submerged himself completely in Stravinsky when he was on the podium. And finally, the insurmountable opposition from musical directors and orchestra managements, many of whom continued to hold Robert responsible for Stravinsky's persistent refusal to share the podium with anyone else, kept my efforts on his behalf from being successful.

This situation could only produce a tinge of bitterness on all sides, including my own, and I knew that sooner or later it would have to come to a head. But in the meantime my chief worry, beyond Robert and beyond Mrs. Stravinsky, was the composer, and for this reason I disregarded many requests that were made in 1965 for realization during the following year, not even reporting them to the West Coast, and keeping everything over which I had direct control at a minimum. This also meant that I had to scramble around a bit for my own wherewithal—my arrangement with Stravinsky had always been on a commission-and-expense basis, and at this point in our association it went against the grain to discuss money with him. Our relationship had never admitted the subject of a regular salary; it was on another level entirely. Mrs. Stravinsky, of course, knew my problems, and when I would come to Hollywood to stay she always insisted on giving me "tooken" (token!) sums that would take care of my needs. But I didn't like the whole idea, and began to take more assignments during periods when I was not with the family.

The Stravinsky/Craft contracts I had written for the beginning of 1966, with the Hurok office as booking agent, included one each in Minneapolis and St. Louis in January and February, a Los Angeles concert between those two, and one with the Rochester

Philharmonic in March, scheduled during a week in which the
Eastman School of Music devoted itself to a festival of Stravinsky
works. These were not too difficult, and provided a few unusual
moments.

In Minneapolis we were bound in five feet of snow, and it was
twelve below! Stravinsky told me that when he had conducted in
that city a quarter of a century before (and in the same Northrop
Auditorium, which he referred to as "a prehistoric cave"), the snow
had reached a height of ten feet and there was no heat in the hall,
due to a "burst engine" (*sic*). Further: "The harp strings froze . . .
yes, really! . . . It was a performance *glacé!*"—looking at me with
that wide-open-eyed "honest" expression as I helped him make
ready in a now impossibly overheated dressing room (the older
generation of stagehands, still on tap, had remembered).

But snow, of course, is part of the municipal dress of the Twin
Cities, and therefore nothing kept five thousand people from shaking it off their coats and stamping it off their boots in the Northrop
lobby. The ovation (for *Fireworks* and *The Fairy's Kiss*) raised
the temperature to volcanic level, and it was equally so for Robert's
performance of the *Rite*. But the latter's comment, as Mrs. Stravinsky and I congratulated him backstage while the thunderous applause was still going on, was as self-deprecatory as usual: "They're
just trying to keep warm."

Between Minneapolis and St. Louis Stravinsky flew home, and
five days later fulfilled the first of three engagements scheduled
during the year in Los Angeles—four, really, for the initial one
involved a pair with the Los Angeles Philharmonic. This program
was particularly important for its "non-popular" elements. Stravinsky conducted his own transcription of Bach's *Vom Himmel
hoch Variations* and the *Symphony of Psalms*, while Robert opened
the program with Schoenberg's transcription of Bach's *St. Anne
Prelude and Fugue*, followed this with Stravinsky's *Symphony in C*,
and as a bonus offering his fifty-five-year-old cantata *King of the
Stars* (*Zvezdoliki*). I was sorry to miss this concert, which was a
major event in Los Angeles music life (the program! the program!),
for as part of my new policy I was busy earning some money "advancing" Sherwin Robert Rodgers's national tour of Rolf Hoch-
huth's controversial play *The Deputy*, which was having an interesting success. Though this permitted (because of the convenient

nearby "stands") a trip to Minneapolis and later to St. Louis, the West Coast was not feasible.

The conductors *sans* Mrs. Stravinsky joined me in St. Louis on February 1. We stopped at the Chase Park Plaza and did not leave our rooms except for rehearsals and the concerts, taking advantage of that hotel's celebrated Tack Room, where Robert nightly satisfied his insatiable appetite for steaks and shrimp cocktails (the former like sides of steers). Stravinsky telephoned his wife every night—she was alone in the house (it was a servantless period) and he was concerned. But he usually didn't reach her until the later hours of the evening—she was having a wonderful time all by herself, dining out with Lawrence Morton, visiting with friends, shopping with Miranda, painting, lunching in Beverly Hills—in short, she didn't miss any of us a single bit, and let us know it! The gentlemen were a little nonplussed, I remember, in the manner of all gentlemen who cannot understand why their absence from home does not result in the dissolution of the universe. Once, when Mrs. Stravinsky did not answer our call until the immoderate hour of 10:30 P.M., Stravinsky actually said to her peevishly, "Where *were* you all night?"—exactly like any other husband.

Stravinsky knew the music director of the St. Louis Symphony —Eleazar de Carvalho—from his South American visits, and liked him very much. De Carvalho had a young and very beautiful Brazilian wife who had a career herself as a concert pianist under her maiden name, Jocy de Oliveira. The composer paid her a great compliment, and also acknowledged a friendship, by having me write on June 25, when I sent the program to William Zalken, who was in charge of the concerts, that he would like to have Miss de Oliveira play his *Capriccio.** I say "compliment" because this was one work about which he was particularly exacting as to performance requirements—which is not to say that such an attitude was absent in the case of his other works, but he had, after all, been soloist in this one many times himself. In fact, I had heard him voice very negative opinions about past performances by other pianists. Moreover, only a few weeks prior to the St. Louis engagement, he had raised strong objections to Columbia's choice

---

* The remainder of the program included the *Pulcinella Suite*, led by Stravinsky, and the Brahms-Schoenberg *Quartet* in G minor and Stravinsky's *Variations*, led by Robert.

of a well-known European pianist for a recording of the *Capriccio*. With incredible stupidity Columbia had ignored his wishes; Stravinsky refused to attend the session and never conducted this work on records,* and this incident was added to the list of grievances which later ended his contract with Columbia.

There was a very human note in the St. Louis story, contributed by de Carvalho (who, incidentally, was guest-conducting elsewhere and was not in St. Louis during our stay). He sent us a telegram which not only expressed his deep appreciation at the honor paid his wife, but also asked that we make it very, *very* clear in our correspondence with the Symphony management that the suggestion for a soloist came directly from Stravinsky and was not influenced by himself. I did, indeed, write this letter, and quoted the composer exactly as saying he "would never have suggested the *Capriccio* with Madame de Carvalho as soloist if I had not been most eager for her to perform it."

Madame de Carvalho gave a fine performance, and Stravinsky's approval was very warm. The ovations were standing (which, of course, we usually expected they would be), and there had been no quarrel about the generous number of rehearsals—six!!—awarded the two conductors. Mr. Zalken was found to be another "*gentle*-man". The only unpleasant note was a story in the *St. Louis Post–Dispatch* printed the day before our arrival (and captured in time, thank Heaven, by me) from the pen of an aging reporter, who concluded his brief history of Stravinsky by criticizing his "lack of melody" thus: "A composer whose melodic inventiveness is blocked is a handicapped composer, and there are no two ways about it. . . . It is fair, I believe, to say that Stravinsky is an incomplete genius." Well . . . !

I collected one other little St. Louis "water color." We had booked three adjoining bedrooms at the hotel, with Stravinsky occupying the middle one. One night, as I sat up in bed very late (it was after one, I think) writing some release or other, he tapped on the connecting door and entered. He explained that he had seen my light and begged pardon for having disturbed me, but could he use my reading lamp, which seemed brighter than his? Then he sat down in an armchair, opened the Simenon he was carrying, read

* As piano soloist Stravinsky did record the *Capriccio* (Paris, 1930, for French Columbia).

for half an hour (while I pretended to continue working), and finally closed the book, waved good night, and left. I felt as if I had just had a visit from someone who was afraid of the dark.

Stravinsky/Craft fulfilled five more contracts which I handled in 1966; at the Hollywood Bowl (July 5); with the New York Philharmonic (July 24); the Louisville Symphony (September 17); the Columbus Symphony (November 29); and a pair in Chicago on December 28 and January 1, 1967.* Of these I suppose the July 24 concert would be considered the major event (in a biographer's eyes, at any rate), since it climaxed a three-week-long Stravinsky Festival at Lincoln Center.

Except for the Rochester trip, which brought them East, the Stravinskys remained quietly at home in Hollywood throughout March and April, where Stravinsky worked hard on *Requiem Canticles*. My tour with *The Deputy* kept me in Chicago and other midwest cities until the end of March, and because Stravinsky had finally consented (after a long, long correspondence and a large, large fee) to conduct *Oedipus Rex* at the Athens Festival in Greece and later in Lisbon, and was planning to be abroad for the major part of May and June, I signed a contract to take the national company of *Barefoot in the Park*, starring that exquisite lady Miss Myrna Loy, to Philadelphia and Washington. During one of our two trips to Chicago the previous year, the four of us had seen the play at the Blackstone Theater, and that evening was probably Stravinsky's closest approach to a state resembling hilarity. He wore his loud grin throughout the three acts. (Neil Simon's other long-run opus, *The Odd Couple*, which we saw at the same theater in 1966, did not amuse him quite so much, but the Scotch that company manager Clayton Coots smuggled down to him in a paper cup during intermission did!)

The spring period at home was rewarding for the composer. Between the first and fourth weeks he completed more than half of the new work, and would undoubtedly have finished the rest if the

---

* Stravinsky and his colleague conducted the San Francisco Symphony on February 23, 24, and 25—a contract made directly with the orchestra's management. The composer led *Vom Himmel hoch* and the *Symphony of Psalms;* Robert the *Rite* and *Variations*. Robert Commanday, in the *San Francisco Chronicle*, reported that "from the roar that went up . . . you would have thought it was the first time San Francisco had heard *The Rite of Spring*."

European trip had not intervened. That voyage bothered me in other respects, for Robert, it turned out, had been encouraging Paterson to go ahead and book whatever concerts he could get, and Paterson had done so in East Berlin, Luxembourg, and Strasbourg. Stravinsky was also committed to make appearances in Oxford in connection with the Bach Festival—on which I compiled a huge exchange of cablegrams with its enterprising organizer, Lina Lalandi. It all seemed too much, and when I flew in from Washington on May 8 to meet their plane from Los Angeles, I was certain it was, for Stravinsky seemed frailer than ever. His wife was very worried. "We will cancel everything," she said. "Wait and see."

But in the four days before they flew to Paris, after several talks with Dr. Lewithin, Stravinsky appeared to improve. He actually seemed to be looking forward to the Athens trip, and talked animatedly at the Pierre with Carlos Moseley about the programs for the forthcoming festival in New York.

The first of Mrs. Stravinsky's predictions came true early in June, when Robert, writing on the sixteenth from the Hotel Lotti in Paris, told me that Luxembourg and Strasbourg were cancelled because Stravinsky had a very bad flu and Robert was sick, too (which latter bit of information did not surprise me at all; in New York, Robert had worn the look of someone who had spent several days in the company of a vampire). I also learned by transatlantic phone that the mayor of Strasbourg was a follower of the school of skeptics, for either he or someone purporting to be his deputy paid an unannounced visit to the Lotti suite not long after news of the cancellation had reached Strasbourg, and penetrated as far as the bedrooms! The French doctor had strongly advised rest, but the Athens and Lisbon money was much too tempting, and they were determined to go.

Still, both of them ill at the same time! In one telephone call to Mrs. Stravinsky, when I caught her alone, I was sure I heard her weeping, although she vehemently denied it. But I could visualize how she must have been kept running from one room to another with tea or pills, or newspapers or books, answering dozens of telephone calls, calling room service every five minutes; and I could imagine her husband's *"Vera!"* and Robert's *"Madame!"* recurring with the consistency of the thirty-two *fouettés* in *Swan Lake* if she should happen to sit down in a chair for one moment. I entertained some wild notions at this point—of abandoning Miss

Loy and flying to Paris to drag them all home by force. I even
went so far as to have TWA issue me a ticket, which shows that
even after seven years of association with this truly unpredictable
trio I was still not accustomed to the fact that it was unpredictable.
For two days later, when I called to say that I was flying to Paris
to help (fearing that the surprise might be too much for them),
the *concierge* relayed the message that they could be reached in
the Ritz dining room!

Nevertheless, my mind was made up on one point. I would book
no more concerts either at home or abroad unless forced to at gun-
point. (How many times in the last year had I made this resolu-
tion?) Robert and I exchanged several letters on this subject during
these weeks, and it was clear to me that there would be very few
European concert tours after this one. It had finally been driven
home that, despite the one or two financially rewarding engagements, fees were always too low and taxes and expenses too high.
Neither of us voiced what we were *really* thinking; but when, a
little later, East Berlin and Oxford were also cancelled, I could read,
between Robert's sometimes peremptory appeals to secure contracts, his despairing "How much longer, how much longer?" It
was as though his own life were beginning to slip away from him.

The Athens and Lisbon concerts came off well, but the conductors did not. They both contracted an ailment with the
romantic-sounding name *fièvre de Malte*, from eating Greek goat
cheese, and were uncomfortably confined to bed again in Paris.
On June 22 the wanderers returned to New York somewhat the
worse for wear. Although I was still under contract to the *Barefoot*
company, I secured a few days' leave to fly to Hollywood with
them on July 2 to to look after matters for the Hollywood Bowl
concert on the fifth. This, Stravinsky's last appearance in that vale
of stars, was accompanied by some unforgettable experiences apart
from those his presence always provided. For one, he was conducted onstage by another octogenarian, S. Hurok, who, having
made certain that Stravinsky could reach the podium alone—although so much more slowly, haltingly, painfully than he had only
one year before—then stepped modestly to right stage. There he
stood at attention, like a benevolent general reviewing a visiting
troop, while Stravinsky conducted his own (once-banned-in-
Boston) orchestration of *The Star-Spangled Banner*, and the audience behaved as though the Los Angeles Dodgers had just won

the World Series. In the dressing room, after saluting Robert, who was just then leaving to conduct *The Song of the Nightingale*, Stravinsky said to me dryly, "Who were they applauding, *me* or Hurok?"

The other event occurred after the concert. Mrs. Stravinsky rarely came to the Bowl and on that evening had arranged to meet Robert at Chasen's following his own chore, which, this time, was the *Firebird Suite*. Mr. Hurok, Stravinsky, and I were to join them for a later supper. The black Lincoln was parked directly outside the stage entrance, surrounded by—at quick estimate—at least five hundred cheering fans. The guards, commanded by George Fowler, had a great deal of trouble clearing a way for us, but finally the two elderly gentlemen were settled in the rear seat and I was safely installed behind the wheel. We were immediately surrounded again. This time our protectors had to exert a little pressure to make a lane so that I could drive out, and when this was done they signaled emphatically for me to come ahead. But I didn't come ahead—the car had been parked in reverse. The crowd scattered as though the father of a family of skunks had decided to take his progeny on a sightseeing tour of the Bowl. As I shifted to "D," a second short of backing into the wall that formed one side of the musical director's dressing room, the only persons who remained calm were my two passengers. The conversation, while I drove away as non-chalantly as anyone could who has just missed committing the crime of the century, went something like this (and in English, *not* Russian):

Hurok: Tell me, Igor Fyodorovitch, how much are you insured for?

Igor Fyodorovitch: Not enough.

Hurok: How often do you employ this driver?

I.F.: All the time.

Hurok: I'll send my insurance man tomorrow.

I.F.: Good. [Pause] No. Tonight. Tell him to meet us at Chasen's. We need to be insured for the drive home after dinner.

And they labored this joke like a pair of conspirators to such a point that I took the wrong turn on the boulevard and headed freeway-wise toward San Francisco. Sheer luck, in the form of a detour, brought us to Chasen's an hour later.

This final Bowl concert did not do much to improve the situation with Columbia. Stravinsky's recorders were now fully aware

that the composer was not feeling well-disposed about the treatment
he had been receiving, especially since the January incident of the
Capriccio. They were anxious to improve the situation and to secure as many discs as they could before it was too late—and, incidentally, they wanted to record the Los Angeles Philharmonic.

Therefore John McClure had requested that *The Song of the
Nightingale* be included in the program, as this was one of the
works not yet satisfactorily documented. He also planned to record
whatever other Stravinsky pieces would be performed—and he
promised Robert a Schoenberg recording as well. After a flood of
cables, phone calls, telegrams had passed between Paris (Stravinsky), New York (Columbia), Washington (me), and Hollywood (the extraordinarily understanding Jaye Rubanoff—cooperative, peace-loving), we reached an agreement on the program.
Schoenberg's *Chamber Symphony* would be taped, as well as *The
Song of the Nightingale*, the Fourth Tableau from *Petrushka*, and
the *Divertimento* from *The Fairy's Kiss*. Then, three weeks before
the concert, Columbia backed down. Too expensive, said they—
meaning the Schoenberg, of course—and gave as an excuse that
they had exceeded their budget on the *Perséphone* recorded in May
at a cost of thirty thousand dollars. Robert wrote me from Paris
that McClure had said the Schoenberg project was at an end, to
which Robert had answered that in that case so was the Stravinsky
project. He was bitter, and I did not blame him. The budget excuse
was hardly valid; Columbia had *wanted Perséphone* and should have
foreseen its costs. Furthermore, it could never have been made
without Robert, whose compensation would have been his own
recording session.

Robert's "revenge" lost some of its force, however, because it
came too late. Columbia Records had used him well to secure the
Stravinsky library and, despite his anger, were to use him again in
October and January. But even if it had been possible to smooth
matters over, Stravinsky himself was destined to make only one
more record, the *Firebird Suite*, in January 1967.

Two days after the Bowl concert Mr. Hurok came to lunch,
which was served by a cook named Dagmar. Dagmar not only
could cook, but also looked like a Scandinavian movie star. The
impresario always stayed at the Beverly Hills Hotel when he was
in Los Angeles, and I went to fetch him in the black Lincoln. After

lunch Stravinsky told me in a whisper to be sure to use the white Lincoln for his return. As Mr. Hurok started to climb into the front seat, a startled expression crossed his face. He said nary a word until we reached the luxurious *porte-cochère* of his hotel, and as he disembarked he looked at me and commented slowly, "You know, I could swear the Stravinskys had a black car!" Stravinsky was enchanted when I reported the success of his ploy but later asked George Fowler, who came to take me out to dinner, to be sure to expose his trickery at an opportune moment because "I would not wish Hurok to worry about losing his memory—not with all *his* contracts!"

I returned to *Barefoot* and Washington the next day, acquiring a wrenched shoulder en route by virtue of a porters' strike at the Los Angeles airport and three extra pieces of baggage carried in advance of the Stravinskys' July 14 arrival for the festival at Lincoln Center.

The festival, however, had been underway since June 30, and thereby hangs another tale. During the previous fall, prior to our trip to Cincinnati, Carlos Moseley, then managing director of the New York Philharmonic, had met with us all at the Hotel Pierre to discuss the 1966 summer festival at Lincoln Center, which was to be dedicated to Stravinsky. The plans he outlined interested the composer, for within three weeks important works from every "period" and examples of each "style" in his career would be performed within a frame of ten orchestral events and three chamber-music concerts. The programs would also be planned to include works by masters who had endowed Stravinsky with some of their wealth, and works by contemporary composers which displayed that they were Stravinsky's musical beneficiaries. Lukas Foss was artistic director for the Festival; Leonard Bernstein, the Philharmonic's musical director, would conduct the opening concert; and the concluding one would be a Stravinsky/Craft concert, with the composer conducting *Symphony of Psalms*.

And the guest conductors for the other programs? Well, Kiril Kondrashin, conductor of the Moscow Philharmonic, for one: nod of approval; Lukas Foss for another: nod of approval; and (pause) Ernest Ansermet for another: long pause on the Russian front, then a brief but determined polemic, a turning towards the bedroom, and the discussion was left to be continued animatedly by Carlos,

Robert, and myself. But Stravinsky could not have vetoed in any case, apart from the reason that an unnecessary scandal would ensue, and in connection with an event in his honor. He was not the artistic director, and such decisions were not within his jurisdiction. He could have refused to appear, of course, but this would have caused an even greater scandal. Besides, he did not want to refuse. He liked the whole idea of New York formally paying major attention to a panorama of his works. The meeting ended optimistically, and the drawing of the contract was left to me. The fee offered by the Philharmonic was lower than that I was then asking (and receiving) for Stravinsky, but it was augmented by one thousand dollars for Stravinsky's definite commitment to be in attendance at the opening program on June 30.

It was also assumed at the time that he would certainly attend some, if not all, of the others, or at least put in an appearance. There was actually no reason for him not to. When we signed the festival contract on October 29 nothing—not even the Hollywood Bowl concert—was definitely booked for the following July. But even then I knew that Stravinsky had started to think about how he could avoid being in New York at the time Ansermet would conduct. We would have to wait and see, however, for the programs had not yet been made final, nor had the conductors been formally signed. One other point was touchy. Stravinsky was sole controller of his own program, of course, but Robert asked me to insert a clause into the contract that would grant the composer the right to approve the other programs, particularly the selection of non-Stravinsky works. I believe the Philharmonic management would have conceded this (as, indeed, it should have done), but Lukas Foss would not, and as artistic director it was entirely within his province to refuse. Stravinsky did not belabor the point. It was, in fact, of more interest to Robert than to him—especially that program that would be concerned with "Stravinsky and Recent Years." However, Foss did "consult" once or twice, and finally permitted the modern music program to be more or less selected by Stravinsky/Craft. This ultimately included two works of Webern (*String Trio* and *Kinderstück*) and one each by Carter (*Études and Fantasy*), Varèse (*Octandre*), Foss (*Echoi*), Boulez (*Éclat*), and Babbitt (*Ensembles for Synthesizer*)—the last-named performed during intermission on the Grand Promenade beneath the Lippold sculptures of Orpheus and Apollo. Of this entire list,

probably the only works with which Stravinsky was really familiar
were the Boulez, which he himself had recommended for inclusion
on the program, and the Varèse, which Robert had recorded. But
he gave the nod to the inclusion of the other compositions. His own
works on this particular program were the *Fanfare for Two Trum-
pets* (composed for Balanchine and Kirstein) and the *Introitus* (a
New York première).

At the opening concert, the audience rose as one when Stravinsky
entered the manager's loge at the left of Philharmonic Hall; he sat
patiently while Leonard Bernstein conducted a program entitled
"Stravinsky and American Music," beginning with the composer's
arrangement of *The Star-Spangled Banner*, which was followed by
Samuel Barber's *Capricorn Concerto*, Aaron Copland's *Dance Symphony*, and Revueltas's *Sensemayá*. Mr. Bernstein was at his spectacular best, and audience excitement mounted with the performance of each work. By the time the Revueltas was over,
Stravinsky's influence on American music was quite clear, and—in
my opinion—all three non-Stravinsky composers would have fared
superbly if *The Rite of Spring* had not been the concluding work
of the evening, reducing everything that had gone before to a faint
echo.

Bernstein had surpassed his own image in the *Rite*, and as he
turned to face the principal loge, with arms outstretched toward
Stravinsky, the cheering threatened to break the Philharmonic's
new multi-million-dollar sound barrier. The composer, after a
brief acknowledgment of the homage, moved from his seat, leaving
the spotlight and another quarter of an hour's applause to the conductor of the evening.

Dressing Room Number 2 had been assigned (thoughtfully) to
the composer for his use during the entire festival. It adjoined that
of the music director, and there he, Mrs. Stravinsky, and I sat and
waited patiently until Bernstein arrived from stage level, flushed,
excited, and escorted by at least two dozen worshippers in various
states of ecstasy. He knelt at Stravinsky's feet to receive the composer's embrace, which was warm and delivered with a deeply
affectionate smile. Then, as he started to rise, Stravinsky leaned
toward him, raised an admonishing finger and said, "I do not agree
with your *tempi*. All *wrong!*"

The Ansermet problem, scheduled for July 9 and 12—"Stravinsky and French Music": Machaut's *Hoquetus*, Poulenc's *Organ*

Concerto, encircled by *Symphonies of Wind Instruments* and *Perséphone*—was totally eliminated by the Hollywood Bowl concert on the fifth. Obviously Stravinsky required at least a week to recover from *that* strenuous summer evening, and his "doctor insisted" that he could not travel to New York before July 14. The first program he could conveniently attend, therefore, was "Stravinsky and the Dance," on Friday evening, July 15, co-conducted by Lukas Foss and his assistant, Richard Dufallo. This all-Stravinsky program was a sore point with me, for it included a rather novel presentation of *The Soldier's Tale*, in which the speaking parts were assumed by three gentlemen whose usual business was composing, not acting: to wit, Aaron Copland, John Cage, and Elliott Carter as—respectively—the Narrator, the Devil, and the Soldier. In our earlier communications, Lukas had suggested that Robert share the podium with him in one of two concerts that were contemplated, and when we were advised of this particular plum, I had taken it for granted that it would be given to Robert. When the decision was made known, Robert said little, except that he did not want half of *any* concert save the half he was to do with Stravinsky. But I was annoyed and spoke of this with the composer, hoping he would express his own displeasure. He demurred, on the basis of the accepted authority of the artistic director, pointing out at the same time that, although the festival was built around him and his works, *he* already *knew* his works, and his interest now was only in the program *he* would conduct and in which Robert was to lead the first New York concert performance of *The Flood*. Stravinsky was always consistent in this respect: he was not a good listener at performances, and especially those of his own music.

He did not feel well on the evening of the "Dance" program—the transcontinental adjustment in time always affected him—but he attended for a special reason: his friend Balanchine had choreographed the *Elegy* and *Ragtime* (*Elegy* would have its première). Suzanne Farrell, who later caused some public stir by deserting Balanchine and the New York City Ballet to get married, was to dance both, the second work with Arthur Mitchell. Balanchine was eager for the composer's opinion on the choreography and the ballerina; it turned out, fortunately, to be very pleasing in both instances. As for the *Soldier's Tale* presentation, Stravinsky rose in the loge wearing the broadest smile possible, to thank the performers and accept his share of the applause. But if one were close enough, there was the faintest hint that his expression came from

the Commercial File. (He did, however, receive a visit at the Pierre
from John Cage—their first encounter—and gave him a sheet of
manuscript for a charity auction.)

There was no smile at all for the program five days later, the
"high point" of which was a visual presentation of *Oedipus Rex* by
Larry Rivers, who placed that tragedy of patricide and incest
within the confines of a boxing ring, clothing the predestined perpetrator of these crimes in the trunks and gloves of a heavyweight
champion fated to lose his title. I don't think it is anywhere recorded that Stravinsky ever attended a prizefight (although he
might have, in the Paris days), and, to put it as simply as possible,
he did not like the sport.

While Jason Robards (Narrator) and singers Shirley Verrett,
Ernst Häfliger, Heinz Rehfuss, and Thomas Paul were engaged in
this contest, Robert was rehearsing *The Rake's Progress* in Santa Fe,
where he was also contracted that summer to conduct three performances of Berg's *Wozzeck*. The difficulties of arranging his
arrival in New York on July 22 in time to take a 10:00 A.M. rehearsal (to be followed by another at two, to be followed by the
dress the next day at ten, to be followed by the concert at eight-
thirty, to be followed by his immediate return to Santa Fe) were
aggravated not only by the fact that John Crosby could not release
him until after an important rehearsal on the twenty-first, but also
by an airline strike of all carriers save American. At that company's
Columbus Circle office, where a line of one hundred or more air-
happy people formed on the street two hours before the ticket
desk opened for business, I employed every devious method I
could think of (short of an ancient and dishonorable one) and
finally secured a ticket on a plane out of El Paso for New York,
leaving at midnight on the twenty-first. Santa Fe is not within walking distance of El Paso, however, and a private plane had to be
chartered to deliver Robert there. At 4:00 A.M. on July 22, I met
this worn-out, hungry, pale, and Cessna-deaf "music fanatic," who
was so confused when he saw me standing at the gate that he said
in a daze, "Gee, it seems awfully dark for eight o'clock."

Robert held onto his energy throughout the *Symphony in Three
Movements* and *The Flood*. The distinguished poetess Marianne
Moore was originally to have been Narrator for the latter work,
but she bowed out at the last moment on the grounds that her extremely soft voice did not project, and John Hollander took her

place. The performance was esthetically satisfying, and the applause was—satisfying. I sat with Stravinsky in Dressing Room Number 2 and heard the music over the speaker transmitting it thereto; he made no comment at all, but gave Robert a hearty kiss on both cheeks when—in a state near-collapse—he stumbled in, snatched up his belongings, and returned to Pierre. There he packed and then kept himself awake by sheer force of will, so that he wouldn't miss his early flight to Santa Fe.

The *Symphony of Psalms* that evening will, I think, never be forgotten by the full house that heard its creator conduct this noblest praise of God in twentieth-century music—the last appearance he would ever make on the podium in New York City.

Outside his dressing room and in the adjoining Green Room, there was an impossible jam of people. Stravinsky was perspiring heavily and was very tired, but he was also obviously happy. He received the tributes of the privileged—those whom I knew should be admitted—relaxed, drank Scotch, kissed several ladies, had a smile for everyone. *Time* magazine's photographer Alfred Statler crept about and caught him bending low over Miss Moore's hand, embracing Elliott Carter, toasting Lukas Foss and Carlos Moseley, greeting the French conductor Jean Martinon. There was one shot he did not catch, however, and that was when I refused entrance to someone who was asking for "the Maestro." Without looking to see who it was, or recognizing the voice over the din, I said, "Sorry, no more visitors," and slammed the door very tightly shut on Mr. S. Hurok!! *

* He gained access by another route, along with Goddard Lieberson.

CHAPTER FOURTEEN

TWO days after the conclusion of the festival, the Stravinskys and I flew to Los Angeles, where I remained with them for a month. Robert was in Santa Fe during this period, save for the final three days of my stay. (It was the longest amount of time he had ever spent away from them, and he telephoned daily— sometimes twice a day.) His absence had two immediately notice-able effects: one on me—my eyesight improved; the other on everyone—tranquillity prevailed. Robert's endless store of nervous energy and his ever-bubbling "hot spring" of ideas, however fascinat-ing, could make one feel that it was necessary to live each of the sixty-one minutes he crammed into every hour as if a deadline loomed ahead. Stravinsky, delighted to be back in his studio, oc-cupied himself immediately with his work on *Requiem Canticles*. His wife relaxed, slept late, visited her dressmaker. Even the de-parture of the glamorous Dagmar, whose visa expired within three days of our return, provoked no crisis. Mrs. Stravinsky had an enormous collection of cookbooks, and I supplied accessories to her main courses. I also started a concentrated hunt for a new servant, enlisting the aid of Miranda.

Dr. Edell prescribed a series of bleedings to reduce the platelet count, which he found high, but otherwise the composer's general condition was pronounced good. Mrs. Stravinsky, however, was discovered to be overweight, and a program of exercise (swim-ming) and diet was in order. This was always a real hardship for her, chiefly because she was convinced she ate very little, and would tell you this seriously while consuming three or four pieces (one after the other!) of French bread with butter, or some other simple but deadly snack. But she was subject to high blood pressure, and the danger of heart strain was always present. The staircase didn't help either. One of her greatest charms was her complete lack of any talent for organizing her thousands of "little things," as opposed to her husband's genius at coordinating his. The result was that letters, checkbooks, accountings, sewing materials, recipes, address books, photographs, etcetera, etcetera, were scattered throughout the house on every floor in a half-dozen different desks, credenzas, or bureaus. Every now and then she would set aside a day to "make order," as she called it, and would start with her dressing-room closet, but then she would become so intrigued with boxes containing packets of old correspondence, *cachêts* of tulle veils, ribbons, *passementerie* collected over the years, unfinished scrapbooks, hoards of costume jewelry that the project would be abandoned and chaos would reign for days in her bedroom. But she never lost anything—that is, permanently. This was all due to St. Anthony. Should a key or a ring or an address book vanish, she would promise St. Anthony a candle if he would only help her find it, and St. Anthony never seemed to fail her! Now, she told me, she was going to ask him to help us discover a cook. However, I put *my* faith in Miranda.

Stravinsky, pleased with his progress in the studio, was more than ever inclined to relax in the evenings. I looked about for some good movies (Hollywood was always devoid of them) and presently found *Khartoum*, which had just opened. If Stravinsky had been head of the Academy Award Committee, this film would have received every prize on the list. And if the term "enthusiastic" could ever have been applied to one of his moods, it would have been the modifier describing his reaction to this spectacular, in which Charlton Heston as Lord Gordon and Laurence Olivier as the Mahdi brought to life some of the events Stravinsky had avidly and repeatedly traced in Alan Moorehead's books about the Nile. From the moment he left the theater, and for several days thereafter, he talked about it constantly, outlining it in detail to Bill Brown, who came for lunch; to Miranda, who dropped in for coffee; to Christopher Isherwood, who came for dinner; to Dr. Edell during a medical discussion. It was recommended, in fact, to everyone who happened by, and Milène knew the scenario (which was expounded to her on two successive visits) by heart. Robert, of course, was told over the phone that the first, the very first thing he must do on his return was to direct his steps immediately to the Cinerama Theater.

What struck me about these seemingly unprofound circumstances was the simplicity of his pleasure. He behaved exactly like a child who had stored in his mind a fantasy based on tales he might have read or been told, and who was suddenly confronted with its concrete realization. I thought, of course, as I talked to him, of the wealth of Russian folklore, of the stories of Hans Christian Andersen, of the *Ice Maiden* and *The Emperor and the Nightingale*, which had been part of his own childhood and had ultimately found their way into his music. One night after dinner, we spoke of fairy tales and he commented on the complete fearlessness of children, who accept them in all their gruesome details—giants chopping off heads and hands, witches burning little boys and girls in ovens, poisoned apples, fiendish tortures—as part of a "special kind of life." He believed, he said, that if this unsophisticated approach to cruelty could remain with us as adults there would be no wars, for all our aggressions could be consummated in this unreal world of brutality. "The fairy tale supplies the necessary element of form."

While Robert was away, there was no record-playing and Stravinsky did not ask for any, although once or twice, when I was working in the library, he came in and looked at several albums lying on the table. His answer to my query as to whether he would like to hear some music was always negative. And I don't believe he ever would have played a single record if Robert had not been there.

During this visit I worked a great deal on Stravinsky's correspondence, and one particularly trying aspect of it was the handling of a delicate situation that had arisen in Europe. Everyone engaged in the business of concert management has had to deal with the problem of concellations from time to time, but up to this point Stravinsky had never been a source of trouble, to me at least (though very often I had wished he would be). Such European cancellations as had occurred the previous year in Strasbourg, Luxembourg, Oxford, had been in no way directly connected with me. From 1963 on Hurok had entered into some "yes-no-yes" negotiations for concerts in Rumania; these never came to pass because either the money or the traveling conditions made such voyages totally impractical as well as hard on the aging composer, and therefore they could not be considered cancellations. For example, had the Stravinskys gone to Bucharest (one of the areas they had requested) before Warsaw—which was to have been the arrangement—the concert in the latter city might never have taken place. Stravinsky could not have made two visits to two Iron Curtain countries within a few days of each other, according to Robert's correspondence out of Poland. He wrote that they were terribly spoiled after the comfort and luxury of Paris. The Bergen *Perséphone* concert had not been Stravinsky's idea at all, but had been sought by Vera Zorina, to whose pleas Robert had yielded; Stravinsky's initial reaction to the size of the fee (very Old Style) had from the start instilled misgivings in me that the project would never come to a proper conclusion.

Nothing I ever had to do professionally for Stravinsky embarrassed me in the slightest degree (occasional jousts with the public or "certain persons" excepted). I always felt he had a right to make whatever demands, whatever refusals, and whatever excuses he chose to make. This arose not only from my total belief in his special mission on this earth (in which feeling I was far from alone), but also from the normal reaction one has to someone who is generally a man of his word. If Stravinsky had to, or wished to, change his mind about anything, he never looked for a subterfuge. *That* was always provided by the people around him, and in professional matters, very often by me. It always infuriated him that he could not say outright, "The reason I am not going to come to your city to conduct is because I have changed my mind," which to him (I am sure) was a sentence that should be included in the "Act of God" clause in all contracts. He would also have been perfectly willing to say, "You must forgive me, but when I committed myself verbally (and therefore, morally) to do your concerts, I was full of some excellent Scotch and therefore very optimistic about all proposals"; or, "*I* did not promise; someone else promised." And if the argument were that "someone else" was close to him and therefore assumed to be expressing his wishes, his response would have been, "Close to me, but not *me*."

Yet even if *I* were not embarrassed, an embarrassing situation *had* arisen involving Robert Paterson, who had seen the Stravinskys during their spring trip abroad for the Athens Festival, and who had been told by Robert (as a telegram received from Paterson on August 4 clearly indicated) that he should definitely arrange some concerts for October. Indeed, the Stravinskys had planned to return to Europe in the fall; the composer's Italian impresario and old friend Adrianna Panni had his promise that he would conduct, with Robert, performances of *The Soldier's Tale* and *Renard* (at a fee he would never have agreed to on one of *my* contracts—

twenty-five hundred dollars for each concert, including broadcast rights!). These were to take place at the Accademia Filarmonica in Rome during the second week in October.

It was obvious to me at the time of the Lincoln Center festival that another trip abroad that soon was out of the question for Stravinsky, especially if he were to keep a promise made to George Barati, musical director of the Honolulu Symphony, to go to Hawaii for two concerts in November. (Mr. Barati and Hawaii had been waiting patiently on the composer's doorstep for several seasons.) Besides, the Honolulu engagement would provide a fine vacation for our swimming champion and would be minus the pressures of that clutch of well-meaning but demanding Europe-dwelling friends. But Paterson's cablegram, which he had sent after several negative (for him) transatlantic telephone calls, required an immediate confirmation of several engagements he had booked on the strength of Robert's authority. Stravinsky told me to send a three-word message: "No, thank you," which would have settled matters neatly and pleasantly. But this could not be done—doors must always be left open, at least for the less influential of the two conductors. After a talk with Mrs. Stravinsky, and her own telephone conference with Robert in Santa Fe, I sent a long cablegram including the following: "He [Stravinsky] cannot and will not interest himself in anything you propose prior to March 1967. Please do not persist." The reply to this (in the form of a letter berating me soundly for my "vindictive" communication!) had, attached, a beautiful clipping from the *London Times* in which its Rome correspondent reported all the lovely plans for *The Soldier's Tale* at the Accademia in the first part of October, immediately before the dates we had just refused Paterson!

Signora Panni was one of Stravinsky's *in-fact* friends, and therefore I had still not communicated with Rome, the reason being, of course, that there was hope in certain quarters of the household that this trip might yet be made. But friend or not, Stravinsky now put his foot down. He was not going to go to England, therefore he could not go to Rome. I communicated with Dr. Edell. He supplied me with the necessary ammunition for the exercising of *force majeure* (which, incidentally, he sincerely felt *should* be exercised, as he did not recommend Stravinsky's return to Europe at this time), and I cabled Signora Panni, regretfully cancelling. She responded immediately, her message containing nothing except concern for "Maestro's health" and the hope that he would be well enough to return in 1967—no reproaches, no tale of personal hardship in *this* cablegram (although she was presenting a fully-staged version of *The Soldier's Tale* with *décor* by Manzù, choreography by Maurice Béjart, and direction by Sandro Sequi).

While all this was progressing, Stravinsky quietly completed *Requiem Canticles* and on August 13 handed me the manuscript pages of the final movement to take to the photostater's. He was feeling very content and quite ready to enjoy *Khartoum* again by way of celebration. But his wife suggested we wait until Robert came home before we made a second visit "to see all that killing," and instead we went to a revival of that Italian film gem *Seduced and Abandoned*, which—for those who are unlucky enough to have missed it—is hilariously concerned with the emotional antics of a middle-class Sicilian family whose youngest daughter has been led astray before marriage by the scion of another provincial household to whom she has been betrothed for years. There is one moment in this film in which the local magistrate, half driven out of his mind by a series of confrontations with the excitable parents, turns to a map of Europe on the wall and places his hand over Sicily, obliterating it completely. Stravinsky, whose shoulders had been silently shaking throughout, lost himself so completely that he seized my bag of popcorn and unconsciously consumed a good part of it in a few minutes. He had already eaten half of his wife's supply (she only liked the top salty part), and that night he was very, very uncomfortable. Like all remodeled houses, this one had not yet lost its newness, and the echo of his padding footsteps reached me in my room two floors below, by way of a route of creakings and soundings. (I am not a heavy sleeper, and in any case whenever I was with Stravinsky I only half-slept.) The footsteps finally stopped after about ten minutes, but I decided to see what it was all about and crept upstairs as quietly as I could. Some lamps were always left burning on the first floor—a useless precaution against burglars, who could have entered easily and soundlessly through any of the numerous French doors or casement windows by merely flicking the lock with a finger. Mrs. Stravinsky's door was closed, but her husband's was ajar. He was not in bed but across the hall in his little private office, standing there in his pajamas and beret in front of a table-height filing cabinet. He was leafing through a portfolio of old photographs from the years in

France, which I had been arranging that day. I brought him his
dressing-gown, for it was chilly; put it on his shoulders; and stood
quietly beside him while he turned them over, one by one, without
more than a second's glance at each, as though he were counting
the years. At length he snapped the folder shut and placed it neatly
back in its appropriate space in the file drawer. "I did not feel well
from those little yellow nuts [popcorn!]," he said by way of explaining his sleeplessness. "I have had a bad diarrhea. We have not
awakened Vera, I hope." I thought not, but he walked carefully
to her door, where he listened intently, then nodded to indicate
that all was well and went back to bed. I bent to kiss him good
night, and this time I could not keep from holding his small frame
close for a moment. He did not seem to mind, but took my hand
and held it fast until he had settled himself comfortably and closed
his eyes. Light was beginning to seep into Los Angeles, and I went
back into the office and sat there watching it grow brighter for an
hour or so, until I heard Mrs. Stravinsky moving about in her room.
I went downstairs to make some coffee and only then realized that
my face was wet.

We were unable to find a cook for the first week-and-a-half of
my stay, but we managed very well. Stravinsky was generally easy
to please, provided one avoided custards or floating islands or stews
of any kind. Mrs. Stravinsky always said that he was "an angel" as
far as her cooking was concerned, and certainly he seemed to enjoy
every dish she prepared for him, always telling her that the om-
elettes were "wonderful" and her Russian cutlets "better than anything at Chasen's." Apart from these two dishes, *risotto*, a vegetable
soup, and a fish soup that would have stood up well against any
Marseillesian *bouillabaisse*, Mrs. Stravinsky preferred to be a smör-
gasbord-type cook. She loved to load the table with cheese, salami,
smoked salmon, and quantities of bread, butter, sour cream, and
kasha. The traditional balanced meal was an absurdity as far as
she was concerned, and the meat-and-potatoes syndrome was "for
Americans." Now, with Robert away, she could indulge herself in
her own dietary fancies as much as she liked (I am half-Russian,
and she didn't have to worry about me—we were alumnae of the
same cooking school).

When Robert was at home, however, it was a different matter.
His appetite was healthy and standardly American (except when

he traveled abroad, when it was standardly whatever country he was in), which explained the real urgency of finding a cook *before* he conducted the final *Wozzeck* in Santa Fe on August 24. In the almost-daily lunch conferences we had with Miranda on the subject (apparently the making of two cinema extravaganzas—one was *Ship of Fools*—had temporarily depleted the actors' unemployment line), Mrs. Stravinsky would repeat over and over that she could get along very well if we didn't have a "growing man" in the house! The already grown man in the house, who, on one of these occasions, sat patiently consuming another of my Waring Blendor specialties—this time, a fairly successful avocado soup made from the fruit of the owner's tree—merely grunted that he hoped we would not hire a cook who would give the "growing man growing pains . . . he has enough of those already."

Relatives and friends came to the rescue, of course, and Mrs. Stravinsky and I took turns so that we were not confined to the kitchen very much. During this period, on a visit to the Marions, I had my first experience with one of Milène's dinners, which began with an incredible *mousse* whose main ingredient was a Milène-made goose-liver *paté*. The *pièce de resistance*, a rack of lamb with blue grapes, was a masterpiece, and so was the dessert—a banana Bavarian cream with cognac that belonged in the *Arabian Nights*. The house was small but charming, with examples of Milène's handiwork everywhere: chairs she had upholstered, frames she had made, lacework, drapery. Her "stone-jewel" laboratory proved to house all manner of equipment for sewing and carpentry as well.

There was, in fact, very little Milène was unable to do with her hands. She undoubtedly could have had an outstanding career in some craft or design field had she been the daughter of another father. But I am sure she suffered from the same foreordained feeling of limitation on her abilities as her brothers must have experienced, with the additional disadvantages that her sex and the over-protective atmosphere of her childhood (due to her now-cured tuberculosis) had created. Mrs. Stravinsky was really entirely responsible for "bringing Milène out," as it were, and had gradually and patiently overcome the feelings of hostility toward the "step-mother" that Milène still entertained when she first came to the United States. She had offered encouragement and sympathy; had made contacts for Milène with designers; was the interceder with *père* for financial help when it was required. By the time I met

Milène, she and Mrs. Stravinsky had what could be described as a
sisterly relationship, if not a deep friendship. They discussed their
mutual domestic problems; Mrs. Stravinsky gave advice (but never
too much); they were very open together on the subject of *père*
and "Igor." And of course whenever Stravinsky's nineteenth-
century "spare the rod" attitude came to the fore, Milène always
found his wife to have a comforting shoulder.

Her husband, André, however, was regarded by the Stravinskys
as difficult. After the manner of most parents, who believe no one
is good enough for their offspring, they felt that Milène had married beneath herself in choosing a husband from the French prov-
inces. They never made any effort at all to understand him, although their manner with him, during my days in Hollywood,
always appeared to be friendly if a little formal. It is no secret that
Stravinsky did not entertain any deep affection for the mates of his
children, nor would his feeling have been different no matter
whom they had married: marriage meant a division of allegiance.
But of all of them, André was perhaps the furthest removed from
Stravinsky's world, although he had been the composer's traveling
companion on tours many times in the fifties and acted as his business manager and accountant right up to the time the Stravinskys
left Hollywood forever. He continued to take care of the major
part of the composer's business correspondence until the fall of
1966, when Marilyn Stalvey (Robert's part-time typist) was hired
on a permanent basis as secretary, and Robert was thereafter able
to dictate most of the letters. André was not an "amusing" man in
the Stravinskyan sense of the word, nor was he a conversationalist,
at least on subjects that were of interest to that household. He did
not participate in discussions on music, books, the artistic life.
He was a proud and practical Frenchman, perhaps a little hard-
headed, and Milène's whole life was wrapped around his wishes. He
did not like the subservient role in which he had been cast—the valet
aspect of touring, the clerical aspect of the correspondence, the full-
time obeisance to his employer. And he gradually "resigned" (except for the accounting), beginning with the tours. After several
tries at various enterprises (in which the Stravinskys were of some
financial assistance), he had settled for the travel business and was
working with a good agency on Wilshire Boulevard when we
finally meet.

André is a gourmet. He appeared to have more reliable knowledge of good food and wine than the Stravinskys. But as a matter of fact, Mrs. Stravinsky was the only member of the trio who knew anything about wines at all; Robert's *sagesse* is an acquisition from his association with the other two, and he tends to Lafite-Rothschilds and Chateaux Margaux of pre-war years and forbidding prices. Therefore, this was the area of André's self-defense; he shone in it, and I admit it used to amuse me to hear him catch one or the other of his "opponents" in some glaring error about the locale of certain vintages and the grapes from which they were derived.

When the Stravinskys dined out with the Marions, the Montaperts sometimes came along, and vice versa. André had been responsible for Stravinsky's retaining William Montapert as his lawyer, and it was entirely due to the latter that the composer's tax burden was then relatively light. For example, Montapert had advised making gifts of certain manuscripts to the Library of Congress, and suggested investment in mines for the purposes of development (a project with the intriguing name of "Verigor," incidentally); had arranged the purchase of orange groves in Arizona (some of which Robert also owned), which were later given by the composer to his children. Stravinsky's frequent professional conferences with the Montaperts always reminded me of those scenes in sophisticated movies where the head of some industrial empire receives his legal advisers and formally makes known his wish to decimate another industrial empire or cause a panic on Wall Street. The meetings usually took place in the library, sometimes behind closed doors. But on those occasions when I was present to supply a bit of information on contracts, Stravinsky would deliver a brief but pointedly dictatorial talk on the matter at hand, with specific emphasis on the indifference—nay, hostility—of the Bureau of Internal Revenue toward anything connected with the arts, after which he would obediently and rapidly sign every paper placed in front of him. Madame Montapert customarily outlined their contents in rapid French, but by that time the composer was eager to return to his studio or have a Scotch, and it was all a matter of form. This struck me, of course, because in the preceding years he had always been so careful about the examination of anything given him to sign, and his wife agreed with me (when I remarked on the speed with which these signatures were achieved) that he had, indeed, changed in this respect. I had noticed, of course, that he was becoming less and less concerned with business of any kind, leaving it in the hands of people he had come to trust. On very small matters, however, his native suspicion never left him. "*Who* has taken one of the two handkerchiefs I left here?" . . . "*Who* has removed my scissors?" . . . "*Who* has vanished with my dictionary?" And the accusing questions exempted no one as the possible "thief" . . . not even his wife.

Stravinsky, like most cat-lovers, had long been familiar with Edward Lear's little charmer *The Owl and the Pussycat*. A French version, *Le Hibou et La Poussiquette*, delightfully translated by Francis Steegmuller, had been discovered once by Mrs. Stravinsky in *The New Yorker* magazine, which published it in 1961. For a long time she searched for a copy of the French edition but was unsuccessful until a few months before I came for this visit, when she presented the little volume to her husband. Immediately after he finished *Requiem Canticles*, he began to work on what was to become his last original composition—the song set to Lear's original (English), and created for his wife. It was Mr. Steegmuller's French translation, incidentally, which decided the composer to grant that author permission to examine and use his correspondence with Jean Cocteau, for a biography of the latter on which he was then engaged. Obviously here was a man in whom one could have confidence! When Mr. Steegmuller paid a visit to the West Coast house in April 1966, Stravinsky promptly sought out the Cocteau file and dropped it into his lap!

While the composer was thus occupied with owls and pussycats I was busy reorganizing (according to his instructions) the contents of the filing cabinets in the little second-floor office which, within a year, were to become part of a Boosey & Hawkes microfilming project (although I did not know this at the time). I was also concluding arrangements for the fall concerts, listening to pleas for 1967, and keeping in close touch with Robert, who, despite Alban Berg and *Wozzeck*, was wretched at having to be away from the center of things for so long. The greater disappointment was, naturally, that Stravinsky could not go to Santa Fe—there was a threatened airlines strike and he was tired—to see his colleague conduct this rarely performed work. Robert, in fact, was the first American conductor to lead a fully-staged version,* and

* Dmitri Mitropoulos conducted a concert performaance of the work in New York in 1951, which Robert once described to me as "all wrong and superb."

he could not conceal a forlorn note in his voice on the telephone. But for once Mrs. Stravinsky did not give in. Her husband's need to remain quietly at home for a good spell was beginning to be very clear. His back continued to trouble him, and a very close check was being kept by Dr. Edell on his polycythemia. The letters I received from Santa Fe were dismal. Robert was very disturbed about the small number of concerts scheduled for the remainder of the year; there were bookings only in Louisville, Honolulu, Columbus, and Chicago. Since the October trip to Europe had not been cancelled until we reached Hollywood, it was impossible for me to find substitute engagements on such short notice, even had Stravinsky been willing to regard October proposals with favor— which he was not. At this time no date or place for the world première of *Requiem Canticles* had yet been determined, and we did not know that this would come about at Princeton in October.

But, oh, those wails from Santa Fe! Anything else besides Louisville this Fall?, Robert would ask. New Orleans? Baltimore? Nashville? Any of the Texas cities? Salt Lake City? Detroit? Boston? Buffalo? Pittsburgh? Buenos Aires? Even $5000 would be acceptable, I was told, and then he would raise that sorrowful question: will a year from now be possible? Anything was possible where Stravinsky was concerned, of course. I had thought a great deal about this during the New York Festival, for although the composer had required pianist Paul Jacobs' arm for his walk to the podium, his conducting had been as vigorous and exact as ever. Age might have established a permanent residence in his body, but the terms of the lease were still controlled by his mind.

Stravinsky relaxed his studio hours somewhat during my 1966 visit. He would come downstairs about half an hour earlier than usual, both before lunch and dinner. Our walking periods grew longer in the afternoon, and the cocktail hour extended itself enough to fuddle us all nicely before dinner. If we didn't go to the movies or for a drive in the evening, we would play cards. Jack Quinn often made this a foursome and Casino was the preferred game in these instances—preferred by Mrs. Stravinsky, that is, for she aways seemed to attract the "Big Ten" or the "Big Two" or all the aces. Her husband would become very annoyed with his bad luck and after a few rounds of this pastime would decide to

---

Staged versions, previous to the one at Santa Fe, were conducted by Stokowski in 1926 in New York and Philadelphia, by Joseph Rosenstock at the New York City Center in 1952, and by Karl Böhm at the Metropolitan Opera in 1959.

play Patience. He was a poor loser (he did not like anything he could not keep within his control!) and if these solitaires did not improve his position, he would become disgusted and begin to cheat just a little. Mrs. Stravinsky always told him that he would never win if he did not "speak nicely to the cards." Her conversations with the cards, on which her husband and I would frequently eavesdrop, were enlightening. "Behave properly. . . . Take your turn. . . . No, no. I need a black seven! . . . You are a nice girl [to the Queen]. . . . Do not be a bad boy [to the Jack]. . . ." She would maddeningly win one game after another, never forgetting to give the willing deck a few pats of thanks. Stravinsky would then make an attempt to follow her advice, but he was usually unsuccessful, whereupon Mrs. Stravinsky would tell him that his tone of voice had been "insincere." "You cannot fool the cards. You must *mean* your good manners, or they will not ever believe you." His reply to this was that of course she had more influence than he, for the cards were undoubtedly all "male" and the *"Pique Dame"* obviously a "transvesitite" (*sic*).

At long last, after I had served up a tragic duck dinner (roosters masquerading as waterfowl) to the Marions, the numerous agencies to which I had been appealing, Miranda notwithstanding, produced a cook—this time a lady of Irish-Scottish ancestry in her early forties. Her references indicated that she had been satisfactorily employed as housekeeper for a lengthy period at the home of a movie producer who was now leaving Hollywood. She was very straightforward in her answers to us about her culinary abilities (good American cooking), and it was also apparent that her intelligence would extend to the understanding of recipes for foreign dishes: the word *soufflé* did not throw her, and she knew all about *aspèrges hollandaises*. There was one slight drawback in the presence, during this interview, of her small son (let us call him "Billy"), who was about nine or ten years of age and who, naturally, went along with the package. He was bright-eyed and eager; and, after a few moments of conversation, it was clear from his college-level vocabulary that he had an IQ of respect-commanding proportions. But he was a *little* boy, and little boys occasionally shout, upset things, play hard, and require the companionship of other little boys, especially since it was still "no-school" time. Quiet, particularly during rest periods and studio hours, was a vital factor in Stravinsky's life, and although this youngster was already displaying the interest of a Rhodes Scholar in the thousands of books that framed us as we talked in the library, I could not visualize him poring over volumes, however fascinating, while the hot sun was making magic drawings on the water in the swimming pool.

But actually my doubts as to the success of this domestic contract had arisen more on Mrs. Stravinsky's than on Mr. Stravinsky's account. She can tolerate children, but not when they are in the immediate vicinity for prolonged periods of time. Besides, not ever having had any herself, her notion of children is all tied up with impressions received from her husband's offspring—for her love affair * with Stravinsky had begun in 1920. Milène was not yet seven, Soulima was ten, Theodore was just thirteen, and Ludmilla (who did not survive) was eight. It was quite natural for her, from that point on, to regard all youngsters in the light of the problems engendered by the particular situation in which she was involved. Children were sickly, complaining, demanding of time and affection, and terribly expensive. They deprived one of the right to remain attractive and made life messy and complicated. By the time she married Stravinsky in 1940, even had he not been the figure he was, a change in attitude was both impossible and undesired.

As for the head of the household, he was drawn to any small thing that had life in it, provided it remained within the boundaries laid down by law, natural or otherwise (ants and bees were wonderful, but outdoors, not in). Therefore, I was fairly certain that this new "little creature" would receive the same consideration, if he observed the rules.

At any rate, Mrs. Stravinsky was agreeable to "trying things out," and two or three days later "Mrs. B." and son drove up in a neat second-hand sedan and moved into the guest house ground-floor apartment. Mrs. B. was indeed a very good plain cook, and also willing to learn. Billy seemed a model of good behavior. He was cherubic with regard to the swimming pool restrictions, for at first he was only allowed to splash about when naps were over. We made a test one day and discovered that if he did not sing, or shout "Mum" suddenly, he could even swim sometimes during the morning studio hours. His manners were very good, and he would scramble out of the pool and vanish instantly when Mrs. Stravinsky

* So described by this remarkable lady on National Educational Television's broadcast *Stravinsky Remembered* in the Fall of 1971.

appeared for her late-afternoon regimen, recognizing (without being told) the invisible line that separated her neighborhood from his. Every day, when Stravinsky arrived for lunch, Billy would come in from the kitchen, where he had already eaten his, bow to the composer respectfully, shake hands, and be off. Stravinsky acknowledged that he was an unusual boy and after a day or so he began to detain him a bit to find out what wonders he might have discovered during his morning adventures. Billy, on his part, fell into the habit of bringing Stravinsky small souvenirs of his expeditions—a toad one day, a handsome butterfly the next, a stray cat another time. Even the two or three lapses, in the form of a slammed door or a wild dash across the patio in pursuit of Public Enemies One through Five, were overlooked. In fact, Milène's visits in the afternoon now included a sojourn with her father on the second-floor terrace adjoining the swimming pool, so that *père* could watch Billy defeating fleets of pirates who had trapped him on his rubber raft, or guiding, on that same inflated barge, the stray cat (now obviously Cleopatra) on a voyage down the Nile.

Moreover, the presence of two additional human beings on the premises was reassuring. Hippies, followed by other, more dangerous, intruders, had now moved further up Sunset Boulevard. Their active entrenchment in 1966 extended to within a block of North Wetherly Drive, and after six o'clock, outside the innumerable "body shops," rock-and-roll paradises, and "trip" joints, hundreds of long-haired, long-bearded males, and females clad in body-stockings and little else, would assemble. Traffic was dense, and not in any way alleviated by the motorcycle police, who, as the hours passed and the consumption of "maryjane," LSD, and other more potent euphoria-producers increased, generally had their hands full chasing stolen cars and trying to prevent vandalism. A pre-Manson crime wave was underway at that time, and every day some new and frightening report would reach our ears. A wealthy friend of Jack's, living not five minutes away, had opened his door to a "workman" and found himself immediately thereafter bound, gagged, and locked in the trunk of his car. A woman whose house was one block above Miranda's had been raped and beaten and left lying senseless in her totally wrecked bedroom. It was nerve-racking, and Mrs. Stravinsky wished a dozen times a day that Robert were back so that there would be a "man" in the house (what she meant, of course, was a *younger* man). But I confess this wish did not console me much, since I was sure that if a cry for help should penetrate the walls of Robert's sanctuary, he would probably shout back: "Wait a minute! I have to finish writing this paragraph!"

Late one night, a prolonged ring at the front doorbell terrified us all out of bed, and brought me dashing up to the foyer. Mrs. Stravinsky, wrapped in her bright-green satin evening cloak, was poised halfway down the staircase, like Tosca in Act II, clutching a dainty ivory paper-knife. Her husband, a step above, was almost completely hidden behind her (she was protecting him!), but his bereted head peered over her shoulder, and he held his cane aloft to indicate that he was prepared for battle. I motioned to them to remain where they were and went to the door, which was now being belabored by a heavy fist. Through the small, grill-protected square of glass, I could see a very unsavory face, easily identifiable as that of an *émigré* from the Strip. A car was parked in the drive, and from the sound of voices I deduced the presence of two compatriots. When he saw me the intruder stopped banging and began a speech of the type usually associated with obscene telephone calls, at the same time fiddling dangerously with the door-latch. In the firmest tones I could muster, I told him to make himself scarce, that I had six brothers, that the maid had just gone downstairs to wake them, and that, furthermore, the police were on their way. I then dashed to the phone in the reception hall to make this final threat come true, while praying that the door would hold. Sounds of a car motor revving up and receding indicated that the visitors had decided to accept my word. The Stravinskys then sat down with me in the living room to await the arrival of the police (one hour thereafter, by which time we might easily have made the next morning's headlines). The two officers, who seemed well aware of the respect due the head of this particular house, displayed extraordinary courtesy in their questions, and did not insist on my being specific in front of the Stravinskys about the monologue directed at me by that character out of Kraft-Ebbing. But after they had left, assuring us that "these types never come back to the same place," I had a great deal of trouble persuading the Stravinskys to go to bed, and it dawned on me that they were nervous because of the two floors separating us. I casually mentioned that I planned to spend the rest of the night on the living-room sofa because "I am afraid to be alone so far away from

you." And at that they marched bravely up the stairs—Mrs. Stravinsky first, her husband at her heels—and both suddenly seemed
to me so very lonely and so very young.

Stravinsky may have been completely apart from everyone in
his studio, but once outside its door his wife was the forefront of
his world; if she were not there, first of all the excuse must be a
good one, and then, if her absence were prolonged, he would begin to worry. A few days before the criminal attack on the Stravinsky's front gate, our lunch guest was George Fowler. Mrs Stravinsky had an appointment in Beverly Hills that morning and had
told us not to expect her until one o'clock. George (who always
had to tell people that he was *not* television's most famous used-car
dealer, Ralph Williams) was a welcome guest because of his immediately discernible good breeding and complete ease in Stravinsky's presence. Also, he was the perfect straight man for the
composer's occasional sly digs at Hurok and how many millions
he must be making "in the ballet business." The strange part of this
pointed jocularity was the tinge of respect that colored it—respect,
that is, for a Russian of another class (and a religion that had added
to the discomforts of early life in his native country) who had,
without formal education, elevated himself to a position in the
world where he could dictate terms (in certain quarters, that is!).
   Stravinsky descended that day a quarter of an hour before the
usual time to indulge in a bit of such repartee with George over a
double Scotch. When his wife had not returned at quarter past one,
he asked me where she was; I explained, adding that the heavy
traffic on Santa Monica Boulevard had undoubtedly delayed her.
This satisfied him for about five minutes; then he looked at his
watch and murmured: "How strange. She should be here." In
the next fifteen minutes he made three or four trips to the front
door to scan the driveway. Then he sent Billy to stand at the post-
box and keep watch on Wetherly Drive so that word could be
brought as soon as the Lincoln turned the corner just below. He
lost interest in the conversation. He did not finish his drink. At
length Mrs. B. and I persuaded him to sit down to lunch (although
I was beginning to be very concerned myself), on the promise
that I would telephone all the shops Mrs. Stravinsky generally
visited, provided she did not arrive within the next ten minutes.
He was obedient but sat without saying a word or eating his food.

Shortly thereafter his wife arrived, looking rather pale and breath-less, very apologetic for her tardiness. Her husband reacted in the normal manner: his great relief at having her safely back turned to anger, and from the tone of his Russian, she was being roundly scolded. Her reply in English, after a moment of listening, created consternation. "I had an accident," she said with studied calm, "on Santa Monica." Stravinsky changed very noticeably from red to white. Her account—the car had suddenly stalled; another car had therefore bumped into the rear of the Lincoln; it was a jolt; that was all; she had left the car, which would be towed, and had come home by cab—caused his hands to shake. He grasped hers and began to pat them, but she pulled away and said almost pettishly, "I am perfectly all right," and began to talk about how much she loved Paris at this time of year.

But she was not all right. It was gradually revealed that the jolt had thrown her forward and she had undergone a shock. Despite her protests, sedatives and bed were in order for at least twenty-four hours. Her husband abandoned all his activities and hovered outside her room, poking his head in every now and then to see if she were resting comfortably. He did not realize that every time he did this she woke with a start. That evening he sat by her bed holding her hand and stroking her arm while Mrs. Stravinsky, who has always preferred to suffer her little illnesses in solitude, kept assuring him with growing impatience: "I am *fine*. I only want to *sleep*." Finally I was able to urge him downstairs for some supper, explaining that Dr. Edell had said a night's rest would turn the tide, and all would be well again. From that moment until he went to bed (after a final look at her through the slightly ajar door) he conducted his con-versation with me in whispers, although by that time nothing short of a cannon could have roused the sleeper from the effects of a potent tranquilizer.

"I do not want her to drive that car again. She should not drive anymore alone," he told me. I did not voice my silent agreement (Mrs. Stravinsky was a very erratic chauffeur and could be absent-minded about signals), for I knew that such a restriction would break her heart. Driving was one of her greatest joys. It was her personal method of escape, the means by which she released her-self from the confinements of her life—the music, the concerts, the arguments, the perpetual pressures, the temperamental out-bursts, the submission to laws she must obey as the wife of a man who belonged to the world. To be alone behind the wheel of her car had the same effect that whisky or champagne has on other Nepenthe-seekers.

And I also knew that her state of shock had in great measure been brought on by her constant fear that The Law might step in and revoke her driving privilege because she was no longer young. She had already been involved in several minor incidents—creasing someone's fender as she backed out of the always jammed super-market parking area (this happened a dozen times a day to others), making a left turn from the middle lane on a three-lane road (though there was no obstructing car beside her). Her name was inscribed on the books as someone who had paid fines; her age—in 1966—was touching seventy-five, and her operator's license was about to expire. She kept her anguish over these things to herself, but her husband did not, and the next day he repeated to me (*almost* within her hearing), and with renewed firmness, "I think she must now stop driving." He did not refer to the reason *why*, of course, but it was there in his tone, and it was the first time I had ever heard him even remotely imply that his "Vera" was beginning to show the mark of passing years. Robert, who was told the story on the phone that night, was grimly definite: "Let them take her license away. It'll be the best thing. She should have stopped driving years ago." (Heartless creature!!)

But Stravinsky's fright had gone very deep, and for the remainder of my stay that summer, his first words in the morning were, "How is Vera?"—whereas formerly he usually accepted his matutinal tea with the information that "I have a headache. . . . I do not feel well. . . . I did not sleep," and *then*, after a sip or two, "How is my wife?"

About a week before Robert returned from Santa Fe, Christopher Isherwood and Don Bachardy came for a visit. Christopher was now one of the two sole California survivors of the Stravinskys' circle of literary friends of the forties. The other was the late Gerald Heard, tragically struck down not long after by an al-most total paralysis. Christopher came to see the Stravinskys as frequently as work would permit, usually accompanied by his friend Don, whose talent as a portrait artist is sometimes visible in *Vogue* and *Harper's Bazaar*. Stravinsky was totally relaxed and very informal during their visits. He would recline comfortably on the white sofa at the side of the living-room fireplace, Scotch in hand, and enjoy the brilliant Isherwood wit as though he were at a play. I think what he liked about the writer's remarks (the meaning of many of which must have escaped him—he never really understood or was deeply interested in Anglo-Saxon humor) was the laconic style of their delivery. Christopher usually sat on a hassock leaning against the wall, quietly listening as Don and Mrs. Stravinsky chattered away about people, books, movies, plays, fashions, and then, at a strategic and more or less serious point in the conversation, would make some comment or other that sent us into gales of laughter. He was rather like a supervisory imp, more often mischievous than demolishing, and on the few (alas) occasions when I saw him, I was certain he was snapping away with his literary camera, catching us all in pictures we might not want to enliven.

Christopher and Don were also two of the four or five people who called Stravinsky by his Christian name (except for Russian friends, who addressed him traditionally and formally as "Igor Fyodorovitch"). "Hi, Eager," said Christopher when he arrived and was saluted with a double kiss. Whenever this occurred, I would experience a slight sense of shock. The form of address was so peculiarly the property of Mrs. Stravinsky, and when used by anyone else it brought to my ears (and Robert's also, as he once said) an echo of disrespect. Of course this was never intended—the British custom of ultimately acknowledging a friendship (after a good period of thought, of course) by switching from the formal "Mister" to the Christian name, was at its root, but I think it always startled the composer as much as it did the rest of us. He was not a person one knew on a first-name basis, and even his non-Russian friends would sometimes use the Russian form of address if they did not call him "Mister Stravinsky."

This particular visit remains in my memory for reasons apart from the fact that it was my initial encounter with the author of *I Am a Camera*. Stravinsky became very drunk, fell asleep on the sofa, and snored peacefully away while we talked. At one point Mrs. Stravinsky, Don, and I made a brief visit to the garden, which, at that twilight hour, was always full of a heavenly scent. We found on our return that Christopher had tucked himself up on the right end of the sofa, was also sound asleep, and was breathing gently. Reading from left to right, the two reminded me of Ariel and Puck.

Later, when I helped Stravinsky to bed, still somewhat under the influence, he said to me in an exact imitation of Christopher's manner, "You know—he is one great guy!"

Robert finally came home on the twenty-fifth and was met at the airport by Jack and his new boxer puppy, an animal of proportions and weight that exceeded Stravinsky's (the only creature, incidentally, that ever aroused a certain feeling of timidity in the composer—it took quite a while and several rather overwhelming *rendezvous* under the *porte cochère* and on the patio before a few cautious pats were administered). We had a great deal of business to discuss: arrangements to make for the conclusion of the United Airlines film recording, programing for the fall concerts, and a new project—a tour of *The Soldier's Tale* proposed for the spring of 1967 by Glynn Ross, director of the Seattle Opera Association. Mr. Ross had contacted Robert earlier in Santa Fe and had been told to come and see me in Hollywood. He had some rather original ideas for the production—*décor* by Saul Steinberg, Cary Grant as Narrator (Jason Robards was an alternative), and Anton Dolin as the Devil. He wanted Stravinsky to conduct the initial Seattle performance and Robert the half-dozen others he planned to take on the road; he had hopes that the composer would attend some of the latter, of course. I named a very high fee (all those stellar notions certainly pointed in that direction) and gave him something to think about for the next few months. The project of a tour that would solve some of Robert's financial problems was appealing, although the prospect of Stravinsky's going along for the ride was not, nor did I think for one moment that he would consent to it. In fact, he evinced no interest in the Seattle production at all at the time, but did ask me to try to work it out for his colleague.

I was to leave for Mexico City on August 27 to do some advance work for another Hurok–Ballet Folklórico tour, scheduled to begin shortly after the Louisville concert. On the eve of my departure, Mrs. Stravinsky and I entertained Stravinsky and Robert with a fashion show. She had spent a good deal of time (after a good deal of pushing from me) with her dressmaker, Madame Rose, who had an unimpressive little shop off Third Street (where some of the most impressive French sewing was turned out at relatively modest prices) and had acquired the first really extravagant wardrobe she had owned in several years. (She also bought me a slinky blue taffeta!) Mrs. Stravinsky loved beautiful clothes but was always loath to spend money on them—in fact, had a real block about spending money on anything that had to do with herself. (On matters relating to the comfort of her two charges, limitations were unheard-of.) She owned some "small" furs when I first met her—a mink stole, some silver fox, and a black Persian coat that had already lived through several seasons. The jewelry she wore was more often than not composed of semiprecious stones, each one of which had been either a present from a friend or a memento of a trip. She had designed two or three very striking crosses out of these bits of chrysoprase, moonstone, garnet, and so on, and wore them a great deal—whenever, that is, she did not have to ask St. Anthony to find them. Otherwise, her most "precious" jewels were a string of black cultured pearls acquired during the 1959 Japanese tour (always worn with two strands of imitation white ones), a small aquamarine ring framed in tiny diamonds (her father's gift), and a gold link bracelet with a charm which, when spun rapidly, revealed the legend "I love you" (from her husband). Her passion, however, was for junk jewelry, and Beverly Hills shopping expeditions were climaxed, as a rule, by trips to Woolworth's or Kress's or to novelty shops for additions to her treasure hoard. Stravinsky, needless to say, regarded everything she ever wore as richer by virtue of her beauty (it could be, as it often was, a twelve-year-old housecoat or a chiffon dress from the early thirties). Once only, when she flourished an enormous five-dollar "diamond" ring, did he raise any protest, and promptly made her get rid of it. But it never occurred to him to urge her to buy what she might want for herself, or himself to buy presents *for* her. Part of this thoughtlessness was due to his automatic reluctance to spend hard-earned money on non–tax-deductible items, but more of it, I am sure, was pure ignorance of the fact that his wife might entertain a yearning for fripperies.

At this point in his life Stravinsky had almost stopped questioning the *spending* of money. Only the continued *earning* of it, and the prompt arrival of everything that was due, concerned him. True, he always asked, "Can I afford it?" but would be readily satisfied with an affirmative answer, and that was that. He no longer studied the right-hand side of the menu when he went to dinners at Chasen's or Perino's or The Bistro, although they could amount to two or three hundred dollars at a time, depending on whether the Marions or the Edells or the Montaperts or Miranda joined us; nor did he dwell long over the expenditures for new cars, nor the limousines, nor the suites at hotels or the room service on trips, which often mounted into the thousands. But of course most of these outlays were permissible on the IRS's Long Form, since 90 percent of the time the guests constituted business or medical deductions, or the expenses were connected with tours, and the proper notations would be made on the little daily calendar. I prided myself on being Stravinsky's best tax deduction (he could take all of me off), and I would sometimes tease him by saying that that was the only reason he tolerated me at all. At which he would become very wide-eyed and serious, would take my hand and assure me sincerely that this could never, never be so, "although it is nice that the other advantage accompanies you!"

The fashion show was a great success for the two gentlemen, but it wore the models out. One part of our audience was reading Simenon in bed on the second floor, and the other was occupied with those everlasting sheets of yellow paper in the living room. We floated up and down the stairs, like showgirls in a Ziegfield extravaganza, receiving polite but brief applause, until we lost our breath, changed back into our old clothes, and drove to Will Wright's to have tangerine mint ice-cream sodas.

When we returned and I made my customary bed-check, Stravinsky, lifting his eyes from his page, regarded my creased slacks and old sweater (which I had worn at least three times a week) for a fleeting second, and said courteously, "That is the best one of all."

CHAPTER FIFTEEN

STRAVINSKY was greeted in Louisville as though he had won seven straight Kentucky Derbys. He opened with *Fireworks* and closed with the complete *Firebird*, but a pyrotechnical display that almost matched the overture occurred at dress rehearsal, when he saw that Leeds had sent the usual error-filled materials for the second work. (The poor acoustics in the auditorium didn't help either; every note sounded as though it were being played at the top of Mount Rushmore.) Nevertheless, it was heartening to see him wrap his fury in the old vigor—for he was walking badly and constantly complained of weakness—and when he thrust the *Firebird* score into my hands (the orchestra manager had more than gladly turned this rented music material over) and outlined graphically what he wished me to include in the letter to its publisher, I was happy. Robert conducted the *Rite* at this concert with such splendor that the city's principal critic wrote him a fan letter, delivered the day we left (I have kept it as a testimonial that such things *are* possible). As for Mrs. Stravinsky, she had a charming reunion with an old beau whom she had not seen for some years. He was a baron who now lived in nearby Lexington; he spent the entire Louisville stay with us, and it was quite clear that his adoration had been not one whit dimmed by the passage of time.

However, Louisville provided *me* with a few agonies, for I had made an unforgivable mistake in a moment of absent-mindedness and quoted the committee a fee of seventy-five hundred dollars instead of the ten thousand dollars Stravinsky had been led, from my previous conversation, to expect. The sponsors, with true Southern courtesy, tried their best to remedy the situation by suggesting that a tape be made of the concert as a permanent document, for which they hoped to raise the additional twenty-five hundred dollars. This fell through because of those terrible acoustics. I told one tale after another to Stravinsky to gain time. Long after, the money was produced and acknowledged with thanks from the West Coast. Stravinsky bothered me a little about this, but not as much as he had on that other occasion when money was delayed long ago in 1961. He knew me well enough now to be aware that I would not take advantage of him, and he realized I had fallen into some kind of morass and was afraid to tell him the truth. My "optimistic nature" and my "certainty" about securing huge fees on all occasions were the two things he would chide me about, but that was as far as it went. Still, the fact that my feeling for him was so deep that I would have done almost anything to remain near him is hardly an excuse for the stupidity I demonstrated on this occasion, and it remains one of those memories (within the experience of everyone, I think) whose recollection instills a passionate desire to be concealed forever from view under six feet of heavy black earth.

However, the inner suffering this affair caused me became tinted with a slight cynicism in October when I was asked by Robert to draw up a contract for a concert he had arranged independently with the Beverly Hills Symphony. This was to take place the following February (1967) in, of all locales, the International Ballroom of the Beverly Hilton Hotel. Stravinsky was to conduct *Fireworks*, excerpts from *Petrushka*, and *The Firebird*; Robert, the *Rite*. The fee was four thousand dollars! I could hardly believe in Stravinsky's acquiescence, but, according to his co-conductor, this was a favor for an old friend. The old friend's organization, however, went bankrupt, and the fee was never collected, which prompted a comforting letter to me from André, who had been aware of my protests over this contract and my gloom over Louisville.

October was the month of a more significant event: the world premiere of *Requiem Canticles* at Princeton on October 8, a performance arranged by Robert, who applied himself, immediately after Louisville, to securing the sponsorship. His determination to obtain hearings as rapidly as possible for Stravinsky's new music found its catalyst this time in Arthur Mendel, chairman of the Music Department at Princeton, whose efforts brought the project to fruition. The concert was subsidized by funds from the Seeger bequest, and was coordinated by Claudio Spies. At Princeton, Stravinsky saw Dr. Robert Oppenheimer, whom he had met in 1959 at the time of the Fromm Seminars, and that gentleman then expressed the wish that the *Requiem Canticles* be performed as part of the memorial service that would be held when his own death occurred. Only a tragically short time thereafter, his request was fulfilled.

And it was with rehearsals for this concert that Arnold Newman began his series of photographs, some of which were to see daylight late in 1967 in a book entitled *Bravo Stravinsky!* * Mr. Newman is one of America's better-known genii of the camera. He is also a persistent artist, who had been pursuing me for some time with his project of capturing Stravinsky at home, abroad, on tour, at play, etcetera. The composer's attitude initially was very negative; he had had enough of being "captured" by people who followed him about for a full year. Finally, Mr. Newman caught up with me by telephone in Louisville, and because his suggestions involved writing and a respectable financial benefit to Robert, I took the matter up again, this time receiving a "Yes."

I was not to have personal contact with Mr. Newman until I went to Hollywood in the month of December (October and November were spent "advancing" the Ballet Folklórico), but periodically Robert reported that the cameras were snapping away at the Henry Hudson Hotel, on Fifty-seventh Street, the scene of the Princeton rehearsals (a floor of enormous black and white marble squares exposed the composer like the King is a game of chess); in New York at the Hotel Pierre (at breakfast, lunch, dinner, supper, reading, writing, packing, unpacking—Stravinsky told me that he, personally, was prepared to supply some excellent shots in the bathroom); at North Wetherly Drive during a week including Halloween ("Maestro," "Madame," "Mrs. B.," and "Billy" carousing with paper hats and bogy accessories in the dining room); at the Columbus concert. By the time Mr. Newman and I met on his second trip to Hollywood, he had already shot a few thousand pictures, and Stravinsky gave me a few hundred words of advice on how to deal with the situation during the remainder of his stay. The effective technique, evolved by Mrs. Stravinsky, was based on almost total disappearance: "He is sleeping. . . . He is working. . . . He is bathing. . . . He is thinking. . . ." And to Mr. Newman's plaintive "Then what shall I do now?" Mrs. Stravinsky would reply, "Some still life." "What still life?" And then there would emerge some of the creative processes that, in another way, have made her an outstanding painter of fantasies of nature, and she would come up with one idea after another to distract him from the chase. Sheets

* Cleveland: World, 1967.

of music, scrapbooks, groups of accessories, Mrs. Stravinsky, Robert, Marilyn, and I were photographed as never before, and in between Mr. Newman waited around corners for the moment when the composer, hearing no sound, would poke his head out of his studio or bedroom or other hiding place. Then Mrs. Stravinsky would entice Mr. Newman into the dining room with promises of all manner of delicacies. But when Stravinsky was finally forced to return to civilization, he was photographed—at his viewing of the United Airlines film; at Chasen's, kissing Greer Garson, brought to our table for this purpose one night when we dined with the Edells and others (earlier I had had to refresh his memory, although he *had* met her before, by recalling the entire story of *Mrs. Miniver*); at the posh penthouse restaurant of the Dorothy Chandler Pavilion, where he sat absorbing Scotch and finally concealed his face entirely by supporting his sleepy head with his hand.

One day I brought Stravinsky a Siamese kitten that I thought he would like for Christmas, and we sat together for an hour at the living-room card-table while the tiny creature struggled and yowled protests at the camera, but quieted down remarkably whenever Stravinsky held him. (The kitten was destined for another comfortable home, for the composer's allergy was cat-shy, and the doctors said no.)

But there is no question in my mind that the greatest photographs made of Stravinsky in the final dozen years of his life were snatched by Mr. Newman's various very costly lenses.

Before all this, while I was traveling in the South, a recording session took place on October 11 at Manhattan Center in New York. It was an extremely important one, based on the Princeton concert: *Symphonies of Wind Instruments, Mass, Variations,* and *Requiem Canticles*—all part of the *Stravinsky Conducts Stravinsky* project—were scheduled. I had been in touch with the family by phone very frequently after Louisville—sometimes twice a day, for Stravinsky felt ill on his arrival in New York. On the day of the recording he remained in bed in the morning, and Robert departed to begin the sessions, reporting, on his arrival at the studio, that the composer would be there "later." But as the afternoon wore on and Stravinsky did not appear, Claudio Spies, who was attending as he customarily did, was asked by Robert to telephone the Pierre Hotel and explain to Mrs. Stravinsky the need for the composer's im-

mediate presence. She replied that her husband was not well enough
to come; in fact, that he would not come at all. Robert himself
telephoned, had a rapid and intense conversation in French, and
around five o'clock a grim and silent Stravinsky appeared, escorted
by his wife and Ed Allen, who had been visiting at the hotel. He did
not participate in the recording, of course, and remained only for a
brief period, during which the *Symphonies* and a part of the *Mass*
were taped. Claudio, one of the engineers, and a musician with
whom I spoke later were unanimous in their impression that Stravinsky's attitude clearly showed he was there against his will. And I
am sure this is true. I am also sure that the "forcing" on Robert's
part was entirely motivated by the knowledge that if the composer
were *not* present, there would be no more Stravinsky records, and
consequently no Craft records either. Stravinsky, it should be remembered, apart from feeling ill on that day, bore a grudge against
Columbia for its employment of an unapproved soloist for the
Capriccio recording the previous January, as well as the cancellation of plans to record the Hollywood Bowl program in July.

However, he snapped back rapidly, and within a day the family
left for Hollywood, where the composer happily took up his work
on *The Owl and the Pussycat,* completing it within a week or so
after his arrival. Its surprise première on Halloween Eve at one of
the Monday Evening Concerts in the Los Angeles County Museum's Bing Center Theater—with Stravinsky's friend Ingolf Dahl as
pianist, and soprano Peggy Bonin (who learned the score in two
days)—was interesting for another reason. Lawrence Morton, artistic director of the series, had outscored Diaghilev by one in presenting his twelfth Stravinsky world première.*

Robert had succeeded in persuading Marilyn Stalvey to extend
her secretarial services from part- to full-time, and beginning in
November, from nine-thirty to six each day she labored over yellow
sheets of paper and cartons of correspondence. From this point on

---

* At that time, that is. Actually, Mr. Morton was to present one more première—the Wolf songs—on September 6, 1968. However, in a letter to me he
modestly pointed out that Diaghilev's list included such major works as *Firebird, Petrushka, Rite of Spring, Renard, Pulcinella, Oedipus Rex,* etc., while
his list consisted chiefly of arrangements of earlier works. Nevertheless, he did
première such significant pieces as *In Memorian Dylan Thomas, Three Songs
from William Shakespeare, Elegy for J.F.K., The Dove Descending,* etc.
Robert conducted all of the premières.

Robert undertook the dictation of replies to practically all except
the most personal letters received by Stravinsky, thus finally reliev-
ing André of a burden, although the latter continued to keep the
books. Marilyn was married to Dorrance Stalvey, a musician who
sometimes played in Robert's concerts. They had a son and daughter of primary-school age and lived a twenty-minute car drive from
the Stravinskys. Between taking care of her family and fulfilling the
decoding demands of those manuscripts, she still had strength to remain calm and thoughtful at all times, even though Robert's habit
of dropping "just these few letters" on her typewriter as she was
preparing to depart for home was infuriating. Marilyn worked for
the Stravinskys until I came to close the Hollywood house in
January 1970. Or, rather, she worked for Robert. Every secretary
ever employed by that household somehow or other immediately
became Robert's exclusive property, for in order to maintain pace
with his flow of prose, there was no alternative to keeping one's
wrists tied to the typewriter, with fingers in a state of perpetual
motion. Marilyn loved Mrs. Stravinsky, who represented to her
everything connected with the glamor of fame. And she regarded
Stravinsky as a kind of mysterious god. "I don't understand what he
is," she said to me once in a moment of confidence. "I know he is
something that is great, but I don't understand it at all," and therein
innocently voiced what many people who claim expertise *really*
experienced when they were with the composer.

Marilyn was responsible for the complete restoration of my vision
(as well as that of many another of Robert's correspondents, I am
sure), for now all letters sent from Hollywood arrived neatly typed
and, of course, assumed a much more official air. (It is vital that a
secretary, more than anyone in professional life, must receive a
good first impression of one's authority!). I began to collect a series
of legal-sounding missives from Robert (implying to those present
that he had met me only yesterday), and my replies would be in
kind. Our exchange—that is, what there was of it in the next two
years, since telephone calls were now almost daily occurrences
when we were not together—reads like a file of correspondence between two administrative assistants at IBM and General Motors,
along such lines as: "To resume, steps must be taken immediately
to insure, etc., etc."—rather than "Let's get the hell after that contract"—to which I would answer, "There is no validity in any of
the points you refer to in yours of, etc., etc."—instead of "What in
God's name do you expect me to do about, etc., etc."

In any case, Robert and I were now more prone to lose our tempers with each other, and if he were really angry with me, he would have Marilyn apply some of the rules laid down for those beyond the fringe. "Mr. Craft is not here. . . . Mr. Craft is out of town for two days. . . . Mr. Craft is editing tapes . . . please give me the message," as happened to me when I once called from Florida about a deadline for an orchestra contractor and another time from New York about overtime on the United Airlines recording. These ruses did not deceive me—I had myself used them too often on Robert's behalf. And of course, out of sheer perverseness I would *not* give the message but would wait until Mr. Craft, out of sheer curiosity, would return from "editing tapes" or leave off partaking in "conferences." This habit of instructing everyone to relay such important-sounding excuses when he did not want to take telephone calls, or having the party call back every fifteen minutes for the same negative answer, is one of Robert's most maddening quirks. (Of course, the pot shouldn't berate the kettle—*he* hated *my* habit of saying everything was "urgent.") I have never, never understood why he finds it impossible simply to send word that he is "too busy to talk now." Or, if someone calls to whom he really does not *want* to talk, to have that person informed that *he* will call whenever he is free. (He rarely does, of course.) When help was not about, Mrs. Stravinsky would frequently deal with the same credulous caller (usually female) six or seven times a day.

But though Robert and I disagreed more often now, our arguments never lasted longer than a few hours or a day or so at the most. He knew I understood the terrible feeling of insecurity he was perpetually combating, and I knew he understood my love for Stravinsky; and those were the grounds on which we always met, right to the end.

November 1966 began with a long-promised concert to celebrate the seventy-fifth anniversary of the founding at Pasadena of "Caltech," which was then in the process of helping to send Man to the moon. But, as one reporter pointed out (he of the celebrated sweatshirt!), Stravinsky did not offer a parallel by programing any of his recent "path-breaking advances in technology"; instead, he conducted the *Pulcinella Suite* and Anne's aria from Act I of *The Rake's Progress*, turning over the *Dumbarton Oaks Concerto*, originally scheduled for himself, to Robert. On the twelfth the trio flew to Honolulu, where for a week or so they drank in a pineapple-tinged sunshine (Stravinsky told me later he was sure his laundry had been done in "pineapple-water") prior to the pair of concerts arranged there by Barati.

Early in November, when my tour with the Ballet Folklórico came to an end, the Stravinskys asked me to return to Hollywood; in fact, André sent me an air ticket on Stravinsky's instructions. But since Marilyn was now working full-time, my bank account was overdrawn, and Hurok had offered me a goodly sum to look after the D'Oyly Carte Company, I wrote Robert on the fifth that Columbus would probably be our next meeting-place. I note that this same letter indicates my receipt of concert inquiries for the fall of the following year from St. Louis, Oklahoma City, Cleveland, Houston, and New Orleans, and that I said "unless you tell me definitely that Maestro wants to do them, I am reluctant since the last time Madame and I spoke in New York, she felt she didn't want to think too far ahead." From the general tone of my letter I deduce that Robert and I must have been having one of our twenty-four-hour periods of coolness, for I also suggest (with what I thought then was thinly veiled irony, but which now sounds like lead-encased verbiage) that apparently he no longer had faith, since he was dealing with Glynn Ross directly on the *Soldier's Tale* tour —an accusation with absolutely no foundation except my own pique at not yet having heard a word from the Seattle Opera.

Alas for Robert! He was usually denounced for the wrong things, while the right things escaped one's attention completely. For example, after the Columbus concert on November 29, which an airline strike kept me from attending, thereby eliminating my only chance to hear that famous thrice-changed lecture *The Genesis of a Masterpiece*, I learned quite by accident that the trio had flown to Portland, Oregon. Robert, without saying a word to me (for fear deep melancholia would occur!) had booked a pair of concerts with a West Coast "lady impresario" who had been doggedly pursuing this goal for years. She used to turn up at the oddest moments and in the most unexpected places, and regard us from a distance in predatory silence. As an instance, when Stravinsky, Robert, and I were traveling to Washington for the *Abraham and Isaac* concert in 1964, she suddenly decided to walk back and forth in front of our open compartment between Newark and Baltimore. (I was instructed by Robert to disregard her presence and close the door— Stravinsky wore a faint grin as he read his book without looking up.) But there they were in Portland, and, moreover, I had to reveal my knowledge of their whereabouts because Miami required immediate confirmation of a request from manager Francis Mayville for a concert in February 1967. It *was* embarrassing—but not for me!

My work for Hurok was to bring me back to the West Coast before the end of the year, and at Mrs. Stravinsky's invitation I returned to their house on December 9. The composer was in excellent spirits, though his face seemed more gaunt and his frailty compelled the feeling that one must handle him as one would a piece of bone china. He was beginning to be very fearful of the stairs, I remember, even though his walk, strangely, had improved. His chief complaint now was, "I do not hear so well." This did, indeed, seem to be the case, but usually only when more than two people were engaged in conversation around him. (He had always had some difficulty, if the talk were entirely in English, in comprehending everything as rapidly as his wife did, and he depended on her asides in Russian to keep him *au courant*.)

Mrs. Stravinsky looked flourishing but was cookless again, for Mrs. B. and Billy had gone the way of all flesh, and not in a cloud of glory, either. I had suspected trouble when news about the Portland trip had been given to me on the phone by Mrs. B., who announced at the same time that Mr. Craft had said at lunch that day, "Tell Lillian she's fired." That, in itself, did not perturb me much at the time; Robert's favorite expression, after "I'll be right there" (two hours later), was "Tell Lillian [or Marilyn, or the gardener, or whoever] she's fired!" First of all, he never meant it; secondly, in my case it would have been a poser, since I was not on salary. But Mrs. B.'s delivery of this charming bit of gossip (apart from the enormity of its repetition) was made in a voice replete with some strong beverage. In any case, Mrs. Stravinsky told me the situation had become intolerable. Billy had begun to break ground rules as soon as school started, and the air was filled, at the wrong hours, with a sound equivalent to that which might result from the spontaneous release of all inhabitants of San Quentin. He also was "all over the house"—that is, what was left of it when he had finished devouring slices of it in the kitchen. But none of these reasons would have surrounded the departure with the unpleasantness caused by the real one, for one day, in reply to a very mild reprimand about disciplining her son, Mrs. B. leveled accusations against the family that resembled those published in the *Protocols of the Elders of Zion.* Stravinsky was not at all unaccustomed to hearing from time to time that he was Jewish. (His childhood summers had been spent in Ustilug, where every family except his *was* Jewish, and all his life Jews had figured prominently in his circle without its being a case of "some of my best friends.") I had heard that he "definitely is" long before I ever met him, and afterward, this was usually one of the questions asked of me by the super-inquisitive.

Stravinsky never bothered to deny this theory, any more than he did the other ridiculous fiction that he was anti-Semitic. The first would have required time for an exposition on Genesis, leading to the dogmatism that *everyone* was Jewish, and the second could hardly have entered his scope of thought. Such inventions were not his affair, in any event, but were strictly the property of those who created them.*

But if he *were* going to be identified with that ancient religion, it was certainly not to be in Mrs. B.'s terms, which, in the minds of both Stravinskys, could have been given voice only by someone whose approach to life was exceeding strange. The woman and her child—a wide-eyed and wondering Stravinsky told me—had been "a pair of *moan*sters!" Miranda was now scouring the movie colony for another cook—a man, this time—and in the interim, Mrs. Stravinsky had returned to her fish soups. I went back to the Waring Blendor.

Robert was very busy with a series of articles, and also with the British edition of *Dialogues and a Diary* (which contained some of the material from the just-published fifth American book, *Themes and Episodes*). I helped out occasionally with a little deciphering in the evenings after Marilyn went home. Robert was also working with singers for the Schütz *Christmas Oratorio,* which he was to conduct at the Bing Center Theater on December 19, and the rehearsal guest room sometimes gave forth the sounds of a long-

* Stravinsky's 1952 *Cantata* has occasionally come under attack, since one of the four fifteenth- and sixteenth-century English lyrics used as texts contains some lines which identify the Jews as deicides. The composer was not conscious of this implication of the text during the composition period and received quite a jolt when he first heard his piece performed. He changed the words immediately and amended the music for a new edition which has not yet been published. Robert has assumed responsibility for carrying out Stravinsky's wishes.

ago holiday praise of God. Mr. Newman arrived on the twelfth and began his watchful waiting-and-snapping.

Four or five days after I arrived, the Russian poet Yevgeny Yevtushenko paid a call on the Stravinskys. The enormous amount of publicity accompanying his tour of the United States had stirred Robert into declaring that this visit was part of the whole planned campaign, and would be the biggest feather in the poet's cap (all true, of course). Despite Mrs. Stravinsky's entreaties, Robert retired to his room, and, backed by Mr. Newman, I opened the door to the celebrated visitor. A very attractive gentleman wearing a neat white shirt and an old school tie, coat on one shoulder, swept in (followed by two other men, one holding a camera) as though on a favorable wind. He enveloped the Stravinskys, who stood in the hallway wearing welcoming smiles, in a huge embrace, and literally held them captive for a moment or two while the meeting was documented. The visit took place in the living room, complete with Mr. Newman, during which time I remained alone in the library, but within earshot of the explosion of Russian which was thereafter sustained throughout the hour. I could hear Stravinsky's (sonorous) and his wife's (gay) voices, responding with an enthusiasm I could not recall from any encounters they had with anyone else within my experience—even their oldest Russian friends. At one point Yevtushenko began to declaim, and then I could not resist stepping into the hallway for a peek. Clearly, he was reciting some of his poetry, and in a tone that contained all the vibrato capable of being produced by the string section of a large orchestra. It had the pianissimos of Debussy, the fortissimos of Beethoven; and in between it ran a gamut of Wagnerian, Mozartean, and Stravinskyan *arpeggios*. He sat on the sofa for the lyric passages and rose for the dramatic ones. His audience was enthralled. Mrs. Stravinsky, leaning forward, looked, from where I was hidden, as though she had just had her twentieth birthday party, and Stravinsky also leaned forward, chin on his cane, his gaze fixed on the performer, his mouth pursed to an *o* of concentration. It was a marvelous show. What a pity I didn't understand a single word of it!

Toward the end of the visit, a light footstep sounded in the kitchen; Robert had apparently descended from his den and was prevailed upon to enter and be introduced. And immediately thereafter, on the same west wind that had brought him, Yevtushenko and friends blew away in an easterly direction.

At dinner, while Mrs. Stravinsky was reliving every moment of
the interview and translating every line of the poetry for my benefit,
Robert and she argued about Yevtushenko's talents; he did not share
her enthusiasm, and she retorted that how could he expect to when
he did not know Russian and could therefore neither appreciate nor
criticize the work. Robert fell silent, as he usually did when she
leveled this charge about his ignorance of the Russian language, and
I sympathized with him—in this case particularly, because although
the first part of her statement was true, the second was not. He
certainly knew Yevtushenko's poetry, on which he had given me a
thorough and fascinating negative critique the day before, although
with reservations because, of course, he knew it only from trans-
lations. But Robert always had his defenses up when the Stravinskys
were involved in anything directly connected with their native
country. During the argument my mind went back to a letter he
had written me in 1962, just prior to the Russian tour, in which he
expressed anxiety about being totally dependent on *them* once they
reached the USSR because he could not speak the tongue, and they
would readily find guides in other people. Sometimes this fear of
not being needed was so strong in him that he would take the opposing side in discussions about anybody or anything they praised,
even if the matter was of minor importance. For example, during
our April 1965 visit to Chicago for the concert that included the
premières of *Variations* and *Introitus*, we went to the Chicago
Opera House to view another first—Jerome Robbins's *Les Noces*,
performed by the American Ballet Theater. The Stravinskys were
deeply moved by it, and the word "superb" was used in connection
with the choreography, although I cannot now remember which of
the two voiced it. On the drive back to the hotel Robert began a
critical analysis of the production in which some of his points were
valid. I recall, for instance, that he was particularly not in favor of
the ballet's final movement, wherein the bride and groom "symbolically" consummate their marriage in perfect synchronization
with the "tolling bell" chords that make the ending of Stravinsky's
work miraculous; Robert felt this was a "commonplace use of the
music," and said so repeatedly and vehemently. By the time we
reached the Ambassador East the Stravinskys were thoroughly dis-
gruntled, and Mrs. Stravinsky departed for bed with an annoyed
"You never like *anything!*" Yet Robert remarked to me in the liv-

ing room before I left the suite, "Jerry Robbins is by far the most original choreographer around!"

Stravinsky's two final appearances in Chicago took place at Orchestra Hall on December 28, 1966, and on January 1 of his eighty-fifth-birthday year. I had booked the Royal Suite at the Drake (where Queen Elizabeth had resided during her American visit) and it lived up to its name, with its draperies of deep-blue velvet, handsomely carved gilt wood, ormolu, ebony and marble furnishings, and regal service. Mrs. Stravinsky loved the colors, and Stravinsky and Robert sampled every fish dish on the hotel's world-famous menu. The suite's grand salon, where the Stravinskys sat while Mrs. S. talked to an Associated Press reporter (and Mr. S. permitted photographs), overlooked Lake Michigan, on which a three-day snow-and-ice storm had laid down a crystal floor. We celebrated a belated Christmas here, as well as Mrs. Stravinsky's "American" birthday (which falls on the twenty-fifth).

Robert and I decided that Stravinsky's present to his wife that year should be a new fur coat—a blonde mink to match her hair—which I found in one of the elegant shops on Michigan Avenue. It took our combined efforts to convince her that her husband's purchase of it would not immediately send them all to the bread line. She had not then, and has not now, any concept whatsoever of what an annual income well into six figures means, nor that the hotel bill for that five-day stay, with its continued room service, large lunches and dinners, wines, long-distance calls, telegrams, and cables (the norm on any Stravinsky trip), would almost exceed the price of her present. Stravinsky's approval of the coat was all that could be desired; he kissed his wife half a dozen times and told her over and over how beautiful she looked, and in the next breath said to me, "Have I enough money to pay?" When I assured him he had, he returned, satisfied, to his reading of Chekhov.

John Stravinsky paid his grandfather a visit during this Chicago stay (remaining for the concerts), and received a Christmas check that was entirely his step-grandmother's doing. She used her powers of persuasion to good effect on her husband, who had regarded the visit as prompted by this motive alone. But of course Stravinsky always did suspect that everyone must want something from him—and his family seemed to him no different from anyone else in this regard. I suppose he felt that he had made enough gestures in the past, with his gifts of houses, cars, and allowances to one or the other. Nevertheless, the present to John created a degree of cheeriness, since the boy's visit to Chicago in 1964, at the time of the July concert, had been a disaster. John had stopped overnight at the Ambassador East (as his grandfather's guest, of course), and a hue and cry had arisen over an extra dinner charged on Stravinsky's bill—entirely my fault; I had told John to charge it. A family coolness resulted, and silence from the Urbana section for a long time. But now all appeared to be repaired, and John, who is a very intelligent young man, amused us with stories of his efforts to break into the theater, including plans for finding an apartment in New York, for which my aid was enlisted.

Except for the business that had brought us to Chicago, a few forays into the hotel restaurants, and *The Odd Couple*, Stravinsky caught up on his reading in bed during this blustery stay. But one evening, before the first concert, we went to Maxim's for dinner as guests of impresario Harry Zelzer, who likes to hear himself identified (as he often is) as "the Hurok of the Middle West." Mr. Zelzer is exactly the same height as Stravinsky was, and every one of those five feet two inches is staccato. Dinner included an interesting barrage of jabs, stabs, picks at everything in the concert business, particularly the unions, which were "running it." Mr. Zelzer had bumped into trouble with the Chicago Symphony when he sought to recruit it for Stravinsky's concerts. Some of its members claimed that money was still due them from the Stravinsky session in Orchestra Hall on July 20, 1964, when the composer had recorded *Orpheus*. On that same day—in fact, prior to the *Orpheus* taping—Robert had recorded Schoenberg's transcription of the Brahms *G-minor Piano Quartet*. The orchestra attested that this constituted two sessions, not one; it had worked for two conductors—therefore compensation should be in accordance with union regulations: double! The problem had not been solved in 1965 when the *Variations* concert took place on April 17, causing the cancellation of Columbia's plans to record that program. Furthermore, it was still unsettled now—although whether the obligation was Columbia's or Stravinsky's was never made entirely clear to me. Doubtless Columbia felt that because the trouble had arisen over Robert's recording, the rightful payor should be the composer.

The orchestra Mr. Zelzer had finally assembled consisted, in the main, of the finest musicians Chicago could supply from both the symphony and other groups (an opinion shared by the conductors, who found occasion to express themselves on this point within a day or so after that dinner), but several members of the Chicago Orchestra had refused to be recruited. Mr. Zelzer's battery fell on sympathetic ears, particularly since it contained, within its range, an imprecation of the press that made the celebrated Stravinskyan demolitions seem like eulogies. (Mr. Zelzer is famous in the concert business for the punishments he metes out to members of the Fourth Estate—critics out of favor must *pay* for their reviewers' tickets.)

Stravinsky, who had come to dinner with a slight grudge because Mr. Zelzer had only allowed two rehearsals (alas! this happened with other managers, too), decided now that his local sponsor was a man of good sense, and from then on it was *Carthago delenda est.* The materialization of a well-known and more-than-casually-interested columnist from the *Chicago Sun-Times,* who stopped to say hello, brought the discussion (which might well have continued, regardless) to a hasty conclusion, for I almost knocked Robert out of his chair as I leaped up to greet "Kup" Kupcinet with the best "small world" air I could muster.

Almost every aspect of these last Chicago concerts I will remember with joy for the rest of my life. Stravinsky, despite his now very halting walk, commanded the podium with the vigor, firmness, and youthfulness of that night in the thirties when I saw him at the old "Met" for the first time. He drew pictures of *Petrushka* and *The Firebird* with that orchestra which I had never seen before, and as though he were working with a palette of colors freshly mixed for what he instinctively knew in advance would be masterpieces. And with *that* orchestra!—which, in forever unpardonable rudeness, showed greater respect for its union colleagues than for the man now among those immortals whose creations made it possible for them to form unions, by failing to rise when this eighty-four-year-old master was led, so slowly, to his appointed place.

The Craft portion of the program is also in my total recall. Itzhak Perlman, the Israeli violinist, played Stravinsky's *Concerto.* This young artist, who is a virtuoso not only on his instrument but in his display of courage in triumphing over poliomyelitis, had performed the same piece in the earlier Honolulu concerts, and Stravinsky told me later that he would not be averse to "having Perlman play in every subsequent concert in which I appear." The audience outdid itself in cheering this work not usually programed by concert violinists, since its beauties are more subtle than spectacular (although it contains some of the most difficult stretches in the repertoire, according to Samuel Dushkin, and a lyric movement that gives the player an opportunity to be a poet as well); and Stravinsky, sitting in the wings with me, was moved, and embraced both soloist and conductor with deep appreciation.

The second performance on New Year's Day was even better than the first. This time the entire orchestra rose at the proper time. But the anticlimatic tribute was doubtless due to the grapevine, along which word had traveled (on lightning wings, apparently) of Stravinsky's telegraphed reply to the editor-in-chief of a Chicago newspaper whose critic, in his adverse review of the first concert, labeled the orchestra "a miserable band." The telegram was composed by Robert in Stravinsky's bedroom, approved and signed by Stravinsky, and sent off by me. Its contents were notable, and it concluded with the words: "Wednesday's orchestra was a credit to Chicago. Your reviewer is a local disgrace."

So much for those who might claim that offenses to Stravinsky would ever prejudice his *musical* judgments! And so much for duels with the press—for this was the last time Stravinsky himself was to entrust to my hands the dispatching of such communiqués.

CHAPTER SIXTEEN

1967! Stravinsky will be eighty-five in June. Before that he will conduct for the last time, record for the last time, and though he will continue to work at the creation of music, think it, and live it beyond this birthday, and the next, and the next—and beyond even his eighty-eighth—there will be no more original compositions.

This is also the year in which he will begin to gather all his resources for a long campaign against an adversary whose victory is inevitable, and who has the additional advantage of determining the time and the place.

The Stravinskys and Robert flew to New York immediately after the Chicago concerts, and I did not see them all again until their return to Los Angeles on January 12 (Robert had actually arrived a few days in advance, to prepare for a "Monday Evening" concert at the museum.) I was already there, due to my Hurok commitments, and living, this time, in my little apartment (Hurok's orders —no distractions!). Mrs. Stravinsky told me that in New York Stravinsky had received favorable pronouncements from Dr. Lewithin on his general condition, following a series of x-ray treatments. The trio had dined with Marcel Duchamp (Mr. Newman was there!) and had visited with several old friends. Stravinsky looked well to me, and indeed felt well enough to attend Robert's Monteverdi concert at the museum and his concert of Wagner and Beethoven in Inglewood. And on the eighteenth of the month the composer stood, for the last time, beneath the microphones that now carried the 1945 *Firebird Suite* to the sound booth where John McClure sat.

But according to Dr. Edell his blood did not show a safe balance, and several bleedings were prescribed—something like four or five in as many days, if my memory serves me correctly, for I recall

Mrs. Stravinsky's almost daily calls to Dr. Lewithin in accordance
with the normal East-vs.-West–West-vs.-East procedure. The number of bloodlettings indicate that Dr. Edell apparently preferred
to draw very small amounts of the composer's vital fluid each time,
rather than a pint (the customary portion) all at once; perhaps the
growing sclerotic condition of the arteries made the punctures difficult—I cannot say. Dr. Edell knew his patient well; he had been
treating him for many years—ever since, in fact, the Aldous Huxleys had first called the Stravinsky's attention to him in the forties.
The doctor was Viennese, and five minutes with him exposed a
brilliant and cultured mind, which thoroughly encompassed fields
of study other than medicine. He spoke fluent French and English
as well as German, using the latter language frequently in his talks
with Stravinsky, who regarded him, as did Mrs. Stravinsky, with
great affection. His conversations dealt with music, art, literature,
psychology; and in this last field he excelled in handling his patient,
for he recognized and understood the complete hypochondria of
the man, and did not treat it lightly. In my opinion he was far and
away the best of the doctors who treated Stravinsky, at least during
my association with the composer. And, like the greatest of his
professional brethren, he was human.

When Stravinsky arrived in Miami for his first and last concert
there, the hotel I had chosen sent an oxford gray Rolls-Royce, complete with highly-liveried chauffeur, to meet our flight from Los
Angeles on February 19. This set the tone (as well as the size of the
tips) for our entire stay, and it was all wrong from the word go.
Rooms commanding a magnificent view of the ocean—after all,
why travel to Miami, fees notwithstanding, if not for a look at the
Atlantic!—had figured prominently in our prior discussions. Out of
the array of new palaces facing the beach, I settled on an "exclusive" older model. Its lobby was relatively small and convenient
to elevators, and its decoration (by comparison) was discreet. The
management recommended the penthouse apartment—the only accommodations available, in fact, and no wonder: even among those
devil-may-care, purse-happy denizens of America's Playground,
there were not too many who wanted to pay upwards of two hundred dollars a day for a place to sleep, deductible or no.

But the suite! All in "gorgeous" red velvet and modern rococo.
Mrs. Stravinsky hates red rooms (although her husband and Robert

both loved the color), and her displeasure the moment she crossed the threshold was acute: "Awwfool!" Robert didn't help much either. He told me his room (somewhat more subdued, but in green cretonnes, which *he* hates) induced in him a slight feeling of nausea. Stravinsky, the angel, made no comment about the interior decoration—he always obediently took the room assigned to him after everyone else had chosen his—but he did about the probable bill. All in all I was a complete failure, although the crayfish and crab (I had nothing whatsoever to do with *those*) were somewhat ameliorating.

There had been some orchestra trouble here, too. A Philharmonic Ball was scheduled on the same night and at the same time as the concert, and the orchestra manager (with whom we had had previous dealings when he served the Philadelphia Orchestra in the same capacity) advised in strong terms that Stravinsky should change his date or he would not have first-desk musicians. This suggestion, made in letters addressed to the Hurok office and to the composer, expounding specifically in two pages what the conductors would be up against on the date chosen, had an effect exactly opposite to its intent.* Rather than change *his* date, Stravinsky would have cancelled, particularly since he was half-hearted about leaving his home at all—a feeling that was growing more and more marked each time he returned to Hollywood. It was curious, too, because that other fear—that he might not be *able* to travel— was now very apparent in the effort he made to overcome it. In any case, the president of the Miami Philharmonic partially resolved the conflict in a diplomatic address to the orchestra, and Stravinsky was granted forty-one first-desk players from that body, including its concertmaster. Thirty others were contracted from (in the words of one reporter) "top rank-and-file players"!

But the Philharmonic Ball was undoubtedly a more attractive proposition to the Miami residents and vacationers, and although Dade Auditorium was full, a great part of the audience represented the labor of our local manager (Francis Mayville) at a last-minute

---

* The list of trials Stravinsky would have to endure, in addition to the absence of the Miami Philharmonic's first-desk men, included: 1) the absence of twenty-one string players who were playing nightly in an orchestra for Frank Sinatra; 2) the absence of "many other musicians" who were playing in hotel orchestras; 3) the absence of "many community leaders, music lovers and contributors to the Philharmonic," etc.

distribution of complimentary tickets (a fact of which we were quickly made aware by members of the orchestra).

The concert itself—*Firebird* (1919 version), *Petrushka* (fourth Tableau), *Symphony in Three Movements* (Robert), for which only two rehearsals were scheduled, was not the best, and there were a good many "clinkers." Stravinsky's mood was angry, for he felt that overtime should have been allowed for better preparation, and he sat fuming in the dressing room while Robert conducted the *Symphony*. But the audience was warm and the critics even more so, although all of them reported on the "gentle" manner in which Stravinsky now led the orchestra, a great change from his former "commanding" air, and—for the first time—emphasized his frailty *on* the podium, more than in his walk as he approached it.

Mr. Mayville lost a goodly amount of money in this venture, but when he delivered Stravinsky's check for seventy-five hundred dollars at intermission, no one could have detected a single trace of anything is his manner except the gratitude he felt at having had the privilege. The composer yielded and actually said, "I wish we could have done better for you." (This was the one and only time in my experience I heard Stravinsky express himself thus to a manager.)

There are two Miami footnotes. Stravinsky gave me a billet-doux he had received from a self-described "retired widow," now living in that sunny clime, who recalled to him a flirtation they had had in the lobby of the Grand Hotel in Paris almost forty years before. "Do you remember?" was its final sentence. And then in the postscript, again an echoing "Do you remember?" and following this, in a large, clear hand, she had written her telephone number.

The other: Miami was the last time I was to have the honor to serve Stravinsky backstage.

"Stravinsky in a Smoked-Filled Room" conducted *Fireworks, Firebird*, excerpts from *Petrushka* on February 27 at the Beverly Hilton Hotel in Los Angeles, while the audience ate, drank, and puffed away at cigars. I read this review in my own far less splendid hotel room in Minneapolis, where I was starting the final lap of the Mexican Ballet tour, which was to keep me occupied for Hurok until May. The description of the atmosphere surrounding this concert did not depress me so much as the phrase that occurred a little further along in the column, lamenting "the increasing insecurity of his conducting." The day following this event, which was also to prove a *débâcle* financially, the family flew to Seattle, where the

composer conducted *The Soldier's Tale* for Glynn Ross and a large
audience on March 1, but when I spoke to Robert two evenings
later in Hollywood, he told me "he" was "not near par," and that
his conducting had been very erratic and vague.

There were several contracts pending for 1967, and one I had
already signed (for an eight-thousand-dollar fee) with the Music
Department of the University of Kentucky in Lexington, scheduled
for April 11. The others included a CBC concert in Toronto in
May, a later one in Ithaca, and another in Buffalo; and we were
even negotiating with the St. Louis Symphony for 1968. Also,
Hurok was bringing the French National Orchestra to the United
States in the fall, and this organization was extremely anxious that
Stravinsky be one of its guest conductors. The hope (of course)
was that this might open the doors he had shut so tightly on all
French concert halls after *Threni*, almost a decade before. The pro-
posal that Stravinsky and Craft should guest-conduct the French
Orchestra in Boston was brought by Hurok's vice-President,
George Perper, whom the Stravinskys always had liked. It was
also regarded with favor because their friend Madeleine Malraux,
wife of the French writer, was a concert pianist and wished to appear as soloist.

All of these important matters prompted me to ask Robert, when
I heard the dismal note in his voice after Seattle, whether it would
not be wise to cancel everything then and there. I was certain that
most of the concerts mentioned, if not all, would take place without
Stravinsky on the podium. But Robert thought we should wait, because he felt that to suggest these steps to Stravinsky at this moment
would have a traumatic effect, and I reluctantly went along with
him. When I recalled those last splendid concerts in Chicago, I
wished with all my heart that they had marked the termination of
the composer's career as a performing artist.

But I was plagued by doubts about the attitude I had taken, for I
knew Robert and his tendency to ruminate on anything that might
be at variance with his own views, sometimes to the point where he
would exaggerate even a suggestion out of all perspective. The person who expressed any contrary opinion might come to represent,
in his mind, the "obstinate opposition."

In March, Theodore came from Geneva to visit his father and
stayed with him for ten days. Robert left for Boston during this
period to fulfill a contract I had drawn with Sarah Caldwell's Opera

Company of Boston; he was to conduct three performances of *The Rake's Progress* in a new "black and white" staging. And I continued to pile up my average of a hundred thousand air miles per annum "advancing" for Hurok.

But the news from Hollywood was not good, and on March 26 I gloomily cancelled the Lexington concert. Hubert Henderson, director of the university's School of Fine Arts, came through with the engagement nevertheless, accepting Robert as the sole conductor, and doing so with enthusiasm. Robert also agreed to deliver a lecture. The fee was reduced to fifteen hundred dollars, but it was all Robert's, and it was a help.

Our communication during Robert's absence from the West Coast was neurotic. He would phone Mrs. Stravinsky from Boston or Lexington, and I would phone her from various points in the Midwest, and then Robert and I would speak in the evening, or between his rehearsals, or after his performances. We would compare notes and have one argument or another about the dates that were still pending. Mrs. Stravinsky, who spoke frequently now of her husband's weakness and age, did not regard the Canadian concert scheduled for May 17 with favor, and neither did I—in fact, I had not yet drawn up the contract, using the lame excuse that my jumps between cities were so rapid that I could not find time to type it. Yet it was almost upon us, and, moreover, the CBC director was Franz Kramer, a man of whom we were all very fond and who should not be let down. He had usually been in charge of all the artistic arrangements for the previous dates in Toronto, and had always handled everything with particular efficiency and consideration, prompted by his own feelings of love and respect for Stravinsky. For this reason, Toronto concerts were anticipated with pleasure because they were a source of great esthetic satisfaction to the two conductors.

But when Robert returned to Hollywood from Lexington on April 12, I had still not signed the CBC contract. The suggested program was for Stravinsky the *Pulcinella Suite*, and for Robert the *Oedipus Rex*, which he wished to record. I received a series of typed letters beginning on April 14, in the first of which he emphasized that both Stravinskys seemed much better than they had been a month ago, but that he (Robert) had a sense of terrible sadness facing the reality of their ages. He reported that the composer seemed undeniably older and weaker than at the concerts in Chicago. He then went on to tell me that Stravinsky feared his inability to conduct anymore, although he was clutching at every project of a concert as if it were life itself. Robert thought that the *Pulcinella Suite* in Toronto would be very easy for him to do, would be a great tonic for him, and would restore his self-confidence, which at that point seemed to be entirely destroyed.

So I signed the contract and sent it off, despite the handwriting on the wall. I knew now that Robert would begin to look in every possible direction for someone else to secure engagements, all the more because the Hurok office had grown very wary about Stravinsky's health, only halfheartedly following through on the various suggestions I passed on. The Hollywood Bowl refused us. The Vancouver Festival was afraid of a last-minute cancellation, and so on. In addition, Mr. Hurok did not like the rumors that had reached him from the West Coast about Robert's direct dealings with independent managers, although he could hardly be blamed for trying. But no one did *that* with Hurok! And I was the composer's personal manager and *connected* with Hurok. The impresario was also very specific on another point: "Why do they want to drag that poor sick Stravinsky around to perform? He should not do any more concerts! Leave him alone"—which, indeed, had been his opinion for almost a year, and my own for a longer period. Still, no one could really know exactly how Stravinsky himself felt about it all; and although Robert would realize at one moment that it was perhaps useless to go on, he would, in the next, refuse to believe that the clock could not be turned back. As for Mrs. Stravinsky, she was beginning to build a mental block against the future, and would usually give up very quickly, leaving the decision to Robert.

Before the Toronto engagement rolled round, Robert had asked me to investigate recording possibilities for the *Oedipus*, which was to have a stellar cast headed by mezzo-soprano Marilyn Horne as Jocasta. Relations with Columbia Records were poor and it was apparent that the contract would soon be cancelled, but even if this had not been the case, Miss Horne was a London-Decca artist and complications would have arisen. However, I called Decca to propose that they record it, and received the first blow: even though, in accordance with Robert's instructions, I indicated that they would be able to advertise the record as having been made "under Stravinsky's supervision," there was little or no interest. CBC, in the meantime, was making plans to televise the concert—a project that

filled me with dismay when I met the Stravinskys at their Toronto
hotel very late on a May evening, five days before the concert.
The composer looked ill and drawn, and he was silent in his wheel-
chair though he held my hand tightly as I walked beside it through
the long promenade to the elevators, giving it an occasional squeeze
by way of showing he was pleased to see me but too tired to talk.
Robert was in pain from a kidney infection, and as for Mrs. Stravinsky, for the first time she allowed me to relieve her of some of
her perpetual parcels and coats, and her own progress was so weary
that we stopped several times to wait for her.

The Ballet Folklórico was performing at the O'Keefe Center, so
I was able to be with Stravinsky during the *Oedipus* rehearsals and
at the Park Plaza Hotel. His wife had recovered her vitality after
a good night's sleep (she has remarkable recuperative powers) and
told me all about the new cook—finally recruited by Miranda after
a series of mishaps drawn from a film with a cosmopolitan theme:
Jamaican, French, Polish, etc. "He is Japanese, his name is Hideki
Takami, and he is very cute and amusing." The last adjective gave
me confidence in the possibility of Hideki's tenure. (I was right—
except for one or two necessary departures, Hideki was to remain
until the move to the composer's final home on Fifth Avenue.) And
Stravinsky added that "he is littler than I." Looking at him, so
shrunken and feeble, I could hardly believe this.

Still, at rehearsal, which took place in an ancient theater converted into a studio in a rather run-down neighborhood, he seemed
his old self as he followed the score, and his greeting to the singers
was hearty. He always had entertained an extremely high opinion of
Miss Horne's voice; now he was particularly pleased with her ren-
dition of Jocasta's aria (it was, indeed, wonderful!), and he gave her
a smacking kiss that was a real accolade. But afterward, when he
took my arm, he needed support on his right side as well in order to
maneuver the upgrade of the aisle. In the car, he remarked to me
that he thought the condition of his blood was bad, and his eyes
seemed to be troubling him more than ever. His description of his
symptoms made me think of the series of little strokes that had
troubled my mother before her death in 1962, and I thought he
might have suffered such a minor embolism very recently.

I did not want to attend this event in Massey Hall, and I made an
excuse to the Stravinskys about having to leave for Mexico that
evening with the director of the Ballet Folklórico, although actually

our departure was scheduled for a day later. Mrs. Stravinsky would be backstage, and in Toronto her husband always had a dozen caretakers who would have done anything for him.

But after the concert had begun, I crept in at the rear of the auditorium and stood there unseen while Stravinsky was led to the podium—the *Pulcinella* was in the initial half of the program. For the first and last time in his career, he sat down to conduct. And after a few moments, when it became so apparent that the orchestra could not follow his beat and that all was confusion, I rushed out and ran for several blocks, pushing through crowds that were gathering to catch a glimpse of a member of the British royal family. I ran a good distance before I thought to stop a taxi.

The rest of the year is part of my own mental block. The Stravinskys went to New York on the eighteenth, and I departed for Mexico to prepare a project conceived by Amalia Hernandez, director of the Ballet Folklórico, for the Olympic Games in that country. I wondered then how much longer my relationship with the family would last. My professional usefulness to the composer was at an end. And our personal relationship? Well, when we were together, there was no doubt in my mind that we had a rapport—he rarely showed me anything but the loving side of his nature even when he was angry, and he had become accustomed to my being there when needed. But if I were away, I could never be sure how strong this habit was, because now he depended entirely on people around him to make decisions on everything not connected with his music.

Stravinsky underwent a series of medical tests in New York during the remaining week-and-a-half of May, which did nothing except prove what was already known—that his brain showed not a single sign of age or deterioration, and that his body was rapidly succumbing to the advances of both. I kept in touch by telephone from Mexico after their return home. Robert's occasional letters echoed bitterness at the lack of acknowledgment by Los Angeles that its most distinguished resident would soon celebrate his eighty-fifth birthday. Lawrence Morton wanted to do a concert in the composer's honor, which was to serve at the same time as a benefit for the victims of the floods that had wrought so much destruction in Italy, but apart from this and Martin Bernheimer's remarks on the event in his column in the *Los Angeles Times,* nothing had been planned—not even the programing of any Stravinsky work in that huge outdoor theater on Highland Avenue.

Robert's letters also stabbed in my direction. He would attack by telling me of marvelous offers that were being made, ironically pointing out, for example, that the University of California at Berkeley would dedicate its new multi-million-dollar Zellerbach Auditorium in May 1968, and had invited Stravinsky to "open it for them at fifteen thousand dollars"—something of an exaggeration, by the way, since, as it turned out, the fee was to cover *four* "openings" on four non-successive evenings. When I read such sentences, even though (knowing the writer) I understood their intent to spur me on, I would force myself to believe that Stravinsky's conducting career was not over, and I would make another effort. I proceeded as ordered with the contracts for Louisville and the French National Orchestra, knowing perfectly well that they could never, in these terms, be fulfilled.

At the same time, on my return from Mexico in the latter part of June, I redoubled my efforts for Robert. Several universities in the midwest had expressed an interest in having him come for lecture-concert dates; I started a series of files which today are quite interesting: on certain instances when I was able to secure a good date in the next two or three years, Robert would say yes and would wait until the last minute; then Mrs. Stravinsky would telephone me and ask me to exercise the *force majeur* clause. "He has the grippe. . . . He has the flu. . . . He is so overworked the doctor says he will collapse. . . ." It was such a curious conflict in him. While he wanted more than anything else to stand alone, he seemed to be plagued by constant self-doubt.

July passed in a heat wave, and I felt more and more remote from the West. Robert had been in Santa Fe most of the month working on the American première of Hindemith's *Cardillac,* and we had spoken together but had not written. Mrs. Stravinsky and I talked frequently. "I am all right but my husband is not very well," she would say most of the time. "Still, he works." That was always good news, of course, yet I could usually detect the sound of loneliness in her voice, despite the list of social activities she would recount to prove that life was full. Once Stravinsky picked up the telephone (which he almost never did in those days) and gave me a brave "Haloo" and a heartening "When will we see you?" that filled me with happiness for a week. It was obvious though, even with Mrs. Stravinsky's constant emphasis on the fact that everything was "so peaceful . . . no arguments," that Robert was profoundly missed.

The "adopted son" came to New York in August to do some recordings, and I told him of a commission I had just secured from Fratelli Fabbri Editori of Milan for an article under Stravinsky's byline, which would appear as the Preface to Volume IX of their *Storia della Musica* series.* It was a brief piece—some two thousand words—and each word, in terms of the financial receipts, was pure gold. (Robert, incidentally, in order to meet his deadline, dictated the text to me in two of the most expensive long-distance calls he ever made from Hollywood.) I knew Stravinsky would want Robert to have all of this money, and the lunch we had at the Plaza that day—with a very attractive lady who had been, for a long time, instilling other than literary ideas in Robert's mind—was an extremely gay one.

But on the same evening Mrs. Stravinsky telephoned Robert with the frightening news that her husband had been rushed to the hospital with a bleeding ulcer. He dropped his work and left for Hollywood on the first plane he could get.

Then followed a nightmarish two weeks, all the more so because every time I spoke with Robert (Mrs. Stravinsky was usually napping, worn out from the visits to the hospital) he would feel impelled to give me a complete clinical report, down to the last drop of medication administered, while I—captive at the other end of the wire—held my breath until he came to the point of saying that Stravinsky was improving. He did this each time, as though he himself wished to live through the experience of every needle-puncture and transfusion, and from this first hospitalization down to the end he was thus to engrave on his memory every detail of the various crises through which Stravinsky was to pass. It is a foolish analogy, perhaps, but those calls, and the letters arriving thereafter, always brought to mind the identification in nineteenth-century literature of man with some natural force—Kathy in *Wuthering Heights* saying, "I *am* Heathcliff!" as the heavens crash and flash with thunder and lightning above her head.

Stravinsky, I knew, had once before been hospitalized for a

* This article is reprinted in *Retrospectives and Conclusions* (New York: Alfred A. Knopf, 1969), p. 102 ff., under the title *Some Perspectives of a Contemporary.*

bleeding ulcer (May 1958) and, although he had undergone heavy transfusions at that time, his recovery was rapid. Now it was not; he was depressed for days following his release from the hospital on September 4, and he had lost a great deal of weight—eighteen pounds, to be exact—which he was never totally to regain. We cancelled the concerts with the French National Orchestra, by this time expanded to two at Carnegie Hall, one at Rutgers University (where Stravinsky was to have received an honorary degree),* and one in Boston. I took the file of Robert's letters, removed a recent one in which he had asked me to pursue a concert possibility in Marrakesh, and tore it in two.

The next time I saw Stravinsky was at Mount Sinai Hospital in Los Angeles, in November—but he did not see me. He was then gravely ill.

While Stravinsky was recovering from his ulcer attack I was traveling between Indianapolis and Chicago promoting the first tour of the American National Opera Company. This organization was under the artistic direction of Sarah Caldwell of the Boston Opera, and was partially subsidized by the United States government through the new Performing Arts Division, then headed by Roger Stevens. My job was important and held some promise of engagements for Robert, and since Stravinsky appeared to be regaining strength despite his depression, I concentrated on the business at hand. Pierre Souvchinsky, Stravinsky's closest surviving friend from earlier years, was to arrive from France in late October for a ten-day visit, engineered by Robert as a morale-booster. Also, the philosopher and writer would be able to help with the organization of the archives for microfilming by Boosey & Hawkes. Before his arrival Georges Balanchine, whose ballet company was on the West Coast, had been a caller. In the interim, I was reading in newspaper clips, sent me by the Hurok office, that Stravinsky—notwithstanding his illness and the three-month rest ordered by the doctors

---

* Stravinsky actually held only one honorary degree, with which he had been "surprised" during his engagement at the Eastman Music School Stravinsky Festival. After he had been defeated in his nomination to the French Academy in the thirties, he continually refused any such offers, though there were a great many of them both in the United States and abroad. The last request came from Columbia University in 1970.

—was still planning to open the Zellerbach Auditorium at Berkeley in May and—surprise!—that he and Robert would conduct some concerts in Oakland in February. But such information was no longer surprising. It was clear that Robert did not need me, and I despaired of ever seeing Stravinsky again.

I pretended not to notice, however, and kept up my stream of telephone calls. After we finished with the medical report, which now seemed to be concentrated on pains in the composer's left hand ("gout, they say"), we would discuss business. Sarah Caldwell had come up with the idea of having Robert conduct some performances of *Lulu* and *Tosca* in Chicago and other stops on the tour. This didn't please him, since other performances of the same works were to be conducted by someone else. (Still, it *was* a repertory company, after all.) Each conductor has a different way of doing things and a new conductor means new rehearsals, he told me by way of refusing. Sarah had indicated her willingness to schedule extra rehearsals, but Robert was firm. If he couldn't do all, he would not do any. (He *was* difficult!) He had not been too happy with Sarah's last-minute choice of him as conductor during the April Boston Opera season, and had accepted because it was the *Rake*. In that instance, he was justified. Sarah's talent as a director of opera (probably one of the best in the world today) was almost matched by her talent for securing major artists at the eleventh hour, and even though her "finger-snapping" was always for something artistically worthwhile, it was hardly flattering.

Then, on the evening of November 3, an Associated Press reporter reached me in Knoxville, Tennessee, to ask if I could throw light on a report that Stravinsky had been hospitalized with a serious illness the day before in Los Angeles. I knew nothing of this; my last call to Hollywood had taken place only two days before, and the composer, despite his "gout," was reported by his wife to be enjoying Souvchinsky's visit. I was, in fact, a little worried about *her*—she had sounded extremely fatigued, and complained about the difficulty of having to be a smiling hostess all the time. "It is hard to converse all day," she said, and I knew what she meant. It was always the same with any visitor who stayed at the Stravinsky house more than a few days. It would become tiring, in some cases "boring." And she could not be blamed, for the constant intellectual hammering that went on during such visits (everyone was a potential source of information about Stravinsky's past—if he had known him pre-1948) could flatten anyone who longed for a little gay table-talk.

I tried unsuccessfully to reach Robert for two days, calling at all hours and receiving only the most cautious information from Marilyn during the day. But finally, on the third day, he responded to my entreaty for some news. Mrs. Stravinsky picked up the extension, and between the two of them I learned that Stravinsky's illness had been incorrectly diagnosed as gout. The fingers of the left hand had suddenly become black with gangrene, and the dreadful possibility of amputation still hung over their heads. How had this happened? The prescribed anti-gout medicines had had a disastrous effect, but now a team of specialists had been called in, among them a well-known Californian hematologist and a new "general man," and the counter-treatment for circulation blockage (the correct diagnosis) was having some positive effect. The details of that "wrong" medical guess were dealt with bitterly, and my own reaction was equally bitter at the time. Since then, I have learned from two doctors in New York and one in Boston that the symptoms of gout and circulatory blockage are so similar, in certain cases, that this error could have been made by any expert at any time. Perhaps the real mistake lay in the fact that consulting physicians were not called in until it became absolutely necessary, but then this is not an uncommon thing in the medical profession, even in these days of extreme specialization.

I asked if I were needed and was told no, there was nothing I could do. Stravinsky was on drugs most of the time, and it would be useless to come since I could not even see him. Robert advised me to telephone as often as possible.

One day toward Thanksgiving time, I could no longer bear being away and I impulsively caught a plane to Los Angeles. My excuse when I telephoned Mrs. Stravinsky to say I was in Hollywood was that I had business to investigate for a Hurok tour. She, Robert, and I went to Mount Sinai Hospital. I remained outside the door of Stravinsky's room, which was partly open, while they went in. I saw him lying there like a tiny, aged doll in a huge bed, and I could trace with my eyes the figuration of his skull, so thin was he. An intravenous apparatus was performing its function on his right arm, and I also noticed the rubber tubing of what was probably a catheter. The heavy sedation usually was wearing off at this hour, I had been told, and I could see through the door the sleepy, loving smile he gave his wife. Robert bent over and talked to him, telling him how everyone was waiting for his return home, and repeating my name and the fact that I was waiting too.

After a bit Stravinsky closed his eyes, and they left the room. The three of us had dinner together that evening, and I caught a plane back to New York at midnight.

CHAPTER SEVENTEEN

STRAVINSKY left the hospital on November 28, but he would never really be well again, and from then on doctors and nurses would gradually encroach on his life more and more. He was now to undergo a slow and devastating process of physical decay, all the more terrible because of his complete awareness. As a result of the thromboses, he had lost some peripheral vision in both eyes, and his hearing was affected to the point where not much later he would have to use a hearing aid in his left ear. None of these things are uncommon in old age, even without the incidence of strokes. But they were happening to an uncommon man with an uncommon brain; the depth of his mental suffering for most of the next two years, as he watched himself degenerate, cannot possibly be understood—let alone described—by anyone, except in the prosaic, detached terms of medical reports on the external manifestations of disease.

I was with Stravinsky a great deal in 1968. From mid-February until mid-April I lived in my little apartment in Los Angeles while working on the West Coast tour of the American National Opera Company, and I spent every free moment during the day with him, and most evenings when I did not have to cover performances. In late May, I went to Spain, and on my return at the end of June Mrs. Stravinsky called to ask if I would come to stay with them. Marilyn was planning to take a vacation for part of that time, and—wonderful words—"We need you." During July, August, and half of September I lived at 1218 North Wetherly and was very close to Stravinsky, and, in the hours that he worked or rested and Marilyn wasn't around, I typed Robert's manuscripts for *Retrospectives and Conclusions*, the sixth and final "collaborative" volume—although at that point it could hardly be thus described. This book was to be published in the fall of 1969; apart from Robert's diary excerpts covering certain periods between 1948 and 1968, it was composed chiefly of reprints of articles that had appeared or were shortly to appear in a number of newspapers and periodicals, including the *New York Review of Books* and *Harper's* magazine.

But before my February arrival, I had seen Robert in New York in December when he had come to do a concert at Ithaca College— one of those contracts I had drawn up for both conductors but knew at the time of signing only one would be able to fulfill. He reported then that earlier treatments of radioactive phosphorus seemed to be helping the composer, but that his sight was so bad he could not read at all, and probably would be thus restricted for six weeks. It was, therefore, difficult for him to work, and his greatest pleasure now, according to Robert, came from the evening record-playing hours in the library. We talked about the future, passing lightly over the concerts scheduled in Oakland and Berkeley for February and May. Robert felt that Stravinsky would be able to be "in attendance" at least, and I could still detect in his voice a trembling conviction that he might be able to conduct as well.

The composer *was* in attendance at Oakland for Robert's concerts, and the first time I saw him was at dinner at his home on the sixteenth, the day after his return. For me, who had last glimpsed him lying in that encumbered hospital bed at Mount Sinai, it was a pleasant surprise. He had regained some of his lost weight and this seemed to have had an effect on his stance, for his walk was much improved and he held his head high, eyes straight ahead, in the old way I loved.

At the card table he told me that he had become "the plaything of nurses." One was the day nurse, Mrs. K., "who is almost six feet" (she was actually five-nine), and then there was another, who was both nurse and therapist, "and requires herself therapy on her vocal chords, which are constantly in action." "Miss Therapist" administered exercises to bring some life back into his poor, belabored left hand and to strengthen his legs. He also informed me that he was sure he had had "*several* thromboses, or else why am I always so sleepy?" In fact, I did notice after a few days that he slept a great deal longer and more often than before, although I thought much of this could have been due to the many variegated medications he was taking: drugs to keep the red blood cells from multiplying, pills for his appetite, capsules to relax him, others to keep him awake, vitamins, diuretics, counter-allergents, and, from time to time, antibiotics. One day at lunch there were six different specimens of the pharmacist's art resting on a napkin beside his plate. What was amazing to me, knowing of his tendency from youth to use medicines as a normal part of his diet, and having had experience on tours with his special carrying case for the dozen or so neatly labeled bottles, was that he had not already acquired an immunity to drugs of *any* nature. The ones that had the worst effect on him were the antibiotics, which he had to take rather often because of those inexplicable sudden rises in temperature, chronic for years. Sometimes these would be accompanied by chills, sometimes not. But when antibiotics were prescribed, the days were hard, for his Scotch was taken away, and being deprived of anything he wanted—let alone this symbol of conviviality, this representation of the hours when he could relax and forget his "miserable ailings"— would put him in a black mood. I would color his soda water or ginger ale with a drop or two, and then wait to hear him say with contempt, "What is this *merde* you are giving me?"

However, pill-absorption in that household was not his sole province. Everyone was on tranquilizers—in 1968 it was Librium— but the outsize amount consumed was positive proof of this drug's harmlessness, at least in Robert's case. Right after Oakland he had dashed off to New York for a week to finish his Gesualdo recordings and edit tapes, and, as he said, to make a final decision about the proposed cancellation of the Columbia contract, about which we had been talking for weeks. (We all suspected the presence of a glamorous lady.)

During his absence we went to see *The Graduate*, which Stravinsky couldn't comprehend at all (and no wonder!—the generation gap was, by this time, a canyon to him), but Mrs. Stravinsky giggled throughout the two hours, and I knew this was a film that would be seen again (once more, in fact, when Robert returned, as against twice more for *Khartoum*.) We went to quite a few movies during February and March. Two that stand out in my memory are *Bonnie and Clyde*, which Stravinsky found "horrendously noisy," and *Guess Who's Coming to Dinner?* The latter film was particularly enjoyed because Stravinsky liked Katherine Hepburn and his wife was fond of Spencer Tracy, but neither could understand the fuss over the central problem. These entertainments were usually followed by trips to the Sunset-and-La Brea branch of Pancake House, which were usually followed by diarrhetic attacks because of the composer's fondness for blueberry pancakes.

Robert flew back, and away again on March 8, this time to Boston for rehearsals of the *Rake*. Sarah Caldwell had decided to take her new "mod" production on the West Coast tour, and I had contracted Robert to conduct all performances of it: one in Phoenix, two at the Los Angeles Music Center, and two in San Diego.

Stravinsky did not yet have a regular night nurse (though one was on call in case of emergencies), and when Mrs. Stravinsky could be persuaded to go off and enjoy herself at dinner with some friends, I would come early and spend the evening with him. During one of these periods he talked a great deal about his "files" and said that he had to "work in them," as they were "perhaps mixed together since the photographers." He was referring to the microfilming (though he never used that term) of all his archives, which had been begun by Boosey & Hawkes during his November stay in the hospital. "They thought I was not going to come back so soon," he said to me, pursing his lips in his "wonder" expression, but there was a sly glint in his eye.

The files and their handling seemed to be a matter of great concern to him, but the impression I received was that it was far less over the form of publication of their content than the possible disarray they might have suffered at the several hands through which they had passed. I was reminded of Francis Steegmuller's visit in 1966 in search of permission to see the Stravinsky-Cocteau correspondence for his book; Stravinsky had promptly gone to his files, located the orange folder that held the letters in question, and handed it over to the author without any time limitation or restriction on when it should be returned. The action demonstrated his complete willingness to make any of his material available to the proper people, in order to guarantee the correct dissemination of information about himself and his activities.

As is now well known, Stravinsky had given Boosey & Hawkes all publication rights not only to his musical manuscripts (most of which rights they already held), but to his archives, which included all photographs, correspondence, programs, clippings, contracts—in fact, everything that had been preserved since his departure from Russia, where much valuable correspondence and other material still remains. These rights had been given with no remuneration to the composer whatsoever (a circumstance that would later be troublesome to his heirs). I have always wondered what fantastic spell was woven to secure this pot of gold, although I am fairly certain Stravinsky's ready acquiescence was partly due to the composer's complete faith in the late Dr. Ernst Roth, director of the London office for many years, and a man whom he regarded as his dear friend. It also seems to me an indication that he placed not a financial but rather a historic value on the archives. In any case, the original letter granting the rights appears (from the correspondence) to have been signed during the period of Souvchinsky's visit, when the composer was recuperating. At the same time it was agreed that Souvchinsky was to receive an annual stipend as an editorial consultant on the archive project, to be paid by Boosey & Hawkes out of the composer's royalties. No mention of Robert (who would naturally be expected to do a great portion of the work—at least, on the American years) was made in this original letter, nor was there any clause in it containing the right of approval or veto by the composer or his heirs on any of the material that would be published.

Stravinsky took it for granted, as we talked of the archives, that I knew all about the photography, whereas Robert had not informed me about it at all. But I had learned of it from Mrs. Stravinsky, who innocently told me one day that she had removed a large batch of her early personal letters to her husband before they were noticed and documented. However, since I knew very little and did not wish to put Stravinsky in an embarrassing position, I quickly changed the subject and we retired to Mrs. Stravinsky's room to watch a revival of *King Solomon's Mines* (lots of animals!) on television.

It seemed obvious that for some reason or other the project was to be shrouded in secrecy, at least for the present, although I knew quite well how carefully and for how long a time Robert had been collecting material for what would be the most important musical archives of the twentieth century. I also knew that Marilyn had instructions from Robert to make a daily search through every wastebasket. I don't know how fruitful these siftings were, knowing how expert the composer was at pulverizing any scrap he did not wish other eyes to see, but they may have yielded something. Perhaps when the archives are ultimately published or made available to scholars, some new light may be shed on Stravinsky's creative processes by way of deduction from what he threw away—but I seriously doubt it. *This man never wasted anything.*

Robert did not talk with me about the archives until much later—in fact, not until he became an editorial consultant in 1969 by virtue of his appointment at that time as the composer's "business manager." He then began to receive a fixed salary higher than any he had earned before on a regular basis. Boosey & Hawkes rewrote the agreement acknowledging Robert's position, and inserted a new clause giving Mrs. Stravinsky the right to approve or veto any material to be published.

I fell madly in love with the new cook, Hideki, the moment I saw him, which was at that first dinner after the Stravinskys' return from the Oakland concerts. Save for his costume—very "groovy," consisting of tight trousers and a pinstriped sport-shirt, tucked into a waistband that could not have exceeded twenty inches in girth—he might have stepped from a kakemono scroll. His features, hands, feet, everything about him, seemed drawn with lightning strokes by a very fine Japanese brush dipped in pale ivory and black inks. He moved with the same speed—flashing soundlessly from his room in the guest house to the kitchen and back, and up and down Robert's staircase, like some shy, woodland creature. But I loved him especially for the delicacy and courtesy with which he handled Stravinsky, helping him on with his coat or his sweater, or handing him his cane, almost without touching him, and as though if he had touched him it might have caused pain. At lunch or dinner he would stand at the composer's side until the first spoonful of soup or whatever was tasted, and retire only when he was sure there was no need to run for salt or pepper or some other condiment. Nothing was too hard for him, even after a long day; I used to see his lamp lighted until all hours to show us that he was awake and ready to be of service.

Hideki was not the greatest cook in the world, and since vegetable dishes were relatively unpopular with the Stravinskys, he inclined a bit toward starches. Robert and he got along famously, particularly since Hideki had early discovered Robert's sweet tooth. So well did he satisfy this (along with Mrs. Stravinsky's and mine) that all of us were forced to undertake periodic diets. Stravinsky, who never suffered from an overweight problem, would not gain a single ounce, but then he had a controlled appetite for sweets: a *petit beurre* or ice cream was almost as far as he would go beyond Jello or rice pudding. Hideki's only fault was a tendency to store leftovers carefully for long, long periods of time. The little gardens that occasionally grew therefrom were as carefully tended as the fresh flowers he arranged with the instinctive and unsurpassed art of his country. Stravinsky always said of these bouquets, "How wonderful!," even in that last moment when he left the Essex House, not to return. Bless Hideki! For wherever the man he served now is, I am sure this name is in his orisons.

During these early months of my 1968 stay, the one marked change I noticed in Stravinsky was in his voice. Its deep, melodic strength was gone forever; now it was weak, sometimes falling to a whisper, although even that whisper retained a suggestion of the old *timbre*. On the other hand, his animation and vitality made it difficult to realize that he had been near death. He was working, despite the continued trouble with his eyesight, and his appetite was excellent. The walks in the garden were briefer now, but still exploratory. And he was sometimes able to use the staircase without any extra aid beyond his cane and his own hand on the balustrade.

On March 19 we flew to Phoenix, where Robert conducted the first of the five *Rakes*, and except for Stravinsky's frailty it was almost like old times. Throughout the flight, which passed over one of the most scenic air routes in the West, he disregarded his book, constantly calling my attention to the extraordinary difference of lights and shadows first on the mountains and then on the desert.

Accommodations had been made for us at the Casa Blanca Inn, a famous resort hotel in startling white stucco—domed, minareted, and resembling some fantastic Oriental palace, albeit with modern conveniences. It was priced equally fantastically—the Arizona State University at Tempe, on whose campus the performance took place, was footing the bill. This time I lived in the suite with the Stravinskys, so that I would be nearby in the night, and Robert sought shelter elsewhere. Mrs. Stravinsky had not been sleeping well at all in Hollywood—she now kept her door open at night and was always on the alert—and the strain imposed by her husband's first serious bouts with the inevitable was beginning to show its signs.

Stravinsky had heard a great deal from Robert about Sarah's "black-and-white" production of the *Rake*, in which several changes had been made since the Boston performances. The composer had always respected Sarah's talents—her first production of this opera in 1953 (in a period setting) for the Boston University Opera

Workshop still ranked high in his esteem; until he saw Ingmar
Bergman's production in 1961, hers had been the only staging that
he accepted as displaying a comprehension of his ideas. Now he
watched the opera in a "mod" decor: hippie clothes, overalls, gurus,
psychedelic lighting, "Killer Joe" Piro choreography, multimedia
staging, audience participation, and the Rake himself passing to his
Bedlam through the whole panorama of life as it was being lived
on—say—Sunset Strip, complete with Hell's Angels motorcycles,
discotheques, barkers, and a final chorus of lunatics. It was inven-
tive, it was stunning, it was musically a fine performance. And I
have absolutely no idea to this day what Stravinsky *really* thought
about it; nor, do I think, has anyone else.

He did not say a word when the rehearsal was over, but asked
me to take him out to the lobby, where he waited in a corner office
while I went to fetch Sarah. She sat huddled up and disappointed
that he had made no immediate remark to her, which he easily could
have done; she had been sitting in the row directly in front of us
as he watched. His greeting was affectionate, his words were complimentary, and he wore his "commercial" smile. I recall that he
made one or two suggestions about certain inconsistencies between
what was happening on the stage and in the pit, but these had been
due to mistaken cues rather than to lack of understanding. He
praised James Billings's performance as Sellem, the auctioneer (who
was elevated in guru posture on what looks like a pogo stick), and
the casting of a countertenor in the role of Baba, the bearded lady,
had impressed him. (He had missed entirely, although he didn't admit it then, the projection on a movie screen of Leonardo's *The
Last Supper*, in which Baba appears as one of the Apostles, and
when the performance was repeated at the Los Angeles Music
Center he asked me to be sure to point it out to him.)

At the hotel, Sarah and a group of singers joined us for a cocktail
get-together. The host, dressed for bed, was genial, smiling, very
tired, and left us after half an hour.

He was in attendance for two performances at the Los Angeles
Music Center, but did not go with us to San Diego. The ovations
were painful to him, for he had to rise from his seat in the row to
receive the applause, and he was infuriated that the audience could
see that his wife and I had to assist him to stand.

I was to leave Hollywood in mid-April and expected to see the
Stravinskys in New York the following month, before they went to

Europe. Mrs. Stravinsky had been talking with me about her desire
to leave Los Angeles forever, but I attributed a great deal of this
wish to Robert's now almost perpetual lament over the lack of any
intellectual stimulus on the West Coast, the downgrading of the
neighborhood, the air pollution, and the general boredom of life
in a city devoid of all old friends save one or two. But Mrs. Stravinsky loved her house on North Wetherly Drive. Her studio had been
redecorated; it was full of light and full of privacy and, in her eyes,
perfect. How could she ever transfer to any other area the atmosphere she had worked so hard to achieve? She was torn. As for her
husband, he had never expressed a desire to leave what he considered his permanent home, and he was certainly not thinking in such
terms now.

Still, Robert's arguments were highly logical, and I supported
him, but more for his reasons that the house and its staircase were
becoming too difficult for Mrs. Stravinsky to manage, and that, by
moving East, Stravinsky would be closer to the major centers of
medicine in New York, Boston, Baltimore, and so on (Max Edell's
exit had made this an important factor). At this time, however, it
was Europe rather than the United States that was being considered
as a permanent residence—Paris, probably, the city which Mrs.
Stravinsky yearned to revisit more than any other, and where there
were still a few old friends. Talk, usually carried on when Stravinsky was not present, began to center around a trip to Zurich in May
or June; Paul Sacher, director of the Basle Festival, had invited the
composer to come there in that latter month, and this provided a
good excuse for a European trip. Moreover, meetings in Paris with
Souvchinsky and Rufina Ampenoff about the archive project were
planned, and while in that city Mrs. Stravinsky could look about for
a house or an apartment. When I left Hollywood in late spring, this
was the decision. I cancelled the St. Louis concerts, in which Stravinsky could not have participated under any circumstances, and
from whose management no suggestion was forthcoming about
having Robert as sole conductor.

Nothing worked out as planned, because Stravinsky, following
that twelve-day trip in May to San Francisco to "attend" the concerts that opened the Zellerbach Auditorium, was thereafter practically bedridden for five weeks with what was diagnosed as lumbago.
He was forced to wear a special harness encasing his waist, back,
and shoulders and weighing a murderous eight pounds. When I

came to stay in July, in response to the plea "Come and organize us. We are to pieces!" he was still "tied up" but despite great difficulty was walking about by himself. Bach was heard occasionally in the studio; and, in fact, before the "lumbago" attack the composer had completed his arrangement for chamber orchestra of a song from Hugo Wolf's *Spanisches Liederbuch,* which we used to listen to in the Fischer-Dieskau recording, and he was now finishing another.

But the other changes that had occurred in two months were great. Whereas before I had chiefly thought of Stravinsky's physical weaknesses in terms of his various illnesses, I now was forced to see them in the light of his age. His voice was extremely soft, and his speech was much slower. He guarded his words carefully, as though he did not wish to waste an atom of his small store of strength. And he used a hearing aid, except when he listened to music or did not wish to listen to what was going on. These days, when he ascended and descended the stairs one of us walked either behind or before him; his fears of falling were sad. And something else was very noticeable: he no longer liked to be alone.

Mrs. Stravinsky had said, "Organize us!" And as on that long-ago day in 1965 before the recording sessions, I started by shooing her off to her studio, which she had barely entered since her husband's first trip to the hospital. From then on, with very few "slips," she worked at least six hours a day and began to look happy again. She was thinking about a new exhibition of her works in Europe, as well as one in New York. Robert, who had been nervous about Marilyn's forthcoming two-week holiday (it was finally reduced to a few days!), relaxed about the typing: two fingers or no, I was fast. Mrs. K. came in the morning and remained until her patient's after-lunch nap, which he now took in the conservatory, for the most part; he never failed to ask, when I bent to kiss him, "Where will you be?" or, "In which room will you work?" And Hideki watered his gardens in the kitchen.

The routine had changed. Stravinsky rose later. An hour was about as much time as he could spend comfortably in his studio in the morning, and an hour and a half in the afternoon, if the weather were not too hot. The studio was air-conditioned, but he rarely used the unit now because of his inordinate fear of chills, although only a year before one's nose and ears turned red after five minutes within. The harness irritated him terribly. He often refused, hands down, to wear it at all, furiously pushing it to the floor, and giving it so sturdy a kick with his good leg that it went flying. But he always knew he would finally have to submit, and then he would look at Mrs. K. and me so despairingly and with such a sorrowful "Why?" in his eyes that one day, when we were all sweltering by 10:00 A.M., I said impulsively, "I don't see any reason why," and removed that instrument of torture from his sight. He was none the worse for its temporary absence, either. Mrs. K. confided to me that she didn't think it helped at all, because his bones were so brittle that the weight of the garment could itself do some damage. (Much later, it was thought that the trouble had been caused by a possible tumor, but an exploratory operation would have been too dangerous.)

An essential part of Stravinsky's current life was exercise, so that the left leg would not become totally inactive. At twelve-thirty Mrs. K. would help him downstairs, and he and I would take a turn in the rectangular space between the guest house and the front door, an area always left free now by parking the cars in the outer part of the drive. Several times a week the therapist came to apply her art to his left hand, still not quite normal, and to his legs. She had the manner of an English games mistress, and should have been one. I would listen to the cheering section from the bottom of the stairs: "In position now, My-*stro!* Let's rally round, My-*stro!* . . . On your mark . . . we're off! With a one-and-a-two-and-a-three. . . . Right-oh!, My-*stro!*" And she would continue this encouragement, ending up fifteen or twenty minutes later with a hearty "Good Boy!" The deep groans and explosive grunts and sounds of abysmal annoyance that would issue from "Good Boy" she fortunately took as expressions of frustration that he hadn't won his letter but was determined to make the varsity or bust!

Oh, how Stravinsky dreaded that therapy hour, for all its physical benefits! A few minutes before four he would ring the tiny dinner bell I had found in the kitchen and, when I dashed upstairs, would ask apprehensively, "Is *that* one here yet?" And then, hopefully: "She is a little late. Maybe she isn't coming!" If I happened to be in the library and he in his studio just above, I would hear the piano sounds stop and the scrape of his chair as he pushed it back, and then I knew he was moving to his front window to see if the motor he had heard roaring up the street came from her car. I believe he would have locked himself in a closet if he had not been sure it would have been useless.

The therapist welcomed my presence in the house because I represented another ear. (I had earlier learned that, as the hour of four approached, Mrs. Stravinsky would suddenly be seized with an impulse to "make order" in the basement storeroom.) She was an authority on every branch of psychiatry, and was particularly well versed on the subject of kidney diseases and the artificial-kidney machine. What she didn't know about dialysis was not worth a fig! Usually I could escape after twenty minutes, on the grounds that Stravinsky was alone and might need me upstairs, but that ruse worked only while the Marions were away for two weeks on their summer holiday in Cambria, on the California coast. Milène's daily visits were resumed as soon as they returned, and she invariably arrived at the conclusion of the therapist's duties on the second floor.

Surcease came in the reduction of the therapist's visits to twice a week. On the other afternoons I exercised with Stravinsky on the upstairs terrace. We would circle it once in silence as he strained every muscle to lift his left foot slightly off the ground (he was a good pupil) and set it down firmly. His tremendous will to help himself, to win his own victory over his physical disability, was so stirring that I would try to loosen his clutch on my arm, so convinced was I that somehow he would. There were days when he did walk very well, and we would make as many as six turns around that small balcony before he gave in to fatigue. On these good promenades he would talk principally about the books he was reading—a Simenon or, during this period, histories and biographies of the French court, which his wife had recommended. The favored one then was Nancy Mitford's *The Sun King:* Colbert, the minister of finance, *that* was a genius! And the political intriguing of Mazarin and Richelieu was, he thought, not only superior but far more elegant than what had gone on at the Yalta conference.

There were also very poor days, when his bad leg would not obey him and he was forced to shuffle it forward instead of lifting it. Then after one circuit he would say, "I cannot." And at the end of the second one, "No, I *will* not." I never urged him on at these times but helped him back to his bed, where he would tear furiously at the front snaps that fastened the harness, pushing me away as I tried to assist; and then, finally, when I was able to release him, he would sink back on his pillow exhausted and reach for my hand to kiss it in a silent "Pardon me." Once or twice, discouraged by his lack of progress, he took his cane and threw it against the wall in protest against this symbol of his own failure. To the end of his life, even in semiconsciousness, he never gave up trying to do everything by himself.

On the second day of my visit Robert told me to get rid of the extra-heavy white Lincoln, which had really been a white elephant, and buy a new car (the black one was still Mrs. Stravinsky's favorite). "Let's try something else this time," said he, "Maybe a Rolls. A Rolls would be very comfortable for Mr. S." There was no denying that, of course, but Lincolns were also comfortable, and since these instructions did not resemble a request to "pick up a copy of *Time* magazine on the way back from the Beverly Hills Post Office," I decided to consult Mrs. Stravinsky. Rolls-Royce lost a potential customer in less than two seconds, but she did agree that there was no need to stay in a "Lincoln rut." I therefore suggested a Cadillac, pointing out that this make of car was now a rare sight in Hollywood, since everyone, including the assistant manager at the Beverly Hills Hotel, was driving a Rolls. "Bring it back with you," were Robert's parting words as I drove off in the now ignoble white Lincoln. (It *was Time* magazine!)

The handsome black Cadillac that I brought home an hour later, complete with a rather startled salesman (and all the extras, including a stereo hi-fi that would not be used), was examined by Mrs. Stravinsky as she leaned out of the library casement window in the contemplative attitude of a Carpaccio lady, and, more practically, by Robert, who sat behind the wheel for two minutes to record the fantastic dashboard in his mind's eye. Forthwith a large check was produced (the Lincoln, not being a member of the "proper" family brought less than we had thought it would), despite the protests of the salesman, whose past experience had been only with "charge-it" customers. Transactions completed, Robert drove the black jewel around the block twice and pronounced it perfect.

As for the master of the house, who had been standing with Mrs. K. at *his* window above while this was going on, he merely gave his wife his usual loving smile when she asked him if he liked it. It did not matter to him one way or the other, so long as the bill was paid immediately; transportation was a deductible item. Almost every evening we took a drive in this car, and—as with all possessions that became familiar to him—Stravinsky had his pride in this one. Before he took his front seat he would scan the body quickly for any marring, and if so much as a twig or mud spot was discovered on the hood or chrome trim, he would ask me to secure Hideki and his polishing rag immediately.

Before we left Hollywood in September, this princeling of General Motors—which had toted up only a few hundred miles—was loaded down to the ground with cartons, suitcases, crates of pictures, and other paraphernalia, and driven East at (the mechanics later told us) an average speed of a hundred miles per hour by that attractive composite of a movie star, who blew all four tires, among other things. Later Ed Allen drove it back, similarly loaded. He was much too polite to say it was ready for the junk heap, but he did gently insinuate that it was doomed.

The next car the Stravinskys owned was a snappy red Lincoln Mark III, purchased in Hollywood at the end of the year. My first ride in it occurred in May 1969, when Robert drove me home one day from New York Hospital, where Stravinsky lay near death.

But in general it turned out to be a good summer, for Stravinsky did regain some strength and Mrs. Stravinsky hopefully occupied herself with plans to make the European trip at the end of September. The doctors apparently approved, and a resort in Switzerland seemed the best idea. She kept in touch with Denise and Theodore, who undertook the task of investigating deluxe hostelries.

Robert was busy with *Retrospectives and Conclusions* and also with plans for one of Lawrence Morton's museum concerts on September 6, at the Bing Center Theater. This was to be an "Homage to Stravinsky," and would include the Los Angeles première of two preliminary versions of *Les Noces;* the final version would be played as well. Stravinsky's arrangements of the two Wolf songs, and *Symphonies of Wind Instruments* (in both original version and 1947 revision) were also programed. It was an important concert and one the composer looked forward to hearing—itself a rather unusual thing.

The fact that we hoped Stravinsky would be present at the Los Angeles concert was also part of the reason Robert had cancelled some summer seminars he was to have given at Harvard on the subject of *Les Noces*, which were to be climaxed by a similar concert; not wishing to be away from the composer for a prolonged period was the rest of the reason.

I had my own notions as to his subconscious reason, however.

Robert's reactions to campuses appeared to be regional. The Midwest, the Far West, the South were on his preferred list. But something about the atmosphere of Eastern universities—the so-called Ivy League—always seemed to make him throw up his defense barrier. Back in 1959, just after I had begun to work for Stravinsky, Robert was scheduled to deliver some lectures in a three-week Fromm Seminar at Princeton. It was an appointment that should have delighted him, not only because of its prestige but also because he was concerned with establishing his identity apart from Stravinsky. His accident at Santa Fe excused him from the first week of his commitment, but then—after his arrival at the university—he delivered only a few of the planned lectures, and these consisted largely of playing test pressings and tapes of his performances. The disappointment of the seminar participants (as reported to me) may have been the cause of his request for a release from the remaining lectures, and he arranged for Stravinsky as a substitute! (Elliott Carter kindly filled in for another one.) In the present instance (Harvard) I was instructed to call Claudio Spies at the last moment to take Robert's place, a thankless task because of the enormous amount of preparation involved, but rewarding in that Claudio had the world première performance of all four preliminary versions of *Les Noces*.

In California, Gregg Smith prepared the chorus for the "Homage to Stravinsky" museum concert, and the Stravinsky library was lively with daytime conferences. The usual guests came for lunch—Miranda, Jack, Bill Brown. One day Bill brought playwright William Inge, a tranquil man who talked quietly and humorously about his lack of ambition and the joys of sedentary life in an almost-deserted Hollywood (which made me despair of our ever again having another wonderful evening at the theater from him!). Mr. Inge loves birds, and later, when the Stravinskys left for New York and Europe, he became the adopted father of that noisy canary in the conservatory.

We went to Chasen's fairly regularly on Sunday nights, but Stravinsky was now exercising caution with his diet, and lamb chops or something equally simple were generally the order of the day. And we went to one or two dinner parties, although he tired quickly and would ask me to take him home in advance of the others. Once there, he would sink into bed and either reach for his book or doze until the sound of the car arriving with his wife and Robert awak-

ened him. He needed assistance in making ready for bed; buttons
gave him trouble, for his fingers were no longer so facile, and it
was difficult for him to bend to remove his shoes and socks. But he
also loved to be fussed over, particularly on good nights when he
felt perfectly capable of helping himself, and then he would emit
small moans and breathe hard to inspire sympathy so that I wouldn't
abandon him too soon. He would never put on this act when he
really needed help.

Movies that summer included *The Thomas Crown Affair*, which
we attended because Robert had such a passion for Faye Dunaway
that he was willing to eschew his yellow pages for an evening, and
Rosemary's Baby, which was a poor choice. The Stravinskys and I
went to see it alone, and although I knew the book and had
warned them in advance, its effect was devastating. Both of them
had nightmares. Mrs. Stravinsky was depressed for a full day, and
Stravinsky warned us to warn Mrs. K. (who was then in the
seventh month of her pregnancy) not to dare to see it! Later in
New York, when we would take a drive now and then, Mrs. Stravinsky would avert her gaze every time we passed the Dakota, on
Central Park West. And when the time came to look for a permanent residence in Manhattan and this building (which is one of the
most interesting of all apartment dwellings in the world) was suggested by Robert, she said in horror, "I won't live in a place with
all those witches!"

As Robert had told me, Stravinsky's greatest pleasure now was
the evening record-playing. He would begin to anticipate these
sessions hours ahead. When Robert raced noisily down his staircase
to join us for dinner, the composer would greet him with a look of
anxious inquiry and would then wait quietly, restraining an almost
boyish impatience, until Robert's plans for the evening were made
known. For the most part, no matter how much writing he had to
complete, Robert managed at least an hour, very often two, in the
evenings. That was generally sufficient for Stravinsky as well, and
he would retire satisfied. When Robert had an important deadline
and was working around the clock, Stravinsky's disappointment was
keen. He would snap the cards down in his game of solitaire, or
would say to me querulously, "What is he doing up there? . . .
Cannot he come for half an hour? . . . I want to hear some music.
. . . Why cannot he come? . . . " and so on. Explanations were
sometimes difficult—the use of the phrase "important work" was to

no avail; he did not consider anything more important than music, even if it were writing about music.

That summer we listened chiefly to the late Beethoven quartets (although once or twice the "Rasumovskys" took precedence), and passages, particularly from the E-flat-major and C-sharp-minor quartets, would be repeated over and over. Stravinsky's changes of expression and the occasional word he uttered were as fascinating as the wonders of the sound: the sudden rise of the eyebrows in question on a passage, the affirmative nods, the little smile, the whispered "Incredible"; "Wonderful"; and again, "Incredible!" And now and then a fleeting frown of disagreement. Handel's *Messiah* was a favorite as well, and once in a while a portion of Debussy's *Pelleas and Melisande*. (The sudden resurrection of this work came about after an evening some months before when Robert had played it and the composer had remarked, "I like it better now than the last time I heard it." Upon being asked when that was, he had replied, "When Debussy played it for me.") We did not listen to any opera, though in previous years parts of the Mozart operas had many hearings, and Verdi's *Falstaff*, particularly the closing fugue, which Stravinsky never failed to designate as a "marvel." (In the first years of our association, we had gone once to the Thirty-ninth-Street "Met" to see this opera—the only production at that august establishment I ever heard him praise.) He always preferred sonatas to concertos. "Music for small places, for private places," he would say, implying, of course, music for those who know. The *Hammerklavier Sonata* and the *Goldberg Variations* were works he would listen to at almost any time. But it was the Beethoven quartets that seemed to send Stravinsky into his private world of joy—the works of Beethoven's maturity that must have been composed in the bright, clear light of day, after experiences that had plunged him to the depths. Watching Stravinsky and listening to Beethoven during these happiest hours, I would always think of a third who might have joined them—he who produced *Lear* and *Macbeth* and *Hamlet* out of some terrible suffering, and emerged to create, in his last years, the supreme expressions of the meaning of living in *The Tempest* and *The Winter's Tale*. Looking at Stravinsky across that library table, frail, old, but concentrated in the processes of his mind, I would think how much music there must be left in him, and pray that there would be time for it to be heard.

Recordings of his own works were never played at all that summer. And if one wanted to listen to any Stravinsky, one turned on the record player *piano, piano, piano* during the day, when he was closed away in his studio.

We had another visit from the police toward the end of August, only this time Stravinsky actually enjoyed it. The lady impresario who had an inclination for promenades on railroad trains turned up out of the blue one afternoon, rang the front doorbell, and asked to see Robert. Upon being told that he was not at home (the usual answer), she replied, in Douglas MacArthur tones, that she would return. A hasty consultation by phone with Robert, who had witnessed her arrival from his window, brought forth instructions to tell her that he was making a concert tour of the Andes in areas unequipped with telephones. Thereafter all was peaceful until cocktail time, which came and went with no sign of either Robert or the peripatetic lady. Mrs. Stravinsky and I wondered, but Stravinsky did not, merely remarking that "Robert will return from South America in time for the first course." Twilight crept in, and no light shone from Robert's room. If it hadn't been for the fact that I had not ordered any plane tickets from André, I would have begun to believe that he *was* rehearsing somewhere in Bolivia.

The telephone rang. A distant, barely audible whisper: "Put Madame on. Quick!" I protested that she was busy fixing the soup (it was the cook's day off). Whispered desperation: "Tell her to come to the phone or else no one will ever see me again!" (My God!)

Mrs. Stravinsky came running, applied her ear to the receiver, listened with difficulty for a minute: "I can't *hear* you. Speak louder! Why are you whispering?"—while Stravinsky and I sat, spoons poised. Finally she hung up and turned to me excitedly: "Lillian . . . *do* something! She ["Mrs. Douglas MacArthur"] is sitting in front of Robert's door since she first came. He cannot move because he does not want her to know he is there. *Do* something . . . he will starve!" Stravinsky thought this unlikely, and resumed his soup.

I walked casually across the patio as though I were in search of the sprinkler with which to water the garden, and expressed great astonishment at discovering the visitor installed on the top step, back against the balustrade post, feet pressed firmly on Robert's door hinges. Two magazines and a newspaper on the step below sug-

gested she had armed herself against the *ennui* of a long wait. Our
conversation was not illuminating:

"Well . . . hello! I didn't know you were still here. But there's
no point in waiting. Robert won't be back for several days." (Robert, whose screen door could easily have exposed him, was lying
flat on the floor to avoid this contingency.)

"I'll wait."

"But you can't wait here all night."

"Oh, yes I can!" (She looked healthy, and I was sure she could.)
"I'll sit here until he comes out. I *know* he's in there."

"Mr. Stravinsky wishes you would leave, please."

"Oh, he does, does he!" (Well!)

"This is his property. If you don't leave at his request, you are
trespassing."

"I'm staying here until Mr. Craft comes out. I have some business
with *him*, and it's none of *your* business!"

It was an impasse, and I left, saying it would probably be necessary to call the police. When I announced my intention as the only
possible solution, Mrs. Stravinsky said "Oh, *la!*" but Stravinsky decided he would go to bed and read. He thereupon mounted the
stairs very slowly but with no assistance, and did neither of those
promised things, but took up a position at his bedroom window,
which provided an excellent view of the proceedings.

This time it was an hour and a half before a patrol car turned
up, and Mrs. Stravinsky was fearful that the body on the floor was
by now, in truth, a body on the floor. Fifteen minutes were required to convince the unwelcome camper that if she had a griev-
ance, squatting was a far less effective method of achieving justice
than courts of law, and might, in fact, be misinterpreted as va-
grancy. The policemen gallantly offered her a ride to the railroad
station so that she could immediately entrain for her home (in a
city celebrated for its bridges)—or, if she preferred, there was an
alternative.

The ride was accepted. Robert was then signaled by phone to
catch the next plane home.

Upstairs, I found Stravinsky in bed with a book, looking as
though that was where he had been for the last two hours.

"She has left?" (Innocent inquiry.)

"Yes."

"And Bob? He is well?" (Slightly less innocent inquiry.)

"Very well. He is back from his travels and having his dinner."

"Poor fellow! To have to make such a long flight in so few hours. Conductors have a complicated life."

And this time he gave me a loud, *loud* grin before he kissed me good night.

But though Stravinsky may have wished me to assume (or perhaps really thought) that this was an *affaire du coeur*, I was fairly certain it wasn't. Robert did indeed have a complicated social life—he would make three different appointments at the same time, or he would be not quite out of love with one damsel while he was falling in love with another—but his business life was even more involved. Every time he ventured alone into the field of non-artistic negotiations, trouble followed. His approach was intellectual, never practical. He would read contracts not for their content but for their prose style, and instead of studying a clause to make sure that he was to receive a fee within a reasonable period of time, he would criticize the phraseology and forget about other requirements. Returns home from solo engagements were usually occasions for an announcement that "they didn't give me my check. Do you think you could call them?" A split infinitive in a letter would drive out of his mind the question of whether his expenses were to be paid. "What'll I do? My costs were bigger than my fee." For a man who shared Stravinsky's opinion of concert managers, he was guillible; and though in almost everything else his nature was one of the least optimistic I have ever come across, he regarded every proposition made to him—no matter how fantastic—as recorded in an ethereal "letter of agreement." The only time he would ever raise a question about the good faith of management was when the written contract spelled his name with a *K*.

The trouble with the lady impresario had arisen from just such impulsive (or compulsive) desires to accept anything in order to conduct, and had resulted in a disagreeable financial argument, which was (I believe) finally resolved.

Moreover, because he wasn't a businessman, and because he was motivated by the absolute belief that Stravinsky's conducting days were not yet over, he would always promise too much. A case in point was the Zellerbach Auditorium opening, when his ears had caught the sound of an enormous figure and he had not stopped to realize what it covered. He had involved himself and Stravinsky in a contract stating that the composer would definitely conduct, and a concert which was falsely advertised right up to performance time, when patrons entering the lobby read a sign saying that Stravinsky would be "in attendance" instead. The management had known about the change long before (Robert had suggested Ansermet as an alternative),* and Robert had never doubted that it would "be worked out." The entire affair caused difficulty for both conductors—but for Robert it was mortifying since the audience had come to watch Stravinsky, not him.

When Robert was finally compelled to admit, during that summer of 1968, that Stravinsky would never again be able to lead an orchestra (though I am sure inner hope had not actually left him), he would thereafter sometimes promise that the composer would be "in attendance" at his concerts. This was *never* done to secure an engagement, but always and only because he could not conceive of his own existence without Stravinsky.

One of the greenest memories of my life with the Stravinskys was provided by a small dinner at home, on the occasion of a friend's birthday that was traditionally celebrated at 1218 North Wetherly when the family was in residence. A substitute "chef" had been summoned (to add a festive note), and she turned out to be a lady down to the tips of her toes. Clearly, times had once been a bit more prosperous, for the lace that trimmed the white apron she wore over a neat black dress was Brussels, and her white collar was fastened with an eighteenth-century French lapis and rose diamond brooch. Something else caught my attention on several visits I made to the kitchen to check on the progress of the canape tray: a bottle of Scotch, set aside as reserve, kept lowering its liquid level like an ebbing flood. Mrs. Stravinsky, too, had remarked this interesting fact, but with true Russian philosophy had indicated that as long as dinner was on time and good, why worry about a nip or two? As for Mr. Stravinsky, had he taken any notice, such a predilection would have endeared the kitchen's temporary occupant to him forever.

The birthday boy duly arrived and his present was delivered—a handsome cashmere sweater, which the proud recipient promptly donned and refused to remove for the remainder of the evening, although the California "cool" had become California "heat." Since

* As sole conductor, that is—a suggestion that was refused.

the *hors d'oeuvres* were not forthcoming at the appointed time, I went "backstage" where I found the beautifully arranged tray, but no trace of the lady. I presumed (correctly) that she had "left the room." When she re-entered it noticeably later to say that dinner was served, her approach resembled that of an unseasoned traveler promenading the decks of a ship at the mercy of a rolling sea. But by then this was noticeable only to me (I was on antibiotics, and off alcohol, because of a bad tooth) and the host, who calmly spooned up the wild rice, destined for his plate, that had found its way into my lap. However, the atmosphere had been so "carefree," due to our lady's delay, that this incident passed over the heads of the other four completely, and they never knew that two squabs had fallen to the floor. Stravinsky advised me later that since his twenty-year-old Ambassador (he had switched from Chivas long before) hadn't been involved, it was all right with him. But we made the mistake of relating the lapse to Robert, and after that he periodically checked all the bottles in the racks that formed a make-shift wine cellar at the foot of the stairs leading to the guest room— where *I* slept!

Homage to Stravinsky at the Los Angeles Museum was bright with television lights on September 6, when a very happy lady needed no extra assistance as she held her husband's arm for the brief walk to the Stravinsky seats in the front row. The composer was much better than he had been at the beginning of the summer, even though he now wore a hearing aid (removed for the playing of music, of course) and the press found him "wizened," "hunched over," "skeletal." But then its members had no way of knowing in detail the victories he had won during the preceding weeks. For us it was enough that he was there, and in the warmth of his response to the audience and his applause for the performers, he seemed to be expressing his own thankfulness (perhaps astonishment) at having survived a major crisis.

Columbia Records, which could have recorded this important event, failed to do so, and Stravinsky gave orders that his contract be formally cancelled as of September 18. (Arnold Weissberger carried out these instructions on that day.)

Two days after the concert we flew to New York. Stravinsky spent time with Dr. Lewithin during the two weeks before their departure for Europe; the doctor seemed to approve of the trip.

Denise and Theodore had recommended the Dolder Grand in Zurich, and reservations had been made for a month, after which the trio planned to go to Paris to see Souvchinsky and perhaps inquire into real estate possibilities. In New York, Stravinsky took an occasional very brief walk with me on the Sixty-first-Street side of the Hotel Pierre. Mrs. Stravinsky prepared a good many meals in the tiny kitchenette, but otherwise we ordered from room service. George Perper came to visit, and so did Lucia Davidova and Ed Allen. There was no movie-going, although Stravinsky did venture down to dinner once or twice. One day we went to La Grenouille for lunch as guests of Arnold Weissberger. Attention was focused on our table by a group of ladies seated at an adjoining one, and the composer gave me a gentle dig in the ribs as a warning. Finally, a member of that party, no longer able to contain herself, leaned toward me intent on autograph, and as I leaned toward *her* to prevent her from thrusting her sheet of paper in front of Stravinsky, she said breathlessly, "Pardon me, but aren't you Carol Channing?" Stravinsky, in a hissing whisper: "Sign it! Sign it!"

On September 24 I walked beside Stravinsky's wheel-chair as the porter pushed it down a long dirt path leading to the Swissair parking gate at Kennedy Airport, where waited an as-yet-unoccupied jet, bound for Zurich. There was a photographer there whom I will remember, for he averted his eyes and his camera as two stewards half-carried the composer up the narrow entrance staircase, and he did not reappear until Stravinsky was completely and comfortably settled and ready to smile. Mrs. Stravinsky, whose misty eyes told me she had never believed they would really be able to go, sat in the window seat this time, and Robert, across the aisle, was visibly shaken as the hour of parting drew near. I knew he was inwardly praying that he had been right in persuading the voyage.

As I bent over Stravinsky to say *au revoir*— how many times in how many years?—I wondered if these simple words would come true, and perhaps he did as well, for as he put his arms around me and kissed me twice he said, "Come with us . . . come with us. . . ."

CHAPTER EIGHTEEN

WE DID meet again in late November in Hollywood, after Stravinsky's return from Zurich and Paris. I waited at the foot of the staircase and watched him—shrunken, clothes hanging loose on his wasted body—as he slowly and carefully closed the door of his studio, turning the knob back and forth several times with the caution of the very old. Then he began his laborious journey downward. His new Danish nurse, Rita Christiansen, who had been engaged in Paris, walked beside him now, her left arm around his waist in firm support. He paused on every step for a moment, his forehead drawn into a deep frown of concentration. But when he reached the bottom he stood almost erect, triumphant, and stretched his arms out to greet me in that wonderful way he had of making one feel that he was encompassing the whole world.

At lunch I sat next to him and he held my hand in one of his while he raised his glass of red wine—"it strengthens the blood"—in a toast to all of us, a gesture he was always willing to make as long as he had the power, no matter to what extremes his illness was to bring him.

Later, when he was helped up the stairs to his room, he paused on the landing and threw kisses to me, in a parody of our little joke of other days when, at the bottom of the stairs, I would salaam his descent in the Oriental manner, touching my heart, mouth, and forehead.

And that was the last time I would ever see Stravinsky in the home he had grown to love dearly, and where I know—as certainly as I know the place of his grave—he thought he would live his life out, making music in his studio, until that moment when he would be summoned to discuss its creation with the very few others who truly understood the sound of the spheres from which it came.

I was not with Stravinsky very much in 1969. I was not needed—except when the composer came to New York in April to be in attendance at another "Homage to Stravinsky" on the twenty-seventh of that month, at the State University at Stony Brook; *Les Noces* was again to be the feature, and Robert would conduct other works as well. Originally, this concert was to have been subsidized by the composer and presented at Carnegie Hall by S. Hurok on January 10, 1969. Out of Zurich I had received $4500 for what were described as "preliminary expenses," and Columbia—in an effort to re-establish relations—was planning to record the program. But it was obvious from the beginning that the financial success (that is, the avoidance of too great losses) of the concert depended on Stravinsky's presence, and reports reaching me from Europe on his general weakness pointed toward the judiciousness of a cancellation. Mr. Hurok thought so, too—he was extremely reluctant "to present" by "using a sick man" (his words). On November 6, after talking long-distance with Robert, I cancelled the contract for the hall.

But in February Robert wrote me from Hollywood for assistance with the project at Stony Brook. And from another letter (March 11), I noted that Columbia had definitely re-entered the picture. He reported that Weissberger, on Stravinsky's and his instructions, had notified Columbia that the recording contract could be renewed only if the *Noces* preliminary versions were recorded, but then he went on to question if Columbia did in fact care whether or not the composer's contract was renewed at all. He further said that Goddard Lieberson had been there the week before, had seen Stravinsky three times, knew there would never be a possibility of Stravinsky's conducting again, and had not even mentioned the word "music," let alone "recording" (although I was certain that Mr. Lieberson had tactfully avoided bringing up those subjects). It was sad, but even sadder that, although the contract *was* reinstated on April 11, Columbia failed again to keep its promise, and the concert at which the composer made his last public appearance was not recorded (at least "officially").

Five days after Stony Brook, embolisms of the left leg struck Stravinsky down, and he underwent three operations in two days. My half-hour daily visits to New York Hospital then did no good for *him*, who lay there suffering in a world apart, but only for me, who did not want to endure the possibility that he might have slipped away in the night. I would walk from my apartment to the hospital in the morning, because Mrs. Stravinsky or Robert would usually go in the late day, when the patient was at his best. Most of the time when I came, after he had been moved from the Intensive Care Unit (Rita would come out to give me news of him during that period), he lay peacefully or dozed, and on a few joyful (for me) occasions he took my hand and brought it to his lips, and said my name. Mrs. Stravinsky was not very well; her blood pressure had elevated alarmingly, and the trips to the hospital were hard on her. Natasha Nabokov would substitute for her on those days when the doctor ordered bed, and would amuse the patient with her stock of Russian stories. And Soulima came once but did not return, although he remained in New York two days longer—he said later he could not bear to witness his father's anguish. Theodore cabled from Geneva but was told by return cable not to come, as the doctors felt it would be too traumatic an experience for his father.

For the rest, I could only contribute by keeping the many people who begged to see Stravinsky far away from that room where this man of supreme dignity had to submit continually, and consciously, to the indignities of his illness; and by maintaining with the press the perpetual fiction that the Master would soon be returning home to compose more music.

And even while I was saying this, I half believed it. Stravinsky had, after all, been occupied with orchestrations of three preludes and two fugues of Bach (from *The Well-Tempered Clavier*) in the weeks before he entered the hospital—had, in fact, been working on Bach in the Pierre living room on the afternoon Donal Henahan had participated in that "interview that never took place." At the time of my November visit to Hollywood, Stravinsky had been at work for part of the morning, and he continued to spend daily hours in his studio until the onset of a painful attack of shingles just before Christmas.

But I feared this was all wishful thinking. For although Stravinsky recuperated physically, in fact with an astonishing rapidity (and moreover, weathered, during this same period, a dangerous pulmonary congestion), to me—untutored though I am in these things —it appeared that he had begun to withdraw into regions none of us would ever be able to enter.

It had seemed so as early as the Stony Brook concert, which he should never have been permitted to attend. Apart from the fact that Dr. Lewithin thought it ill-advised because the weather was not at its best, his infirmity made it necessary for Rita and me to

push him in a wheel-chair through corridors crowded with bystanders, to the stage-side of the hall, where a few difficult steps brought
him to his seat. It was a dreadful experience for him; he kept his
face hidden with his hand. And later he did not recognize two old
friends—one of whom had sat beside him through many recording
sessions. Afterward, when I told him who they were (in answer to
his own anxious query), he said *"Quel dommage!"* and shook
his head in self-reproach.

But his inner hold on life was tenacious, and it brought him back
to the Pierre Hotel on the day he was eighty-seven. And just as
tenacious was Robert's hold on life *for* him, for from that moment
on his own compulsion to keep the curtain from falling on the final
act moved him to create a "living" man from a dying genius.

Stravinsky himself began this legend while he was still in the hospital, for his drive to continue his work was demonic. By sheer
force of will he worked, and had the doctors not acceded to his
demands that he be lifted out of bed and placed near a table, he
would somewhere have found the strength to accomplish this without aid.

But the tragedy is that the will was not enough; the great master
no longer had the power to sustain that will beyond the copying of
notes with a trembling hand. And he did not realize yet that he was
tired. One day he reported to Robert with pride the number of
measures he had been able to score; on another day he talked with
him about the need to have the works published immediately. He
spoke of the scheduled performances of the first two preludes and
fugues, which the Berlin Festival had already announced for its
October 2 program—Nicolas Nabokov, director of the festival, had
asked Robert to conduct them. And Robert forced himself to believe, right up to the morning of the dress rehearsal in Berlin, that
it *would* be possible to give these orchestrations a hearing. Yet some
months before—in a moment of truth—he had told me that the
work was confused, and that it would require a great deal of editing. And indeed, one day in the hospital, he had to assist the composer in transposing a clarinet part. Robert had hoped, of course,
that Stravinsky would recover sufficiently to be able to straighten
out the confusions. But he did not regain that kind of strength, although he did have enough to refuse the assistance of a collaborator;

and at the very last moment Nabokov and Robert decided that the works must not be performed.

The Stravinskys returned to the West Coast on July 11 with another nurse (Rita had left for her home in Copenhagen), and until September 15, when I met the last flight the composer would ever make from Los Angeles, I had to rely on the telephone or an occasional letter for news of his progress. It was costly, for Hurok business took me to London in the first part of August, but I learned that a final decision had been made to go to Europe in mid-September—Paris directly, this time, where Rufina Ampenoff had been asked to reserve rooms. I gathered that Mrs. Stravinsky and Robert had more or less decided that the house on North Wetherly Drive must eventually be abandoned. Ed Allen was there helping with the packing, and planning to drive the Mark III East with as large a load as it could carry.

According to Robert, Stravinsky seemed to be gaining back some of his strength, although immediately after his return home in July he had suffered a frightening rise in temperature and another congestion of the lungs similar to the one that had occurred in New York Hospital. The Los Angeles doctors now seemed to think that the attacks were due to a flare-up of his old tuberculosis (this diagnosis was to crop up continually in the course of the next year and a half, when he was subject—all too frequently—to recurrences). In point of fact, and according to one of the nurses who attended him during this period, the tests for tuberculosis were positive—that is, they showed the reopening of old lesions. But after he left the West Coast no such medical proof (at least that I know of) was ever offered when he suffered similar congestion.

And then, just before the door at 1218 North Wetherly Drive was bolted and arrangements made for Jack to keep an eye on the property and Marilyn to pick up the mail, Robert sent a final letter from Hollywood. It gave the hour of the plane's arrival and asked me to reserve him a room at the Plaza Hotel, where I was installing the Stravinskys (Nixon's permanent residents had finally driven them out of the Pierre). The letter ended with the saddest news he had ever written me:

Stravinsky suddenly didn't want to move.
But he had to.

At the end of the year I was needed, and from then on, except for a few unhappy months after my departure from Évian, I did not leave Stravinsky again until he was covered with a blanket of black earth in San Michele.

Stravinsky did not go to Europe. His doctors forbade it, at least for the time being. Instead, Mrs. Stravinsky and I and a half-dozen other friends began to look about for a suitable hotel apartment with service, in which the trio could live until a permanent New York residence would be found. The Wetherly Drive house had taken its toll of Mrs. Stravinsky as well as her husband; she was now suffering the effects of having had to mount and descend the staircase at least a dozen times a day. Besides, what Robert had pointed out was quite true: the isolation had become unbearable.

Not too many hotels provide three bedrooms and three baths as well as a large salon facing Central Park, but at last Arnold Weissberger came up with a solution that seemed within reason, at the Essex House. It did not fulfill all the requirements—its rooms did not front the park, and the one assigned to Stravinsky was very small—but there were advantages. The composer's bedroom was so located that it could be closed off easily from the eyes of a visitor or a servant. Its door was directly opposite the one leading to his wife's room, which was large enough to accommodate her work tables, painting equipment, and dozens of boxes of mementos and photographs—in fact, everything she had refused to leave behind in Hollywood, as though knowing they would never return. Between the two bedrooms was a reception area used for dining. Robert's room lay to the right of the small, square entrance foyer that led to the dining space, thus affording him some privacy. The salon, as well as Robert's quarters, looked out on West Fifty-eighth Street, which in the spring of 1970 was to undergo a complete and noisy rejuvenation of its pavements. There was also a tiny kitchenette where, until the arrival of Hideki, some weeks after the Stravinskys had taken up residence, Mrs. Stravinsky prepared "little meals."

The family moved into the Essex House on October 14, a week or so after Robert returned from the Berlin Festival. Mrs. Stravinsky had signed a lease for two years. She did this because she felt at least that much time would be needed to find a comfortable house or apartment in New York where she, her husband, and Robert could establish new roots and begin life once more.

I telephoned the Baldwin Piano Company and asked that they send a muted upright to Stravinsky until we could bring his own from Hollywood.

The first three services I performed for Stravinsky in this final year and a half of his life were acts of conclusion. I witnessed his last will and testament, went to Los Angeles to receive his manuscripts transferred by a relative he never saw again, and closed his house on North Wetherly Drive forever.

Stravinsky had executed several wills before this decisive evening on December 9, 1969, and it was somewhat ironic that I should have been witness to the first and last that were ever drawn. And there was irony, too, in the contrasting circumstances of each occasion. Back in 1966, during my stay at the composer's home, the Montaperts had come one sunny afternoon with a lengthy document. Stravinsky was in good health then, and his attitude did not admit the implication of this ceremony. He knew he was going to die like everyone else, but that would not be for many, many years. Still, since the subject was one that had never figured in any conversation, to accomplish the project even at that time required a little doing! The principal argument for the wisdom of a will was that while the composer certainly had a long lifetime ahead of him, accidents could occur. He traveled so much; planes were uncertain; and in the event of an unforeseen disaster, his affairs would be in a mess and his children might suffer. Moreover, the likelihood that his wife would be traveling with him indicated that the will should be a mutual one. He agreed. The document was read to both Stravinskys behind the closed doors of the library, and I was summoned at the appropriate time to sign my name above those of the Montaperts, who were the other two witnesses. Thereafter Stravinsky emerged, relieved that the business of the day was over, and he and I toasted each other in Scotch and vodka (respectively), while I thanked him for the honor of being his witness, and he thanked me for writing my name so clearly!

The contents of this will, as well as those that were to follow (including the final one), were never known to me; and though in the ensuing years Mrs. Stravinsky asked me on several occasions to read them, I always refused. However, she did talk to me about the first one (it had been a new experience for her as well), and volunteered the information that Stravinsky had rewarded Robert by leaving him the full rights to all the literary collaborations. She also indicated that she felt his children would be satisfied with their legacies.

There were two more wills that I did not witness—one drawn the following year, when I was not in Hollywood, and another in November 1969 at the Essex House, when I was traveling in Montreal for Hurok. After Stravinsky's death, when I became involved in handling some of the estate affairs, it was made known to me that in every will from 1967 on, Robert had a status comparable to that of each of Stravinsky's children, their spouses, and their issue. Arnold Weissberger, who became Stravinsky's sole attorney on October 14, 1969 (receiving from the composer on that date the power of attorney hitherto held by William Montapert), told me that he had never seen the will of 1966, which was not included in Stravinsky's papers when they were sent from Los Angeles to New York. Mrs. Stravinsky—who cannot concentrate on legal documents of any nature—has no exact recollection of its details, but she is fairly certain Robert's status was the same in that one as well.

The night Stravinsky signed the will that was to stand, I had come to the Essex House to have dinner with his wife, who wanted to unburden herself about the problem that had arisen over Stravinsky's original manuscripts, still in California. An action had been brought in Stravinsky's name for their recovery from the custodians, Montapert and André, who had refused to release them on request (for reasons about which I was to learn more after that evening). In fact, the suit had received some newspaper publicity in certain areas on November 19 and 20 (the *New York Daily News* and the *Post* printed brief stories). No references were made to this unpleasantness, however, while Stravinsky was in the room. Arnold brought the will, which (I was later told) differed from the one of a month earlier only in certain references to taxes and the omission of André's name (although this could in no way affect him—he was Milènc's husband and what was hers was his, even if he remained anonymous). Stravinsky was wheeled into the living room by his afternoon nurse, Miriam Pollack, who had attended him at the New York Hospital and at the Plaza Hotel. He did not read the will, although I was informed that Arnold had previously discussed the changes in it with him. He was cheerful and—for the record—"of sound mind." (*Absolutely* of sound mind, for when we greeted each other he whispered, "My dear, I would like a

Scotch.") During the formalities, he was serious and silent as he bent low over the document, initialing pages and affixing his signature in the places indicated by Arnold. And though his hand now trembled slightly, he completed the task with a flourish and returned the pen to his lawyer with a cavalier-like snap on the latter's palm. Arnold then said to me, employing the foreboding sentence used by good attorneys at such events: "Lillian, this is the last will and testament of Igor Stravinsky. Are you willing to sign your name as witness to his true signature on this document?" (How exact he was! The Montaperts had only said, "Please witness Mr. Stravinsky's will.") A repetition of the same for Miriam Pollack and for the visiting Ed Allen, and all was over. I brought Stravinsky his Scotch.

He retired to his room a few minutes later, to rest before room service delivered its usual expensive dinner. Nor did he have very much to say during the meal, but listened carefully to our conversation—which was only casual table talk—and missed most of it, because after the ceremony of the will he refused to wear the hearing aid he hated. We had a brief look at television, and he was off to bed.

Except for one more document he executed for his wife, the signing of the will was the last piece of business in which Stravinsky evinced any interest at all. In the months following, although everything of importance concerning his affairs was always carefully explained to him, he could no longer spare the time to become involved. The only things he did care about were the moments when he was well enough to sit at his piano, and the moments in which he knew there was someone nearby who loved him. His need for both was very great.

On December 28 I went to Los Angeles to bring Stravinsky's manuscripts back to him. What transpired before and after this trip was the cause of much unhappiness and widened the rift between Mrs. Stravinsky and her husband's children, which at the time of this writing, shows no signs of being repaired.

When the decision was made in September that, regardless of where the Stravinskys would finally settle, they would not return to the West Coast, it seemed practical to centralize all the composer's affairs in New York. This involved not only matters relating to his financial life (taxes, income, change of residence, etc.), but also his life as a creator of music. Therefore, on September 25 Arnold Weissberger drafted a letter to André Marion (in the latter's capacity as Stravinsky's accountant and business manager) for Stravinsky's signature, making known these wishes, and requesting that all pertinent material, including the manuscripts, be shipped to New York. There was no immediate reply to this letter, for what were probably quite logical reasons—at least in the beginning. Montapert still held the power of attorney; he was then occupied with many of Stravinsky's financial affairs abroad; matters in Hollywood required settlement; and some further explanation of the action might have been anticipated on the West Coast.

But nothing much happened in October, either. And when, no longer Stravinsky's attorney, Montapert visited Mrs. Stravinsky at the Essex House on the twentieth (during which meeting Robert and Arnold were both present), his answers to questions about the delay seemed to indicate a fear on the part of the Marions that this transfer of all business meant that the deed of gift bestowing the Arizona orange groves on the children, drawn a year or so before, would be revoked. Mrs. Stravinsky protested, of course. Such an idea had never entered anyone's head. And at the same time she mentioned the oddity of not having had an acknowledgement of this gift from either Soulima or Theodore.

It was arranged, through a series of letters and telephone calls following this meeting, that the manuscripts and tax records would be given on October 31 to Ed Allen, who would bring them by car to New York. Ed was now quite accustomed to this coast-to-coast motor-commuting and could easily have qualified as an estimator of truckload-weights-and-measures. A Los Angeles attorney, David Licht, who had been appointed to settle Stravinsky's California taxes, was to supervise all formal aspects of the transfer—such things as insurance, for example (although what good this would have done if the manuscripts had been lost or destroyed I do not know).

November, however, brought surprises. The Marions had themselves appointed an attorney, who on their behalf requested Stravinsky's signature on a release that included the usual legal hodgepodge about protecting the custodians from any tax or other governmental claims or lawsuits. I doubt if any trouble would have arisen at all if the papers had limited themselves to this type of request—very few releases are devoid of them where valuable property is concerned, according to lawyers whom I have questioned on this point. But the writer of this one was carried away—or else his client felt it necessary to protect himself against any and all contingencies, having had innumerable experiences with his father-in-law's tendency to argue about the minutest accounting details in his dealings with other people. Whatever it was, the release was worded in such an unfortunate way that it made André sound as though he expected to be accused.

But the bigger surprise was the discovery from the Marions' lawyer that the orange-grove deed of gift had made no specific mention of an equal division between the three children, but had transferred the total property directly to the Marions. Mrs. Stravinsky was taken aback, since this had never been Stravinsky's or her intention, but she did admit that neither her husband nor she had perused the paper carefully to see if their desire had been clearly understood before they signed it. (This did not astonish me. I had witnessed in later years the nonchalance with which several legal papers were executed by both Stravinskys. But I *was* somewhat surprised that it had escaped Robert's attention. After his unfortunate experiences with the San Francisco concerts, he had begun to scan carefully any legal documents relating to Stravinsky's business, although he still neglected those concerned with his own.)

This revelation provided the straw. On November 7, on instructions from the Essex House, Arnold advised André's counsel that the gift of the orange groves was to be divided immediately and the manuscripts turned over, or Stravinsky would not sign the release. As soon as he had taken this action, Arnold reported at once to Robert in a telephone conversation, and it was then decided to bring suit for recovery of the manuscripts. In order to accomplish this, Stravinsky's affidavit was required so that the California courts could order the custodians to turn over Stravinsky's property.

I was not present when the purpose of the affidavit was explained to the composer (although I heard about it later from Mrs. Stravinsky and Miriam Pollack), but knowing his detestation of *any* public airing of his private affairs, my own conclusion would be that he may not fully have understood what possible consequences might result from taking such a step. If it had been a matter of custodianship only, he could not have cared less about anyone's feelings: two men were holding something that belonged to *him*. But in this instance one of the men was Milène's *husband*. I think he might have *threatened* to sue, to scare everyone to action, but that is as far as he would have gone.

Arnold undoubtedly felt the same way, for he sent the signed affidavit to the California counsel, Mr. Licht, with instructions to telephone him on receipt, before presenting it to the courts. Licht, however, not being as close to the situation as the rest of us, was worried that the manuscripts might be moved by the custodians to some place where they would not be found for a long time; he consequently disregarded the instructions and asked for the restraining order immediately. The affair was thus tragically made public, and it terminated Stravinsky's relations with his daughter and son-in-law.

The manuscript dispute had another aspect. The works composed before 1940, the year in which Stravinsky married his second wife, represented a more important part of the children's legacy than those composed after, and among these was the most valuable manuscript of all—*The Rite of Spring*. A fear undoubtedly arose, when the delivery of the manuscripts was requested, as to the ultimate disposal of this collection of originals in the event Stravinsky should suddenly die.

To avoid further trouble, however, the release André had requested was signed on December 22, the manuscripts were duly given over to David Licht, and Mrs. Stravinsky asked me to fly to Los Angeles and bring them back.

Before I undertook the trip (which was made in a single day), a dozen or more telephone calls passed between Mr. Licht, Marilyn (who was to meet my plane), Arnold, and me. (Robert was spending Christmas in Florida with his family.) Everyone suddenly decided that the strictest protective measures should be taken to guarantee my safe return with the precious cargo. Everything was suggested—from a Pinkerton man as a guard to a special permit so that I could carry a gun. (Nothing was said about my trip *to* Los Angeles, or what might happen if there were a plane crash—and no reference was made to the once-placidly-regarded project of a drive across the country with a carful of cartons.) Mr. Licht had vetoed my plan of arriving Friday evening, December 26; relaxing on Saturday; and flying back Sunday morning. He did not want to be custodian any longer than was absolutely necessary, and he confessed to perpetual sleeplessness so long as the manuscripts were in his house. Therefore, on Saturday night I went to Stravinsky's bedroom, put my arms around him, and told him that I would be back the next night with his beloved possessions. "Are you going to the bank for them?" he whispered with concern. "Do you have the key?" I assured him all was arranged and that his job would be to provide some sun for my return (snow was piled high in New York), which he solemnly promised to do.

American Airlines was the carrier and its West Coast office had been let into the secret, although requested not to discuss the honor until I was safely back in New York. Two first-class seats were reserved on the return flight, so that the six cartons could be within my view the entire time. (Since it was a non-stop flight I wondered who would have been foolhardy enough to make off with them in mid-air; a hijacker would have been too busy.)

My arrival in Los Angeles almost matched that accorded a movie star! Marilyn led a welcoming committee composed of Mr. Licht, a major official of American Airlines, a slightly less major official of American Airlines, two porters, and an airport guard.

There was no sign of any manuscripts. Apparently Marilyn (who had made all the V.I.P. arrangements with the airline) was there to identify me to Mr. Licht *et al.* before any turning over was to be done. Once satisfied, Mr. Licht departed to effect their delivery into my custody. And where had they been all this time? In his car in the public parking lot, along with approximately ten thousand other cars from which, daily, a nice business in filching is carried on!

Ed Allen, wearing a look of such sympathy and understanding that I mistook his hat for a celestial aura, waited at the Kennedy Airport gate. At the Essex House Stravinsky was already asleep, but the next day, a little bone-weary, I watched him as he sat tucked in a corner of the sofa, extra pillows supporting his back, leafing through the pages of one of his sketchbooks for *The Soldier's Tale*. And suddenly six thousand miles in fourteen hours became the shortest minute in my life.

After the first few days Stravinsky no longer paid much attention to the presence of his manuscripts. If he thought about them at all, it could only have been in connection with the arrangement originally suggested by Montapert: that eventually most of them along with the material in his archives, would be given to the Library of Congress in exchange for tax benefits over a period of many years. The business of listing and cataloguing each page of what was now in the Essex House was begun not long after by a gentleman whom Stravinsky never met—for which Heaven be thanked: in conversation he had referred to the work that caused the Paris riots as *The Firebird*.

In mid-January 1970, I went to Los Angeles again—this time to ship everything East except some items of furniture, bric-a-brac, and clothing that Mrs. Stravinsky did not wish to keep and had asked me to sell. For two weeks Marilyn and I put up with an invasion of second-hand furniture dealers and souvenir hunters as we stripped the house. I would handle these greedy individuals while she typed the yellow pages that Robert mailed daily to California. Finally, everything saleable and not transferable was gone, including Mrs. Stravinsky's magnificent philodendron (for which a movie mogul paid a hundred dollars); boxes of old clothes, veils, feathers, gloves, shoes were sent or given to those to whom Mrs. Stravinsky had assigned them; bins of unimportant papers, recipes, old Christmas cards, magazines, newspapers were burned or hauled away. Two mammoth boxes filled with hundreds of pharmaceuticals— bottles, tubes, jars of pills, pastilles, unguents, drops—were offered to and rejected by every hospital in Los Angeles, and were finally incinerated. Lawrence Morton inherited some kitchen equipment (he is a great chef), and Marilyn a vanity table. And then in four days the packers made almost ten thousand books disappear into 250 cartons, hundreds of pictures into dozens of crates, multitudes of faience and silver into barrels. It took a day and a half to load the van. The very last room to be emptied was Stravinsky's studio, and the last item to leave the house was his upright piano.

It was impossible, of course, to move everything into the Essex House. Most of the books, and all the furniture from Stravinsky's studio, were stored, under Robert's and my supervision, at the home of his parents in Kingston, New York, where the Stravinsky library alone filled almost the entire garage. The remainder of the furniture was placed in a warehouse in Manhattan. To the Essex House came some of those things that Mrs. Stravinsky loved to have around her —the screen made from the photograph of the Villa Manin, the early American ducks that had guarded the old fireplace, pieces of treasured china and silver, her husband's favorite teacup and saucer, her own paintings, the Léger and a score of other pictures, her *gros point* rugs, the crystal obelisk Robert had once bought for her birthday, her "pet" small tables, the closet-chests in which she kept those thousands of little objects and letters and notebooks and scraps of memorabilia that reminded her of her youth. The movers brought Robert his huge black leather armchair—the one he would sink into, usually, when he was ready to correct the final draft of a manuscript.

For Stravinsky—whose bedroom was soon to take on the total aspect of a hospital room—there was not very much we could do except hang the pictures that had been on his wall and place the lambskin rug he loved on the floor. I had promised to bring him his own piano and the book cabinets from his studio, but to move them into that small space was not very practical, and they were stored away with the other furniture "until," Mrs. Stravinsky said, "we will find a place to *live*."

One of the terrible things about prolonged illness is that after a while it becomes routine—but for those who surround the sufferer rather than for him who suffers. In order to survive the continuing threat that the end may come at any moment, one's natural instinct is to carry on daily as though that possibility does not exist.

And that was the way it was during the first few months of 1970. Mrs. Stravinsky marketed, saw friends, "made order," discussed plans for the future, arranged her room like an *atelier*. Robert worked on letters to the *New York Times'* and other critics; on book reviews; on the series of articles on "The Performing Arts" for *Harper's* magazine in which Stravinsky, as contributing columnist, was critic, philosopher, essayist, commentator on life. I exchanged the Mark III for another full-size Lincoln—dark coffee color this time—and otherwise performed the duties of a glorified house-keeper-typist-budgeter-buffer. There were endless telephone calls, endless bills, endless discussions with the bookkeeper at Arnold's office, endless correspondence, and endless arguments about the difficulty of living in the noise of New York and the necessity to save money by dining at Pavillon (where the food was expensive and good) instead of the Essex House (where the food was expensive). Another concert was planned—for Alice Tully Hall in February— and cancelled.

Talks were also begun about securing an evaluation of the manu-scripts in an event an offer was made for them, and visitors included representatives of Parke-Bernet, Sotheby's, and others supposedly expert at such things. In the meantime, twenty-eight cartons containing the archives arrived in March from another storage house in California and were stowed away in Robert's bedroom closet, until—a few months later—Mrs. Stravinsky granted Francis Steegmuller permission to examine them for his proposed book on the composer.

Stravinsky himself gave the least trouble of all. And when there *was* trouble, the nurses called Dr. Lax (who had succeeded Dr. Lewithin when the latter fell ill). Those days the principal anguish for the patient was his leg. He could hardly walk, and the chief task of Helen Tzvao, the nurse who relieved Rita (Robert had summoned her back from Copenhagen in November), was to make him take this exercise. (He had had another circulation blockage in that limb in January, detected by his night nurse, Ruby Edwards, who noticed and reported immediately an unusual coolness in his leg; three days later anti-coagulants were successfully administered.) He practiced at these times with a walker, bravely and resignedly following orders.

Ruby was a black woman who reminded me of those hospital nurses assigned to cuddle foundlings in their arms, lavishing love that would normally be given by the natural mother. Then there was a series of relief nurses who came when the "regulars" had their days off. Another (less voluble) games mistress arrived twice a week to administer leg therapy, and there were frequent visits from the laboratory technicians who kept track of the patient's blood. (Stravinsky had a favorite finger for this nuisance, and even when it had arrived at a stage where the puncture could only be extremely painful, he would insist that this be the only source for withdrawal; I was sure, then, he would never give up the combination to the vault where he had stored his private reserve.)

My days at the Essex House began before 8:30 A.M. and ended somewhere between six o'clock and midnight, depending on whether I stayed with Stravinsky in the evenings when the others went out for a change of scene. But this was my own choice; no one ever set this schedule for me, although for the next eighteen months Robert's articles for *Harper's* magazine and the *New York Review of Books*—each word of which drew another breath for Stravinsky—established a continuing series of deadlines.

Rita would usually be serving Stravinsky his breakfast when I arrived, and there he would be, in his pajamas, robe, and slippers, a cushion beneath his feet, eating away and enjoying every minute of it. Breakfast had always been a satisfying meal for him—the "most voluptuous meal of the day," he had once said. He would look up from his porridge just long enough to give me a kiss. Then I would vanish to the corner of the living room—which I had organized as a small office—so that he would not stop eating, for I knew his instinctive courtesy would distract his attention from the food. Even his wife, after a time, did not disturb him at his breakfast, for when *she* was there he had neither eyes for nor interest in anything else. After breakfast he would be wheeled back to his room to be bathed and dressed, doing as much by himself in those early months of 1970 as he could. On the good days he then would sit down at his piano.

But the truth of the matter is that every day he withdrew a little more. Oh, yes, he lunched with us when we stopped our work, and would have room-service dinners with his wife and Robert or with me or his nurses. In the beginning he even made one or two descents to the Essex House dining room, but they were not very happy: the dinner music bothered him. The Nabokovs came and so did Natasha and the Liebersons; Ed came from Connecticut for weekends, and from time to time one or two others. And sometimes he would agree to a drive in the new car through Central Park or up the Hudson. Other times Rita would dress him up, complete with borsalino and muffler, and the three of us would "take a walk" on Central Park South, not for "fresh" air, but to get him out of that tiny, confining room. (Occasionally, we only got as far as the elevator when he would whisper firmly, "I want to go back to bed" —he hated to be seen so helpless.)

Once in a while there were bursts of the old spirit—a flash of the sly wit—a smile for a visitor if it was someone he had known for a long time, and only if he were able to see him in the living room (never in his bedroom). He entered into the spirit of the thing, playing three-dimensional tic-tac-toe, admiring the plastic-cube games people sent as gifts, opening a book obediently, looking at pictures, and "fighting" with his nurses as was expected of him.

Still, he was slipping away all the time. And not in the sense of any mental degeneration—but because he was aware he could no longer maintain his position as the focal point of the household. Life was proceeding as usual around him, but *without* him. He was

unable to participate in the leisure hours of that life, and he realized
that he could not deprive others of their right to it.

Even so, I think he would have reconciled himself to the loneliness. He had always been—in a particular sense—a lonely man, for
there were so very, very few with whom he could really talk about
the one thing that mattered to him above all else. What made him
withdraw and permit the final act of dying to begin—although he
fought bitterly and hard against admitting to himself that it *was*
final—was the anguish that filled him as he began to believe that he
could no longer work.

On one awful day, when we had left his bedroom door open because the nurse had gone out to make a long distance call and I was
alone in the apartment, I saw him sitting at his piano, hunched over,
arms pressed against his body, his gaze fixed on a piece of white,
pencil-marked paper that he had set against the open score of Bach's
Well-Tempered Clavier. He stared and stared at the paper for fully
five minutes without moving a muscle or uttering a sound. Then he
placed on the piano ledge a pencil he had been holding, took the
paper, and carefully tore it in half; and then he placed the two
pieces together and tore them again in half, dropping the pieces on
the floor.

I did not move, and he did not notice me. The nurse came back
just then and went into his room and closed the door.

Dr. Lax came to see Stravinsky very often. Recommended by
Nicolas Nabokov and known to Balanchine, he had tended many
people in the world of the arts and had apparently been close to
Bartók at one time. Mrs. Stravinsky liked him very much, and it was
well that she did, for she needed medical care herself. One of the
principal reasons, apart from her tendency to high blood pressure,
was an inability to sleep. But understanding and reassuring as Dr.
Lax was in the face of a difficult situation (after all, he had inherited
a patient of international importance whom, he must have known at
first glance, he would be unable to save for long), he could not
supply the remedy for that. It was not ordinary insomnia, brought
on naturally by natural worry and strain over her husband's illness
—not an insomnia that could have been treated with sedatives a
little stronger than the ones she already used. It was an aggravated
wakefulness, and the aggravator was Robert, whose own agony for

Stravinsky made him appear to me to be on the verge of a nervous breakdown.

Robert was very fearful of the future. The armor which Stravinsky had forged for him during the good years was invulnerable only so long as Stravinsky was there to resupply him with any parts that might have been destroyed in the lists. He saw himself now as the central figure in a tournament, defending his dukedom to the death against a dozen or more challengers. And these challengers, in his mind, took the form chiefly of Stravinsky's children, who according to Rumor (and Mrs. Stravinsky's "friends" were masters of "Rumor") regarded him with nothing but acute hostility. He was "a usurper," and now that "father" was ill and helpless, and since the affair of the manuscripts, he had become in their eyes a "monster" who was the root of all evil perpetrated against them. Furthermore, because he had been treated like a son and defended against attack by Mrs. Stravinsky, she must realize that they considered her a "monstress," and one day both of them would wake up and find themselves in the street, because if anything happened to Stravinsky, it would be *their* fault—but principally *Robert's!* And while *he* could stand it, what was going to become of *her!*

Thus did Rumor speak. Robert, however, had a greater tendency toward exaggeration than Rumor. It had been well known for years, of course, that Stravinsky's children did not look upon him as a beloved "adopted brother." But whatever they felt, none of them, to my knowledge, had actually demonstrated by any positive action (or word, in fact) that they did not accept the now-twenty-three-year-old relationship as one of those things one accepts with resignation, if only because there was nothing they could do about it.

Like Stravinsky, Robert had long ago established certain regulations governing his daily life. He slept until ten-thirty or eleven and, except for meals, worked until Mrs. Stravinsky was ready to retire for the night. That was the time, according to *his* schedule, when all pending and potential problems engendered by Rumor were to be taken up with her. Every plan or decision or project that had been acceptable during the day was now to be reversed. Everything that was being done was being done *wrong*. Well—how could she make it right if it was wrong? This was the signal for Robert to make a hasty departure, since he was usually as much at a loss as she. And then she could not sleep.

The maddening thing was that although Robert could harass a

person to the point of distraction, his worries (apart from predictions about the lengths to which his enemies might go) were about matters of genuine concern. Mrs. Stravinsky had absolutely no notion of how much money was being spent weekly, nor where it came from, nor how long it would last. So long as there was enough to take care of her husband, everyone had a place to sleep, and no one went hungry, she did not permit herself to think about the future or what might happen to her at the moment when Stravinsky could no longer write his name on a check or a letter. "I have friends," she said. "I will not starve." And while this was true so far as some of us were concerned, it was hardly practical.

Angry as I would be at Robert when I arrived in the morning to find Mrs. Stravinsky lying on her bed, pale, her face drawn and wrinkled, her eyes red and tired, I was forced to admit that something must be done, and rapidly. While Arnold Weissberger did hold the power of attorney to receive certain royalties, which were then administered by him to take care of Stravinsky's bills, two major sources of income still required Stravinsky's endorsement. I knew Robert could not make a move to discuss this situation because of his special position in Stravinsky's household. I decided to do it myself. My motives could not be questioned. As a witness to Stravinsky's wills since 1966, I could not possibly be an heir, and as for salary, the money I drew each week covered my transportation, cigarettes, and an occasional trip to the hairdresser's. (Mr. Hurok never believed it!)

I called on Arnold Weissberger and secured a power of attorney for Mrs. Stravinsky so that in the event her husband should die suddenly, she would immediately be able to draw money on which to live. This was explained to Stravinsky, and he signed the power of attorney on February 25, 1970.

Like any person of his age, especially one suffering illness that required many different types of medication, Stravinsky experienced occasional periods of disorientation. When he woke up from a nap, for example, he would think he was in his bedroom in Hollywood, or he would ask one of the nurses to "run downstairs and call my wife in her studio." He was forgetful, too, as one is when day and night are marked by no changes of events, and would be distressed to discover that he *had* already eaten his lunch, or that he *had* already listened to records in the living room. Time telescoped itself. "How is your dear mother?" he asked me one day, as he had used to before she died. And: "Where is my wife? Where is Vera?"— although Mrs. Stravinsky had just been in to tell him that she must be away for half an hour to do a necessary errand.

Lapses such as these were completely understandable, and startling only because they were happening to this particular man. But this man's own anguish, when he would realize his error, went so deep that it soon became apparent that he should not be exposed to such embarrassments in the presence of visitors, and this had a great deal to do with the excuses we began to make to all except the very few friends of many years.

On April 6, 1970, Stravinsky was rushed to the Intensive Care Unit at Lenox Hill Hospital with apparent symptoms of heart failure and the severest congestion of the lungs he had thus far suffered. The physicians looked grave. I located Robert, who had left for Florida only the day before, and told him to come home. For several days Stravinsky "hovered" above us. Theodore and Denise flew in from Geneva, and the world—represented by the members of the press with whom I dealt for the greater part of each day— prepared to say *adieu*.

This time Stravinsky had been much closer to death than ever before. In fact, as Rita and Helen were preparing him for the ambulance journey to the hospital, there was a split-second when he left us entirely, and it was only their rapid reaction—the repeated shouting of his name, the shaking of his body, the rubbing of his hands and his heart—that brought him back.

In the hospital, after his first crisis he suffered another, even more dangerous, one—a kidney complication which, in almost any other human being, would have been too much to combat. Yet *he* was not prepared to say goodbye to anyone, and on April 29 we brought him home, using the back routes of the Essex House as we always did, so that no one would see him . . . for *his* sake. He knew he did not look his best—that astonishing man!

And because he had survived this worst of all experiences, his wife and Robert began to believe that he would never leave them. Routine was re-established, even though Stravinsky now slept in a hospital bed at the Essex House, and all the necessary equipment for

any sudden changes in his condition (which he would *naturally*
weather) filled his room.

And the days began to fly—for everyone except him.

One of the exercises devised to keep Stravinsky close to everyone else's life was the signing of correspondence and autographing
of records or photographs. It was a practice I hated (although it
may have been good for him), and I would have nothing to do with
it. Each day Robert would turn over the most important of these
requests to Rita. A sheet of paper would be placed before the
patient and he would be told to practice writing his name until he
arrived at the point of facility at which a proper specimen might
result. Sometimes he obeyed out of sheer boredom, and other times
he deliberately scrawled as illegibly as possible. There were times,
too, when he would not write at all. Helen, who spent every minute
of her swing-shift duty (four to eight in the afternoon) keeping
Stravinsky busy, made him practice by signing magazines, books,
pictures of her friends, birthday cards, Christmas cards she had had
the foresight to purchase well in advance of the holiday season, and
—most ingenious of all—letters to her relatives in Bulgaria. (I
would give *anything* to know the opinions on life Stravinsky expressed in these daily epistles to Middle Europe!)

Helen was remarkable in other ways. She created a social calendar
for her lonely patient. Every afternoon he would be taken on a
promenade through the apartment in his wheel-chair to visit me. I
would stop typing "Stravinsky's" comments on the Beethoven sonatas, new plays, new ballets, the Panthers, maxi-fashions, prizes
awarded to Beckett and other playwrights, and we would hold
hands and talk—that is, I talked and he would listen with a slight
vague smile as I recounted the latest antic of Pusspartout, or enu-
merated the list of delicacies Mrs. Stravinsky had gone to buy for
him at Colette's, or told him that Robert had planned a long record-
playing schedule for that evening (this always made his face light
up).

Another amusement was the telephone. There was still an extension in Stravinsky's room, for outgoing calls only. Helen would arrange to have him "call Lillian up," or sometimes he would call Rita
from my phone, and he would say "Halooo!" in that fading but still
resonant whisper, and then, slowly, "Come and see me sometime!"

Or else he sat on the sofa in the living room with a book in his lap while I went on typing because, most of the time, even this did not disturb the silence he had built around himself.

Or he watched television. In the evenings he dozed over it with me in the living room if the others were out to dinner. There were times, too, when I would discover him sitting in his wheel-chair watching the set in his bedroom, his nurse beside him, while the New York Rangers conducted their duels on ice with the Toronto Maple Leafs, or the Mets cavorted across the tube in their spring training.

One day at lunch it was decided that a summer in New York would be unendurable. Europe was the only solution, provided Dr. Lax felt Stravinsky was well enough to go. It appeared after a time that he would be, and the change "would be good for him." Évian, on the French side of Lake Geneva, seemed the most attractive spot. Besides, there were many hospitals, doctors, and nurses in the immediate vicinity, as well as Theodore and Denise, who would be of great help in securing them. The hotel selected was the celebrated Royale.

On June 11 a small ambulance brought the patient, his wife, Robert, and Rita to Swissair at Kennedy, where I was waiting with airlines officials. We flew to Geneva with eighteen pieces of luggage and the electric typewriter. I carried the composer's little bag, in which all the materials for composition were packed.

The only one who had not wanted to leave New York was Stravinsky.

In Évian, from the balcony of his suite, Stravinsky could see the mountains beyond which lay Italy, and off in another direction was the road to Clarens, where he had worked so hard so long ago on *The Rite of Spring*.

But most of the time he did not know where he was, and when he knew, he did not seem to care.

CHAPTER NINETEEN

STRAVINSKY'S suite at the Hotel Royale—an "international" palace-resort suggestive of a lighthearted "Haus Berghof"—faced Lake Geneva, and when mists were absent Lausanne and its back-rest of mountains appeared clearly on the opposite shore. All our rooms had balconies jutting out over the walk that led on the right to the dining terrace, and on the left to the swimming pool and tennis courts. Directly ahead, handsome lawns with formally arranged flower beds and clusters of poplars and oaks sloped down to a stone wall bordering the road that led to the town below.

For the first few days Stravinsky did not enjoy the view, for he was confined to bed with an alarming weakness. The doctor whom Theodore and Denise had secured in Geneva diagnosed severe anemia; transfusions were to be the recurrent treatment from this point on, whereas hitherto they had been part of the hospital procedures only. The patient's polycythemia—which might have made such a prescription dangerous—seemed, curiously, to have vanished permanently. No trace of it had been detected during the weeks following his discharge from Lenox Hill, and this had radically diminished (at least in clinical eyes) the possibility of embolism.

Stravinsky was in a state of extreme agitation, in pointed contrast to the calm he had shown during the flight. (He had not been moved from his seat throughout; Rita and I had helped him whenever he required assistance of a physical nature, concealing him under a tent of blankets.) His face was flushed and blotchy; he thrashed about nervously and reached desperately for the hands of whoever happened to be at his bedside.

Theodore, who came daily with his wife, was shocked. During his April visit to New York his father's occasional wandering had not disturbed him so much (although he had raised questions about it). As most of us preferred to do, he accepted the lapses as an aftermath of the protracted hospital stay and the continued administration of calming medications during the recuperation period. Now, however, he was unable to face with equanimity the change in his father. In his anxiety to prove to himself it was not true, he tried repeatedly to engage the patient in conversations about his works, about music, about the surrounding country, where the composer had experienced one of his greatest periods of creative activity.

Stravinsky remained indifferent—even after he had adjusted to the change of locale and was beginning to feel more relaxed; even during those periods when he was extremely alert (and they did occur), although Évian itself meant nothing to him, for he had never been in that exact spot before. Indeed, attempts to engage him in small talk irritated him altogether. He rarely spoke now at all except in very laconic whispers, and his responses and reactions were interpreted by us through his facial expressions—always more articulate than any words. A stubborn protrusion of the jaw and drawing-down of the mouth meant "No, I will *not* be sociable!"—and his son grew to understand it. Raised brows and closed eyes indicated "I am so bored . . . so bored," and that was sometimes worse. Most of all he wore that wide-open look of astonishment, asking the unanswerable "Why?"—and that was the hardest to take. But the smile of love was also there, especially when he wakened from a dream and found one of us beside him.

Nurses—a whole string of them that changed constantly at first—were provided by nearby clinics, and later one came fairly regularly in the afternoons, and another at night. Rita looked after the patient until four, as she had done in New York. When toward the close of the first week he regained some strength, the breakfast hour assumed its former importance as a source of pleasure. I would come at eight o'clock to find him seated in his wheelchair at a table Rita had placed on the threshold of his balcony, French doors opened to admit the fresh, sunny air. She would crumble a roll on the balcony railing and within a moment a dozen or more winged guests (mainly sparrows) would arrive to breakfast with the gentleman who understood their chatter and listened with respect. To our delight he would consume huge amounts of food at these times—quantities of fruit juice, porridge, eggs, *brioches;* and when he was through he would seek our approval with a look that said, "You see, I *am* cooperative. . . . I do my best. . . ."

During these breakfast periods Mrs. Stravinsky rested. The strain

of the past year began to vanish from her face. Just to be in France
with her husband was enough for her, and she closed her mind to
anything else.

And Robert? Except that he now worked in a French Provincial
bed, he might just as well have remained in the Essex House, for
nothing had changed: the paraphernalia on his coverlet was the
same, though his slump was perhaps a little more pronounced because of the low wattage of European electric bulbs. An analysis of
Les Noces was occupying his attention now. A few months before,
he had concluded arrangements with the Harvard University Press
for the publication of a fascimile edition of all preliminary materials
—some seven hundred pages of sketches, a full score of the thirty-
instrument version in the Rychenberg Stiftung at Winterthur, and
several other incomplete versions. He was writing a detailed description of each folio and its verso, and for this reason he had insisted
we bring the non-portable electric typewriter. I deciphered and
typed for an average of nine hours out of every twenty-four.

The typewriter, transported over everyone's protest (the Hotel
Royale could have supplied us in an instant with the most up-to-date
IBM masterpiece) represented, to me, one symbol of Robert's
determination that no single thing in the established pattern of daily
living around Stravinsky was going to be changed in any way. The
other symbol was the brown Lincoln, also transported, but via the
S.S. *Queen Elizabeth*. The fact that limousines and chauffeurs were
even more readily available in that paradise of the wealthy (whether
ailing or indolent) than in Paris did not cut any ice with Robert.
The "American" car must come to Évian because, he said, Stravinsky was accustomed to it. (Stravinsky had had exactly four rides
in the Lincoln since its January purchase, and during these he had
either slept or expressed a desire to return home.) A more logical
reason, in my opinion, was that Mrs. Stravinsky would be able to
enjoy herself as she used to, driving in safety on the deserted
country roads (she did, later, regaining almost all of her self-confidence). Accordingly, I had arranged for the car to sail "as a
passenger," and Robert announced in New York that he would
take a few days off to retrieve it at Le Havre, where it was expected
to arrive in the early-morning hours on June 17. We all knew, however, that this was one of his momentary fancies. Once settled at his
writing, nothing involving too much movement could budge Robert.
Therefore, two days before Stravinsky's eighty-eighth birthday, I

was to go west, stopping in Paris for the insurance card (the decision to ship the car had been a sudden one). An overnight stay in Le Havre and a 375-mile drive back to Évian (which I could not make in one day on unfamiliar roads) would bring me back too late to celebrate it with him.

When I went to Stravinsky's room on the morning of my departure to say *au revoir* and explain where I was going, he indicated that I should hand him his jacket, which was hanging on the clothes horse. From the side pocket he produced two of his favorite cough pastilles and a one-dollar bill (one of those I had stuffed in his pockets just before we left the Essex House in response to his distressed "I cannot go. . . . I have no money!"), pressed them into my palm, and then drew my hand to his cheek to say good-by.

I returned late on the eighteenth after his birthday dinner, to which Denise and Theodore had come, and I learned that in my absence Kitty and Kitty's three-year-old little girl—Stravinsky's great-granddaughter—had paid a visit. He whispered to me that she had worn a red dress "like a small flower," and then he held my hands and called me "Bertha." Rita comforted me by relating that during the day he had asked: "Where is Lillian? She has not come to say 'Happy Birthday.' "

There were days that were very good at Évian. On occasion, wearing one of the pale-blue shirts we had found in the village—the color so enlivened his face now, for his eyes had begun to change, and blue was clearly visible in the gray-brown iris—Stravinsky would descend, sometimes with me, sometimes with Rita, in the small fretwork *ascenseur* into which his chair, the operator, and I fitted like tight gloves, and we would "take a walk" on the terrace, topping the excursion off with an *aperitif* at the outdoor bar near the pool. The personnel was super-discreet, greeting the composer with deep, respectful bows, taking our order, and then leaving us pleasantly alone. Stravinsky no longer swallowed his drink in largish gulps (although he easily could have), but sipped it slowly, as though to prolong those moments when he was not suffering real discomfort. He was generally very quiet, but once he pointed to the right, in the direction of the mountains, and whispered, "Over there I used to live," emphasizing the final word ever so slightly. Another time he remarked, at the sound of the ferry whistle, *"On va à Lausanne"* (he knew! he knew!).

When the Lincoln arrived, we went for a few drives in the late afternoon whenever I could be released from typing. These expeditions (on which one of the Swiss nurses usually accompanied us) were best limited, I soon discovered, to half or three-quarters of an hour, for that was about as long as Stravinsky was able to sit in the front seat without becoming restless or acutely uncomfortable. (In the hotel, in fact, he would keep the nurses jumping with a call every fifteen minutes to have his position in the bed changed; or he would want to be moved from the balcony to the bed or the salon and back again. This habit of clutching onto reality by summoning another person to his side persisted, with rapidly diminishing intervals of quiet, until his death.) Once, when Mrs. Stravinsky had expressed a wish to "drive over a small mountain," I lost the road, and the search for a descent that would bring us back to Évian took almost an hour, covering expanses of Alps that grew in my mind— along with the increasing intensity of Stravinsky's groans—to the size of those that must have confronted Hannibal. To keep my attention riveted to the treacherous hairpin turns and sudden declines —even though Mrs. Stravinsky and the nurse kept reassuring me throughout that the moaning was more for effect than anything else—was agonizing. After that, whenever I drove the composer anywhere, I made sure that we took the flat five-to-ten-mile stretch on the French side of Lake Geneva.

If Stravinsky felt well enough we lunched on the terrace; and occasionally Mrs. Stravinsky, Rita, and I would don our resort finery and dine downstairs with our two gentlemen in the manner of the other cosmopolitans who were sampling everything on the clogged menu. (Robert always and deliberately kept his back to a table occupied by a lady who changed her jewels to match the changes in the weather and never failed to eat four different desserts.) Stravinsky was tranquil and happy, at least through the entree, but then he generally became restless and Rita would take him upstairs. He did obviously prefer the coziness of the little salon in the suite, and the majority of our meals were served there by a superb waiter called Marcel and his assistant, a handsome teen-age lad from Sardinia who perpetually wore a look of extreme cynicism. During my stay, apart from Denise and Theodore and the doctor and nurses, there were no outside visitors except Arnold Weissberger, who drove over from Zurich with a vacation companion. Stravinsky was glad to see him. News came, though, that Stravinsky's niece Xenia expected to travel to Évian from Moscow, and Lucia and Natasha wrote that they might come. No word arrived, however, from Soulima and his wife, who were visiting less than two hundred miles away.

During our second week a record-player which Robert had asked Theodore to secure from Geneva was delivered, and then there was music during the "good hours," day or night. It was ruffled a bit in the evenings by the strains of the dance band floating up from the terrace, but that did not matter: Robert sat next to Stravinsky on a little sofa and they listened together, holding the same score, the younger man's finger moving along the measures—the older one's hand following jerkily, hesitating. Robert was at his happiest then, if he could ever have been called happy. Otherwise, he was a bundle of nerves, and his state of mind showed clearly in his manuscripts, which were almost impossible to decode. Furthermore, his anxiety was aggravated by the fact that he had fallen in love again, and this time I knew it was very serious. For without wishing to face the future, he found himself dwelling on it, and in his bursts of confidence to me the forlorn cry "What shall I do? What shall I do?" recurred constantly. He was fearful that he would never be able to recapture his right to a "normal" life—to a wife and children—lost irretrievably so many years before when he had answered a vocation, so to speak. He wanted that right back, or at least what would be left of it when the "voice" that had called him was gone.

Stravinsky had the first two of several blood transfusions before I left Évian. These were given at the hospital at Thonon, a spa in the direction of Geneva, about twenty minutes' drive away from the Royale. On the second trip I sensed that he was not feeling well when we started out; he grew whiter and whiter as I sped along, and by the time we reached our destination he was quite helpless. Orderlies and interns moved him rapidly upstairs with Mrs. Stravinsky, Rita, and me in their wake. After a while the doctors said he would be able to return to the hotel later in the afternoon. Mrs. Stravinsky and I left for Évian to collect some fresh clothing and articles he needed; Rita stayed with him.

We had been driving about ten minutes when suddenly Mrs. Stravinsky began to laugh. Tears were running down her cheeks, but she could not stop laughing. "And Bob wants us to take him tomorrow to that great French restaurant near Montreux," she cried, wiping her eyes with shaking hands. I pulled over to the curb and put my arms around her.

On July 1 I left Évian. Mrs. Stravinsky had asked me to stay, and I hated to leave, but the typing had become too much; besides, my job of organizing accounts, nurses, routine, weekly disbursements was completed—that part of the sojourn would run more or less automatically. In any case my departure would somewhat reduce the enormous hotel bill; I was far more aware of it than anyone—these days nobody else was inclined to concentrate on anything relating to the spending of money. I typed out a list of "don't forgets" for Mrs. Stravinsky, and we sat together in the bar for two hours while I explained it, becoming (as she put it) "a little intoxicating."

Robert had only begun to make inroads into the *Les Noces* writing project—I was sure it would go on for a long time, and he was sure he would ultimately need a collaborator for certain aspects of the text. An addendum to his diaries had occupied us as well, part of which had a publication deadline in London, and numerous letters had been answered or composed—one of them, addressed to a Los Angeles critic, expressing what might have been Stravinsky's sentiments some years before. Robert and I arranged that he would send his handwritten pages to me in New York. I was to type, and return them to Évian.

I went back to work for Hurok, at least until the summer ended and the family returned. The trail of yellow pages, along with news of various brief visits (Souvchinsky; Xenia; Lord Snowdon, photographer; Miranda; the Patersons; Natasha) followed me on my travels for the impresario to Mexico and the West Coast. And then one day a letter containing a batch of these pages was lost, probably somewhere between Europe and the United States. Robert was beside himself, and I couldn't blame him—he had labored long and hard, and the date of delivery was nigh. The material had apparently concerned a study of the French waiter Marcel, and it was a pet piece of writing. All the pent-up misery in Robert—his agony over Stravinsky, his worries about his personal life—found its mark in me. The hurt went deep this time, and I told Mr. Hurok I was willing to advance Rudolf Nureyev's forthcoming tour with the Australian Ballet. Work on this was to begin in November.

But at the end of August, when Évian had become as ghostly and boring as Los Angeles, Stravinsky came back. Frequent talks with Mrs. Stravinsky finally straightened everything out, and Robert and I had a reconciliation. Still, I could not request a release from my contract with Hurok until several weeks later, and even then I was unable to return permanently to the Stravinskys until after the first of the year. This time I was put on a salary of $300 a week, determined by Robert and Arnold Weissberger, since I was now additionally involved in a large amount of work that would later be pertinent to the estate.

The final threescore days of Stravinsky's life were lived for him by his wife, Robert, and me. He had already determined that he could no longer accept his present environment and had almost decided on another. From time to time he would let us know in various ways that he was doing this. He only rarely called anyone by name now, although he became more whisperingly garrulous with his nurses. There were moments, too, when he gazed at each of us—save for his wife—as though we were strangers. Bored tolerance characterized his attitude toward his own routine: he permitted himself to become a puppet and gave in to anyone who chose to manipulate the strings. He was busy finding others who would love him, though he still welcomed our love—almost apologetically, as if to say, "Thank you, but you will not be able to satisfy my need much longer."

During January and part of February, when he could still sit at the table with us, he concentrated his attention on his plate or on Hideki (forever beside him) or on the nurse, who told him he must eat. The arguments we had (and they were frequent, for everyone's nerves were on edge) no longer provoked his former slightly sardonic smile of dismissal. He took his afternoon promenades with Helen and did not notice that I had changed my locale—Robert had moved down the hall to another room for some privacy and quiet, and I now worked in his old bedroom. A few times he held my telephone receiver and tried to say "hello" to Rita. Almost no one saw him—Ed Allen on weekends, Natasha for some minutes each week, once Dominique (Nicolas's wife), who entered his bedroom—and perhaps one or two others whose pleas Mrs. Stravinsky could not resist.

In the night, as he lay sleeping, he would sometimes conduct a

concert for another audience, his right arm striving on the counter-
pane to make those clean, precise gestures of instruction to the
orchestra. "Take this down," he used to whisper to Ruby as he
corrected the music. But Ruby had been gone since Christmas, and
now he did his work in silence.

When Robert played records, he sat with his arm around Stravinsky's shoulders, holding him close, stroking the listless hand that
lay on the score.

We maintained the pretense. Mrs. Stravinsky "pretended" that
her husband was beside her in taxis when she went shopping for
articles for the new apartment she had found on Fifth Avenue in
November, and on which she had promptly paid a large deposit;
or when she dined out with Robert and Rita and Ed, or walked
around the corner to the CBS studios for private screenings of
movies Goddard Lieberson would arrange. Robert "pretended" he
was carrying on interviews with the composer on "new music" and
the state of the arts, on euthanasia and other timely subjects. And I
"pretended" when I phoned the editor-in-chief for whose publication these pieces were destined, requesting deadline extensions "because Stravinsky must approve the copy."

The biggest pretense was the new home . . . the home that
Stravinsky was to live in happily ever after. There I spent part of
each morning for six weeks, smothered in rubble, plaster, paint—plead-
ing with twenty or more workmen to rush their reconstruction of
the apartment with which Mrs. Stravinsky had fallen in love after a
five-minute tour because its three bedrooms provided a beautiful
view of Central Park. "He will be able to see the trees all day long,"
she told me with a joyful smile, "and we will only have to take the
wheel-chair across the street. . . . He can sit in the park. . . . It
will be wonderful. . . ." Who could scold her then for not having
noticed that there wasn't enough electricity and that special risers
would have to be brought up from the street (requiring special
permission from the city); that the air-conditioning was totally inadequate; that a new kitchen was necessary; that the plumbing had
to be entirely refurbished, with resultant broken walls and floors;
that the fireplaces had to be remarbled and made workable, and
the whole place painted, scraped, tiled, and recarpentered before
anyone could live there. She was so full of the future that I could
only share her pleasure—even when I brought her the check that

had to be certified to make the apartment really hers; the check that she signed without so much as a glance at its six figures, telling me proudly at the same time that she had saved money that morning by finding a chaise longue for ninety dollars! Rather than disillusion her, I went ahead with the work, and only when it was fairly near completion did I allow her to take a hasty walk through the premises.

We dealt with other problems, too. It was becoming more and more apparent that if Stravinsky survived, large amounts of money would be needed to maintain the way of life that his illness dictated; and if he died, a very large amount of money would be immediately necessary to meet the enormous inheritance taxes. Offers for the manuscripts had been solicited by the House of El Dieff, handlers of rare books and papers (appointed by Arnold Weissberger as agents for a possible sale); one offer, purportedly from the USSR, had received coverage in the *New York Times* on December 1—released on whose authority I never could learn accurately, nor was I able to discover who had really placed the quoted evaluation of three and a half million dollars on the collection. The figure made me doubt (as I told Mrs. Stravinsky) that the Russian offer was based in fact, since it seemed unlikely that that government would allocate so large a sum toward only one aspect of cultural activity— however important—when it required much larger sums for its all-important economic program. In any event, Stravinsky's children were highly disturbed at the news that the manuscripts had been put on the world market. Letters passed between Theodore and Mrs. Stravinsky, and they were no longer friendly. (Communication with Soulima and Milène had, of course, ceased long before.) In one letter from Geneva that Mrs. Stravinsky had asked me to read, written that same December, Theodore protested strongly, beginning with his agony over the fact that he had not been allowed to come and see his father in 1969, when he was confined to New York Hospital, and that now, for months, he had not had any direct news of his father's condition. He went on to say that this proposed sale had been undertaken without Stravinsky's permission —in fact (Theodore felt sure), without his knowledge, because at Évian he (Theodore) had realized that the composer was totally incapable of conducting any business or understanding any proposals regarding the sale of his manuscripts—that, indeed, he had often not even recognized his own music. And finally, he condemned Robert for having used his father's name on articles in which the latter had had no part. It was a sorrowful letter, tinged with bitterness, and yet it concluded on a note that sought some explanation—seemed even to beg for one in a desire not to close all doors. Mrs. Stravinsky replied later in February, also bitterly (it was Robert's bitterness, too), rebutting Theodore's implications, fighting loyally for Robert, and pointing out that Stravinsky had sold many manuscripts in his lifetime, and what was left would undoubtedly come to forced auction later to cover the taxes, if no sale resulted now.

It was still an armed truce—had been since the time of Theodore's visit to New York in November 1969, in fact, when Mrs. Stravinsky had asked him to question Milène about the reason the orange-grove gift had not been immediately divided. Theodore's answer was that he could not do this. But later, after he had been in touch with Soulima, his attitude changed, and it became apparent that from that point on he would no longer discuss with Mrs. Stravinsky his brother's or his sister's or his own reason for anything. (We did learn that the orange groves had been accepted by the Marions as a trust, to be managed by André for all three children.)

The archives were the source of another problem. The little piece of paper Stravinsky had signed in the hospital back in 1967, transferring all publication rights to Boosey & Hawkes, now spelled trouble. Who would buy the archives without being able to publish them? No one—unless it were a collector who lived as a hermit and would be satisfied simply with pride of ownership. Solutions were proposed and discussed with Arnold: the breaking of the agreement with Boosey & Hawkes on technicalities—Mrs. Stravinsky, under California law, was half-owner and had not "approved" the original transfer of rights; the recipients of these rights had not paid the one-dollar fee required on the execution of such an agreement; and so on—all rather tenuous and easily contested, it seemed to me. There was a saving grace, of course: the 1969 revision of the original letter of transfer gave Mrs. Stravinsky the power of approval or veto over any material to be published, and she could exercise this power in all cases (save if the publishers themselves had already vetoed a request from any other source). But that would come to the same thing—if she "forbade" Boosey & Hawkes, there would still be no money, and the precious historical materials would be lost to the

general study of scholars and students, destined to be seen only by
very few privileged eyes.

These problems were discussed night and day with everyone who
came and went and telephoned—with everyone except the only one
who mattered.

Since Évian, Stravinsky's bronchial cough had grown increasingly
worse. By mid-February, the suction pump had to be put to use
almost nightly, and sometimes during the day as well. He coughed
dreadfully, especially after taking liquids—and yet these were essential to his sustenance. The spells induced terrible fears in him,
for with this filling of the lungs he was experiencing the panic of
final suffocation. Now, when he was confined to his bed he could
remain quiet only for minutes at a time—and if he were left alone
even for a few seconds, his heart-rending "Halloo" for the nurse
echoed throughout the suite. When he lacked the strength to call
out, he would tap fiercely on the iron bed-railing with the gold
wedding rings he wore, and as time passed that clanging sound
became for me a vital part of the atmosphere, and I would listen
for it.

On the afternoon of March 18, Dr. Lax told Mrs. Stravinsky that
her husband would be better off in the hospital, and instructed Rita
and Helen to prepare him for Lenox Hill. Neither Robert nor I
were in agreement with this move, nor was Rita. From a medical
standpoint, it did provide a more convenient milieu in which to treat
the patient, but from a human standpoint it provided nothing except
an ambience filled with strangers—impersonal, too busy, perhaps
indifferent—among whom Stravinsky might die. Rita said that there
was nothing the hospital would supply that could not be installed
at home. And at home he had what he needed most—people who
loved him. But though Rita disagreed with Doctor Lax, she felt it
was not her place to advise. As for Robert, he was afraid to speak—
the responsibility was great; he might be wrong. He asked me to
protest, pointing out that "as a member of the family" I had the
right. Knowing in advance that my arguments would be set aside,
I begged—in vain. They took him away.

While Stravinsky lay at Lenox Hill, I rushed the workmen to
finish the apartment and ordered the furniture brought from storage
on March 28. Baldwin promised to send a grand piano for the living

room, and the carpenter raced to complete the new bookshelves that would hold part of the Stravinsky library. Mrs. Stravinsky went in search of plants and flowers and a canary. And Ed and Hideki packed the belongings at the Essex House. Ironically, we could not bring his studio furniture from Kingston because the moving companies went on strike—it did not matter, though, for it could not have been contained within the little room where he was to sleep the last.

But his own upright piano *was* there.

At four o'clock on Tuesday, March 30, Mrs. Stravinsky brought her husband from the hospital to his new home. Iago, the canary, welcomed him piercingly. That evening Robert, with feverish eyes, wheeled him about the apartment, pointing out where they would sit to play records, showing him the view of the park in near-twilight, calling his attention to the coral color on the walls of the room I had made into an office. Wystan Auden came later, when the composer was in bed, and went with Mrs. Stravinsky and Robert to Pavillon.

On the last day of March and the first three days of April, Stravinsky ate fairly well and even took two or three steps with his walker in the bedroom on two of those days. On April 1, with only a little assistance, he brushed his teeth, used his electric razor, and tried desperately to trim his mustache. On the evening of April 3 he began to yield, and the next morning—Palm Sunday—he no longer had the strength to speak, and did not speak again save in little sounds. Once more Doctor Lax suggested the hospital—but this time Mrs. Stravinsky said no.

He fought so hard on Monday that I could read in her eyes the belief that he would win. So strong was this that Rita went back to her room at the Essex House and Ed returned to Connecticut. The four of us were left there—with two nurses and an intern.

After midnight it was Tuesday, April 6.

STRAVINSKY, of course, does not come to an end. And in the long run, whatever has been or is or will be said or written about him is of little importance—swallowed up, as it has to be, in the light he sheds on the world. For those of us who, by fortunate chance, were privileged to bask in the warmth of its rays a little more than others, everything is a personal memory and almost everything is, therefore, contradictory.

The one constant, incontrovertible truth is his own mark—not to be described or interpreted in terms other than those he set down.

In Venice, in the Church of San Salvatore, where Stravinsky must sometimes have gone, there is an *Annunciation* by Titian, painted—tradition tells us—after he was eighty-five. Below his name the artist has written words in Latin which mean "*He* did it. . . . *He* did it."

And thus, Stravinsky!

New York City
January 15, 1972

INDEX OF WORKS

Note: This index includes works, by Stravinsky and other composers, to which reference is made in the text.

INDEX OF NAMES
AND PLACES

(All listings are alphabetical except for names of buildings, concert halls, restaurants and the like, which are indexed under the city of their location.)